How can I live when . . .

*I keep committing the same sins...someone I love is dying...
my family is falling apart...the enemy seems stronger than my
faith...I really don't love myself....*

All of us have points of real need. But perhaps our greatest
need is to develop roots of understanding deep in God's
Word. It's a journey that promises an honest view of our
Father, ourselves, and our problems. It's a journey into
prayer that knows *what to say* and faith that knows *what to
do,* through all of life's twists and turns. It's a journey that
takes a lifetime, but you can take the first step today. Join
Kay Arthur in seeking *God's* answers to your question,
"How can I live?"

*"A rare combination of practical principles with potent
power. These pages reveal the character of God and
how we can live in relation to knowing His character.
Few writings so reach the heart and convict the soul.
I have read it, I have grown."*

June Hunt

How Can I Live

A Devotional Journey with

Kay Arthur

Power Books

Fleming H. Revell Company
Old Tappan, New Jersey

Library of Congress Cataloging in Publication Data

Arthur, Kay, date
  How can I live.

  1. Devotional calendars. I. Title.
  BV4811.A77   242'.2   81-17827
  ISBN 0-8007-5077-2   AACR2

CONTENTS

CONTENTS

The Lord Is My Shepherd I Shall Not Want

Do you long for contentment? Do you crave peace? Are you afraid of what the future holds? You shall not want if the Lord is your shepherd.

Confidence To Enter Through The Veil

Covenant, Volume I
   How can I explain it to you except to say that once you really see it, your Christianity will take on a whole new dimension and you will never be the same. This is the testimony of the multitudes who have heard this teaching as I have shared it across the United States.

Come And Dine . . . I Call You Friend

Covenant, Volume II
   Do you ever feel lame in both feet when it comes to being what you should be for God? Are you destined to be nothing but a clod? No . . . not once you learn all that is yours because of the covenant cut for you.

The Promises Of God In Him Are Yea And Amen

When everything around you is failing, there is one thing that will stand . . . the promises of God. But promises must be claimed! This is the key. It's hard to claim that which you do not know is yours.

I Sought For A Man To Stand In The Gap

Have you ever seen a picture of children . . . adults . . . with horribly bloated bellies protruding from skeletons covered with dark wrinkled sagging skin?
   Have you ever felt the flush of anger and righteous indigna-

tion as you've heard of the massacre of thousands by ungodly, power hungry warmongers? Have you felt helpless and thought . . . *but there's nothing I can do.* There is . . . you can pray . . . around the world as we visit country after country.

The Righteous Has Hope In His Death

If death should come, what then? What is it like to die? What happens to you when you die? Does it hurt to die? If a man dies, will he live again? How do you live with the dying? How do you survive the death of your loved ones?

All these questions and more are answered this month as you learn how to handle death. Depressing? No, blessing beyond measure.

You Shall Teach These Words When You Sit, Walk, and Rise

"Talk to me!" "What do you want me to say?" Communication . . . the barrier or the bridge to every relationship . . . especially the family. A month of specific hows, whys, do's and don'ts on communication.

Born To Die That You Might Live

Jesus. Born to die that you might live. But live now . . . how can I live? A December journey through the life of Christ that you might experience life . . . life as only He can bring . . . life abundant . . . life eternal.

INTRODUCTION

I don't know what kind of a book you are looking for as you pick this up and flip through it, but let me say, beloved one, that if you want or need answers to the question, How Can I Live? then you are one of those for whom this book was written. This is a how-to book.

Published previously on a monthly basis, it has been test-marketed, so to speak, by thousands. And the letters have poured in telling of transformed lives. They told of now being able to handle death, trials, immoral thoughts, fears, grief; they told of knowing freedom, cleansing, release, comfort, salvation, peace; they told of restored relationships with mates, children, family, God; they told of insight, conviction, and a new appreciation of God's Word; they told how the devotionals had been used of God to develop consistent, profitable, daily quiet times; and they told of their outreach to prayer groups, businesses, offices, Sunday schools, clubs, prisons, and ministries.

This is more than a devotional book. To be frank, I'm not the devotional type. Rather it is a combination of good solid teaching on various subjects with gut-level practical answers to situations and problems we all face in life. Nothing is spared, not even my reputation, if it will minister to you. If you can learn from my mistakes, if they can give you hope, I will gladly share them.

You and I will talk together for a year . . . day by day if you can take it that way. Or, if you are like most, each month will be read the first time at one sitting. Anyway . . . however . . . we'll become friends. I cannot think of anything more exciting!

So quit browsing and buy it if you need practical answers to the question, How Can I Live? Look at the table of contents. It was written for you . . . for you are precious to Him.

ACKNOWLEDGMENTS

There is only one true Creator . . . the One who spoke and by the power of His Word formed the world and all that is therein. Thus, this book is not the work of one, but of friends, colaborers, family, acquaintances, teachers, authors, editors . . . people whom I remember and people of whom I am not even aware. Each has contributed in God's sovereign way to bring me to the point of obedience . . . obedience in writing these words as a ministry to the body of Jesus Christ.

To mention everyone would only bore you and yet I must mention just four. First, my husband, Jack. Not because I am his wife, but because as one we seek to labor in undistracted devotion to the Lord. God knew we needed one another. Then I want to mention Jan Silvious and Evelyn Wheeler, both visionaries who care only that our Lord is glorified. There have been times when I could write no more—alone I could not meet the deadline. But I was not alone, they wrote with me . . . for you and for Him. Evelyn also served as editor, and then God sent Gwen Ingraham, a bookkeeper with, of all things, editorial experience. So ultimately it is all of Him "for from Him and through Him and to Him are all things. To Him be the glory forever. Amen" (Romans 11:36 NAS).

JANUARY

Beloved, before we begin to share I need to tell you something so you will better understand what I am saying. The material in January's devotions, in a sense, is hard to start off with; perhaps May would have been better. January is hard because it is not typical of the remainder of the book. The rest of *How Can I Live* is filled with love, compassion, understanding, and the practical how-to's of life. But January . . . well, January is a month of cleansing . . . a month of soul-searching . . . a month of making everything right with God and man. And that's not always easy, is it? Yet, it is January's message that has been used of God to bring revival to lives and to many churches. So if it seems a little heavy . . . read May first, then come back to January.

* * *

As you go through this first month's devotions each day, there are some terms that you need to fully understand. These terms have been simply and briefly explained below; but before you read the definitions to these terms, pray and ask your Father to open the eyes of your understanding so that you can grasp the full meaning of each term. Your understanding of the full meaning of these terms will be essential if you are going to act upon the truths shared in this Prayer Guide!

Oh, how we pray that you will not shrink back from anything that your Father would do in your life this month! As you go through January's devotions, please remember that you have been prayed for.

Sin is independence from the control of God's Spirit. It is transgression of the law or breaking the law. It is knowing what you should do . . . knowing the right thing to do but choosing not to do it. Sin is an action which reveals an attitude or a condition of the heart.

Repentance is changing your mind about sin. It means, also, that the change of mind will result in a change of direction, and that direction is toward God! Repentance is, simply, the changing of directions!

Confession is to agree with God regarding a sin you have committed. It is a verbal acknowledgment that you have done wrong. Confession of sin is the result of seeing yourself in the light of who God really is and what He requires of you. The word, *confess,* literally means "to say with" or "to say with God the same thing He says about your sin."

Forsake means to renounce your sin, to give it up, and to have nothing further to do with that sin. Forsaking is the act of "burning your bridges" so that you cannot return to that sin!

Forgiveness is the releasing of negative feelings, attitudes, or responses that you have against an individual. Forgiveness does not consider whether your feelings, attitudes, or responses are the result of a legitimate cause; it does not take into account who is right and who is wrong! Full forgiveness involves the positive aspect of healing in a relationship which has been broken.

Restitution is to make good any loss, damage, or injury for which you are responsible. It means returning stolen goods, borrowed things, and replacing what you damaged, lost, or took as earnest money. If you are going to have a clear conscience and if you are going to be totally right with men, you must make restitution. Read Leviticus 6:1–5 and Ezekiel 33:14–16.

Cleansing is the act of being washed in the precious blood of the Lamb, which takes away your sins! Cleansing is the end result of confession and necessary restitution!

As you go through this Prayer Guide, remember three things:

1. If the sin is against God, confess it to God; then, make things right with God.

2. If the sin is against another person, and that person is aware of the sin, confess it to God and to the other person; then, make things right with that person.

3. If the sin is against a group, confess it to God and to the whole group; then, make things right with that group.

A good rule to remember is, "As wide as the sin, so wide should be the confession."

If there is full confession of sin, there will be complete cleansing.

It is the precious blood of Jesus Christ that cleanses you from sin *not* your own efforts or prayers. The joy of the Lord will follow. "Blessed are the pure in heart: for they shall see God" (Matthew 5:8).

January 1

How committed are you to God? That commitment can be measured, beloved, by your desire to be holy even as He is holy. Your commitment to God cannot be measured by the time you devote to your church, to other Christians, to Bible study, or to prayer, for all of these, as worthwhile as they are, will be absolutely worthless without the longing, the desire, the determination to be holy. Hebrews 12:14 says, "Make every effort . . . to be holy; without holiness no one will see the Lord" (NIV).

Because Christian men and women, for the most part, have ceased to be men and women of the Book, they have fallen victim to a great delusion of the enemy. That delusion is the equating of true spirituality with busyness for God. We think as long as we give some of our time to God to do His thing for Him that we are walking in a way pleasing to Him. This thinking is not true. It is deception! There is only one way you, or I, or any other Christian will be found pleasing to God, and that is by being holy even as He is holy (1 Peter 1:16).

Are you holy? Do you desire to be holy? Is holiness the longing of your heart?

If you cannot answer even one of these three questions in the affirmative, then, beloved, there is something desperately wrong in your heart or in your relationship with God. Oh, I plead with you to fall on your face and to ask God to rend your heart and to cut away all that has hardened your heart toward Him and toward His command to be holy. Ask God to speak to you this month in a way He has never before spoken to you.

And, beloved, if you could answer affirmatively, thank your Father and ask Him, by His Spirit, to use these devotions to make you holy as He is holy.

Write below, in a prayer to your Father, your heart's desire with regard to being holy as He is holy.

January 2

Do you want to be used of God? Before you answer that question, stop and think about it. Do not answer it lightly. As you consider this question, ask yourself what you think it would cost you to be used of Him. For if you say that you really do want to be used of God, surely you must realize that to be so used will require certain disciplines and efforts on your part.

If you have not done so before, it is time you faced this question realistically. And if you have already dealt with this question, you need to evaluate your progress—your life since you said yes or no.

So today God has brought you face to face with this question, "Do you want to be used of God?" Commit yourself verbally. Write out your answer below knowing that it is God to whom you answer and to whom you give an account and not to man. Remember, if you are truly a child of God, you are not your own, you have been bought with a price. Therefore, you are to glorify God in your body, which is His. You are His workmanship created in Christ Jesus unto good works which He has before ordained that you should walk in! These are the truths of 1 Corinthians 6:19, 20 and Ephesians 2:10.

Do I want to be used of God?

What will it cost me?

God, my prayer is:

January 3

Before you can be used of God for His work, for His kingdom, before you can be an instrument of blessing for others, you need cleansing, forgiving, a right relationship with others, and, thus, a right relationship with God. Are you willing to be made usable for Him, ". . . a vessel for honor, sanctified, useful to the Master, prepared for every good work" (2 Timothy 2:21 NAS)? If you are not, beloved, do you dare call yourself His? On what basis? Is it according to His Word or according to your unlearned interpretation of what you think God's Word teaches that you claim to be His?

Oh, precious one, I do not mean to sound hard, but rather I mean to be honest, to walk in love that cares enough to speak the truth. As I write this before God and at His command, I know that I must ". . . speak to them all which I command you." He says to me, ". . . Do not be dismayed before them, lest I dismay you before them" (Jeremiah 1:17 NAS).

And so I come this month to share many of God's Words with you in order ". . . To pluck up and to break down, To destroy and to overthrow, To build and to plant" (Jeremiah 1:10 NAS). God's ultimate goal for you this month is to do a work of building and planting in your life that will absolutely astound you and others. But to do so, beloved, there must first be a clearing of the ground, thus the plucking up, the breaking down, the destroying, and the overthrowing of all that would keep Him from doing the work He desires to do. Are you willing? If you are, write a prayer to God asking Him for His cleansing work in your life. If you are not willing, tell God on paper why you are not willing.

God, I want to tell You . . .

January 4

What does it mean to be holy? Nowhere in all of the Word, that I know of, is there a definition of the term *holy*. Vine's Expository Dictionary says that the Greek word for holy is *hagios*. It means to be set apart. The words *saint, sanctified,* and *holy* all come from the same root word. But this fact still does not give me a clear definition of what it means to be holy. Does it give you one?

One thing I do know, however, about being holy is the fact that God is holy, and I am to be like Him. Why not take a couple of minutes and turn with me in your Bible, and let's look at Isaiah 6. Read at least the first eight verses of this chapter, and then I will share with you what I have learned about holiness from this passage.

In verses one through five, Isaiah sees God and hears the seraphim crying out, "Holy, holy, holy, is the Lord of hosts. . . ." When Isaiah sees the Lord in the awesome beauty of His holiness, it causes him to see himself and to cry out, "Woe is me, for I am undone! because I am a man of unclean lips, and I dwell in the midst of a people of unclean lips: for mine eyes have seen the King, the Lord of hosts."

To be holy must be to be like God—righteous, uncontaminated, set apart from that which is unclean, and free from sin's taint.

Something very awesome happened to Isaiah when he finally saw his state and, thus, recognized his total ruin. One of the seraphim took a burning coal from off the altar and touched Isaiah's lips with it. Oh, how that must have hurt! The lips are so very sensitive. And, yet, despite the pain, it was worth it all because although pain came with Isaiah's confession of sin, forgiveness also came. "Behold, this has touched your lips; and your iniquity is taken away, and your sin is forgiven" (Isaiah 6:7 NAS).

"Then" . . . then Isaiah heard the voice of the Lord. He knew the will and the heart of God as God said, "Who will go for us?" Then, Isaiah was ready to go, to be used of God.

What does it mean to be holy? One thing is for sure, it means to be cleansed, to be forgiven, to confess your utter ruin, and to know that God takes away your iniquity and, thus, He forgives your sin. And then you are ready to be used to do God's will.

Would you be holy? Ask God to let you see His holiness. Write your prayer to God below.

January 5

Every great revival or spiritual awakening in history has come in answer to sincere prayer from clean hearts.

Oh, wouldn't you like to be used of God to bring a revival to our land? Wouldn't you like to know the power that comes in prayer when your heart is right with your God—free from condemnation as 1 John 3:21 says?

The purpose of these devotions, beloved, is to bring you to that place of cleansing and, thus, to that place of power. It is our prayer that they will be used by God's Spirit to help you open your heart to the gaze of a loving, holy God so that sin might be revealed and dealt with in accordance with God's Word. Just remember, precious saint, when God shows you your sin, it is not for the purpose of tormenting you, but rather it is so that you might feel the same way about sin that He does and so that you might act accordingly.

But let me share with you about the weakness of the flesh so that you might be forewarned and, thus, prepared for the days ahead. When God's holiness is revealed to us through the light of His truth, we have a natural tendency to draw back, to run, to hide, to justify ourselves as Adam and Eve did in the garden. Do not do it, beloved. Face it clearly.

Let yourself be thoroughly cleansed through the washing of the water of the Word, through your confession, through necessary restitution. Whatever it takes, do it. You will never regret it! It feels so wonderful to be cleansed—to have nothing between you and God or between you and others. No guilt! I know because I have done what I am asking you to do, and so have others. And they would tell you the same.

Tomorrow, you will begin your process of cleansing. As you go through each day's devotion, give yourself adequate time before God's throne. Prayerfully listen to God. Gaze upon His holiness. Look up every Scripture reference and let the Holy Spirit search your heart and your mind. Answer the questions honestly.

Remember, dear one, "He who conceals his transgressions will not prosper, But he who confesses and forsakes them will find compassion." "If we confess our sins, He is faithful and righteous to forgive us our sins and to cleanse us from all unrighteousness" (Proverbs 28:13; 1 John 1:9 NAS).

Write below the cry of your heart to God.

January 6

As you begin today, pray back the following Scripture to the Lord. Pray it aloud. God *will* hear you! He promises to hear, and He will answer.

"Search me, O God, and know my heart: try me, and know my thoughts: And see if there be any wicked way in me, and lead me in the way everlasting" (Psalms 139:23, 24).

First of all, I want to ask you what your priorities are in life. If your priorities are out of order, your life will be out of order. So if you want help, be honest. Remember, you must come to the light and not run from it if you are ever to know the glorious blessing that cleansing can bring.

List your priorities below, recording them in the order of their importance.

Have you failed to seek the Kingdom of God and His righteousness first in all things? _____. Matthew 6:33 makes God's will very clear on this issue, "But seek first His kingdom and His righteousness; and all these things shall be added to you" (NAS).

Ask God to show you any areas in your life over which Jesus Christ is not absolute Lord. List these areas below.

Now, write your prayer to God.

January 7

I know you have probably just sat down, but why don't you get up for just a minute and go look at yourself in the mirror. Take this book and a pen with you. After each question, write your yes, no, or whatever is necessary. As you look into that mirror, take a good look at your eyes. Your eyes are the windows of your soul. Are they warm? _____. Do they shine? _____. Are they hard or soft, joyful or woeful, pure or sensual? _____. Now, step back and look at the whole you. Can you accept what you see and live with it comfortably? _____. Are there any changes you would like to make? _____. Are these traits changeable, or is that the way you are built? _____. And if you are built that way—nose too long, chin too prominent, wrinkles too many, and so on, can you accept yourself, thank God, and quit fretting about it or drawing attention to God's "messed up" handiwork? _____. Is your body God's temple? _____. Does He really live inside you? _____. Are you properly caring for this temple? _____. Is it eating nutritiously? _____. Do you keep its appetite under the Spirit's control, or do you indulge its lusts? _____. Are you pushing it or putting it under too much stress? _____. Are you relieving its tension through walking or adequate exercises? _____. Is it getting adequate rest? _____. Are you its slave, or is the body the Holy Spirit's slave? _____. Do you have any personal habits that you know are displeasing to the Lord or that would cause other weak Christians to stumble? _____.

How do you dress? _____. Do you feel it is in keeping with the dress of a child of God? _____.

Are your clothes designed to make you look sensual, or do they fit or expose you in such a way as to detract from God's holiness? _____. Is your appearance neat and as pleasing to the eye as you can make it? _____. Do you groom yourself properly and appropriately for the occasion? _____. Have you given proper attention to cleanliness? _____.

Does all this sound anything but spiritual to you? _____. God tells us in 1 Corinthians 10:31 that "Whether, then, you eat or drink or whatever you do, do all to the glory of God" (NAS). First Corinthians 6:19, 20 says, "Or do you not know that your body is a temple of the Holy Spirit who is in you, whom you have from God, and that you are not your own? For you have been bought with a price: therefore glorify God in your body" (NAS). In Psalms 29:9 it says, ". . . And in His temple everything says, 'Glory!' " (NAS). Does it? _____.

God, what would you have me to do?

January 8

We live in a day and age when people are doing what is right in their own eyes, even as they did in the days of the Judges (Judges 21:25). Why? I believe it is because there is no "King" . . . no Lord in men's lives, because there are no absolutes!

Immorality abounds on every hand, and it has crept into the lives of many who profess to know Jesus Christ as Lord and Savior. And the sin has spread like leaven into the church because the church has refused to discipline its members. Read 1 Corinthians 5 and weep.

It was to this church at Corinth that Paul had to give very

explicit instructions regarding immorality. As he proceeds to do so, Paul tells them *not to be deceived,* ". . . neither fornicators, nor idolaters, nor adulterers, nor effeminate, nor homosexuals, nor thieves, nor covetous, nor drunkards, nor revilers, nor swindlers, shall inherit the kingdom of God" (1 Corinthians 6:9, 10 NAS). Three verses later he says, ". . . the body is not for immorality, but for the Lord." This statement is then followed by a very definite command, "Flee immorality. . . ."

What about you? Do you flee from immorality or from anything that would, in any way, cause you to be immoral in thought or in deed?

God tells you in Matthew 5:28 that if you keep on looking at a woman (or a man) to commit adultery with her (or him) in your heart, you are guilty of the act of adultery. Have you realized that truth, beloved? Do you keep your thoughts under God's control by bringing every thought captive to the obedience of Jesus Christ as God commands in 2 Corinthians 10:5?

Are you guilty of the lustful look, of hanging around to flirt with another's mate, of passing glances, of rubbing knees under the table, of leaving a lingering touch, of sharing thoughts you never should have shared?

Read carefully Job 31:1, 9–12, "I have made a covenant with my eyes; How then could I gaze at a virgin? . . . If my heart has been enticed by a woman, Or I have lurked at my neighbor's doorway, May my wife grind for another, And let others kneel down over her. For that would be a lustful crime; Moreover, it would be an iniquity *punishable* by judges. For it would be fire that consumes to Abaddon, And would uproot all my increase" (NAS). Are you guilty? If you are, repent and confess your sin.

Have you used, or do you use, any member of your body in *any* immoral way? You may say, "What is immoral?" Think upon this verse, "Shall I then take away the members of Christ and make them members of a harlot?" (1 Corinthians 6:15 NAS). Or think upon God's Word in 1 Corinthians 7:1, " . . . it is good for a man not to touch a woman" (NAS). The word, *touch,* in classical Greek meant to light a fire. Are you lighting fires with your touches that should only be put out in the marriage bed?

What have you been doing with Christ's temple? With Christ's eyes? With Christ's hands? With Christ's body?

January 9

God was the One who made us male and female. He is the Master Designer of your sexuality. And in His mind and in His economy, your sexuality is something very beautiful. It is the highest of ways for you, as a man or as a woman, to celebrate your oneness when you leave your mother and father to cleave to your marriage partner and become one flesh. This physical union is an act of beauty and consecration, and, thus, God says, ". . . rejoice in the wife of your youth. As a loving hind and a graceful doe, Let her breasts satisfy you at all times; Be exhilarated always with her love." "Let marriage be held in honor among all, and let the marriage bed be undefiled; for fornicators and adulterers God will judge" (Proverbs 5:18, 19; Hebrews 13:4 NAS).

How have you regarded the sexuality given to you by God? Examine your heart before God by answering this series of questions that deal with this vital aspect of being a man or a woman of God. I'll ask, and you answer in truth before your God remembering, beloved, that the Word of God is your judge. And if you would judge yourself, you would not be judged by God (1 Corinthians 11:31, 32).

Have you accepted your sexuality, the fact of being a man or a woman, and do you live according to your role as a man or as a woman? ———. Or have you denied your maleness or femaleness and turned to a person of the *same* sex to find sexual gratification? ———. God says, "You shall not lie with a male as one lies with a female; it is an abomination" (Leviticus 18:22 NAS). (Also see Genesis 19:4–11, Leviticus 20:13, Romans 1:24–27, 1 Corinthians 6:9–11.)

Have you honored your marriage partner's sexual needs, or do you withhold yourself from him or her? ———. Do you look at this act which God has created as something dirty . . . something to be endured or tolerated, or do you lovingly give yourself to your mate? ———. God says, "Let the husband fulfill his duty to his wife, and likewise also the wife to her husband. The wife does not have authority over her own body, but the husband does; and likewise also the husband does not have authority over his own body, but the wife does. *Stop depriving one another,* except by agreement for a time that you may devote yourselves to prayer, and come together again lest Satan tempt you because of your lack of self-control" (1 Corinthians 7:3–5 NAS, italics added). Are you putting your mate in the path of the tempter by depriving him or her satisfaction of their God-given needs? _____.

Are you guilty of incest, of using a family member to gratify your perverted lusts? In Leviticus 18:6–18, God says that uncovering the nakedness of any blood relative is lewdness. Have you damaged some child, even putting your hands where they do not belong? _____. This act is perversion, and, if unrepented of, it shall bring inconceivable judgment.

If you are guilty of any of these sins, seek God's forgiveness and ask Him to heal the wounds you may have inflicted upon other people.

January 10

God tells you that you are to love Him with *all* of your heart (affections and emotions), with all of your soul (hopes, ambitions, desires), with all of your mind (intellect, thoughts), and with all of your strength (physical ability). This is the foremost of all His commandments (Mark 12:29, 30). And it is in the light of this commandment that *you must ask yourself the following questions:*

Is there anyone I love or desire more than God, His Son, or His Spirit? _____. If yes, who? _____. Now, listen to the Lord Jesus, "He who loves father or mother *more than* Me is not worthy of Me; and he who loves son or daughter *more than* Me is not worthy of me" (Matthew 10:37 NAS, italics added).

Do I love this present world *more than* I love the eternal things that belong to God? God says, "Set your mind on the things above, not on the things that are on earth." ". . . while we look not at the things which are seen, but at the things which are not seen; *for the things which are seen are temporal, but* the things which are not seen are eternal" (Colossians 3:2; 2 Corinthians 4:18 NAS, italics added).

So many Christians live overcommitted lives. They are overcommitted to jobs and professions, to clubs and organizations, to hobbies and sports, to further education and intellectual pursuits. Have you forgotten that God has called you to be a soldier, to endure hardness, to not be entangled with the affairs of this life so that you might please Him who has called you to be a soldier? Are you entangled—so entangled that you do not have adequate time to meet with your God daily for worship, prayer, Bible study, or to minister to your family and to others?

What has entangled you? Ask God to show you, and write it below.

And then write your prayer to God below telling Him what you desire to do about it.

January 11

God says that you are to love Him with all of your mind . . . that in all things Christ is to have the preeminence. What place does the Word of God have in your thoughts, in your mind?

He also tells you that you are to love Him with *all of your heart.* Your affections are to be set on Him. Can you say your affections are set on God if there is no desire on your part, or no discipline on your part, to get into the Word of God? How are you going to get to know God if you do not give yourself adequate time to spend in worshipping Him, communicating with Him, and hearing of His ways and His will through studying His Word?

God tells you—commands you—to desire the pure milk of the Word so that you might grow, and He also tells you to study to show yourself approved unto Him, a workman that need not be ashamed, handling accurately the Word of truth (1 Peter 2:2; 2 Timothy 2:15). He tells you that you are not to be conformed to this world, but to be transformed by the renewing of your mind (Romans 12:2). Have you obeyed? _____. Do *you* desire His Word, and do you study it? _____. Are you learning to handle it accurately? _____. Are you being transformed through the Word? _____. If you are not, stop and tell God why your answer is no. Write out your reasons here so that they will be before you in black and white.

Have you permitted yourself to be put in positions of Christian leadership and responsibility when you know you are not totally committed to God and to the things of His Kingdom *or* when you know that you are still young, a novice in the things of God and, thus, not adequately taught, prepared, and matured for your responsibilities before God? _____.

God says, "and not a new convert, lest he become conceited and fall into the condemnation incurred by the devil" (1 Timothy 3:6 NAS). Do not let others put you into positions of responsibility or leadership, no matter what the need! Even Jesus waited thirty years before His public ministry of three and one-half years began. And in that ministry, you see Jesus constantly going to be alone to pray and to seek the Father's direction. He also knew the Word. Are you greater than Jesus so that you can minister apart from these things? _____.

Are you an elder or a deacon? _____. Do you meet the qualifications of 1 Timothy 3:1–13? _____.

January 12

Thinking again today of the commandment of God to love Him with "your all," have you robbed God of your all by withholding from Him your time, your talents, your money? _____.

Hear, beloved, the Word of the Lord, ". . . And from everyone who has been given much shall much be required; and to whom they entrusted much, of him they will ask all the more" (Luke 12:48 NAS). "And do not neglect doing good and sharing; for with such sacrifices God is pleased." ". . . your abundance being a supply for their want, that their abundance also may become a supply for your want, that there may be equality" (Hebrews 13:16; 2 Corinthians 8:14 NAS). "Therefore be careful how you walk, not as unwise men, but as wise, making the most of your time, because the days are evil. So then do not be foolish, but understand what the will of the Lord is" (Ephesians 5:15–17 NAS).

Every good and every perfect gift you and I have comes down from the Father above. What do you and I have that we can boast about? Was it not given to us or granted to us by the Father (James 1;17; 1 Corinthians 4:7 NAS)? Are you grateful for what you have? Do you ". . . continually offer up a sacrifice of praise to God, that is, the fruit of lips that give thanks to His name" (Hebrews 13:15 NAS)? _____.

Now then, knowing that all you are and that all you have is from God, are you a good steward of all that He has given to you? _____.

God tells us in 1 Corinthians 4 that it is required of stewards that they be found faithful. Write below those areas in which you have failed in your stewardship or in giving God your all.

One last question for today, beloved. Boy, won't you be clean if you persevere! Just think how good it will feel when it is all over and under the cleansing power of His blood!

In making your plans, do you fail to consider what would please your God and your Savior? _____. Is this loving Him with all of your soul? _____. Second Corinthians 5:15 says that you should no longer live for yourself but for Him who died and rose again on your behalf. You are to deny yourself, to take up your cross, and to follow Him. What will it profit you if you gain the whole world and lose your own soul (Matthew 16:24–28)? Have you denied yourself and taken up your cross? _____. Are you following Him? _____. If you are not, tell God why you aren't in a prayer written to Him below.

January 13

What is the only thing on the face of this earth that can save men from death and give them life? Is it not the gospel of Jesus Christ, which is the power of God unto salvation to everyone who believes, to the Jew first and also to the Gentile (Romans 1:16)?

Have you heard the gospel? _____. Have you truly believed it? _____. Have you believed that Jesus the Christ died for your sins and that He was raised again for your justification? _____. Do you have eternal life? _____. Can men apart from Christ, apart from the gospel, ever know life or ever know God? No, not according to John 3:36, Acts 4:12, or John 14:6.

What personal responsibility then does your salvation bring in relationship to others and to the gospel? Paul says you become a debtor to that gospel and that you are to preach it in season and out of season for people will never hear so that they can believe except someone preach it to them (Romans 1:15, 2 Timothy 4:2, and Romans 10:14–17).

Jesus Christ came to seek and to save the lost. Now that He has returned to the Father, He has commissioned you to carry on His work (Acts 1:8; John 17:18). Are you carrying on? _____. Do you believe that men cannot be saved apart from Jesus Christ? _____. Then, beloved, what is keeping you from sharing, from preaching the gospel? _____. Or are you preaching it? _____. If you are not, write out below what is keeping you from preaching it in season and out of season. Then, next to each reason, write down "the cure."

Why I Am Not Preaching The Gospel To Others

The Cause	The Cure

Now, write out your prayer to your Father who saved you and who commissioned you.

January 14

The commandment that ranks second to the one which commands us to love our God with "our all" is the command to love others *as* ourselves (Mark 12:31). You see, God loves people. He loved the world so much that He gave His only begotten Son for it as a ransom for souls. Because of love, He gave the gift of gifts —He gave His all!

And for whom did He give His all? For His enemies, for the hopeless, for the helpless, for the weak, for the base, for the foolish, for the despised, for the ungodly, for the unrighteous—for sinners. And if you are to love others, you are to love the ones He loved as He loved them. You were once one of them, and, by His love, you were redeemed. Your redemption cost God His all, but then that is the price that love, His love, pays.

Have you experienced His love? _____. If you have, you have become a debtor to that love which He sheds abroad in your heart by the Holy Spirit whom He gives you on the day of your salvation (Romans 5:5). And so God's command comes, "Love others" for by this shall all men know you are *My* disciples if you have love one for another. Jesus said that we are to love one another *just as* He loved us (John 15:12). Do you love as Christ loved? _____.

Think about all of those whom you know. List any whom you do not love.

Think about all races of men. Are there any races that you refuse to love? List these.

"But I say to you, love your enemies, and pray for those who persecute you, in order that you may be sons of your Father who is in heaven; for He causes His sun to rise on the evil and the good, and sends rain on the righteous and the unrighteous. For if you love those who love you, what reward have you? Do not even the tax-gatherers do the same? And if you greet your brothers only, what do you do more than others? Do not even the Gentiles do the same? Therefore you are to be perfect, as your heavenly Father is perfect" (Matthew 5:44–48 NAS).

Do you love your enemies and pray for those who persecute you? _____. Do you treat them as God would have you treat them? _____.

January 15

As you prepare for your time of worship today, let me ask you a question. Do you know of anyone who has something against you —legitimately or not? _____. Have you sought reconciliation with them? _____. If the answer is, "Yes, but they would not be reconciled," if you have sought reconciliation in God's way, you have done that which is pleasing to the Lord. You have been obedient. But if your answer is "No," then listen, beloved, to God's Word, "If therefore you are presenting your offering at the altar, and there remember that your brother has something against you, leave your offering there before the altar, and go your way; first be reconciled to your brother, and then come and present your offering" (Matthew 5:23, 24 NAS).

Now, if you are going to be obedient to your Father, what must you do? Write out your resolve below.

If you are going to love others as yourself and as God loves them, then you must extend to them forgiveness—total, complete, absolute forgiveness. But you may say, "How can I? You don't know how greatly I have been wounded. It was so wrong, so unjust, so unloving, so undeserved. I could never forget it. I could never forgive them."

Listen, beloved, as Jesus speaks, ". . . And forgive us our debts, as we also have forgiven our debtors. . . . For if you forgive men for their transgressions, your heavenly Father will also forgive you. But if you do not forgive men, then your Father will not forgive your transgressions . . ." (Matthew 6:12, 14, 15 NAS). And so Paul tells the church, in Colossians 3:13, "bearing with one another, and forgiving each other, whoever has a complaint against any one; just as the Lord forgave you, so also should you" (NAS).

According to God's Word, you cannot receive forgiveness from God if you will not forgive others. So, now, whom do you need to forgive freely and completely? List their names below. Then, ask God to lead you in a prayer of forgiveness for each person. When the forgiveness is given, put a check by their name.

January 16

If you are going to love others as yourself, and as Christ loved them, you must put others before yourself. The love of God has as its focal point the interests and the welfare of others. This truth is brought out so clearly to us in Philippians 2:1–10 where you are urged to "have this attitude be in yourselves which was also in Christ Jesus." It was the servant's attitude—an attitude of submission and obedience that would go so far as to lay down its life. Christ's servant heart in this passage is seen *as a servant in relationship to the Father* not as a servant to man. Why do I mention this fact? Because, dear one, if you realize that you are doing this out of love's submission to the Father rather than to man, you will see how critical, how vital that submission is! Your submission toward man will be held on track because of its higher calling of submission to your dear Father.

Now, in our heart's preparation, listen to God's Word, "Do nothing from selfishness or empty conceit, but with humility of mind let each of you regard one another as more important than himself; do not merely look out for your own personal interests, but also for the interests of others" (Philippians 2:3, 4 NAS) ———.

With whose interests are you more concerned? Yours? Others? ———.

Do you indulge in idle talk or gossip about others? ———. Do you speak evil of others or spread tales about others? ———. Do you pass on prayer requests for the sake of passing on another's faults, failures, or sins? ———. If you have done this, and if you have not sought forgiveness from those about whom you shared or from those with whom you shared, will you do so? ———. "... he who spreads slander is a fool" (Proverbs 10:18 NAS). "You shall not go about as a slanderer among your people..." (Leviticus 19:16 NAS). Do not "return evil for evil, or insult for insult... let him who means to love life and see good days refrain his tongue from evil and his lips from speaking guile" (*see* 1 Peter 3:9, 10 NAS).

Do you call people names, even in jest, or do you try to hurt others with your words? ———. Ephesians 4:31, 32 says, "Let all bitterness and wrath and anger and clamor and slander be put away from you, along with all malice. And be kind to one another, tenderhearted, forgiving each other, just as God in Christ also has forgiven you" (NAS).

If you are guilty of these things, and you have not sought forgiveness, do so as soon as possible. Write below your list of those whom you must seek out.

January 17

God tells us in 1 Corinthians 12 that we, as Christians, are members of one body and, thus, members one of another. In this vital chapter, we also see that as members of Christ's body, bone of His bone and flesh of His flesh, we should have the same care of one another and that there should be no schism or division in the body. Oh, would to God that we would see how our divisions, our envy, our strife, our competition, our demeaning of one another wounds the blessed Holy Spirit who dwells in each of us and makes us one in Him through the unity of the Spirit! We are to so love and to so care for one another that when one member of the body suffers, we all suffer, and when one member of the body rejoices, we all rejoice. To do less is to weaken the health, the strength, the effectiveness of the body, and it is to fail to honor and to obey the Head, our Lord Jesus Christ!

Do you pray for, or do you criticize, your brothers and sisters in Christ? Paul says, "With all prayer and petition pray at all times in the Spirit, and with this in view, be on the alert with all perseverance and petition for all the saints" (Ephesians 6:18 NAS). Peter says, "Above all, keep fervent in your love for one another, because love covers a multitude of sins" (1 Peter 4:8 NAS). And Jesus warns us, "Do not judge according to appearance, but judge with righteous judgment" (John 7:24 NAS). Do you have all the facts right? _____. Are you absolutely sure? _____. Do not make any evaluation until you do!

Do you actively, diligently seek to fulfill Ephesians 4:3, "being diligent to preserve the unity of the Spirit in the bond of peace" (NAS)? _____.

Do humility, gentleness, patience, and forbearance characterize your walk and behavior toward others? _____. Listen to Ephesians 4:1, 2, "I, therefore, the prisoner of the Lord, entreat you to walk in a manner worthy of the calling with which you have been called, with all humility and gentleness, with patience, showing forbearance to one another in love" (NAS).

Do you, "Remember the prisoners, as though in prison with them, and those who are ill-treated, since you yourself also are in the body" (Hebrews 13:3 NAS)? _____.

Are you irregular in assembling with believers for prayer and fellowship? _____. We need one another to support . . . to encourage . . . to admonish one another. What would you do if this privilege were taken away from you, or if it were only at the peril of your freedom or your life that you could gather? In a time of persecution, the author of Hebrews wrote, "and let us consider how to stimulate one another to love and good deeds, not forsaking our own assembling together, as is the habit of some, but encouraging one another; and all the more, as you see the day drawing near" (Hebrews 10:24, 25 NAS). Hebrews 13:17 says to you as a member of a church, "Obey your leaders, and submit to them; for they keep watch over your souls, as those who will give an account. Let them do this with joy and not with grief, for this would be unprofitable for you" (NAS). Do you? _____.

What do you need to say to God today?

January 18

God says that ". . . you are a chosen race, a royal priesthood, a holy nation, a people for God's own possession, that you may proclaim the excellencies of Him who has called you out of darkness into His marvelous light" (1 Peter 2:9 NAS). This is your call to holiness, "Keep your behavior excellent among the Gentiles, so that in the thing in which they slander you as evildoers, they may on account of your good deeds, as they observe them, glorify God in the day of visitation" (1 Peter 2:12 NAS).

Let's take a good look at your behavior in the light of these truths. Ask yourself the following questions by coming "to the light" that your "deeds may be manifested as having been wrought in God" (John 3:21 NAS).

1. Do you have "bitter jealousy and selfish ambition in your heart" (James 3:14)? _____.

2. Do you lie to others (Colossians 3:9)? Be honest now! _____.

3. "Let him who steals steal no longer; but rather let him labor, performing with his own hands what is good, in order that he may have something to share with him who has need" (Ephesians 4:28 NAS). Do you steal? _____. Do you work as you should . . . as unto God? _____. There are so many men today who live off the labors of their parents, their wives, or their government when they could work, even if they made less than the government or unemployment would pay them. If you have stolen anything and you have not made restitution, list it below, and note what restitution is necessary.

4. Second Corinthians 10:4, 5 says, "for the weapons of our warfare are not of the flesh, but divinely powerful for the destruction of fortresses. We are destroying speculations and every lofty thing raised up against the knowledge of God, and we are taking every thought captive to the obedience of Christ" (NAS). Philippians 4:8 tells you the things you are to think upon, "Finally, brethren, whatever is true, whatever is honorable, whatever is right, whatever is pure, whatever is lovely, whatever is of good repute, if there is any excellence and if anything worthy of praise, let your mind dwell on these things" (NAS). Do you bring every thought obedient to Christ, making sure it meets the qualifications of Philippians 4:8, or do you permit all sorts of things displeasing to Christ to fill your mind? _____.

5. "And do not get drunk with wine, for that is dissipation, but be filled with the Spirit" (Ephesians 5:18 NAS). "Now the deeds of the flesh are evident, which are: immorality, impurity, sensuality, idolatry, sorcery, enmities, strife, jealousy, outbursts of anger, disputes, dissensions, factions, envyings, drunkenness, carousings, and things like these, of which I forewarn you just as I have forewarned you that those who practice such things shall not inherit the kingdom of God" (Galatians 5:19–21 NAS). Underline the things mentioned in these two passages that you are permitting in your life. The word, *sorcerers* or *sorcery,* in the Greek, is *pharmakeia,* which means the use of drugs for magical or supernatural purposes. If you are doing any of these things, you are not filled with the Holy Spirit and, thus, you are not being holy as He is holy. "But the fruit of the Spirit is love, joy, peace, patience, kindness, goodness, faithfulness, gentleness, self-control; against such things there is no law. Now those who belong to Christ Jesus have crucified the flesh with its passions and desires. If we live by the Spirit, let us also walk by the Spirit. Let us not become boastful, challenging one another, envying one another" (Galatians 5:22–26 NAS).

Write out an appropriate prayer to God.

January 19

Let's continue today, beloved, with your self-examination by His Spirit through His Word. I do realize that this is not easy. It may even seem wearying, but remember, dear child of God that cleansing is your goal so that you might know the filling of His Spirit!

1. Romans 13:8 says, "Owe nothing to anyone except to love one another; for he who loves his neighbor has fulfilled the law" (NAS). Have you incurred any debts that you are unable to pay? _____. Are you in debt to any man or any woman? _____. If so, list their names, what you owe them, and note your vow to contact them immediately and tell them of your plans to resolve that debt.

I Am In Debt To	I Owe	My Plans For Paying My Debt

2. Is your life characterized by murmuring and complaining when things disappoint you or do not go as you feel they should? _____. Do you disobey Philippians 2:14, 15 which says, "Do all things without grumbling or disputing; that you may prove yourselves to be blameless and innocent, children of God above reproach in the midst of a crooked and perverse generation, among whom you appear as lights in the world" (NAS)? _____.

3. God tells us in James 2 that Christians are not to show personal favoritism to others based on their status in life or based on their wealth. All men are to be held in equal regard. Are you guilty of breaking this command? _____.

4. "Let every person be in subjection to the governing authorities. For there is no authority except from God, and those which

exist are established by God. Therefore he who resists authority has opposed the ordinance of God; and they who have opposed will receive condemnation upon themselves. For rulers are not a cause of fear for good behavior, but for evil. Do you want to have no fear of authority? Do what is good, and you will have praise from the same; for it is a minister of God to you for good. But if you do what is evil, be afraid; for it does not bear the sword for nothing; for it is a minister of God, an avenger who brings wrath upon the one who practices evil. Wherefore it is necessary to be in subjection, not only because of wrath, but also for conscience' sake" (Romans 13:1-5 NAS). Have you been honest in paying your taxes? _____. If not, will you confess and make restitution? _____. Do you obey the laws of the land? _____. What laws are you breaking? _____. How fast do you drive? _____. Are you going to break the speed limit? _____. What Christian stickers do you have on your bumper or car windows? _____ _____.

Write an appropriate prayer to God in light of any sin that He has revealed in your life today.

January 20

How can we be holy if we live as the world lives rather than as God commands Christians to live? Is your life-style different from those who live in the world? How are they going to see the image of God through you if you suppress God's holiness and His righteousness by your unrighteous life-style or deeds? Are you salt that has lost its savor and, therefore, your life does not stop the spread of corruption or cause others to thirst for the Fountain of Living Waters?

Can you sin and get away with it without great conviction? Listen to what Isaiah the prophet said to those who professed to be God's people, "Woe to those who call evil good, and good evil; Who substitute darkness for light and light for darkness; Who substitute bitter for sweet, and sweet for bitter! Woe to those who are wise in their own eyes, and clever in their own sight! Woe to those who are heroes in drinking wine, and valiant men in mixing strong drink; Who justify the wicked for a bribe, And take away the rights of the ones who are in the right! Therefore, as a tongue of fire consumes stubble, And dry grass collapses into the flame, So their root will become like rot and their blossom blow away as dust; For they have rejected the law of the Lord of hosts, And despised the word of the Holy One of Israel. On this account the anger of the Lord has burned against His people, And He has stretched out His hand against them and struck them down, And the mountains quaked; and their corpses lay like refuse in the middle of the streets. For all this His anger is not spent, But His hand is still stretched out" (Isaiah 5:20–25 NAS).

What should you do? ". . . Break up your fallow ground, And do not sow among thorns. Circumcise yourselves to the Lord And remove the foreskins of your heart . . ." (Jeremiah 4:3, 4 NAS). Get rid of your sin and make yourself tender to the Lord. Write out below a covenant prayer to God, asking Him to keep you aware of sin and its insidious ways.

God says you are to walk by faith, not by sight (2 Corinthians 5:7 NAS). You are not under obligation to the flesh, to live according to the flesh (Romans 8:12 NAS). You are to live by ". . . His precious and magnificent promises, in order that by them you might become partakers of the divine nature, having escaped the corruption that is in the world by lust" (2 Peter 1:4 NAS). For by His divine power, He has granted to you everything pertaining to life and godliness, through the true knowledge of Him who called us by His own glory and excellence (2 Peter 1:3 NAS). Are you motivated or directed by the visible, by circumstances, by feelings rather than by the Spirit and by the Word of God? _____.

Do you walk by faith or by sight? _____. Do you live by the promises of God? _____. Do you trust His Spirit, His Word, His power to make you godly? _____.

Write here, in a prayer to God, your heart's desire with regard to a life of faith.

January 21

Self . . . self . . . self! How easily it can get in the way!

"But Jesus called them to Himself, and said, 'You know that the rulers of the Gentiles lord it over them, and their great men exercise authority over them. It is not so among you, but whoever wishes to become great among you shall be your servant, and whoever wishes to be first among you shall be your slave; just as the Son of Man did not come to be served, but to serve, and to give His life a ransom for many'" (Matthew 20:25-28 NAS).

Do you desire to lord over others? _____. Are you in a position of authority? _____. Do you handle that position as Christ would handle it? _____. What would those under you say about how you handle your authority? _____.

Are you self-centered? _____. Do you have to have your way just to prove your point or to establish your authority? _____. Do you seek attention? _____. Do you have to have recognition for the things you do? _____. Do you desire to have more than it is God's will for you to have? _____. "For everyone who exalts himself shall be humbled, and he who humbles himself shall be exalted" (Luke 14:11 NAS). Do you want Jesus to increase and you to decrease (John 3:30)? _____. Or is it just the opposite; do you want to be the Christian superstar? _____. Do you think more highly of yourself than you ought to think (Romans 12:3)? _____. Are you proud? _____. Do you have to make sure others know of your accomplishments for God? _____. Do you brag about yourself and your personal accomplishments? _____.

Self . . . self . . . self! Write out a prayer to God about what you desire with regard to your self.

"I have been crucified with Christ; and it is no longer I who live, but Christ lives in me; and the life which I now live in the flesh I live by faith in the Son of God, who loved me, and delivered Himself up for me" (Galatians 2:20 NAS).

January 22

Did you know that every family in heaven and on earth derives its name from the Father (Ephesians 3:14, 15)? Therefore, the earthly family is to be a picture to the world of God's heavenly family. This truth explains why the family is so sacred to God, and it explains why it distresses God so greatly when family relationships are broken. God wants harmony in our homes because there is harmony in His home and, thus, loving harmony becomes the responsibility of each one in the family. How can harmony be won and maintained? Only as each of us functions properly in our role as commanded in God's Word does harmony exist and persist.

Now, I grant you that there are instances when this peace cannot be maintained because of divisions that the gospel will bring when the unsaved members of a family will lash out at those who have believed in the Lord Jesus Christ. However, that is not the issue before us at this time. Rather what we need to see is whether or not we are living according to God's principles as a husband, as a wife, as a parent, or as a child—this is the issue!

The greatest responsibility for the welfare of a family falls upon the head of the home, the father (1 Corinthians 11:3). I believe with all my being that is why God made a man to differ from a woman in so many ways. He is the stronger of the two sexes, and, thus, he is able to bear the greater burdens and responsibility (1 Peter 3:7). In the light of this fact, let's begin with the man, and as we do, let's remember not to go around telling each other what we are doing wrong. Let's leave that to the Holy Spirit.

God made women, and He knows that every woman has one basic need. If that need is genuinely fulfilled, she will be able to find fulfillment in her role as a woman. What is it that she needs? It is the love of her husband. Therefore, God's command comes to the man, "Husbands, love your wives, just as Christ also loved the church and gave Himself up for her; that He might sanctify her, having cleansed her by the washing of water with the word, that He might present to Himself the church in all her glory, having no spot or wrinkle or any such thing; but that she should be holy and blameless. So husbands ought also to love their own wives as their own bodies. He who loves his own wife loves himself; for no one ever hated his own flesh, but nourishes and cherishes it, just as Christ also does the church" (Ephesians 5:25–29 NAS).

Husband, do you love your wife with the love that God has for you? _____. Do you love her as you love your own body? _____. Do you nourish her and cherish her with the same care you give to yourself? _____. Do you love her unconditionally? _____. Does she know it? _____. When was the last time you told her that you love her? _____.

January 23

Women are so different from men that many times a man will just shake his head and walk away thinking, *Why bother, I will never understand her anyway!* But is walking away the solution? Can a man walking with God just walk away and throw himself deeper into his work saying that it is impossible for a man to ever figure out a woman anyway—"Just let them be women"?

First Peter 3:7 has a clear word for husbands on this matter, "You husbands likewise, live with your wives in an understanding way, as with a weaker vessel, since she is a woman; and grant her honor as a fellow-heir of the grace of life, so that your prayers may not be hindered" (NAS).

No, a man, if he is going to be obedient to God, must seek to live with his wife in an understanding way rather than just walking away and leaving her in her female dilemmas. The husband is responsible for the total welfare of his wife mentally, emotionally, and physically, even as he is responsible for his own body. Is this not what was seen yesterday as you meditated (you did meditate, didn't you?) upon Ephesians 5:25–29?

Husbands, have you diligently sought to understand your wife . . . to listen to her and to hear what she is trying to say to you? Has she asked you to talk to her more? _____. Have you done it? _____. Do you spend some time each week with her when you can be alone . . . unhindered so that you can share? _____. Has she asked you to read certain books that would help you to understand her? _____. Have you taken the time to read them? _____. How important is her welfare as a person to you? _____ _____.

Gentlemen, let me throw in a commercial at this point. If you want to read a book that will really help you understand women, read James Dobson's book, *What Wives Wish Their Husbands Knew About Women.* It's great, and it is not boring! One man read it and said, "I finally understand my wife! I didn't know there was any other woman like her!"

Well, men, let's look at three more questions, and then we'll hit the women tomorrow. Aren't you glad?

Do you pray with your wife? _____. Read 1 Peter 3:7 again. Do you give her honor? _____. Sometimes, men think that because the man rules over the woman that she is inferior or subservient to the man. This thinking is not biblical! And so God reminds the man that his wife is a fellow-heir, one who shares in common the grace of life, and then He warns the husband not to be embittered or harsh with his wife. Are you harsh or embittered against your wife? _____.

Take time today to be quiet before your God. Ask Him, by His Spirit, to reveal to you specific things in which your wife needs understanding along with specific ways you can show her understanding.

January 24

God has given men the wonderful privilege and the awesome responsibility of portraying to the world the relationship of Jesus Christ to His bride, the church. And, thus, men are to love their wives *as* Christ loved the church. When a man fails to love his wife in this way, that man distorts or breaks "the image" of Christ. But where do women stand? Is there not some way in which women can reflect Jesus Christ to the world also? Yes, there is. Women have been given the high privilege of reflecting Christ's image to the world by submitting to their husbands even as Christ submits to the Father. "God is the head of Christ" and "the man is the head of a woman" (1 Corinthians 11:3 NAS), and, therefore, as Christ submitted to His Head, the Father, so woman is to submit to her head, her husband. This submission is not the role of an inferior to a superior, for Christ and the Father are one, even as a husband and wife are one. It is, rather, a submission of design and of loving obedience to God's all-wise ways and sovereign will.

God tells women what His will is for them in Ephesians 5:22, "Wives, be subject to your own husbands, as to the Lord" (NAS). God then repeats this command in Colossians 3:18. Note that it is the woman's responsibility to submit to her husband in cooperation with the Holy Spirit. The verb, *submit,* in Ephesians 5:22 is in the present tense, which implies continuous action or a practice of life. This verb is in the imperative mood, which means it is a command from God. The verb is in the middle voice, which implies that the submission is a joint action in which the subject participates in the action of the main verb. Thus, by God's grace and through God's Spirit, women submit.

At this point, let me say it is the husband's responsibility to rule the wife, but it is not his responsibility *to make* her submit. The responsibility of submission is the woman's.

Wife, are you subject or submissive to your husband as it is fitting in the Lord? _____. If your answer is no write out below your reasons for this answer to God. And then write below your prayer to God regarding what has been said today.

January 25

Women, God has given you such a high privilege in your womanhood. How important it is that you understand your high calling and that you do not despise your position or your role as a woman.

So many women are despising their God-ordained positions as wives, as mothers, and as homemakers, and they are abandoning these traditional roles as set down by God since the creation of the world. What chaos, what disruption, what erosion this abandonment is bringing to families! Women, by the multitudes, are despising God's ways and turning to their own ways as they listen to the deceptive lies of the prince of this world, Satan . . . the deceiver . . . the father of lies. And Satan's way is the way of death.

To whom are you going to listen?_____. Whom are you going to obey?_____. It is time to make your choice. Those who are not for God are against Him. If God be God, then follow Him. To follow God means to walk in obedience to His ways.

God made us male and female. He made us with specific needs, but our needs are basic needs that differ according to our sexuality. Women need to be loved; we have already seen this fact. But what do men need? Men need respect. Men have two basic fears, and I believe these are God-given fears. The first of these is the fear of being subjugated by a woman. Why? I believe it is because God ordained man to rule over woman as seen in Genesis 3:16. That is why a woman is to be subject to her husband. The second fear a man has is the fear of being found inadequate! Why? Because as "the head," he has the ultimate responsibility for the woman . . . for the family. Therefore, he needs the respect, the confidence, and the support of his wife. She is the man's "help meet," his counterpart. She is bone of his bone, one flesh with him! And so God says, ". . . and let the wife see to it that she respect her husband" (Ephesians 5:33 NAS). Do you, dear, respect your husband as God has asked you to do?_____.

Spend the remainder of your time today before your God asking Him to show you specific ways in which you can show your husband respect. As you seek your Father's wisdom, you might want to ask God to show you ways in which you have failed to give your husband the respect you should have given to him. List those things God shows you so that you can keep them before you.

January 26

Have you ever found yourself frustrated as a parent not knowing what to do or how to handle a specific situation with your children? I have, and so I can understand. But, in my frustration, God met me in a marvelous and enlightening way. It was through a principle I saw from the Scriptures. He showed me that at any time *when I could not find a definite answer or a definite way to handle a problem with my children,* I could find the answer another way. What was that way? It was the way of an example. I could look at my heavenly Father and observe how He dealt with or how He handled His children . . . how He behaved, responded, reacted, provided as a Father.

Well, now that I have shared that principle with you in capsule form, beloved, let us move on to examining our hearts and lives before God as parents to our children. Let's begin by reading God's Word to us in Deuteronomy 6:6–9 and then in Ephesians 6:4, "And these words, which I am commanding you today, shall be on your heart; and you shall teach them diligently to your sons and shall talk of them when you sit in your house and when you walk by the way and when you lie down and when you rise up. And you shall bind them as a sign on your hand and they shall be as frontals on your forehead. And you shall write them on the doorposts of your house and on your gates." "And, fathers, do not provoke your children to anger; but bring them up in the discipline and instruction of the Lord" (NAS).

Now, the question comes, "Fathers, as the head of the home, the representative of the heavenly Father, are you bringing your children up in the *teaching and discipline* of the Lord?"_____. God says that *you* are to instruct your children. He does not say that the church or others are to instruct them, but that you are to instruct them when you sit down, rise up, and when you walk by the way. Do you spend enough time with your children to truly instruct them?_____. If your answer is no, how would you excuse yourself before God? You need to answer this question, beloved.

Better to answer now and face the issue, to repent, and to walk in obedience than to stand face to face before your God and to give an account to Him when it is then too late to do anything about it.

Spend time in prayer and then write out below those things God reveals to your heart.

January 27

Do you feel overwhelmed, dear parent, by all of your responsibilities? I understand that feeling also. There is so much pressure put upon us as individuals these days from so many quarters. What is a parent to do, especially a father? The demands of earning a living, the pressures of your business or profession, the pleas of social agencies in your community, the needs of the churches, and the responsibilities of the family, plus your own personal desires —all of these vie for your time and your energies. Then, on top of it all, there is that total commitment asked for by your God if He is to be your Father. What does one do? Is there an answer?

Yes, there is an answer, beloved. And at the risk of sounding naive and simplistic, the answer is to seek first the Kingdom of God and His righteousness and to rest assured that God, who cannot lie, will add to you all the other things a man needs for His family— food, clothing, and shelter. Study and meditate upon Matthew 6:19–34.

In Deuteronomy 6:5–9, you read that you are to ". . . love the Lord your God with all your heart and with all your soul and with all your might" (NAS). This passage is God's command to the parent. So you see, our priority is God. When God becomes your priority, beloved, your life will come into order, and you will have divine direction from the Father. He will then enable you to meet and to handle the pressures of life His way. Then, you will know and fulfill God's will for you as a provider, as a mate, and as a parent.

One more Scripture for the father and the mother, and then tomorrow we will move to the children. The Scripture is Colossians 3:21, "Fathers, do not exasperate your children, that they may not lose heart" (NAS). Are you guilty of dealing with your children in a wrong way . . . of dealing with them in such a way as to exasperate them or to provoke them to anger?_____. As you read the following list, check what pertains to you, and then ask God to help you in these areas. Do you frustrate your children:

with your inconsistency?_____.

by your failure to consider their feelings?_____.

by being too busy to listen?_____.

with your constant reminders of how rough or different it was when you were a child?_____.

with your constant harping?_____.

by expecting them to perform certain tasks without showing them or teaching them how?_____.

by comparing them with others?_____.

by trying to make them what you want them to be rather than developing them according to their personality or talents?_____.

by making promises and failing to meet them?_____.

by not meeting their needs for affection?_____.

by not giving them proper parental direction?_____.

by expecting too much of them for their maturity?_____.

by your failure to care about where they are or who they are with?_____.

Spend the rest of today evaluating your time with your family. Many times, we give them "things" rather than ourselves. The next time you make a major purchase, instead of evaluating it from a monetary perspective, ask yourself how much of your time it will take to pay for it. Then, ask yourself if it is worth it to your family to take that time away from them. Evaluate, also, your time spent in "religious or Christian activities." Does that time make you a better, more effective man or woman of God, and, *thus,* a better parent? Write out below what God shows you.

January 28

Children . . . teens, have you recognized your responsibility before God as a member of the family? Do you realize that God will hold you accountable for your behavior toward your parents?

For too long now, children and teens have shirked their responsibilities before God. You (and I say this in love, and those of you who know me know how dearly I care for you) have been pampered, coddled, and given far too much. I personally believe that we, in the church, are guilty before God of entertaining you rather than training you. I believe many have sacrificed teaching and ministering to the minority of children and teens who mean business for God in order to reach multitudes who only want to be coddled and who will not commit themselves to the discipline to which God calls all of His children. And, in catering to these, the churches have failed to train the youth to be soldiers for Christ. So I challenge you! Do you love God?_____. Do you belong to Jesus Christ?_____. Then, obey Him no matter what the personal cost! Throw down the trinkets of this world and take up your cross. It is time to deny yourself and to follow Christ as a habit of life, even if it costs you your life. I'm willing. Are you?_____. If your answer is yes, we will walk together. If your answer is no, I must leave you behind, and we cannot walk together.

Well, now that I have talked straight with you, let's look at God's Word to you as a child of a mother and a father. Ephesians 6:1–3 says, "Children, obey your parents in the Lord, for this is right. Honor your father and mother (which is the first commandment with a promise), that it may be well with you, and that you may live long on the earth" (NAS). Are you rebellious, or have you been rebellious?_____. Do you fail to honor your father and your mother by giving them the respect and obedience that is theirs because God says so?_____.

Now, listen to Proverbs 6:20–23, "My son, observe the commandment of your father, and do not forsake the teaching of your mother; Bind them continually on your heart; Tie them around your neck. When you walk about, they will guide you; When you sleep, they will watch over you; And when you awake, they will talk to you. For the commandment is a lamp, and the teaching is light; And reproofs for discipline are the way of life" (NAS). Have you observed what your parents have taught you and told you to do providing, of course, it did not go against Scripture nor go against God's definite will for your life?_____.

Write out to God a statement of your commitment to Him and, thus, to His Word. If you are not willing to make this commitment, tell God why not!

January 29

As we approach the end of this cleansing period, there is one more area of your lives that I want us to examine together, and that is your relationship to the world.

God tells you in 1 John 2:15-17, "Do not love the world, nor the things in the world. If any one loves the world, the love of the Father is not in him. For all that is in the world, the lust of the flesh and the lust of the eyes and the boastful pride of life, is not from the Father, but is from the world. And the world is passing away, and also its lusts; but the one who does the will of God abides forever" (NAS). Beloved, before you read any further, take a moment for prayer. Truth must be revealed to you by God's Spirit, so ask God to show you what He means by loving the world.

So many Christians are so confused when it comes to defining worldliness. This fact is shown in a code of decrees—"Do not handle, do not taste, do not touch" (Colossians 2:21 NAS)—but God says you are *not* to submit to such man-made decrees. These decrees have nothing to do with worldliness. Worldliness is sensualism, the lust of the flesh. Worldliness is materialism, coveting what the eyes see. Worldliness is egotism, the pride of life, which keeps drawing attention to self in numerous different ways or that makes you have to be number one. Worldliness is, also, loving the things of this world which will pass away and, thus, setting your affection on these things rather than on Christ and eternal things. Worldliness is not, however, not enjoying the things of this life for He has given you all things richly to enjoy (1 Timothy 6:17). Worldliness is, rather, having the improper attitude toward these things. God tells us in Colossians 3:1, 2, "If ye then be risen with Christ, seek those things which are above, where Christ sitteth on the right hand of God. Set your affection on things above, not on things on the earth."

Are you guilty of materialism or sensualism?_____. Which, if either, of these pertains to you?_____.

Do you try to inflate your own reputation or to show your superiority or importance in any way, even in spiritual things? _____. This is egotism, the pride of life as mentioned in 1 John 2:16.

Write out a prayer to your Father confessing to Him your weaknesses with respect to the world and asking for His help.

January 30

The world desires to squeeze you into its mold. Why? Because when you do not conform to its ideologies, its philosophies, its mores, its standards, you make the world uncomfortable. When Christians live holy lives, as God has commanded them, they become a thorn in the flesh of the world for then the world's cloak or covering for their sin is taken away. The world then has no excuse for its unrighteousness as Christians provide a living testimony to the reality of the fact that it is possible to live righteously in an unrighteous world.

Read what Christ told His disciples in John 15. "If the world hate you, ye know that it hated me before it hated you" (v. 18). Christ's word regarding the world is very clear. He has chosen you *out of* the world. And so God says, "I beseech you therefore, brethren, by the mercies of God, that ye present your bodies a living sacrifice, holy, acceptable unto God, which is your reasonable service. And be not conformed to this world: but be ye transformed by the renewing of your mind, that ye may prove what is that good, and acceptable, and perfect, will of God" (Romans 12:1, 2). Have you allowed the world to squeeze you into its mold in deed, in word, or in thought when it is contrary to the truths of God's Word?_____

Colossians 2:8 says, "Beware lest any man spoil you through philosophy and vain deceit, after the tradition of men, after the rudiments of the world, and not after Christ." Then, God says, "Study to shew thyself approved unto God, a workman that needeth not to be ashamed, rightly dividing the word of truth" (2 Timothy 2:15). Are you spending time on a regular basis renewing your mind through the Word of God, or are you allowing others to feed your mind?_____. Do you need milk and not solid food from the Word of God?_____. "For every one who partakes only of milk is not accustomed to the word of righteousness, for he is a babe. But solid food is for the mature, who because of practice have their senses trained to discern good and evil" (Hebrews 5:13, 14 NAS).

If your answer to this last question was that you are not spending adequate time in the Word, list below those things which keep you from studying the Word. Ask your Father to guide you in dealing with each of these and to show you His priorities for you with regard to each.

January 31

More than ever, we are seeing people who have come under bondage to the enemy. Some have willfully exposed themselves to the powers of darkness, while others have been deceitfully lured into the snare of the enemy. And then there are others—victims of the sins of others and the sins of their relatives of generations past. Sin has taken its awful toll as men have given a place of occupation to the devil through their habitual sin (Ephesians 4:27).

More and more the church of Jesus Christ in the United States of America is awakening to its responsibility to carry on Christ's work to preach deliverance or proclaim release to the captives (Luke 4:18). The church is beginning to see that any fear of Satan is not the lot of the Christian, but rather because our names are recorded in heaven; we have authority over *all* the power of the enemy (Luke 10:19) because greater is He that is in *us* than he that is in the world (1 John 4:4); therefore, even the demons are subject to us in His name (Luke 10:17).

We are to have no part in anything that has anything to do with the spirit world or the world of the occult. God's Word is so clear on this issue. How I would like to write out for you each of the following Scripture references, however, space does not permit. So what I would love to have you do is to stop and to look up each of the following references before you go any further. It would also be a good idea for you to write this list in the flyleaf of your Bible for future reference. Exodus 34:13, 17; Leviticus 19:31, 36, 20:27; Deuteronomy 4:16–19, 23, 12:2–5, 17:15, 18:9; 1 Chronicles 10:13; Isaiah 8:19, 47:13; Jeremiah 10:1–5, 29:8; Daniel 2:24, 4:7; Amos 5:26; Micah 3:6, 7; Zechariah 10:2; Acts 16:16–18; 1 Corinthians 10:20, 21; Galatians 5:20; Revelation 22:15.

Now then, if you would be totally free from any influence the enemy might have gained over your life because of disobedience to any of these Scriptures, you must confess your sin and ask God to take control of any ground gained by the enemy. Renounce Satan's influence over you and command the enemy to be gone by the blood of Jesus Christ. Ask the Holy Spirit to fill every fiber of your being that everything in His temple might say, "Glory!" (1 Corinthians 6:19, 20).

Check the following occult practices that you have participated in and then deal with them as you were just instructed.

__Amulets
__Astrology
__Automatic writing
__Carved images
__Crystal ball readings
__Dowsing
__Divination
__ESP
__Fortune telling
__Horoscope

__Idolatry
__Kabala
__Mesmerism
__Mind or thought control
__Ouija board
__Palm reading
__Psychic healing
__Reincarnation
__Ritual magic
__Seances

__Spells
__Spiritualism
__Sorcery
__Superstition
__Table lifting
__Tarot cards
__TM
__VooDoo
__Witchcraft
__Yoga
__Zodiac

Doesn't it feel wonderful to be right with God, to be restored to total fellowship with the Godhead!

Well, beloved, the month of cleansing is over! Now, your responsibility is to maintain that cleanness through immediate repentance and confession of sin, but better still, beloved, learn to hate sin . . . to flee, for sin hurts God's heart, and it mars His image in the one who bears the title, Christian, which means "little Christ."

FEBRUARY

February 1

It's a disease called "marasmus" . . . wasting away. Have you ever heard of it? It was a disease common among infants who were victims of war or who were poorly cared for in orphanages. Marasmus is caused by being deprived of love. It develops when infants are not picked up, held, cuddled, caressed, kissed, hugged, squeezed, and generally loved. It comes when love or affection is not expressed in some way toward a human being. Children or people who have marasmus do not develop socially, psychologically, or physically, and they often waste away and die. Can you imagine what it would be like to die never having experienced love?

Do you realize that, apart from God's divine intervention, if a baby does not receive expressions of love during the first year of his life, he may be unable to receive or express love during his entire lifetime? We never outgrow our need for love. As a matter of fact, this need will only increase with age.

Have you ever wondered how we learn to love ourselves? Have you ever thought that we gain our perception of our own personal worth or value through the eyes of others—by the way others treat us? Call a child mean, dumb, stupid, ugly, worthless and that is the way he will see himself. On the other hand, give a child love, admiration, a sense of worth—hug him, squeeze him, kiss him, pat him, and he will develop a godly sense of self-esteem. He will see himself as you have seen him.

How many are there in this world who are suffering from marasmus, wasting away because they are not receiving the love and the affection they so desperately need? I think we would be horror-stricken if we really knew the answer to that question. Read the book, *Dorie* (by Doris Van Stone with Erwin W. Lutzer: Moody Press), the true story of a young girl who never knew love or affection from any human being until she became a teenager. Dorie survived only because a church group came to her orphanage one time, and a young woman in that group told her of the love of God. Even then, she almost didn't believe that God loved her because all her life she had been rejected and told how ugly and unlovable she was!

If you could just sit with me and read my mail! Oh, how my heart aches, for there are so many who are suffering the results of having never been loved.

How indebted I am to my mother and my father who so loved me, and so expressed that love, that I do recognize my worth. It is because of their love and God's love that I am able to love others . . . because I love myself. How indebted I am to God for loving me unconditionally—eternally. Oh, how I long to be love's debtor, to reach out to all of you in verbal and tangible expressions of love. Who knows, someone I touch may be suffering from marasmus, and God could use me to keep them from wasting away.

Oh, beloved, will you not join me in prayer asking God to teach us how to love—how to really love others with the love of our precious Lord?

February 2

If we are ever to love others with the love of the Lord, we must understand what love really is. Oh, we throw the term around loosely as we speak of everything from chocolate candy to our children, but do we understand the real meaning of love—love that seeks another's highest good, love that turns the other cheek, love that says, "Nothing you ever do could separate you from my love," love that says, "I understand," love that says, "I'm sorry," love that says, "Although you walk a hard road, I'll walk it with you"?

In my mail this week, there was a letter from a woman who had been raped. Her cry was for love, for understanding. The Christians around her were only giving her judgment. Almost in a desperate, heartrending cry, I could hear from the page as she screamed, "Where are the ____Christians when you need them!" Oh, beloved, where are we? We'll point our fingers, we'll spout correct doctrine, but will we pay the price to love?

Love costs! It makes you vulnerable—willing to be hurt, willing to be misunderstood. It requires commitment. But, oh, the sweetness of wounds healed by the costly ointment of love.

How will the world know we're Christians? What will draw them to our Lord? It is not our doctrines as vital as they are. It is not our correct biblical interpretation necessary though it be. But, beloved, it is our love—genuine, committed, unshakable, and sincere.

What is your life-style like? How does your husband, your child, your neighbor, your boss know that you are a Christian?

"By this all men will know that you are My disciples, if you have love for one another" (John 13:35 NAS).

His Thoughts Toward Me:

My Thoughts Toward Him:

February 3

Within each of our breasts is the capacity to love to one degree or another. That love is expressed in different ways, but it is there. For some, the words *I love you* are not easily or glibly uttered. For others, "I love you" rolls off their tongues with great ease. While the articulate person may find saying "I love you" very easy, the inarticulate or the more reserved individual may find the words difficult to form. Words are so important, but beyond that I want to share with you today what I believe is the deepest point of understanding one can reach when putting love into terms that can be expressed or defined. No matter how often we say, "I love you," if the commitment is not there to back it up, eventually the words will fail.

Commitment is a lost concept in our generation. One hundred years ago, only one in thirty-four marriages failed. Today, one marriage ends for every two that begin. How can this be? Beloved, we have lost our sense of commitment.

Marriage vows are now written, "As long as we both shall love"; no more is it a standard ceremony that includes "till death do us part."

How do we define commitment? Go to the koine Greek with me and look at the definition of *agape* love—God's kind of love. *Agape* love is a love that loves because of the preciousness of and esteem for the inherent value of the object loved. That is commitment couched in terms of love.

It is a love that would keep on loving for the pure worth of the one loved whether any pleasure is derived for the lover or not— or whether any love is ever returned.

I have a stack of current women's magazines that I have been leafing through to get some statistical information for our television program, "How Can I Live?" Over and over, the titles of articles reflect a society that reels from lack of commitment: "Surviving the First Christmas After the Divorce," "Love Crazy: When You Fall Too Far," "The Artful Pick-Up," "One Parent: How To Relate." These articles are from popular, widely read magazines.

In all their racy sophistication, these titles represent a love-hungry, uncommitted society blinded by their lusts to the pain in their own hearts, which cry, "Somebody love me for who I am!"

Is there anyone you love—really love—just for who they are and not for what they can give you? *What do you mean when you say, "I love you"?*

His Thoughts Toward Me:

My Thoughts Toward Him:

February 4

I asked you yesterday if there is anyone you love just for who they are. Let me ask you another question today, Is there anyone who loves you . . . who is committed to you because you are totally acceptable to them just the way you are? If you can't think of anyone, then you probably feel as if nobody really cares about you.

Do you sit at home wondering why the phone doesn't ring, wondering why you don't have any real friends?

Do you long for someone to talk with soul to soul, but you wonder if there is anyone you can really trust—anyone who would really understand you?

Do you feel that people would not like you if they knew what you were really like?

Do you feel ugly, dumb, stupid, or unattractive as a man or a woman?

Do you feel like you are a failure, that you will never amount to much of anything?

Do you dislike yourself? Do you wish you looked different? Had a different life? Were somebody else?

Do you feel unloved? Unlovable? Do you feel empty, sad, lonely?

Do you ever lie on your bed at night just thinking, maybe crying, maybe not, depressed?

When you are out in a crowd, do you try hard not to let people see the real you for fear that if they did they would not like you?

Do you try to be acceptable so that you can be accepted?

When you look at yourself in the mirror, do you see defects—blemishes that you are sure everybody must notice? Or have you been told that you are attractive, but you think that you are really ugly?

Then, my beloved one, you need to know that you are loved just for who you are, because until you realize this, you will never be able to reach out to another in unconditional commitment of yourself in love!

What a privilege to be able to spend time with you telling you that you are loved. First, as I write these words, I cannot tell you the love that flows from my heart toward you, every precious one of you who reads this book; but more than that I can tell you that God loves you. He loves you with that love I've been talking about —that love that doesn't depend on your "lovability." Here's what He says to you: ". . . I have loved thee with an everlasting love. . . ." "I will call them my people, which were not my people; and her beloved, which was not beloved." "But God commendeth his love toward us, in that, while we were yet sinners, Christ died for us." "For I am persuaded, that neither death, nor life, nor angels, nor principalities, nor powers, nor things present, nor things to come, nor height, nor depth, nor any other creature, shall be able to separate us from the love of God, which is in Christ Jesus our Lord" (Jeremiah 31:3; Romans 9:25; 5:8; 8:38, 39).

February 5

Yesterday's devotion ended on a triumphant note, but maybe you're not feeling so victorious right now. God says that He loves you, that He has demonstrated that love in Christ, that there is nothing that can separate you from that love. It's true, and you know that it's true in your head, but your heart is still having trouble believing it. My daddy used to tell me, "Kay, when you know what your problem is, then you have half the battle won!" He said it more than once, and I needed to hear it because I have had a lot of battles. But those words always spurred me on to seek victory rather than to settle for defeat. Beloved, if you are ever to love others with an unconditional, committed love, then you must know, experience, believe, rely upon, and rest in the unconditional love of God for you. If you don't feel loved, it is probably because you are putting some condition on God's love for you.

The symptoms of this problem are poor self-esteem, a dislike of who or what you are, a sense of worthlessness, or an unwillingness to accept God's forgiveness in some area of your life.

The cure for the problem is learning to receive God's love and to see yourself through His eyes as a person of value. If you cannot accept God's love, then you probably have never been able to accept His forgiveness. Until you accept the forgiveness of God, the love that He desires to lavish on and through you is blocked. In order to accept His forgiveness, you must forgive others.

Listen to Jesus' words in Matthew 6:14, 15 and then meditate on what God is saying, really saying to you, "For if ye forgive men their trespasses, your heavenly Father will also forgive you: But if ye forgive not men their trespasses, neither will your Father forgive your trespasses."

Now, take a moment and list those people in your life, past and present, living or dead, whom you have never forgiven. Then, by each name list why you have not forgiven them.

Now, in the quietness of your prayer time and as a matter of your will, tell God that you will forgive each one of them. Then, ask God to forgive you for withholding forgiveness, for as we have seen, it is sin!

If you still are unable to find release, then do as James instructs, "Confess your faults one to another. . . ." Go to a mature, loving Christian and confess your lack of forgiveness. In the process, if your heart is really sincere, you'll find in yourself the grace to forgive. Ask God to never let you forget His forgiveness for your sins.

Beloved, the battle is beginning to be won.

February 6

Beloved, I feel that God would have us spend one more day looking at *what He has to say* about forgiveness. We live in a day and an age of great mutilation. When iniquity explodes in a society, people cannot help but be wounded by its shrapnel. This shrapnel can leave bitter, ugly, repulsive scars, and putrefied, festering wounds, unless it is attended to by the Great Physician.

There is not any wound God cannot heal, but wounds must be healed His way. You cannot cover these wounds with the dressing of man's reasoning, nor can you pretend they do not exist. Shrapnel left within the body undetected can dislodge at anytime and do a destructive work. Therefore, it must be detected and removed. Ask God, by His Spirit, to do a thorough work in your life as you meditate upon His Word.

"Then Peter came and said to Him, 'Lord, how often shall my brother sin against me and I forgive him? Up to seven times?' Jesus said to him, 'I do not say to you, up to seven times, but up to seventy times seven. For this reason the kingdom of heaven may be compared to a certain king who wished to settle accounts with his slaves. And when he had begun to settle them, there was brought to him one who owed him ten thousand talents. But since he did not have the means to repay, his lord commanded him to be sold, along with his wife and children and all that he had, and repayment to be made. The slave therefore falling down, prostrated himself before him, saying, "Have patience with me, and I will repay you everything." And the lord of that slave felt compassion and released him and forgave him the debt. But that slave went out and found one of his fellow-slaves who owed him a hundred denarii; and he seized him and began to choke him, saying, "Pay back what you owe." So his fellow-slave fell down and began to entreat him, saying, "Have patience with me and I will repay you." He was unwilling however, but went and threw him in prison until he should pay back what was owed. So when his fellow-slaves saw what had happened, they were deeply grieved and came and reported to their lord all that had happened. Then summoning him, his lord said to him, "You wicked slave, I forgave you all that debt because you entreated me. Should you not also have had mercy on your fellow-slave, even as I had mercy on you?" And his lord, moved with anger, handed him over to the torturers until he should repay all that was owed him. So shall My heavenly Father also do to you, if each of you does not forgive his brother from your heart' " (Matthew 18:21–35 NAS).

Beloved, "And so, as those who have been chosen of God, holy and beloved, put on a heart of compassion, kindness, humility, gentleness and patience; bearing with one another, and forgiving each other, whoever has a complaint against any one; just as the Lord forgave you, so also should you" (Colossians 3:12, 13 NAS).

His Thoughts Toward Me:

February 7

Love and forgiveness were inseparably linked at Calvary. There, God proved His love by offering up His only begotten Son for us when we were yet His enemies, helpless sinners without hope. And there at Calvary, the One who was made sin for us cried out, "Father, forgive them; for they do not know what they are doing . . ." (Luke 23:34 NAS). Love and forgiveness were inseparably linked at Calvary. They became inseparably one, never to be divorced from one another! *If you love, you must forgive.* You cannot love and withhold or deny forgiveness. Thus God's Word comes to us, ". . . forgiving each other, *just as God in Christ also has forgiven you*" (Ephesians 4:32 NAS, italics added). Therefore, if you love yourself, you must forgive yourself.

If you have *not* believed, received, and accepted God's forgiveness for your sins, failures, shortcomings, how can you forgive others when you see the same things in them? Can you assure them of God's covering love and forgiveness when you are not assured of it yourself?

When I look at my past, I do not have to bury, deny, or suppress the reality of it—my divorce, my adultery, my husband's suicide, the wounds to my children and to my family. I can face them, take full responsibility for them, and still love myself. Why? Because God has said to me, through His Son at Calvary, "Thy sins are forgiven thee." Go and sin no more. And she who was forgiven much, loves much (Luke 7:47–50). If God, the One who was offended by my sin, loves and forgives me, who am I to deny or to refuse that love and the forgiveness that goes with it?

Do you know the love and the forgiveness of God? Have you received His full and free pardon for all of your sins, failures, and shortcomings? If not, tell God this day that you will, *by faith,* fully receive all that is yours because of Calvary. Write out your acceptance below.

February 8

How important are you? Are you loved? Admired? How do others rate you? Do you belong? What is your sense of self-worth?

Oh, how vital it is that you know you matter to someone! You do not just need to hear them say it, but you need to know it with a certainty! This need is a built-in human need, a need created by God in every human being. You have heard the statement, "No man is an island," and it is true. We were built to need one another. God knows this need, and that is why He tells us that we are to love one another (John 15:12), to accept one another as Christ accepted us (Romans 15:7), and to meet together and to encourage one another (Hebrews 10:25).

If your self-esteem is to be kept intact, you must feel that you are a person of worth. You must know that you do count, that you are important. There are so very many who are hurting in this particular area. I believe that the major cause of this pain is the breakdown in family relationships. We are too busy—too over-committed, and in all of our busyness, we have no more time for the individual. So material possessions and gifts have been given to our loved ones *instead of ourselves and our time.* Everyone is too busy, too exhausted, too preoccupied, too strung out to care and to spend time with one another.

Our human engines idle so fast that we have to be doing something or going somewhere. We don't have time to sit, to listen, to share, and in doing so to say, "You matter. You are important. You mean something to me."

You feel good about yourself when you are accepted by others. Lack of acceptance is what causes many to turn to all sorts of way-out groups, cults, or religions that are foreign to their upbringing. Then, their parents or acquaintances say, "I just can't

understand it. That isn't the way they were taught or brought up."
Right, it isn't the way, but apparently their need was not met in
their home, in their church, or in their society. So they went
elsewhere because they had to belong, to feel important to somebody. In their driving need, that is where they ended up—right
or wrong!

How vital it is that you know that you are "accepted in the
beloved" (Ephesians 1:6), and how vital it is that you love and
accept others unconditionally as God accepts you (Romans 14:1;
15:6). This is true love.

His Thoughts Toward Me:

My Thoughts Toward Him:

February 9

By now, you may think that a week is a long time to spend
clearing your love-channels so that the unconditional, sacrificial
love of commitment can flow through you to another! But, beloved, it is so very much worth it! Just knowing the love of God in
your own life can make you useful instead of useless.

In the past year, I have been made aware of two women. These
are two women who were starved for love as children, who suffered from adoptive or foster parent abuse, and who have ended
up telling their stories in books. But here the similarities end!

One of the women was the daughter of a well-known movie star
who writes, "I was claiming the right to tell the truth. I was the
abused child of a famous mother . . . a secret I had learned to
keep." In her book, she introduces the story standing by her
mother's casket whispering, "I know you're not really here with
me any more mother . . . I know your soul is gone already . . . I
just want to tell you that I love you . . . that I forgive you . . ." (from

Mommie Dearest, Christina Crawford: Berkley Publishing Corporation).

And yet 300 pages later, after a blow-by-blow account of abuse and perversion, one is left with the sense of a young woman still struggling—still crying out to be loved. She tried therapy. She exposed it all through the catharsis of her book. She lauds her husband for his loving understanding. But still the bitter pain remains, and the forgiveness and the love have not come, have not been received from the One who knows and loves her best—Jesus Christ. She doesn't seem to recognize that she has been left embittered and embroiled in a continuing search for "reason and identity," a very masked phrase for love and self-esteem.

She has received hundreds of letters. One woman wrote, "No one—except one such as you who has experienced it—can imagine the deep hurt inside that will not go away. Doctors have not helped. Pills have not, prayers have not, but you have. Now perhaps I can go on normally and in time forget."

Oh, how people cry for understanding, and for a short time, it soothes. But people need so much more! The love of God in Christ Jesus is the *only* power that can make the hurt go away.

Tomorrow, the story of Dorie, the girl nobody loved—except One.

His Thoughts Toward Me:

My Thoughts Toward Him:

February 10

You have already caught a glimpse of Dorie. She was the orphan I told you about in an earlier devotional. Even as a child of six, Dorie was told by her mother that her little sister, Marie, was "a pretty girl—she's not like you." Her mother would tuck the little sister into bed and kiss her good-night. Dorie, with pain, remembers, "Without changing my clothes—I had no pajamas—I crawled under the covers next to my sister. Not once did my mother hug me or let me sit on her lap."

From these early experiences, Dorie's life was one rejection after another. She was sent to live in an orphanage, where she was beaten by the orphanage director. When she arrived in a foster home, her hopes for love were dashed as she was banished from the family table—her only food to be the fish heads left from the family's meal. She was beaten by her foster parents; between beatings, she was told how ugly and unlovable she was.

The only light in her life came in the midst of it all when she was told by a college student, who visited her orphanage, that there was One who loved her and that His name was Jesus Christ. Afraid to believe it, but too starved for love not to believe it, Dorie accepted the unconditional love that changes lives and heals hurts that no man can touch.

But, even as a child of God, Dorie was to know more human rejection! Any of the incidents she endured could have crushed the human spirit, but Dorie triumphed knowing the love of her lovely Lord Jesus. Today, she is in His service—a love-slave to Him. Her book shouts of victory. Not a word of bitterness is uttered in the whole account! And today when she receives letters from people who have been hurt, who have known the same pain as she, she can hold out to them the promise of healing, total and complete. She doesn't have to offer them therapy . . . no bitter catharsis, she just offers the unconditional acceptance that heals the deepest wound. "Heal me, O Lord, and I shall be healed . . ." (Jeremiah 17:14).

Oh, how I wish that the writer of the following letter, which was sent to the movie star's daughter, could have talked to Dorie or to some Christian who cared enough to share the unconditional love of Christ that her wounds might have been healed.

Most people with whom I've talked could never understand why I tried for over fifty years to make my mother love me. The sad thing is that all of us are marked—scarred to this day, and so are my own children.

Beloved, do you care enough to learn to love as He does?

His Thoughts Toward Me:

February 11

So far, the only kind of love I've talked about is the kind of love that has its only source in God—*agape* love.

The koine Greek had three other words for *love.* One of those words, *eros,* the word closely akin to our word, *erotic,* was never used in the Septuagint or in the New Testament. Isn't it interesting that erotic love is probably the most frequently used meaning behind our usage of the word love today? It is love based on body chemistry. The basic idea behind *eros* love is self-satisfaction. *Eros* shouts, "I love you because something about you makes me feel good." It looks for what it can receive. If it gives, it gives in order to receive. And when it does not receive what it wants, it becomes bitter and pouts.

Eros love lasts as long as the flower blooms. When the blossom fades, *eros* has found a new field of flowers to stimulate the senses, to satisfy the lustful cravings. *Eros* knows no commitment except to its own desires.

Eros is the teenager who presses his girl, "If you love me, Baby, prove it." *Eros* is the husband who says, "You were good enough to put me through law school, but now I need someone more intellectually stimulating." *Eros* says, "Mom, will you do my wash? And oh yeah, Mom, when I have my party, will you stay in your room, you know how my friends are." *Eros* says, "Son, if you ever get in trouble with the law, don't bother to come home." *Eros* love will allow itself to have an affair—an *eros* affair at that! *Eros* loves as the world loves.

Is there any relationship in which you have been guilty of *eros* love?

His Thoughts Toward Me:

My Thoughts Toward Him:

February 12

The kind of love that most of us experience in our relationship with our friends and acquaintances is *phileo* love. *Phileo* speaks of affection, of fondness, of liking. Wuest defines it as "love called out of one's heart by the pleasure one takes in the object loved." It is a love that responds to love, to kindness, and to appreciation. It involves not only receiving but giving, and it is expressed on a higher plane than *eros* because it is *our* happiness rather than *my* happiness. *Phileo* falls short of *agape,* however, because it can be greatly strained, even to the point of collapse in a crisis! *Phileo* love thrives in fair weather; it holds up well in the rain, but rarely can it stand the stormy gale.

Phileo is a cup of coffee, a few shared intimacies, some happy times remembered. *Phileo* expresses kindness and blossoms brilliantly in the light of appreciation. *Phileo* is not a negative word at all; it is just a word that lacks the strength of commitment. "I love . . . until something happens that prevents my loving you anymore."

Dorie was nineteen when, with fear and trembling, she sent a letter to a Mr. L. Duckworth in Tulsa asking if he were her father. She would never forget his first words when he called, " 'Dorie, honey?' No one had ever spoken such words to me before." He was asking her to come halfway across the United States to visit him. " 'No, Dad,' I protested. 'If you'd see me, you wouldn't want me anyway.' 'Don't be silly. Of course I'd want you.' "

It was at a crowded bus station at the age of nineteen that Dorie was hugged for the very first time in her life. That hug came from her father. Now, she had the love of two friends, God and her father. But only One's love was unconditional. Little did Dorie know that in a few short years her father would reject her because of her commitment to obey God by going to New Guinea as a missionary.

"If that's what you plan to do, then don't unpack your suitcase. From this moment on you are not my daughter."

"Dad, you don't mean it."

"Yes, I do. I never want to see you again."

And with that, he turned his back to her. When Dorie tried to hug him, he stiffened. Dorie's last words to her father were, "Dad, I still love you." But he did not reply. He did not turn around. He had been the only person in the world who had loved Dorie. Now, the storm had come, and *phileo* love was gone in its gale.

Phileo love can walk out. *Agape* love stays—no matter what, it does not fail. *Agape* love endures all things, hopes all things, believes all things. It is everlasting.

"Beloved, let us love *(agape)* one another; for love is from God ..." (1 John 4:7 NAS). With what kind of love would you be loved? And with what kind of love would you love?

February 13

To meet the needs of people who are crying, "Love me for who I am," not only must you love yourself with a healthy self-esteem, but you must go beyond the love of *eros* and *phileo.* You must love with a love that thrives in the face of all of life's hazards and that can survive anything.

The love that began in the heart of God and was displayed in Jesus Christ has the potential to be completed in you.

We will spend the next days considering *how* the love of God can be lived out or completed in you.

71

To love as God loves, we must look at people as God sees them. "Therefore from now on we recognize no man according to the flesh . . ." (2 Corinthians 5:16 NAS). We must learn to look at others as new creations in Christ, as those for whom Christ died, as those who have the potential to become new creations.

Dorie Van Stone went to New Guinea to be a missionary to the Danis, a tribe of stone-age men. She discovered that ". . . the Danis never take a bath from birth to death. They cake themselves with pig grease, rub charcoal on their bodies, and cover themselves with mud during periods of mourning.

"I have often been asked, 'Doris, how could you really love those people?' Because I had experienced God's grace I could give His grace. The Danis had no word for love. I had not known love until God loved me. God seemed to say, 'Dorie, you were like one of them—rejected and ugly. But I loved you and transformed you. I can also transform them.' "

But you don't have to go to New Guinea to find people who are difficult to love! There are plenty of "unlovables" who are part of your life daily.

Spend today praising God that He saw fit to love you when there was nothing to love. And He called you beloved when there was nothing lovely about you (Romans 9:25). Then, ask God to let you see others as He sees them. Ask God to show you specific ways to express His love to those you, at one time, considered unlovable.

His Thoughts Toward Me:

My Thoughts Toward Him:

February 14

Why do we find it difficult to love some people? What causes us to want to avoid certain people or certain types of people? What is it that we find disgusting in other people? What turns us off and makes us want to walk away?

Taking the time to think about these questions and seeking out honest answers could give us great and liberating insights into ourselves. The love to which God calls us as Christians is an *agape* love—unconditional love that is initiated by the lover and is manifested by its behavior toward the one who is to be loved. God's command to us is clearly seen in 1 John 4:11, "Beloved, if God so loved us, we also ought to love one another" (NAS).

If we are His, we have a moral obligation to love one another ... with the same kind of love He has for us. Therefore, if we have trouble loving others, we would do well to discover what is keeping His love from flowing through us in an unhindered way so that we can deal with the hinderance.

As you fill out the chart below, ask the Holy Spirit to use this to cleanse you of all the debris of your self-life.

Things That Turn Me Off In Others	Who It Reminds Me Of

Types Of People I Avoid	Why? What I Think Their Problem Is

Specific People I Try To Avoid	Why?	What Is Their Need?

February 15

Do you realize that much adverse, unpleasant, or obnoxious behavior is a cry for attention—for love? Kids that wear outlandish outfits or hats when no one else wears them, people who are always talking, poking, pulling, joking, showing off, getting hurt, or sulking are crying for attention. A child constantly tugging at a mother's skirt or acting up, a rebellious teenager, a nagging wife, a philandering husband are all, to some extent, crying for attention. Something is missing, something is wrong. Many of these people could be healed if someone would take the time to find out the "why" of their need, and then, in love, would give themselves to the healing of that wound.

Love doesn't react to behavior; love responds to needs. Love pays attention because love desires another's highest good. Whatever the cost, it is not too much to pay. To pay attention to another and to his needs requires the sacrifice of our valuable time and our preoccupation with our own interests. This very act, on our part, shows that person that we see worth in him.

The very fact that you respond instead of react will begin to fulfill the empty groping for love that he needs. So often just noticing someone and patiently waiting for his response will heal a world of neglectful hurts.

There was a young man in a mental hospital who had stared blankly at the wall without saying anything for years. For the most part, he was ignored. But one man visited the hospital and took an interest in him. This man would patiently sit and talk to the young man. This process went on for months. Then one day, the young man turned to the man who had been visiting him and in slow, halting speech said, "I had a pet squirrel once!" A wall had come down. Someone had paid attention. Someone had cared enough to respond instead of react.

His Thoughts Toward Me:

My Thoughts Toward Him:

February 16

"God, teach me the art of paying attention." How this needs to be our prayer in these days when there seem to be so many demands made upon us from so many different quarters!

If we are going to develop the sensitive and neglected art of paying attention, first we have to recognize its vital importance.

Remember, paying attention takes time—yours! Are you willing to pay the cost? Are people worth it? Ask yourself these questions: "What value does God place upon people? Are they more important than possessions, money, recognition, achievement, position?"

If people are more important than all these things, then any investment of your time that is necessary to make them realize their worth to God and to man is a very worthwhile and necessary investment. So then let's look at several things that can be done in helping to develop the art of paying attention.

First, you need to learn to listen with all the intensity and awareness that you can command. Focus in on that person. Look at him. Ask God to show you his real needs. Ask Him to help you hear and discern what he is saying to you. Ask God to show you how to respond to him, how to minister to him, what to say.

Second, you need to listen patiently. This step is where I fail because I find myself so busy because of the demands of the ministry. But I am learning. People need time to express their innermost thoughts, hurts, disappointments and wounds. And then they will become secure enough to be able to share with you and make themselves vulnerable. Patient, sympathetic listening will often bring a person to a point where he will realize his own need just through verbalizing all that he has been through and felt in the situation.

If God finds us of such worth that He listens to us, should we not listen also if we want to convey God's loving care to others? His ears are open to our cry (Psalms 34:15). O Father, may our ears be open, also, to the cries of others.

Tomorrow, we will finish sharing how to develop the art of listening. But as you finish today's devotional, why don't you spend time listening to God.

His Thoughts Toward Me:

My Thoughts Toward Him:

February 17

Unless I honestly care about a person, there is no use paying attention to him for eventually my pretense will manifest itself. Paying attention to a person necessitates being genuinely concerned about that person. Real concern is being willing to share another's hurts, fears, confusions, frustrations, and problems. It is being willing to "bear one another's burdens, and thus fulfil the law of Christ" (Galatians 6:2 NAS).

How do I know God really loves me? Because He was willing to bear all my burdens. He told me to cast all my cares upon Him because what is of concern to me is of the utmost concern to my God and Father (1 Peter 5:7). What touches me, touches Him. That is why Jesus said to Saul (Paul), "Saul, Saul, why are you persecuting Me" (Acts 9:4 NAS). Jesus was touched with the *feeling* of our infirmities, and so we are to be touched with the feeling of others' infirmities. Are you concerned enough to pay attention to others?

Last of all, if I am going to learn the art of paying attention, I will have to learn to put aside my own ego and my own needs. If I am going to give another person the attention he needs, then I cannot seek to gain the spotlight for myself in any way. I have to suppress all or any desire to impress. I have to be willing to listen rather than to use the situation as a platform to express my views or my opinions. Some people counsel others simply because it meets their own ego's needs. Remember, ". . . the Son of man came not to be ministered unto, but to minister, and to give His life a ransom for many" (Matthew 20:28). Those who minister best to others are usually those who are secure and well-balanced in their own lives and in the Word of God. If I am going to love others and give them love's attention, I need to be at peace with myself —to love myself. This enables me to love others and, thus, to focus my attention on them.

Oh, beloved, how I pray that God will use these devotionals to make us more sensitive to the cries of those who so desperately need His attention.

His Thoughts Toward Me:

My Thoughts Toward Him:

February 18

Euthanasia. Do you know what it can be? It can be the killing off of the elderly—putting to death those who are old and who are seemingly of no use to society. Does it sound horrible, inhumane? I hope so! What right has any man to decide when another man is of no value and, thus, shall be put to death? Is it not God who wounds and heals, who kills and makes alive (Deuteronomy 32: 39)? If God does not take away a person's life, then apparently there is some purpose for that person's existence. Oh, we may see no purpose. We may look at them and decide that because they are senile and cannot care for themselves there is no purpose for their existence. As we look at them and consider what an inconvenience, an expense, or a hardship they are on us, then we might consider at least putting them out of the way, out of sight, although we may not believe in the act of euthanasia. I wonder when we put our old people away because we feel they have lost their usefulness if we miss seeing that God has permitted them to live so that He might use them to perfect certain characteristics in our lives—characteristics that would serve to make us more like Jesus, who in love laid down His life for others?

Let's consider one more thing as we talk about the elderly. Have you ever walked through a nursing home and spent time talking to some of the people who "live" there? Many are not complete invalids who are unable to care for themselves, nor do they require constant medical attention. Rather many of these people are human beings who have been abandoned by their families because their presence in the home was an inconvenience of one sort or another. Is this love? Is this laying down your life for another? "But many are senile," you may say. Or you may say, "They are impossible to live with!" And both of these statements may be true.

Let me give you something to think about, and then we will talk about it more tomorrow. It's an important subject because you may live to be an elderly person. In the light of all we have meditated on this month, why do you think people become senile or hard to live with? Write out your thoughts below.

February 19

Old people. Why do so many become senile or hard to live with? Is senility always caused by physical problems? I do not believe so! Let me share a true story with you.

There was a man in a nursing home who required total nursing care. He had to be fed, bathed, and was even incontinent. He did nothing to keep himself alive or to care for his own basic needs or bodily functions. Every morning, he was bathed, taken out of bed, and tied into a chair. There he sat communicating with no one.

The nurses and aides carried on minimal conversations with him, nothing of import was said, only the usual nurse-patient chatter of "Good morning, Mr. Smith, are you going to eat, smile, or whatever?" Inane talk, no more! One day, someone took an interest in that man. Their talk was stimulating, intelligent, challenging. They communicated with him as an adult of worth and value. They recognized that with age went wisdom—the wisdom that years of experience can bring. As they talked and cared for him, they encouraged and expected him to do things for himself. Through patience, and with time, that man was made to see that he still had worth—he still had purpose in life. He began to see his importance, until finally he was up and around not only caring for himself but caring for others there in the nursing home. He became an extension of the nursing staff, even mopping floors when needed.

What had happened? Someone cared for his soul. Someone took the time to instill in him a sense of worth. Someone was willing to patiently persevere . . . to love him. "Love never fails" . . . "is not provoked" . . . "endures all things" (1 Corinthians 13:8, 5, 7 NAS). I know that I do not really love as Christ loved, but, oh, I do want to learn. Don't you? How do we learn? By being given the opportunity. What is your opportunity? Think about it.

Are you one of those people who wishes they had a ministry for Christ? Have you ever thought of going to a nursing home and loving those people with the love of Christ? Oh, not preaching to them but sharing with them—sharing first His unconditional love and care that expresses itself as James indicates in doing good deeds, in meeting their needs (James 2:14–17). Then, when God

tells you to speak, you can share the gospel. It will be more believ-
able and acceptable then for they will have seen and experienced
the reality of God's *agape* love through you, His disciple.

February 20

For God's love to be completed in you, you must accept another
with the same acceptance that God accords to you. In Romans 9:25
God says that He will "call those who were not My people, 'My
people' and her who was not Beloved, 'Beloved' " (NAS).

Wife or husband, when was the last time that you looked at your
mate and thought, *I love you just the way you are?* Over the years,
that perfection you saw in the man or the woman of your dreams
has no doubt been replaced by a more realistic view. The rose-
tinted lenses have been replaced by a magnifying glass which
glaringly exposes every wart or wrinkle, and now it's up to you to
love. With what love do you come to your mate? With:

"I love you as long as you act the way I think you should";

"I have a love for you that will last as long as you love me"; or

"I love you just for who you are"?

You know, the way we love all goes back to our self-acceptance. If
we have a healthy regard for who we are and for our worth in God's
eyes, then whatever our mate does or however he acts will not embarrass us. For after all, what are the qualities that we find difficult to accept? They are qualities which might make us look or feel
bad—which cause us to question something about ourselves.

If *agape* love, unconditional, committed love is our aim, then
acceptance will be the result. In her book, *His Stubborn Love,*
Joyce Landorf tells of the man in her church who accepted Christ
after his wife had prayed for him for thirty-five years. With tears
he told how he simply had to become a Christian because in
thirty-five years he had not seen his wife do one unkind, unloving,
or un-Christian thing. She didn't preach. She loved. She accepted.

What could your husband or wife say about the quality of your
love and acceptance of him or of her?

80

His Thoughts Toward Me:

My Thoughts Toward Him:

February 21

Love is always an active verb not a passive one. Love is more than words—it must express itself if it is true love for true love cannot go unexpressed.

Love has its source in God, for love is the very essence of His being. But man would never know, or even be aware, of that love, nor of its character, if it had not been expressed in a tangible way. Love is tangible. It can be seen, felt, experienced, known. It is more than words, sentiments, feelings, or emotions.

Love is known, primarily, by what it gives and by the way it behaves. First John 4:9 says, "By this the love of God was manifested in us, that God has sent His only begotten Son into the world so that we might live through Him" (NAS). John 3:16 says, ". . . God so loved the world that He gave His only begotten Son . . ." (NAS). Love is measured by what it gives, by the sacrifice it makes. When Paul wants us to fully realize the extent of God's love and commitment to us, he writes, under inspiration of the Holy Spirit, "He who did not spare His own Son, but delivered Him up for us all, how will He not also with Him freely give us all things?" (Romans 8:32 NAS.) Then, in this same chapter, Paul goes on to assure us that nothing shall ever be able to separate us from the love of God, which is in Christ Jesus our Lord (v. 39).

Love gives, it is obligated to meet another's needs as much as possible. In God's case, He is able to supply all of our needs according to His riches in glory in Christ Jesus (Philippians 4:19). In man's case, if we love as Christ loved, our world's goods cannot be withheld from a brother in need. Listen to God's Words in 1 John 3:16, 17, "We know love by this, that He laid down His life for us; and we ought to lay down our lives for the brethren. But whoever has the world's goods, and beholds his brother in need and closes his heart against him, how does the love of God abide in him" (NAS)? And then as if to tell us again that love is not just a sentiment or a verbal expression but rather an active verb, God says through John, "Little children, let us not love with word or with tongue, but in deed and truth" (1 John 3:18 NAS).

Go before the Lord today, beloved friend, and ask God to show you if you are loving others with the love of our Lord—a love that gives, that sacrifices.

His Thoughts Toward Me:

My Thoughts Toward Him:

February 22

Have you ever felt like a klutz? Have you wondered, *How could I be so undiscerning, so self-centered, so insensitive? How could I fail to love?*

That is how I feel at the moment. It tears me up! O Father, will I ever learn? Will I ever be what I am supposed to be? How I hate to fail!

And that is just the problem right now. I have failed a friend— a very special precious friend—because of my insensitivity. I failed because I did not stop to consider that others do not like to fail any more than I like to fail.

You see, when I saw this dear, dear brother of mine feel as though he had failed, I did not go out of my way to reassure him or to protect him in his seeming failure. Why? Because I never stopped to realize that failure could wound or hurt him as it hurts me. I was caught up with myself rather than with his needs.

As I have been in prayer about this situation tonight, God has shown me, also, how I have failed others. I have been more zealous for having things right, perfect, correct, or the way I think they should have been than I have been zealous for the needs of others. I have not been sensitive to how failure affects others.

When I fail, I need encouragement not a continual rehashing of my mistake or of what would or could have been if only I had not failed. Why didn't I realize that others would need the same encouragement in their failures or mistakes? It is because I had failed to look not on my own things alone but also on the things of others. I had not esteemed others before myself (Philippians 2:3, 4).

Oh, beloved, would you pray for me? Pray that I will learn this lesson well. I want my life to be used of God to heal wounds and hurts, not to irritate them. Please, pray for I need to learn to love others with the love of my Lord.

His Thoughts Toward Me:

My Thoughts Toward Him:

February 23

Love—true love, God's love—is known by the way it behaves. God, in His Word, has given us a way to evaluate the reality of our love for others. In these last few days of February, let us spend time looking at how God says love behaves. As we evaluate each facet of our love, let us ask God to cleanse us with the washing of the water of His Word so that we might love as He loved.

Love—*agape* love—is not something that is evoked by others, but rather it is initiated by the lover. "In this is love, not that we loved God, but that He loved us and sent His Son. . . . He first loved us (1 John 4:10, 19 NAS). Thus if we love with the love of our Lord, we will love first. We will initiate the action of love, and that means making ourselves vulnerable to whatever that "love initiative" brings about.

In his pamphlet, "No Longer Strangers," Bruce Larson relates the story of a woman who stood up during a seminar on the subject of broken relationships and asked, "Can God heal a broken relationship that isn't just broken—it doesn't exist?" When pressed, she unraveled the familiar story of a man who comes home from work, eats dinner, watches television, reads the paper, and then goes to bed. Later on, she would go to bed.

"Is it like that every night?" Bruce asked.

"Every night for years," she answered.

"Are you both Christians?"

"No, I am a Christian, but my husband is not."

"Do you love him?"

"Yes," she said tears beginning to form in her eyes. "I love him very much."

"Do you think he loves you?"

"No, I'm sure he doesn't, or he wouldn't be so cold and indifferent!"

"Well," [Bruce] said, "as a Christian, you are the one who must be vulnerable and find out the true nature of your husband's feelings. . . . Perhaps he's hoping that one day something will happen to rekindle the love that you shared when you were first married."

"But what can I do?" the woman asked.

"What are you doing now to try to change the relationship?"

"I keep inviting him to our prayer group," she replied, "and I leave books and pamphlets around, hoping he'll read them."

"Is this working?"

"No," she admitted.

"Then, why don't you try something much more radical and costly to you? . . . "

Bruce encouraged her to put on a pretty nightgown and some good perfume, to sit in her husband's lap, to ruffle his hair, and to tell him that she loved him as much as ever.

Her sheepish response was, "He might laugh at me and that would hurt. . . . "

"This is what faith in Christ is about, lived out in the dimension of marriage. To leave tracts and pamphlets around and to suggest that your husband come to your prayer group really makes you superior and invulnerable. But to do something like this gives him the chance to respond in love or with hostility. Is your faith in Christ sufficient to enable you to take such a risk?"

A note came a few days later, "Dear Bruce, ... He didn't laugh!"

"The point is that we Christians must begin to realize that in living out the dynamics of the gospel, we must become radically vulnerable and love first!"

Is there someone you need to reach out to in love?

His Thoughts Toward Me:

My Thoughts Toward Him:

February 24

How long is your fuse? God says that love is patient and that it has a long fuse, so long that it is never provoked. Love will not walk away in disgust. It will not turn on its heel and slam a door behind it. It will not spew out a hasty word that pierces the heart. Love is kind. It is not rude, crude, cutting, or funny at someone else's expense.

A friend recently shared this story about his mother when she was a young woman. She had always been large, but she kept herself well-groomed and looked good. She dearly loved beautiful clothes, so she bought a bright, flowing caftan on sale. She took it home and tried it on. When she swooped into the room with her family sitting around, her grandfather blurted out, "Evelyn, you look like a covered wagon!" They laughed, and she laughed, but inside, her heart was broken.

Love does not use its tongue to tear down or destroy. James says, "With *the tongue* we bless our Lord and Father; and with it we curse men, who have been made in the likeness of God; . . . My brethren, these things ought not to be this way. Does a fountain send out from the same opening both *sweet* and bitter water? (*See* James 3:9–11 NAS). Oh, beloved, how the tongue reflects the condition of the heart.

What comes out of your cup when you are tipped, when you are bumped? Do you spill brackish, angry, impatient words, or are your words seasoned with the grace and the mercy of the Spirit who dwells within you?

Ask God to show you today the contents of your well. Is your water clear? Is it sweet?

His Thoughts Toward Me:

My Thoughts Toward Him:

February 25

"Love . . . is not jealous; love does not brag . . ." (1 Corinthians 13:4 NAS). Love cares about the other person more than it cares about itself. Therefore, it can rejoice in another's exultation without having to seek its own.

A true test of your love is to check your reaction when someone shares some good news about their child or their mate. Love doesn't jump in with equally good or better news about its child or its mate. Love merely relaxes and rejoices with the object of the love.

Between people who love, there should be the freedom to share personal, good news, accolades, and honors without the labels of "conceited" and "braggart" being tossed around. Real love—unconditional love—would never think evil and would never attribute evil motives to another.

Love is not arrogant, insisting on having its own way. I've just completed reading *Bruchko,* the fascinating story of nineteen-year-old Bruce Olson who struck out on his own to be a missionary to the Motilone Indians in Colombia, South America. When Bruce went as the first white man to the Motilones, who were known killers, he went in love. This love was seen even in the introduction of simple health measures as he approached the Indians in humility through tribal channels rather than as a Great White Father.

The development of the Motilones was considered to be the fastest example of development that has ever occurred in a primitive tribe. How did it happen? The Motilones were not asked to give up their culture and become white men. Bruce presented the agricultural ideas through the elders of the tribe. There were no revolts against the old ways of the elders, and it was the elders who introduced the new way.

Love is never arrogant, boldly pushing its own ideas. Love patiently waits, giving deference to the thoughts and the ideas of others.

Is your love willing to wait?

His Thoughts Toward Me:

My Thoughts Toward Him:

February 26

Love acts with propriety. It does not act unbecomingly. It is, therefore, careful to consider the occasion and the tastes of others rather than to insist on doing its own unbecoming, inappropriate thing (1 Corinthians 13:5 NAS). It will conform to the situation as long as conforming does not offend God by compromising His Word.

I once heard a story told by a young man who remembered an

incident from his childhood that involved his mother and two neighbor women. These two women had just moved to a small community from the hills that surrounded the town. In a neighborly gesture, the boy's mother offered to go by and pick up the women to take them to church. It was winter. When the two women came out of the house, they wore freshly starched pinafore aprons over their thick, cumbersome coats. The boy's mother greeted them warmly and drove them to church with her. No mention was made of their strange attire during the following week. The next Sunday, however, the boy, waiting on his mother in the old horse-drawn wagon, did a double take when he looked up and saw his mother coming out of the house carefully dressed in her best pinafore apron starched and neatly tied over her thick winter coat. She nodded to him with a knowing look, and they drove off to pick up the neighbors.

Love makes another feel comfortable. Love always acts with propriety. It is so easy to become insensitive to the feelings of others, to be careless of actions which would make them feel uneasy. Love is sensitive to the feelings of others. If you had been sitting in the church the day the two hill-women came in in pinafores, would you have whispered and looked askance, or would you have been willing to wear a pinafore?

His Thoughts Toward Me:

My Thoughts Toward Him:

February 27

Anita Bryant, the valiant crusader against homosexual rights, has fallen from her place of leadership. She has fallen, and her fall has been the subject of a media blitz that has equaled that of world news events.

As the gay community giggles a heinous laugh of delight, the man on the street shrugs and says, "So what?" But we're different, and they are to know that we are Christians by our love. As we respond to the news of Anita's fall, what are we to think? How should our love behave?

Love does not rejoice when it sees unrighteousness in any form, but it rejoices with the truth. Love does not write hate mail or anonymous mail! It does not gossip in prayer and Bible study groups about the problem. Love grieves over unrighteousness and prays for restoration of a right relationship, but it does not turn its back. Love has zeal for the truth and walks in truth (Ephesians 4:14, 15). It never lies nor covers up; but on the other hand, it never spreads gossip in the name of truth. Love rebukes in love, but it also forgives and forgives. "If your brother sins, rebuke him, and if he repents, forgive him. If he sins against you seven times in a day, and seven times comes back to you and says, 'I repent,' forgive him" (Luke 17:3, 4 NIV).

Love bears, believes, hopes, and endures all things. Love does not . . . will not . . . cannot fail (1 Corinthians 13:7, 8).

Real love could never form the words, *I do not love you anymore,* for any cause or for any reason.

God says this is His standard for love. How does your love and your way of loving "measure up"? Your heart may grieve for what you have read in the newspapers and magazines, and rightly so because the name of God is being blasphemed. But, beloved, God's love does not fail. Has yours?

His Thoughts Toward Me:

My Thoughts Toward Him:

February 28

I will never forget them as long as I live. I was a nursing student working in pediatrics when they brought the twins into our ward. They were over two years old, and they went wild when anyone came near their crib. They would cry and run into one another's arms for protection. The only one they were not afraid of was the other. All other human beings terrified them. Their little bodies were clean and showed no signs of abuse—physically, that is! Our orders were to love them, hold them, and pet them. When they were fed, they were to be held on our laps.

What was their problem? Why were they in the hospital? They had ceased to mature, physically, emotionally. They were deteriorating as human beings because they had never known love. Virtually all they had was each other, and that is the only reason they had survived as long as they had. Their parents touched them only to keep them clean, and those touches were efficient, mechanical, and brief. They had been bottle fed from day one with a bottle propped up in their crib. Never had they clung to their mother's breast nor been cradled in her arms. They were two precious children who had been damaged emotionally and psychologically because love had been withheld from them. Now, they were wasting away physically.

Love—man cannot survive nor be whole without it. And you, beloved of God, are God's only true channels for the tangible, physical expression of that love.

If you have ever been loved—really loved—then you know what it did for you, how that love caused you to rise to your highest potential.

If you have never known love, real love as God meant it to be, then today your ache must be severe, for you know what you have missed.

No matter where you are coming from or what has influenced

your background and personality, I can declare to you by the Word of God that He loves you with an everlasting love, and that He has chosen you to be a clean vessel through which His love can flow to others.

Can you—dare you—fail to respond to such a love?

Beloved, let us provoke one another to love (Hebrews 10:24)!

His Thoughts Toward Me:

My Thoughts Toward Him:

February 29

He was a waiter. I was praying that I would have the opportunity to share Jesus Christ with him. He was personable and friendly, so when the opener came, I approached him very honestly. His response was unpredictably positive. He ended up sitting at our table, unashamedly admitting that he often thought about God and about his own life-style. He had been through a ruined marriage, and, although from all outward appearances he seemed to have it all together, at the age of twenty-nine his life was really a mess. And he knew it! One of the most poignant statements that he made was, "I really do want to be in love." Wrapped up in that statement and all that he said before was, "I really do *need* to be loved." Then, led by God, I asked him, "Are you committing adultery?" I'll never forget those blue eyes as they locked with mine and I said, "Be honest." I knew that he had to be confronted with his sin that he might see the love of the One who came not to call the righteous but sinners to repentance. I knew where he was; I had been there. I, too, had needed love, and when my marriage had ended in divorce (followed by my ex-husband's suicide) I began searching for someone to love me unconditionally. That search led to adulterous relationships . . . it usually does because we search in the wrong places. For some strange reason we think another human being can fill that God-shaped vacuum within us! How blind we are! How deceived!

He was honest. He even mentioned the women in Miami who went after him for his body. I ached. I thought of so many who become so disillusioned and embittered as they give themselves to others thinking, *This is it . . . this is the love for which I've been searching,* only to find themselves used and thrown away. When all the time there He stands—Jesus the God of love, with outstretched but empty arms. We will not come to the lover of our souls . . . the One who would love us with an everlasting love, the One who would never leave us nor forsake us, the One who through His love would make us more than conquerors (Romans 8:37–39), the only One who can adequately fill that vacuum!

We talked for about twenty minutes. He gave his customers to another waiter. I knew it was a divine appointment. God wanted Chris to know that He so loved him that He had crucified His only begotten Son so that Chris might have life not death, love not wrath, forgiveness—full and free pardon—not judgment. Jesus had sent us hundreds of miles and brought us together just to tell Chris this. Now the decision was his. God had done everything He could. All Chris had to do was believe. All he had to do was run into those nail-pierced arms. But he didn't, not then. There was a weekend party coming up. He almost trembled as he asked me to delay my prayers until the weekend fling was over!

And what about you? **I know you need to be loved.** There the Lord Jesus stands—arms opened wide. Will you run into them or will you try one more "fling," only someday to be flung away in another bitter disappointment? Love waits . . . the choice is yours.

Pray . . . I'm sending this to Chris.

MARCH

March 1

The church has fallen asleep, not on its knees but snuggled up in its bed of apathy. The "snooze" button has been pressed, and the church sleeps on—slumbering, unaware that when she finally does hear the alarm, it may be too late. The demons of hell hover over her bed like ladies-in-waiting. Nothing must disturb the mistress, she needs her rest. They will care for the things of the household! So with the covers pulled over her head, she listens, half-dazed, to their whispers that solace her laziness, not really knowing that they are plotting her demise!

Did you know that people in California have been forbidden to have a small group of people in their home for Bible study? In Colorado, a city was recently taken to court for displaying a nativity scene at Christmas.

Is this Russia, or is this the United States . . . "One nation under God with liberty and justice for all"? What is going on?

The church of Jesus Christ has forgotten that she is at war. She is sleeping instead of wrestling ". . . against the rulers, against the authorities, against the powers of this dark world and against the spiritual forces of evil in the heavenly realms" (Ephesians 6:12 NIV).

We, the church, have forgotten God's admonition through the Apostle Paul that we are to ". . . pray in the Spirit on all occasions with all kinds of prayers and requests. With this in mind, be alert and always keep on praying for all the saints" (Ephesians 6:18 NIV). Are our prayers quick, short, over in no time, "bless, bless, give, give"? Will this kind of praying hold Satan in tight rein? Oh, beloved, let us unite today in corporate prayer for the church of Jesus Christ. "Lord, I will awaken from my slumber. I will get on my knees. Teach me, teach your church what it really means to war in prayer . . . and see the victory."

His Thoughts Toward Me:

My Thoughts Toward Him:

March 2

The enemy has become more brash, more bold, in these days. Unrestrained because of the lack of fervent prayers of saints trained in warfare praying, Satan is like a horse given loose rein. With the bit loosened, he is madly rushing through the trees seeking to throw his rider from his back that he might prance, run, graze as he pleases, where he pleases.

Beloved, when you enter into a spiritual conflict with the enemy, you enter into a different realm of prayer. You enter into spiritual warfare. This type of prayer requires a standing fast, holding your ground and not budging until the victory is won. Satan is like a high-spirited horse. You must let him know who is boss. You must keep a tight rein. You must hold the bit tightly by wrapping the reins of God's truth firmly around your hands, holding on, not letting go until Satan and his demons come to total submission to the truths of God's Word.

The inheritance of every Christian, of everyone whose name is recorded in heaven, is authority over *all* the power of the enemy. Listen to the truth of God's Word:

> And the seventy returned with joy, saying, "Lord, even the demons are subject to us in Your name." And He said to them, "I was watching Satan fall from heaven like lightning. Behold, I have

given you authority to tread upon serpents and scorpions, and over all the power of the enemy, and nothing shall injure you. Nevertheless do not rejoice in this, that the spirits are subject to you, but rejoice that your names are recorded in heaven" (Luke 10:17–20 NAS).

Beloved, you have power over the enemy because you are a child of God. You stand on Calvary ground; you have come to the cross of Calvary where Christ died for you—in your stead. There you also died with Him. The old you died, a new you lives (Romans 6:1–6). You are now a new creation in Christ Jesus. Christ lives in you and because of that, " . . . greater is he that is in you, than he that is in the world" (1 John 4:4).

Beloved, *as long as you remember who you are in Christ,* as long as you recognize your position in Christ Jesus, then *you will never fail* in your power over the enemy. You are seated in heavenly places above all the power of the enemy (Ephesians 1:18–23). But anytime the enemy can lure you away from your position of faith, anytime he can get you to act independently of Christ, then he will run wild with you.

At Calvary, Christ won the victory over the enemy; at Calvary, you, too, will always win. Satan must obey, for you are one with Christ, and Christ is his conqueror. Meditate much on this truth and God will give you great insight.

His Thoughts Toward Me:

March 3

One of Satan's goals is to keep Christians from a knowledge of the Word of God, and he has achieved quite a measure of success. I am appalled at how little the church of God knows of the Word of God; yet many of its members have been in church all of their lives! Even though a great number of college students have been raised in Sunday school and church, during their formative years, a great majority cannot reasonably, logically, or scripturally defend their faith. Worse still, many will not defend their faith or take a strong, uncompromising stand. Why? Because the pressure that comes from the world, the flesh, or the devil seems to be too much. *It is easier to sit in apathy than to stand in conflict.*

Why would one of Satan's primary goals be to keep the Christian from a working, vital knowledge of God's Word? I believe his reason is threefold.

First, it is because our lives are transformed through the renewing of our minds. "And be not conformed to this world: but be ye transformed by the renewing of your mind, that ye may prove what is that good, and acceptable, and perfect, will of God" (Romans 12:2). Our minds are renewed through the Word of God. Therefore, if Satan can keep you from the Word, he can keep you from thinking straight, from seeing life in its proper perspective. He can keep your head so messed up that you really do not know what to think or even how to think. Why? Because, for so long, you have thought as the world has thought. You have spent more time being taught by the world than you have been being taught by the Word. As a result, your thinking is worldly, and it will be until you get into God's Word. Your victory, your power as a Christian, will never be fully comprehended or experienced until you become a man or a woman of the Word; that is one of the reasons why Satan wants to keep you from spending time in the Word of God.

We will look at Satan's other two reasons for keeping you from God's Word in the days to come. But before you go about your day or turn out the light, let me ask you a question in loving concern. How much time in the past five days have you spent in the Word, prayerfully reading and meditating upon it or studying it? How much time have you spent watching television? How much time have you spent reading the newspaper, professional journals, magazines, watching ball games, or reading a good book? God says, "Man shall not live on bread alone, but on every word that proceeds out of the mouth of God" (Matthew 4:4 NAS). Honestly, how are you living? For whom are you living?

His Thoughts Toward Me:

My Thoughts Toward Him:

March 4

Do thoughts of doubt ever come into your mind? Thoughts like, *Maybe Christianity is a hoax! How could that person possibly be going to hell even though he does not pretend to believe in Christ? He is so nice—so good. Surely, a God of love would never send a man to hell; would He? Does God really hear and answer my prayers? It was probably just a coincidence. Maybe God's Word does have errors; maybe it is really not all true; maybe only parts of it are true.*

From where do thoughts like this come? From *your* mind? No, not if you are a child of God! These thoughts come from without; from the same place that dirty thoughts come or thoughts of hatred, envy, or bitterness. In subsequent days, we will talk about the origin of such thoughts; but for now, it suffices to say that thoughts of doubt come from without *not* from within! These thoughts are the fiery darts of the enemy.

Satan has missiles of war targeted toward your mind just as Russia has its missiles directed toward the United States. America's defense against these Intercontinental Ballistic Missiles is strategic missiles that would track them, stop them in mid-flight, and destroy them.

And so we come to the second reason Satan wants to keep you from the Word of God. It is because the Word of God is your defense against Satan's ICBMs. Satan has fiery darts, especially designed for you, designed for the weaknesses of your flesh, aimed straight at your head. And beloved, Satan's missiles are sure to

97

strike their target, unless you catch them in mid-flight with your shield of faith and thus explode them in mid-air.

Therefore, God tells us how essential it is to put on the full armor of God in order to stand firm against the schemes of the devil. Ephesians 6:16 says, ". . . taking up the shield of faith with which you will be able to extinguish all the flaming missiles of the evil one" (NAS). Notice the confidence with which *you will be able*! Why? Because you have a shield of faith! Faith is believing God, knowing truth, and living by it! "Faith cometh by hearing, and hearing by the word of God" (Romans 10:17).

If you will learn God's Word, if you will believe that it is true, you will have a shield that will quench every fiery dart of the enemy. What is your shield like?

His Thoughts Toward Me:

My Thoughts Toward Him:

March 5

My daddy used to tell me that the best defense is a good offense! Beloved, God never intended for the Christian to constantly live on the defensive. The hymn writer so aptly put what our stance is to be, "Onward Christian soldiers marching as to war with the cross of Jesus going on before." We are to storm the gates of hell and demand that Satan's captives be set free. The church of Jesus Christ is to be the aggressor. Satan holds men captive in sin, and he does not release them willingly. Ours is the victory; we are the ones who are more than conquerors. But it is a victory which must be claimed, must be pronounced, must be taken! God's Word says that the gates of hell cannot prevail, cannot stand, against the church; they must give way!

So how do we prevail? What weapons do we need? When you read of the Christian's warfare with the enemy, in Ephesians 6, God clearly tells you that you are to put on the full armor of God. As you read this description of the Christian's armor, you soon realize that it *only* covers the front of the soldier! It allows for full protection as long as you don't turn your back! God never sounds retreat, nor do you ever have to wave the flag of surrender. Why? Because the soldier of Christ has the ultimate of weapons that totally defeats the enemy. It is the sword of the Spirit which is the *Word of God.* Thus, we come to the third reason Satan would keep us from God's Word. The Word of God is the Christian's *only* offensive weapon. It is all he needs—nothing more! With it, the Christian is the victor, more than a conqueror; without it, all he can do is defend himself.

The shield of faith is that by which you ward off Satan's attack upon you, but the Sword, the Word of God, is for conquering, for defeating the foe! It is the same weapon that is used by Christ at the battle of Armageddon. "And from His mouth comes a sharp sword . . ." (Revelation 19:15 NAS).

When you begin to war in prayer, from your mouth must come His sharp sword. Are you prepared? Are you on the offensive or the defensive? An unprepared soldier is a liability.

His Thoughts Toward Me:

My Thoughts Toward Him:

March 6

Does your prayer life seem impotent? Do you get angry at sin, at iniquity? Yet do you feel absolutely powerless to stop it as it rises to flood level? Do you feel like the dam is about to break, threatening to drown all purity and godliness, and all you have is one little finger to put into its leak? Were we meant to feel like, or to be, impotent children of God when it comes to dealing with sin in our society?

Satan would have you to think that you are impotent, but it is not true. Listen to this story which will thrill and challenge your heart. The owner of a Christian bookstore which opened in a section of town that was off the beaten path felt burdened by God to move to another location. After spending much time in prayer, the Lord's direction finally came. He was to move next door to a shop that peddled pornography! Move he did! Then, he began to pray. He watched carefully as client after client entered this place of ill repute. As each one would enter, he began to pray for them —for God's work within their lives. As the weeks went by, his prayer burden lessened until finally there were no more customers. The pornography shop went out of business.

Oh, beloved, I do believe that one of the reasons our prayers seem so impotent is that we cannot or do not freely grasp the power of prayer. We just cannot seem to believe that God would really answer "little ole me," but He does, if we pray in faith believing!

I believe another cause of this impotency in prayer might be a lack of persistent prayer. Satan does not release his captives easily nor does he easily evacuate his strongholds. God tells us in Matthew 7:7, "Ask and it shall be given unto you. . . ." The verb ask is in the present tense, therefore, what God is saying to us, as His people, is to keep on asking. Do not stop until you receive.

There is another reason for impotency in prayer, but we will look at that tomorrow. We have enough to meditate upon today. If your prayer life seems impotent, maybe it is because your faith is weak. If so, then cry out to God, "I believe . . . help thou my unbelief!" And keep praying this verse until you believe!

His Thoughts Toward Me:

My Thoughts Toward Him:

March 7

Do you pray and pray and yet see nothing happen? Do you feel, at times, that God must have favorites, that He is partial, that He is a respecter of persons? Do you feel that is why God answers others' prayers but not yours? Do you sometimes feel jealous when you hear others tell of marvelous answers to prayer? I understand.

I think there is nothing more glorious than praying a specific prayer and seeing that prayer answered in a very definite way. But there is nothing more discouraging than praying and praying without seeing results.

Is there an answer to impotent prayer? Or does God intend for us to pray without receiving answers?

Here is the secret of answered prayer: me abiding in Him and His words abiding in me. God's words are to be in me, at home in me, dwelling in me, remaining in me. If they are, then when I pray I will pray according to the truth of the Word of God. And if I pray according to God's word, then it will be according to God's will, and the promise of 1 John 5:14, 15 is mine. "And this is the confidence which we have before Him, that, if we ask anything according to His will, He hears us. And if we know that He hears us in whatever we ask, we know that we have the requests which we have asked from Him" (NAS).

Thus answered prayer comes from praying according to the promises, principles, or precepts of Scripture.

If I am to have power in prayer, if I am to have recourse with

God so that my prayers are heard and answered, then I must pray according to the Word of God. In John 15:7, Jesus says, "If you abide in Me, and My words abide in you, ask whatever you wish, and it shall be done for you" (NAS). Beloved, to pray according to the Word of God is to pray according to the will of God. If I ask anything according to His will, and I know He hears me, then I have the petitions I have desired of Him (1 John 5:14, 15 NAS). That is power in prayer!

Now, can you understand even more, why Satan's primary concern is to keep you from God's Word? How can you pray Scripture if you do not know Scripture? Will you let Satan keep you in impotency, or will you have power with God in prayer? The choice is yours, beloved.

His Thoughts Toward Me:

My Thoughts Toward Him:

March 8

Satan's target is your mind. Why? Because as a man thinketh in his heart, so he is (Proverbs 23:7 NAS). Therefore, if Satan can gain entrance into your mind, he will have a stronghold, a base of operation from within whereby he can cause you great torment. That is why God says, "Keep thy heart with all diligence; for out of it are the issues of life" (Proverbs 4:23).

Do you have recurring thoughts that seem to torment you, thoughts of evil that seem to plague your mind, thoughts that you cannot seem to shake, thoughts that you relish for a time but that later make you feel so guilty, so unclean? Do these thoughts seek to lead you into overt sin? Is it a continuous, insidious attack that you feel will eventually wear you down? Do you wonder if you will have to live with these tormenting thoughts or desires for the rest of your life?

Oh, precious, precious one, I understand what you are going through! I, too, for years lived with recurring thoughts that would torment me from time to time, thoughts from my past. Mine were thoughts that could breed immorality during the day and then would come as recurring immoral dreams at night. I prayed, I pled, I cried out to God, and finally He showed me the cause. Then, He showed me the cure! And in these next few days, I will share it all with you so that you, also, might have victory over these attacks from the enemy, whatever form they may take! They may be thoughts of fear, rejection, jealousy, insecurity, hatred, bitterness, envy, pride, inadequacy, anger, or whatever—there is victory.

If you have Christ, you have the mind of Christ (1 Corinthians 2:16), and thoughts like these have no place in your mind! You can be set free!

Why don't you take a few moments to talk to God, to tell Him that you want a mind, a heart which is stayed upon Him. Ask Him to prepare your heart to receive what will be shared in the days ahead.

His Thoughts Toward Me:

My Thoughts Toward Him:

March 9

If you are having persistent problems with your thoughts, thoughts you cannot shake or seem to get rid of, then, in all probability, it could be because of a stronghold that the enemy has erected in your mind.

When a man or woman violates God's precepts or principles of life, they reap an awful consequence. It is the law of the harvest ". . . whatsoever a man soweth that shall he also reap" (Galatians 6:7). When we sow to the flesh, then, of the flesh, we reap corruption (Galatians 6:8).

How do our heads get messed up anyway? It is simply because we have not heard, listened to, believed, or obeyed God's Word. God tells us that we are to keep our minds or hearts with all diligence for from them come the issues of life. In other words, what we feed on mentally is eventually what we will become.

It is for this reason that God tells us in Philippians 4:8 what we are to think upon!

> Finally, brethren, whatever is true, whatever is honorable, whatever is right, whatever is pure, whatever is lovely, whatever is of good repute, if there is any excellence and if anything worthy of praise, let your mind dwell on these things (Philippians 4:8 NAS).

Anything I allow into my mind should first meet all of these qualifications. It should be true—not only true but honorable. Some things are true but they are not honorable! What I think on must be honorable—that sure does do away with a lot of thoughts, doesn't it? The thought must also be right, pure, lovely, and of good repute. Whatever the thought, it should have the quality of excellence and be worthy of praise. Then, my mind may dwell or think upon it.

Now, let's get back to the thoughts with which you are having problems. Can these thoughts pass the inspection of Philippians 4:8? Of course not! Well, then, get rid of them. But you say, "that is exactly what I am trying to do, but they won't go away." I understand. Tomorrow, we will start working on them. For today, we need to see that there was a day, a first time, we ever thought that thought which did not meet the qualifications of Philippians 4:8. But we thought it anyway, and that is when our problem began!

Why don't you spend some time with your Father and ask Him to forgive you for going against His precepts (truths) of life. Then, tell Him that from now on you are going to "Philippians 4:8" any thought that comes to your mind!

His Thoughts Toward Me:

March 10

"For the weapons of our warfare are not carnal, but mighty through God to the pulling down of strong holds" (2 Corinthians 10:4).

When we continuously permit our minds to dwell on thoughts that do not meet the qualifications of Philippians 4:8, we are giving the enemy an open door of entrance into the recesses of our mind. And, believe me, there is nothing he likes better. His desire is, thought by thought, brick by brick, to build himself a stronghold within your mind. And it is from that stronghold within that he sabotages your mind, constantly exploding thoughts that are contrary to the mind of Christ or God's principles of life. He tries to wear you down through internal warfare, to get you to succumb to those thoughts and to let them become expressions of sin and disobedience. Remember, beloved, the conception of sin takes place in your mind; if it goes unchecked there, it will eventually be born as sin.

Let me use myself as an example. As a young girl, I was taught to live a moral life. My daddy told me that men dated bad girls, but they did not marry them. *(Remember, I am over forty and times have changed!)* So I determined to be a good girl. I kept myself clean on the outside but not on the inside! What I could not do, I could think—so I thought immorally. My mind had a heyday! Little did I realize that I was walking ". . . according to the prince of the power of the air . . . fulfilling the desires of the flesh and of the mind" (Ephesians 2:2, 3). Little did I realize that I was becoming ". . . a slave to sin . . ." (1 John 8:34 NAS), to immorality—for what we think is what we become. To commit adultery in your mind, according to God's Word, is to become guilty of the sin of adultery. I would see movies, read books, listen to suggestive songs, and picture myself in the role of the heroine being seduced by her lover, unable to resist, unable to help myself, but living happily ever after! All the while, Satan was building his stronghold; little did I dream what destruction these thoughts would bring!

I will share more with you tomorrow, but let me ask you, beloved, What does your mind dwell upon? Is Satan building a stronghold in your mind? Don't let him.

His Thoughts Toward Me:

My Thoughts Toward Him:

March 11

Brick by brick, thought by thought, the enemy will build a stronghold, a place of occupation within your mind and soul.

As I permitted my mind to imagine, to fantasize upon immoral things, little did I realize that Satan was in the process of building a fortress that would someday be occupied by a spirit of immorality. Nor did I realize that from that stronghold would rage a battle that would *seek* to destroy my marriage, my sons, and even, after I was saved, my ministry for Christ.

Repeated disobedience to the principles of God's Word is nothing more than an invitation to an evil spirit to come and take up a place of occupation within your soul or body. Does God not tell us that whoever commits sin (repeatedly) becomes the slave of sin (John 8:34)? For this reason, we are to be careful to guard ourselves from sin. When we sin, we give place to the devil according to Ephesians 4:27. The word "place" in the Greek means "place of occupation."

After years of filling my mind with immoral thoughts and vain imaginations, I became an immoral woman. By the time this happened, I had divorced my first husband, shaken my fist at God, and said, "To hell with you, God, I'll see you around town. I am going to find someone to love me!" (Please do not let this statement offend you, just realize from it the extent of my sin and the abundance of His grace.)

In my pursuit for love, I became all confused by that devious imposter, "lust." My thoughts finally became reality. What I had been taught by my parents about morality was rationalized away. The mind can so easily rationalize that which it does not want to believe, especially if the Holy Spirit is not there to convict of sin, righteousness, and judgment. I was now an adulteress, worthy of death. I became the slave of a spirit of immorality. I knew what I was doing was wrong, that I shouldn't do it. I would resolve that I wasn't going to do it again, but I did. I wanted to be good, but I couldn't. I had never heard ". . . every one who commits sin is the slave of sin." . . . but "If therefore the Son shall make you free, you shall be free indeed" (John 8:34, 36 NAS).

Are you a slave of something—a sin; a habit; a recurring vain imagination; a certain emotion such as fear, hatred, envy, bitterness, jealousy; a feeling that is contrary to God's Word about you such as rejection, insecurity, hatred of self or a poor self-image?

Talk to God about it. I have prayed for you, and I know God will minister to you.

His Thoughts Toward Me:

My Thoughts Toward Him:

March 12

Life is so wretched when one is a slave to sin, when there seems no way of escape. Satan truly held me captive. The web had been woven with such cunning, with such transparency! In the darkness of my path, I walked straight into his web. I knew I did not belong there; I struggled to free myself, but I was powerless, I was too entangled. I could see the ugliness of death crawling toward me, eager to devour its prey; its ugliness revolted me. Surely this was not what life was all about. There had to be more to life than this! Why? Why? How could this have happened to me? It wasn't what I wanted! I had been deceived! What was I to do? In desperation, I cried, "O God, I don't care what You do to me if You will only give me peace." I cast myself upon Him—the God of all mercy, full of grace and peace. Salvation was mine.

"Gracious is the Lord, and righteous; yes, our God is compassionate. The Lord preserves the simple; I was brought low, and He saved me. Return to your rest, O my soul, For the Lord has dealt bountifully with you. For Thou hast rescued my soul from death, My eyes from tears, My feet from stumbling" (Psalms 116:5–8 NAS).

Maybe you are ensnared in a web that holds you powerless. Beloved, our God stands ready to pull away the sticky threads to set you free!

His Thoughts Toward Me:

My Thoughts Toward Him:

March 13

I was saved! It was July 16, 1963. I was twenty-nine years of age. Oh, I did not know, at the time, that what had happened to me was called salvation. I never knew that I *had* to be saved. My church had taught me that my infant baptism had made me a child of God, an inheritor of the Kingdom of God. All I knew was that now I was different. I had a new power within me which enabled me to say no to the desires of my flesh. I had a hunger for God's

Word. The more I read of the Bible, the more I longed to live for my God and for His Christ. I had told Him on the day that I cried out to Him that He could do whatever He wanted with me. Better to put myself in God's hands than to go down into the pit of despair and destruction.

What freedom was mine! The Son had set me free! God had pulled me out of the web of destruction and had set me free from the power of the enemy.

But still, although I ceased to be immoral, at the most inopportune times, immoral thoughts or inordinate attractions would meet me face to face at the door of my mind! We will talk about it more tomorrow. But today, beloved, let me ask you, have you ever been saved from the penalty and power of sin, or are you bearing the name "Christian" but not knowing the life and the power that go with the name? First John 3:10 says, "By this the children of God and the children of the devil are obvious: any one who does not practice righteousness is not of God, nor the one who does not love his brother" (NAS). Beloved, think on these things!

His Thoughts Toward Me:

My Thoughts Toward Him:

March 14

Beloved, before I can tell you how to be completely delivered from Satan's strongholds, I must make sure you realize, know, comprehend what it means to be delivered from Satan's power. To put it another way, before you can ever enter into warfare praying, you must know what your position is as a child of God. You must realize that which was effected at the cross of Calvary in regard to your salvation.

Once you are truly saved, you are set free from Satan's dominion over your life. Remember that verse I quoted from John 8:36, "If therefore the Son shall make you free, you shall be free indeed."

Do you remember several days ago when I quoted Ephesians 2:2, 3? Those verses show us that before we were saved, we lived under Satan's power as sons of disobedience. Hebrews 2:14 then tells us that when Christ died at Calvary, He rendered powerless him (Satan, the devil) who had the power of death. Satan's power was taken away at the cross; oh, beloved, never forget that truth. Because the enemy was rendered powerless, when you continually confront him with the truth and with the blood of Christ, he must back down. The gates of hell cannot stand against the truth!

So, then, Satan was divested of his power over you at Calvary. Next, we turn to the truths of Romans 6, where we learn that our old man—what we were before Christ—was crucified with Christ so that we should no longer be slaves to sin (Romans 6:6). We do not have to let sin reign or rule in our *mortal bodies* so that we obey its lusts (Romans 6:12). We can now walk in newness of life (Romans 6:4) because the Holy Spirit has set us free from the principle of sin and death (Romans 8:2).

Now, this truth may seem a little heavy for you, but "hangeth thou in there, beloved." God will make you to understand this truth in a real and practical way.

When you are saved, you have a new power over sin. The enemy may bug you with bad thoughts, but your body doesn't *have* to give in. These truths are enough for today. Meditate on these things.

His Thoughts Toward Me:

My Thoughts Toward Him:

March 15

Now, I had stopped being immoral. I was saved. I had a new power over sin. When my flesh cried out for entertainment or satisfaction, I could say no. Now that I was a true Christian, I not only knew that immorality was wrong, I could do something about it. But there was more God had to teach me!

Now that I was saved, I saw that whenever I let God's Spirit control me, I had control over the desires of my flesh, just as Galatians 5:16 says, "But I say, walk by the Spirit, and you will not carry out the desire of the flesh" (NAS). *However, I still had a battle with my thoughts!*

Sometimes, dirty thoughts would come to my mind. I would either want to dwell on them, or I would want to vomit. Sometimes, thoughts of pride came such as, *You did a wonderful job. You are fantastic. God can really use you.* Thoughts like this made me sick, too. I knew God could never use me if I was full of pride. Was I full of pride? I did not want to be! *Or* thoughts like this would come, *All this stuff about Christianity is just garbage. It is not real. You are not really saved. You are no different.* But I was! *At other times,* ghosts from my past would haunt me and depression would hover about me as I thought, *How could I ever have done that?* As I tried to reconstruct the events of my horrible past, despair would settle in and heaviness would bog me down. *Or,* all of a sudden, I would remember my first husband, Tom . . . then I would think about his suicide, and I would wonder about that day when he hung himself. I would start to think *if only,* and I would hurt inside.

Oh, I was not overtly walking in sin. When I did sin, I would confess it in a hurry because sinning made me miserable, deep down inside I wanted to be all that God wanted me to be. No, I wasn't walking in sin; but, at times, I had a real battle with my thought life.

It was in these battles that God taught me how to war *successfully* against the enemy of my soul. I saw that these thoughts did not come from within but rather from without, from Satan. What a relief that realization was! These thoughts were external attacks, and all I had to do was to immediately refuse each thought the minute it tried to gain entrance into my mind. This truth is summed up in 2 Corinthians 10:5, "Casting down imaginations, and every high thing that exalteth itself against the knowledge of God, and bringing into captivity every thought to the obedience of Christ." Try it. It works, it is a Christian's prerogative. Oh, you may have to refuse that thought a number of times, but eventually it will go away. It cannot gain entrance, unless you let it!

His Thoughts Toward Me:

March 16

Do you have a pulling within you, a magnetism toward something that you know is wrong, that goes against the character of Jesus Christ? Do you hate it? Have you cried out to God to please help you overcome it? Are you afraid of it, afraid that you will weaken, give in, succumb, sin? Is it a constant battle to deal with it? Have you prayed, wept, pled with God, and still it is there?

I understand. And all I can say, beloved, is that maybe you are where I was. Maybe you have given place, a place of occupation to the devil (Ephesians 4:27). Maybe a spirit has a stronghold within you. If so, he has no right there. He is a poacher, a squatter! Get rid of him. Take away his squatting rights. Tell him you no longer want him or anything that has to do with him.

How? Well, keep in mind all that I have shared with you thus far. I would suggest that you do the following:

1. Draw near to God. Tell God that you hate, abhor that weakness, that sin. Tell Him that you do not want it in your life, but that you want to be all that He wants you to be. Tell God that you want everything in your temple (body) to say glory to Him. When you

do this, beloved, it takes away the enemy's ground for occupation.

2. Now, command that spirit, by name, to leave you. Name it according to its character or work. For example, envy, jealousy, critical spirit, bitterness, fear, pride, etc.

3. As you command that spirit to leave you, come against it on the basis of the following:

  a. your authority over it as a child of God (Luke 10:19). You overcome Satan by the word of your testimony (Revelation 12:11).
  b. the cross of Jesus Christ where Satan was rendered powerless (Hebrews 2:14).
  c. the blood of the Lord Jesus Christ. Revelation 12:11 says that they overcame him by the blood of the Lamb.
  d. the name of Jesus Christ. At His name, every knee must bow (Philippians 2:9, 10) for He is above all principalities, powers, dominion, and every name that is named in heaven and earth (Ephesians 1:20, 21).

4. Tell God you cut and sever every past tie with any association of evil through any acquaintances, friends, or relatives.

5. Then, praise God that He has set you free from slavery to that sin (John 8:34, 36). Ask Him to fill every cell of your being with His blessed Holy Spirit.

His Thoughts Toward Me:

March 17

Well, I finally had learned to control my thoughts. Satan would not defeat me there! I learned to "Philippians 4:8" every thought. When a thought would come to the door of my mind, and it wasn't true, honorable, right, pure, lovely, of good repute, excellent, and worthy of praise, I would not let that thought stay. It had to go.

But, at night, I still had a battle. I had immoral dreams from time to time that would leave me with a heaviness of spirit. The memory of that dream would haunt me during the day. I would have to repeatedly refuse the memory. I tried all sorts of things—reading Scripture before I went to bed, praying, pleading the blood of Christ over my mind—but still I would have these dreams. Also, at times, although I was satisfied in my marriage, I would find that I could not hug a Christian brother for fear I would find myself attracted to him. I had to be careful, too, about working with or praying with a Christian man for, at times, there would spring up an attraction toward him in my mind. During that time, the ministry of Reach Out was just beginning to grow! I knew that we would need to hire men to work with us. And I knew I would never be unfaithful, I had covenanted with God to kill me before I ever let that happen! But still I didn't even want to risk a chance of a mental battle with my flesh and the enemy.

Then, one day, God gave me the key that set me free, and since then it has been used to release many others held captive. One night, I had another immoral dream. The oppression of it weighed me down the next day as I tried to sit through a Bible Conference. I was restless, I had to move, to get out of there. I went to the rest room and locked the door. Enclosed in that most unlikely "shrine," I talked aloud to my God, then to my enemy! "God, I can only assume that I, a Bible teacher, have a spirit of immorality. And right now, in the name of Jesus and by the blood of Jesus Christ, I command that spirit of immorality to leave me alone. Greater is He that is in me, than he that is in the world (1 John 4:4). Satan, you and your demons have no power over me. You were defeated at the cross. And I command you by the cross of Jesus Christ to leave me alone." I unlocked the door and walked out. I did not feel any different. I could not go take a nap to see if it worked! *But, beloved, I was set free!*

It's glorious to be set free! Tomorrow, I will tell you all about it!

His Thoughts Toward Me:

My Thoughts Toward Him:

March 18

"Now when the unclean spirit goes out of a man, it passes through waterless places, seeking rest, and does not find it. Then it says, 'I will return to my house from which I came'; and when it comes, it finds it unoccupied, swept, and put in order. Then it goes, and takes along with it seven other spirits more wicked than itself, and they go in and live there; and the last state of that man becomes worse than the first. That is the way it will also be with this evil generation" (Matthew 12:43–45 NAS).

Now, beloved, when you evict that squatter, the enemy who has no right in God's temple, you can rest assured that he will try to come back. But you need not fear! He cannot come in without your permission. All you have to do, once he has been evicted, is to wield the sword of James 4:7, 8.

1. You simply do the following: *Submit to God.* "God, I know that it is not your will for me to entertain this spirit of _____, therefore, I will walk in obedience to You."

2. *Resist the devil, and he will flee from you.* "Satan, I want no part of you. You are not welcome here. I hate that spirit of _____. I choose God and His holiness. I command you to be gone as Jesus commanded when you tempted Him in the wilderness (Matthew 4:10)."

3. *Draw near to God, and He will draw near to you.* Spend time reading Scriptures that deal with that particular sin or spirit. Spend some time praising and worshipping your God and His Christ.

So when the unclean spirit comes back, just let him know your house is not unoccupied, but rather that it is filled and overflowing with God's Spirit.

His Thoughts Toward Me:

My Thoughts Toward Him:

March 19

"And the Lord descended in the cloud, and stood with him there, and proclaimed the name of the Lord. And the Lord passed by before him, and proclaimed, The Lord, The Lord God, merciful and gracious, longsuffering, and abundant in goodness and truth, Keeping mercy for thousands, forgiving iniquity and transgression and sin, and that will by no means clear the guilty; visiting the iniquity of the fathers upon the children, and upon the children's children, unto the third and to the fourth generation" (Exodus 34:5–7).

Many times, Satan's evil or unclean spirits gain strongholds in a person's life through the sins of the fathers. Iniquity unchecked can pass on from generation to generation.

This fact is oftentimes seen in families that produce nothing but criminals; in other families, you find from generation to generation a line of godly men and women who serve their God whole-heartedly.

The father is like the door to the family or the home. As the head of the household, he stands as the strongman (or weakman) of the house. If the enemy can get the father, then he has access to the rest of the family. This principle, I believe, is shown in Matthew 12:29, "Or how can anyone enter the strong man's house and carry off his property, unless he first binds the strong man? And then he will plunder his house" (NAS).

Abraham's life gives us a clear demonstration of the sin of a father being passed down through the son to the grandson. In

Abraham's life, there was the sin of deception; in Genesis 20, Abraham lies about Sarah being his wife. In Genesis 26:7, Isaac, Abraham's son, does the same thing! Then, you find Abraham's grandson, Jacob, deceiving Isaac in Genesis 27. What weaknesses or sins do you see in your own life that you have seen in the lives of your parents?

Father, what sins have you tolerated in your life? Do you want them in your child's life? If you will repent, your sin will not be visited upon your unborn child! If you already have a child, then when you have repented, you will be able to stand in authority in prayer against sin's power in your child's life.

His Thoughts Toward Me:

My Thoughts Toward Him:

March 20

I could feel my dress sticking to my shoulder, it was soaked with tears. As I sat there with my arms around this young man, tears of awe and gratitude etched lines in my makeup. I sat there overwhelmed, "Father, O Father, it is worth it all for just a time like this, to be able to hold this young man who could be my son and to share with him your forgiveness, to watch his chains fall off, to know that his son will not carry on the sins of his father and of his grandfather."

It was the Sunday morning of our May 1980 Couples Conference at Reach Out. I was speaking that weekend on spiritual warfare. I had shared how God had set me free from the spirit of immorality, and I had given a message that dealt with the sins of the father being passed down to the children. Now, the conference was over, many had already eaten lunch and were on their way home. I was still in our auditorium. I had hugged and prayed with the last person, and I was headed for the dining room, all of a sudden there he was. Lacking discernment, I thought he had just come to say good-bye, so I suggested we walk to the dining hall and talk on the way. Then, the Holy Spirit stopped me dead in my tracks. So we sat in the quiet of that deserted auditorium while the angels hovered at the doors guarding our privacy. The words tumbled out, "Kay, I want you to know that last night God set me free! Oh, Kay, I knew something was wrong; it was like I couldn't help myself. All of my life, I have been immoral. When I dated a girl, I had one thing in mind. Even little girls would come to me. I could not stop. You see, my father was very immoral, even with members of our family. Now, I understand. Last night, I thought about my son. I thought, *O God, I do not want this sin to be passed down to my son!* So I cried out to God, and He has set me free. My son is going to be all right." Then, prompted by the Spirit, I asked how he knew of his father's immorality. The words came haltingly, trembling, fearfully. He had learned of his father's immorality when he, himself, was involved in an incestuous relationship. That same relative had committed incest with his father!!!

"I am so ashamed, so ashamed, I have . . . I have never been able to tell anyone." So with Christ's arms of love about this young man and one hand patting this precious head that poured forth tears of repentance, in Christ's stead, I prayed, praising the Father for the forgiveness which was his through the blood of the Lamb. The chains that held him in sin's awful bondage were gone.

I tell you his story with his permission so that you, too, beloved, if need be, might be set free.

His Thoughts Toward Me:

March 21

Can a Christian have a demon? This question has been the subject of much controversy down through the ages; it has divided many a Christian body or organization. The enemy has rejoiced! For once again, he has succeeded in dividing the brethren, and a house divided cannot stand! (Matthew 12:25).

Can a Christian have a demon? This is a question that needs answering and the sooner, the better. For if Christians can be oppressed by the enemy, how vital it is that the truth be known so that the oppression can be dealt with properly. How horribly sad it would be if a Christian could be tormented by the enemy, and we, in ignorance, denied it!

Satan would have us avoid answering this question. His tactics are to intimidate us, to keep us from taking a stand, to cause us to fear controversy, to keep us silent and ignorant. One day after dealing with a dear person who was troubled by demons, I was told that I had to remain silent about this experience or it would hurt our ministry—other Christians would not understand.

I had just confronted the enemy and found in reality, in experience, the truth of the Scripture that "even the demons are subject to us in His name" (Luke 10:20), and I was to keep silent because of the church's ignorance? No wonder the church is ignorant if no one can speak the truth for fear of controversy! Here I had just seen a precious one delivered from the torment of spirits of lying, fear, rejection, death, deceit, and I was not to mention it for fear of controversy! How the enemy wants to intimidate us, to keep us in darkness for he knows that it is truth that sets us free! I have discovered that there are a host of dear, precious people who are hurting, miserable, desperate, in bondage; they have tried everything, but nothing has worked. Until, that is, someone has shared with them the truths of God's Word regarding the tactics of the enemy.

Can a Christian have demons? We will talk about it more tomorrow. But for today, why don't you meditate on the following verse. Ask God why He wrote this verse to Christians.

"Be of sober spirit [*mentally self-controlled*], be on the alert. Your adversary, the devil, prowls about like a roaring lion, seeking someone to devour" (1 Peter 5:8 NAS).

119

His Thoughts Toward Me:

My Thoughts Toward Him:

March 22

We still haven't answered the question, "Can a Christian have demons?"

Mark Bubeck, in his book, *The Adversary* (Moody Press), answers this question well, so let me share with you what he has to say. (By the way, I cannot recommend this book highly enough.)

He says, "It is my conviction that no believer can be possessed by an evil spirit in the same sense that an unbeliever can. In fact, I reject this term altogether when talking about a believer's problem with the powers of darkness. A believer may be afflicted or even controlled in certain areas of his being, but he can never be owned or totally controlled as an unbeliever can.

"The moment a person becomes a believer, the Holy Spirit brings birth to his spirit. 'Flesh gives birth to flesh, but the Spirit gives birth to spirit' (John 3:6 NIV). The spirit of the Christian is reborn, regenerated, possessed, and sealed by the Holy Spirit in a way not enjoyed by the rest of man's being as yet. The spirit of man thus reborn, becomes the Holy Spirit's unique center of control and operation within man. I do not believe that any wicked spirit can ever invade a believer's spirit. The Holy Spirit's work of new birth and His sealing presence within the spirit of man seems to preclude any presence of wicked spirit control of that part of man's being."

My conclusion in studying the Scriptures is much the same.

Well, then, what can demons do to Christians if anything? Listen again to a quote from *The Adversary.*

> ... demonic forces of Satan can afflict Christians so deeply as to harm their bodies, dictate to them certain attitudes of mind, certain feelings of emotions, and certain expressions of will that are all Satan's doings. To call this possession, in my judgment, is unwise and fails to recognize the difference between a believer's afflictions from Satan and an unbeliever being possessed, signifying total control and ownership.
>
> We must realize, however, that this enemy called Satan can gain a great advantage over us as believers. This advantage can only be broken by the employing of the weapons of our warfare aggressively against an enemy who we are willing to admit is controlling us in any given area.

Now, meditate on what you have read in the light of Ephesians 4:27 as spoken to Christians, "Neither give place [*place of occupation*] to the devil."

His Thoughts Toward Me:

March 23

It was two o'clock in the morning when Mark Bubeck's phone rang. The voice on the other end belonged to a desperate man, and Mark could sense his desperation.

"... you don't know me and I don't know you, but I know what you and your church stand for. Unless you can help me, I'm determined to end it all tonight. I have no idea why I'm calling you. I've been drinking, trying to get up courage to kill myself."

No one had been able to help this man, not even two different psychologists. "I'm a born-again Christian. I've tried to overcome my problem. Oh! How I've tried, but it's no use. I've counseled with several different pastors and Christian counselors, but no one can help anyone with my problem."

"Would you like to share your problem with me?" Mark inquired.

"No, that won't help. I just want to know, if I take my life, will I still go to heaven? I'm not going to fight it anymore. I can't live with the guilt; and I hate it, I hate it. I'm a professional man, and if my associates knew, I'd be discharged in disgrace. I've prayed and I've prayed, but that hasn't helped."

After sharing some Scripture and reassuring the man of God's understanding and forgiveness, Mark asked, "Have you ever considered that this bondage might be demonic?"

At these words, a surge of rage ebbed and flowed through the man; but deep inside for the first time in years, there was a spark of hope.

That night, Mark prayed over the phone with the man binding all Satan's powers that were seeking to destroy the man. Then, in several counseling sessions, the demons were finally uncovered and dealt with. The command to go to the pit was given to the demons, and a marvelous deliverance occurred.

With that deliverance came freedom from his problems plus a whole new ministry. A Christian was set free to serve his God.

Oh, beloved, if you know a Christian who has prayed and prayed, who has tried everything and still not found help, maybe the problem is demonic.

There is victory, but it must be taken, it must be claimed. Stand, take your authority, use your weapons, and he will have to flee!

His Thoughts Toward Me:

My Thoughts Toward Him:

March 24

Men who have been in combat will readily tell you that a primary tactic of the enemy is persistence. Night after night men would defend fire bases in Viet Nam tormented by the illusive but persistent Viet Cong. The enemy of your soul uses the same determined, tormenting tactic.

Perhaps you have prayed for a dear one for years; yet seeing no visible results, you are tempted to give up. Beloved, don't give up. Keep on praying. Intercession on behalf of one held captive *must be persistent* because you're not praying to try to persuade God, but rather you are praying to defeat a tenacious enemy who gives up only what he must.

One daughter relates this story of her spiritual warfare for her dad. "My Dad who is 63 years old has been an alcoholic all of his life. Mom divorced him fifteen years ago; since that time, he has taken a common-law wife who left eleven children to live with him. In this past year, God has given me precious opportunities to visit him and to tell him about Jesus and how much God loves him. At the same time, God began teaching me how to enter into warfare prayer for those in such bondage. Matthew 16:19, 'And I will give unto thee the keys of the kingdom of heaven: and whatsoever thou shalt bind on earth shall be bound in heaven: and whatsoever thou shalt loose on earth shall be loosed in heaven,' was a verse that God used to teach us how to pray for Dad. We brought Dad to the cross confessing his sins of alcoholism, adultery, hate, jealousy, and anger as well as other forms of bondage. We asked God to bind the strongman who had my Dad bound and blinded. God really began to move in response to our family's persistent prayer. I knew the Spirit was really working when Dad confessed his wickedness and asked me, 'Do you really think God could forgive me?'

"Step-by-step, the Lord led and used me as later I led my Dad to the Lord Jesus Christ. Since that night, God has constantly reminded me, His hand is not short that it cannot save and that with God nothing is impossible."

Your enemy, who was a liar from the beginning, would whisper defeat in your ear—give up, there's no hope, you have lost the battle. But, beloved, hold your ground, reject his lies, and pray until you see his death grip loosened from the soul of that one for whom Christ died. Ask God how to pray and then persist until they are set free.

His Thoughts Toward Me:

My Thoughts Toward Him:

March 25

My heart literally aches when I think of all the people who are bound by the enemy and do not even know it! I believe psychiatrists' couches and mental institutions could be abandoned by a multitude if only the church would wake up to the reality of spiritual warfare. Oh, beloved, hear me carefully for I am not advocating an unbalanced ministry or teaching where we see everything as being of the devil, but rather I advocate a balanced teaching where we are taught and are knowledgeable in the whole counsel of God. The Bible is, primarily, the Christian's textbook so that we might know how to live life in a perfect way, thoroughly equipped unto every good work of life (2 Timothy 3:16, 17). This textbook has much to tell us about spiritual warfare! Our problem, for the most part if we are honest, is ignorance. We have not studied to show ourselves approved unto God! So many in the church, in the world, have been taken captive by the destroyer, and we have not even recognized it. Oh, I do pray you will get Mark Bubeck's book, *The Adversary*. There is so much you need to know that I cannot share with you in these brief devotionals.

You see, beloved, our hearts just ache. Our counselors are kept so busy, . . . overworked. People come to us when all else fails. Precious people whose lives, whose bodies, are in turmoil; people who want victory, people who have tried everything and are still defeated, people caught in ruts of defeat! Then, we see them gloriously set free from the bondage, the snare, the occupation of the evil one.

Recently, a woman came to my Atlanta class as a visitor. Her preteen daughter has not slept through an entire night for over a year! They have been to counselors and psychiatrists, all to no avail. A year ago, this daughter went to see the movie, *The Exorcist!* My heart aches, at present the mother is not even willing to consider the possibility of demonic attack. She does not understand. So the daughter goes to bed each night in fear. "In whose case the god of this world has blinded the minds . . ." (2 Corinthians 4:4 NAS).

She is bound by the enemy. Where is the church, called to carry on the ministry of Christ, the one who said "The Spirit of the Lord is upon Me . . . He has sent me to proclaim release to the captives" (Luke 4:18 NAS)?

His Thoughts Toward Me:

My Thoughts Toward Him:

March 26

I have just hung up the phone. I called and asked, "Can I tell your story, Judy?"

"You can tell the whole world if it will help them." I wish I could! I wish this devotional would be used by God to reach around the whole world. I tell you what, I'll tell you, and you tell others—who knows!

I've watched Judy for quite some time now. She is an attractive woman, but her face seemed perpetually clouded, always woeful.

It flashed like a dismal neon sign through a cloud of darkness, on and off incessantly. Depression, Help! Depression, Help! Depression. Only nothing seemed to help. She had good Bible teaching, fellowship, love, prayers, sharing, and counseling; but still the neon sign persisted, accented by the darkness that covered her.

Judy is a Christian. She even served on the foreign mission field until she became so sick that she nearly died. Now, living in Chattanooga, she has become a regular at Reach Out and a close friend of several of our year-long trainees. Once, I heard how one of our girls just felt compelled to go to Judy's apartment. Judy was sitting there on the couch with a gun beside her, debating whether to live or die.

As we just talked on the phone, I learned that Judy has been suicidal since the age of six. Can you imagine? Children of six are meant to laugh, to play, to be loved, to enjoy their childhood, to dream of life and all they will be for God when they grow up. She said that ever since she could remember, she has felt absolutely worthless. When she was eleven, she had to be taken out of school for a while because of a nervous breakdown.

All her life, Judy has felt rejection, from everywhere, and her face showed it! She felt she was nothing but a problem to so many, so why should she live? "I felt like I was completely, one hundred percent in the way. If I died, it would get me out of the way, and it would solve all the problems I was causing others."

Oh, beloved, maybe you know someone like Judy. Maybe you have shared and shared, and still the cloud remains. Or maybe you are like Judy, you're saved but there is still no victory over rejection, depression, or worthlessness. Perhaps the enemy has gained a stronghold and you need to wield the sword of the Lord commanding him to be gone. If you are a Judy, there is victory to be had! If you know a Judy, then, in Christ's stead, "proclaim release to the captives."

His Thoughts Toward Me:

My Thoughts Toward Him:

March 27

After prayer, it was shown to some at Reach Out that Judy's problem was demonic! The devil was having a heyday, running without halter and bit, tossing this precious one to and fro. It had to stop. She didn't believe it would help, she really didn't want to talk about it, but prayer prevailed, and Judy came in for counseling. How I praise God that He is the God of all flesh and that nothing is too hard for Him (Jeremiah 32:27).

As they talked, they saw that Judy lacked security in her position in Christ. She could not see God's love for her. Nor did she think she was of any importance to Him at all. "I could not take authority over anything because I didn't believe I had any authority."

Gently, they led Judy to share with them her childhood asking her how she was raised, her family background, what led to this insecurity. As they listened, they took careful note of her answers. Then, they asked Judy if she was willing to let the Lord do anything He needed to do to set her free. When Judy answered yes they began to pray for her. They quoted Scriptures that contradicted the lies that the enemy had planted in her mind since childhood, then they took a stand against the spirit that was connected with each problem area in Judy's life.

At times, Judy felt that what they said and what she reiterated of the truths of God's Word were just words. "But I didn't realize the power of the spoken word. The truths of Luke 10:19, James 4:7, and verses in Ephesians 6 about our position with regard to the enemy reassured me as we prayed. I also saw the sins that I had inherited, sins in my family that have been visited down through the generations, and so I stood against my family's bent toward evil.

"When we finished praying, I waited for some sort of feeling, but it didn't come until they looked me straight in the eye and said,

'We love you.' Then, I saw what God had done. For the first time, I felt love."

What has God done? "God has shown me without a shadow of a doubt that He can do anything! It's no big deal with Him. All He is waiting for is someone to ask Him. He so wants to commune with us that it is not a matter of asking but receiving. He has accomplished it already."

Talk about being set free! Judy is radiant and mighty in prayer because she has seen the greatness of her God and the power of His Word and the faith which releases it!

His Thoughts Toward Me:

My Thoughts Toward Him:

March 28

The phone that was ringing was not my private line. I was having my quiet time; normally, I would not have answered, but I could not get away from the Spirit's nudging. I knew it was my son, Tom, calling me. He had left his wife and disappeared.

I cried out to God for wisdom and picked up the phone. Oh, how I love my sons! There is something so special about them, something I can't explain. I haven't been a perfect mother. I've failed in so many ways, and it has almost broken my heart at times. But God has been so faithful, as a redeemer not only of souls but of our mistakes, of our failures, of our messed up relationships!

Mary Beth, Tom's precious wife, has said, "Tom, I have never seen boys love their mother the way you all do!" We have our problems but underneath there has always been that love that covers a multitude of sins.

It was that love that now began to desperately fight for the very life of my son. Tom knew too much of God's Word and His ways to walk in such disobedience without being held accountable for such behavior. As we talked, he refused to tell me where he was. *What Tom needed to hear, I did not say.* Instead, I quoted him Scripture. His last words were "You will never see me again, I will never talk to you as long as I live." The awful click sounded in my ear and echoed in my heart.

Now, there was literally nothing more *I* could do. I could not find Tom, I did not know where he was. I couldn't say another thing, we would never talk again unless Tom came home or called me.

I shook my head in disbelief! This couldn't be happening to Tommy! This wasn't like him, not my loving, outgoing, gregarious, warm Tommy, who thrived on love as much as I did! I couldn't believe he would do it!

By this time, I was on the floor in my knee-chest position, crying out to my Father for help.

Where do we run in the day of trouble, to whom do we run for help? I will cry unto my God, my rock, my refuge, my very present help in the time of trouble, I will cry unto the Lord, the God of all flesh who said, "Call unto me, and I will answer thee, and shew thee great and mighty things, which thou knowest not" (Jeremiah 33:3). I cried—He answered.

His Thoughts Toward Me:

My Thoughts Toward Him:

March 29

How could our son leave his wife? Their love for one another was so obvious. God could not have given Tom a more perfect helpmate than Mary Beth, and he was just what she needed. Like Jack and myself, they so balance one another. What had happened? What went wrong? Who failed? Where did they fail? How did they fail? Questions, questions, questions.

As I sought the Lord, He told me how to pray. This was war! Satan desired to sift Tom as wheat, and we had to pray! Second Corinthians said that the weapons of our warfare were mighty through God to the pulling down of strongholds, and I was about to use them! Satan was not going to destroy my son!

As I thought about Tom's life and life-style these past months, I could see strongholds that the enemy had begun to erect in his life. I also saw him caught in the cords of some of my past sins. Mentally, I listed all the sins or leanings toward sin that I saw in Tommy's life. For example, one was avarice or greed. Tom had developed a real drive to get rich quick and had gotten caught up in a "success" sales pitch, the "you can do it if you'll only believe you can" philosophy, that reeks of humanism.

Then, having listed these fleshly appetites, I began to come against them one by one. I would command the enemy to leave my son alone in each particular area. I would bind Satan and all his demons from influencing Tom any further. I would then quote specific Scripture that went against that particular sin. For instance, in regard to avarice, I began praying back to God the truths of 1 Timothy 6:9–11. Then, I would stab Satan and all his demons with the Sword of the Spirit, the Word of God, from 1 Timothy 6:9–11. Jack and Mary Beth did the same. I, personally, found myself praying throughout the day and even at night when I would wake up.

Jack and I were at Mom and Dad's in Florida when the call came. "Mom, I'm at Reach Out, will you come home? I want to talk to you."

His Thoughts Toward Me:

My Thoughts Toward Him:

March 30

Several days ago, Tom and I sat on our porch, talking, crying, laughing, sharing, praying, planning. We would love to write a book. We feel that God could take our mistakes and the things He has taught us in our relationship and use these to give others hope. Who knows! Maybe someday we will!

As we talked, Tom said, "Mom, you would have to write the chapter on the power of prayer. If there was one thing that held me, that brought me back to Mary Beth and God, it was prayer."

Oh, beloved, how much more would I like to write a chapter on how successful, how perfect I was as a mother. But I can't. But I can write on how faithful God is in answering prayer. If only, somehow, some way we could fully comprehend the power that is ours through prayer, then prayer would become the main business of our day, the first thing we would turn to in a time of need.

Satan desires to have us, to have our children that he might sift us as wheat. He hates the family. Why? Because the family is to be the world's living example of God's heavenly home and family. "For this reason, I bow my knees before the Father, from whom every family in heaven and on earth derives its name" (Ephesians 3:14, 15 NAS). Therefore, to hurt and mar earthly families is to hurt and mar God's heavenly image. Many people have problems relating to God today because they have had problems relating to their earthly parents.

What are we to do? Pray and stand against the work of the

enemy. Will it work? It worked with our son, Tom, and it has worked with a multitude of others.

When Christ was lifted up, when He was crucified, judgment came upon this world and the ruler of this world, Satan, was cast out (John 12:31). Satan was rendered powerless (Hebrews 2:14). Now, it is our responsibility, as children of God, to claim and to exercise that authority which is rightfully ours. Matthew 16:19 says, "I will give you the keys of the kingdom of heaven; and whatever you shall bind [*prohibit*] on earth shall *have been* bound in heaven, and whatever you shall loose [*permit*] on earth shall *have been* loosed in heaven" (NAS, italics added).

We, in prayer, are to bind the enemy from working in specific areas of others' lives and ministries. Satan has been cast out, he has been bound in heaven. Now, *we, in prayer, are to execute that binding on earth.* Matthew 12:29 tells us that first we are to "bind the strong man," then we can "spoil" his goods. To spoil Satan's goods is to come against him so that he must desist from his devious work in a person's life. We can say to Satan, "I command you in the name of Jesus Christ and by His blood and His cross to release him and let him go" . . . for even "the spirits are subject to you" (Luke 10:20).

His Thoughts Toward Me:

March 31

Breaches were broken-down places in the walls that surrounded a city. In biblical times, walls stood as a defense against attacks from the enemy. A breach in the wall was an open invitation to penetration by a foe.

In Ezekiel 13:4, 5, God speaks a word against the prophets of Israel. It is a word we, as Christians, need to hear and to heed today.

"O Israel, your prophets have been like foxes among ruins. You have not gone up into the breaches, nor did you build the wall around the house of Israel to stand in the battle on the day of the Lord" (NAS).

I believe, beloved, that we can build walls or hedges of protection, in prayer, around our loved ones whether they are immediate family or Christian family.

Listen to what God says He will do to adulterous Israel. "Therefore, behold, I will hedge up her way with thorns, And I will build a wall against her so that she cannot find her paths. And she will pursue her lovers, but she will not overtake them, And she will seek them but will not find them. Then she will say, 'I will go back to my first husband, for it was better for me then than now'" (Hosea 2:6, 7 NAS)!

If we know someone caught in adulterous desires or relationships, the wall of protection for that family has a breach in it. Can we not pray, "O God, as you hedged up Gomer's way, Israel's way, will you not hedge up _____'s way. Keep _____ from their lover by a hedge of thorns and bring _____ back to rejoice with the mate of their youth."

In Job 1:10, we see that Satan was aware that there was a hedge around Job. Apparently, Satan had tried to touch him and his house, and he had failed because of that hedge of protection. Certainly, Job was a man of faith and prayer (Job 1:5).

In Ezekiel 22, God informs us of the sad state of His people. The people, prophets, princes were filled with corruption. God was going to have to judge, unless perhaps He could find a man, one to pray, one to intercede, one to war in prayer.

"And I searched for a man among them who should build up the wall and stand in the gap before Me for the land, that I should not destroy it; but I found no one. Thus I have poured out My indignation on them . . ." (Ezekiel 22:30, 31 NAS).

Will you become a man, a woman, who will learn to pray, to build up the wall, to stand in the gap? Or will our lives, our families, our country feel the indignation of God's wrath?

It is war—will you stay at home while your brothers go to war? (Numbers 32:6.)

His Thoughts Toward Me:

APRIL

April 1

You may lose peace by what your eyes see or your ears hear when it goes against what your spirit knows. Doubt comes in like a flood seeking to drown that which the Spirit of God has spoken to your spirit.

This is what happened to me recently. The morning of my father's surgery for an aortic aneurysm the Lord gave me Psalm 20. I felt that God was assuring me, through this Psalm, of two things. The first was that my father would be at peace with God, and the second was that my father would live. The assurance of my father's life was not foremost in my heart for death is not the enemy of a Christian. I was not "hoping" that my father would live, but rather I felt that this was God's will and God's Word to me for this surgery. Well, the surgery took six and one-half hours beginning with emergency procedures due to extensive clotting. This was to be followed by two more emergency surgeries within the next twenty-four hours. In each one, I rested in Psalm 20 reminding God of His promises.

Since then, each day of Dad's life has simply been a miracle; medically, he should have died. But there has been a battle with my eyes! Although I saw peace in my father's face since he returned from his second surgery, my eyes have looked upon his body. What my eyes saw totally contradicted what my spirit knew. Conflict came. So back I ran to my little _Christian Life New Testament With the Psalms._ I would take it from my purse, turn to Psalm 20, and pray back God's promises to Him. Then, came the battle of the hearing. My ears would hear, "the graft may be infected" (an aortic shunt); "his foot may have to be amputated" (clots had escaped during surgery to the _right_ leg); "we think he has had a stroke or a spinal infarction" (*left* leg gave no response); "his kidneys are not removing the poisons from his body." On and on came the medical reports that sought to drown what I felt God had said to me. Back would come my words, "I may be wrong, but I feel that God has said my daddy will live."

Three days ago during prayer, I wrote, "You can lose peace by what your ears hear or your eyes see when it goes against what your spirit knows." The conflict was verbalized on paper. The following day, the doctor called to prepare us for "the worst"—in all probability, Daddy would die. Conflict came again between what my ears heard and what my spirit heard, or what I, through my spirit, had heard!

Are you going through that conflict, beloved? I understand. I don't have a pat answer for you; but I'll tell you in tomorrow's devotional what helped me. Until then, "Wait for the Lord; be strong and take heart and wait for the Lord" (Psalms 27:14 NIV).

His Thoughts Toward Me:

My Thoughts Toward Him:

April 2

"For we walk by faith, not by sight" (2 Corinthians 5:7). But it's hard to walk that way; isn't it? Especially when what we see seems to be real or tangible, and what we've heard from God's Spirit, well, we wonder if we really heard it. Maybe we were just wishing or hoping or somehow misunderstood what God seemed to be speaking to our spirit. Do you understand what I'm saying, beloved? Can you relate? As I write this, I can picture some of you nodding, you know; you understand the turmoil between faith and sight. You have, or you are experiencing the turmoil! I can also picture others of you smiling; you have been there and have grown to a deeper maturity of faith. Sight versus faith is no longer a problem for you.

One of the things I keep forgetting is that faith is not faith until it's tested. God's Word calls it "the trial of your faith" (1 Peter 1:7).

As I wrote yesterday, the doctor called to prepare us for the worst. Everything was against my father living. Deep in my heart, I felt, *Well, I guess I misunderstood God's Word to me.* When this happens, and you are a Christian fairly mature in years you can't help but wonder if people, from then on, will doubt your credibility in spiritual matters. I had plainly said over and over again to my family, my friends, the doctors, and the nurses, "I believe God has told me my father will live." Now, I was wrong, the word of the doctor had come!

What happens, beloved, when our faith falters. Will I become a victim of my own frailty, of my own weaknesses? What do I do when this happens? Is all lost because I doubted whether I heard God aright?

I went to my knees. I got all alone with my heavenly Father where I could talk aloud to Him, where I could verbalize *everything* on my heart. I'll share more tomorrow about what happened to my earthly father; but today, I want to share what helped me at this point so that God can use it to minister to you in your prayer life.

When sight or hearing overwhelms your faith, when what you see or hear goes against what God has spoken to your spirit, don't run to man, run to God. It is a trial of your faith. Talk with God, tell Him all of your fears and frustrations; submit yourself to Him for whatever the outcome. God determines the outcome, and He promises that it will all work together for your good. Your frailty of faith will not frustrate God if you take it to Him, but rather it will be used of God to make you grow. Your Father is God, He will use this trial to take you, His child, into a deeper maturity in your faith. Then, someday, you will smile when you read devotionals like this one for you will have been there.

His Thoughts Toward Me:

My Thoughts Toward Him:

April 3

". . . Eye hath not seen, nor ear heard . . . the things which God hath prepared for them that love him. But God hath revealed them unto us by his Spirit . . ." (1 Corinthians 2:9).

Thinking that my father was hovering between life and death, my concern turned to my mother. Never have I seen a marriage where two have so become one as in the marriage of my mother and father. Mom and Dad have lived forty-nine of their sixty-eight years with one another.

I had told Mother that I felt God had said Daddy would live. Now, apparently, I was wrong. Mother's heart was in a turmoil; her faith, also, had been challenged by what she had *seen,* for Daddy had not responded to her at all on her last visit to the hospital. Now, the call had come that once again sought to mortally wound all faith. She had *heard* how hopeless it all seemed.

But all of this God used, for it drew my mother and me closer to one another and to our God. Mother shared that God had confirmed to her heart how temporal things are! She looked forward to heaven and all its promises.

My prayer was, "Answer Mother's prayer, God. Let her communicate with Daddy before he dies."

Oh, beloved, can you imagine the joy in my heart as I sat in that intensive care unit watching my mother laugh in delight as Daddy, through parched lips, in words hard to be spoken but eager to be heard, said, "Kiss me four times." (They have a special thing between them—a kiss for each child and one for them!)

Oh, the joy. Yes, it was joy because of what our eyes saw and our ears heard, but it was joy also because it confirmed what I think God revealed to me in Psalm 20—Daddy would live. There is a word you feel that God has spoken to your spirit, but you can be mistaken. There is *The Word* which God has written for your life, in this there are no mistakes. We, although possibly mistaken in God's will, can rest in God's infallible Word revealed to us by His Spirit.

I am in the school of faith. Since March 17, when this trial began, my prayer, among other things, has been that I would learn all God would have me learn and that I might use it to help others.

Is your faith being challenged? Is it being tried, tested? God has a purpose in it all. Stop now, talk to God about it, tell Him everything you feel; then, tell God you want to learn all that He has for you to learn. And remember, beloved, you may mistake His will, but His Word has no mistakes.

His Thoughts Toward Me:

My Thoughts Toward Him:

April 4

"I am still confident of this: I will see the goodness of the Lord in the land of the living. Wait for the Lord; be strong and take heart and wait for the Lord" (Psalms 27:13, 14 NIV).

It is April 1, as I write this devotional. It has been twelve days of crises with my father since his surgery. But today, he spoke coherently, in a sentence, which showed us he was oriented to his physical status. When Mother and I left the intensive care unit today, I told her I felt like singing the Hallelujah Chorus. (That would be something else!) She suggested we go to the chapel of the

138

hospital, and there we, together, praised our God for we had seen His goodness in the land of the living.

But to see that goodness, we had to wait. "Now, faith is the assurance of things hoped for, the conviction of things not seen" (Hebrews 11:1 NAS). When the things are seen and received, faith for those particular things ceases. Faith involves waiting; this is something that God has been teaching me over the years. I'm a "today is fine" kind of woman. I really don't like to wait, especially when things don't look or seem to be progressing toward the goal. Maybe you are like that, too! If so, we can understand one another.

Why does God make us wait? Do you know I do not doubt for one minute that God could instantly heal my father. I know that God could but speak a word and my dad could rise from his bed completely whole, disconnect all his tubes, and walk out of the hospital. If it would happen, it would not bring forth surprise from my lips but merely praise. But what a clamor it would create in the hospital! Surely some would believe! But would it work that which God intends to accomplish in my life, in Mother's life, and in the lives of others? Apparently, it would not. For if it would, then God would do it! No, there are greater things God can accomplish through the waiting of faith, through the trial of faith. Remember those in Hebrews 11 who "waited" in faith.

Let's join them, let's wait, we shall see His goodness because God never fails. Whatever the outcome, beloved, God never fails.

His Thoughts Toward Me:

My Thoughts Toward Him:

139

April 5

If we have enough faith and if we make what some call a "positive confession," will that bring healing to the sick? Does my faith, does my positive confession with my lips, determine the healing of another? This is a current teaching in some Christian circles today. There are some who would say that any statement from my lips regarding the possible death of my father would be a negative confession that would sign his death certificate.

Each day, Mother and I talk long distance to my brother and my sister. According to those who hold this new teaching of a "positive confession," I would have to tell them that Daddy is well, that he is healed. To give my sister and my brother a verbal report of his current condition would be a negative confession which could cause my daddy to die.

Is this biblical teaching? No, it is a teaching that was born out of a man's experience of healing through a particular Scripture that ministered to him; however, in its biblical context the Scripture does not teach healing for all sickness through a "positive confession." What is the effect of this type of teaching? To some, it has meant healing. To others, it has meant a horrible bondage. The bondage of fear, fear that you would say something that would stop God from healing, from working.

Oh, beloved, a thorough and careful study of God's Word, a proper handling of the Scriptures as we are admonished in 2 Timothy 2:15 will show this teaching of "positive confessions" and healing to be a wrong teaching.

What is faith? Faith is believing God. Faith is taking God at *His* Word. The strength of faith rests in the One believed. Faith is *not* drumming up in my mind and my heart what I want and then claiming it by believing and confessing it to be so.

The ultimate of faith, as I see it now, is to totally and continuously rest in the character and sovereignty of our God and Father. To say with Job . . . "though He slay me, yet will I trust Him." This is where my faith is now, it is in God's sovereignty. And if I fail or falter, my God does not . . . "If we believe not, yet he abideth faithful: he cannot deny himself" (2 Timothy 2:13).

His Thoughts Toward Me:

My Thoughts Toward Him:

April 6

"His foot will have to be amputated." Oh, beloved, I have prayed and prayed over that precious foot. I have crouched down at the foot of my father's bed, stuck my head under his sheet, and prayed for those dark, almost black toes, for his blue mottled foot. I have looked at it and imagined it pink, healthy, and whole. I know God says in Leviticus that the life is in the blood, and I know that Christ is our life. I have cupped that cold foot in my hands and prayed, knowing without a shadow of a doubt that God could heal it instantaneously. And if God had healed it right before my eyes, I would have not been surprised—but I surely would have been excited. At times, I have looked up from my chair to find my precious mother caressing his foot with her eyes closed in prayer. Countless others had prayed for that foot.

But God has not healed my father's foot. He could if it were His will. It's the week preceding Easter as I write. We have been watching "Jesus of Nazareth" on television. As I have watched the recountings of our Lord's life, I have seen some of His many miracles portrayed before my eyes. I know Christ is the same yesterday, today, and forever. He still works miracles, but Daddy's foot will have to be amputated. Has God failed? No! Has our faith failed? No! Oh, some of you may say yes, but, beloved, you are wrong. Our faith has not failed. Our faith is in God, a God who, in His sovereignty, has said no. And we bow before Him, hearts full of worship, love, and trust.

Have you prayed earnestly about something, longing for your

answer? Have you believed? Have you known God could do it if He pleased? Have you wondered about all the verses that say we can ask—ask anything—and it will be done; but it hasn't been done? Have you cried, "What is wrong, God, that you have not heard so as to answer me?"

"And these all, having obtained a good report through faith, received not the promise: God having provided some better thing for us, that they without us should not be made perfect" (Hebrews 11:39, 40).

His Thoughts Toward Me:

My Thoughts Toward Him:

April 7

Yesterday, I wrote about God not answering our prayers, even when our hearts are right before Him, even when we truly believe, even when His reputation seems to be at stake. Let me share a precious story with you. I'm in the process of rereading *Of Whom the World Was Not Worthy,* by Marie Chapian (Bethany Fellowship, Inc.), and this story is from that book. Oh, beloved, what lessons God is teaching me on prayer through this biography. You must read it.

"A young woman from Jozeca's village was struck with a fever, and Jozeca had gone to care for her, her husband, and their babies. Three days passed and Sofia slipped into semi-consciousness. Jozeca's prayers for Sofia's life became frantic as the doctor declared that he could do nothing more. As Sofia's husband cried out, 'God have mercy,' Jozeca grabbed his hand. 'Maybe the doctor can do nothing more, but God can! God will heal your wife with His

142

own hand! You will see!' She fell on her knees by the bed resolving not to rise until Sofia opened her eyes and lifted her head. At seven o'clock, Sofia was dead.

"Why had God not answered her prayers? Why had He not shown this family mercy? Was it because of sin in her life? Was it because of sin in the life of Sofia's husband? Was there sin in Sofia's life? What was the reason? Why had God turned His face and not answered her prayers?

"Jozeca cried out to her husband, 'Why, Jakob, Why?'

" 'The Lord is God. His is all majesty and all power. His greatness is beyond knowing. His glory is beyond our understanding. The Lord is God. He created all things. He created every breath that is breathed. He is the source of all life and energy. He is God.'

"We want faith to be like a wooden door behind which is a table laden with bread. You stand in front of the closed door and proclaim to everyone you know there is a table filled with bread on the other side of the door. The people don't believe you. They say, 'Ah, it cannot be true.' You say, 'Yes it is true. I will prove it to you.' And you fling open the door, and there is a table filled with the finest and most wonderful bread. But faith is not like that. Often we must believe in the bread, and tell people about the bread without even seeing the door flung open." Remember Hebrews 11:39, 40?

His Thoughts Toward Me:

My Thoughts Toward Him:

April 8

It is so hard to look at my father and believe that he could live, his poor body is in such a wretched state. And when I think of one leg amputated, the other paralyzed, his poor vascular system, his almost uncontrollable diabetes, I wonder if it would not be better for him to leave and be with the Lord.

What is better? I do not know, but God knows; I rest in His perfect will. Mother and I want the will of our Lord for we know, as for God, His way is perfect. God has given me much peace, for I know that even these times of suffering for my father and mother are "in His hands."

As I write this, I cannot help but think of Joni Eareckson, a new but very precious friend in the Lord. God has given us the joy of laboring together in some women's conferences; we have also studied and shared together. Many of you know her because your life has been greatly enriched by her books, *Joni* and *A Step Further.*

Joni is a very attractive young woman who was totally paralyzed as a teenager in a diving accident. As I have written some of my thoughts these past days, Joni has come to my mind frequently. I have thought so much of the trial of her faith. So many well-meaning Christians have told Joni that she could walk again if only she would have faith. How brashly we speak with our lips about things we know so little! I have been guilty of the same—speaking brashly, that is! Joni's faith is so beautiful, so solid. God chose life for Joni, life but not healing. Life was better, healing was not.

Joni prayed differently, so did others. Joni prayed for death, God gave life. Joni believed God could heal her paralysis. She prayed and waited expectantly. God said no.

And so Joni lives, entirely dependent upon God and upon others. That dependence is a living parable to me and to others of the complete sufficiency of our God. To me, she is God's answer to those who say a positive confession and undoubting faith can heal anyone. No, Joni's life is God's "something better."

Today, will you not come in faith and completely submit yourself to what God says is best? Whatever it may be, beloved, you can know it will be best. God is for you, not against you. If you are afraid, tell God. He understands.

His Thoughts Toward Me:

My Thoughts Toward Him:

April 9

"Produce your cause, saith the Lord; bring forth your strong reasons" (Isaiah 41:21).

Right now, I am sitting in the Respiratory Intensive Care Unit beside the bed of my father. We are waiting for the doctor to tell us whether he will amputate Daddy's leg (below the knee) today or tomorrow. Because my father is only getting worse, they must take aggressive measures; but, because of Daddy's condition, he is a very poor surgical risk.

Although I do not know what today or tomorrow holds, I feel I must share what has passed between my God and me today.

I shared, previously, that I felt God had said to me, through Psalm 20, that my father would live. However, what my eyes see and my ears hear go against what I feel God spoke to my spirit. So I just prayed. I told God that I would love a confirmation from Him as to whether I understood Him correctly or not. In each crisis we have faced with my father, I have turned to Psalm 20; in each instance, God has quickened a different verse or a particular word to my heart. When Daddy went into surgery for the second time on March 19, I saw his face in utter agony. It was so bad, he was fighting for life. As we waited for the outcome in that waiting room, I sat praying back Psalm 20 to the Lord. All of a sudden, the "him" in verse 6 jumped out at me. "Now know I that the Lord saveth his anointed; he will hear him, from his holy heaven with the saving strength of his right hand." God had heard my father.

145

Oh, the peace, the joy that flooded my heart. And since then, my daddy has had peace.

Today, I again turned to Psalm 20 desiring only to know God's will that I might pray aright. Verses 4 and 5 were quickened to my heart. "Grant thee according to thine own heart, and fulfil all thy counsel" (Psalms 20:4). My heart was that my father would live to bring glory to God; that his living would be a confirmation of what God had spoken to me and I had shared with others. That was my heart, and I was not afraid to verbalize it. Was not this His Psalm, given to me for this time? Therefore, this was God's Word to me; I must act upon it once again. And so I did! I told God what I wanted and why I wanted it. My reasons were for His glory. I presented my case to God; on that basis, I believe God's Word for my father is life. But what if my father doesn't live? Then, I am wrong. And you will know it, for as I write, what I write stands, and you will possibly learn something from my failure to hear God totally aright. But, beloved, I am not afraid to commit myself on paper. Surely, we are not always right, always perfect, but God still uses us. Whatever the outcome, I will grow from this, it will be a stepping-stone toward my goal to be like Jesus, to always and only do those things that please the Father.

Does the fear of failure in being all you should be as a Christian keep you from taking steps of faith? I understand, I have that fear at times, but I'm not going to let it stop me. I'll tremble, but I'll step. My God is greater than all my failures.

His Thoughts Toward Me:

My Thoughts Toward Him:

April 10

"We will rejoice in thy salvation, and in the name of our God we will set up our banners: the Lord fulfil all thy petitions" (Psalms 20:5). This is the other verse God quickened to my heart as I prayed over Daddy's forthcoming amputation. Three things come to my mind in meditating upon this verse at this time.

First is the phrase, "the name of our God." In verse 1 of Psalm 20 it says, "the name of the God of Jacob defend thee." Quite sometime ago, I studied the various names of God. How grateful I am to know His names, for my worship, my praise, and my prayers are directed according to His names. In this present trial, I have called to my JEHOVAH RAPHA . . . "the Lord that healeth." If my father lives, it will only be because our JEHOVAH RAPHA has defended him and shut, for a time, the gates of death to which He holds the key. God has been to me my JEHOVAH SHALOM, "the Lord send peace." What rest this has brought! What calmness! What peace of not only spirit but of soul!

My God is also my JEHOVAH NISSI, "the Lord my banner!" This is the second thing that came to me in meditation upon verse 5. A banner is a standard like a flag, that which you raise and stand under, that which you identify with and give your allegiance to, that about which you rally! The Lord is my banner. The victory is His, by Him, for Him. I will fly His banner and never, by God's grace, shall I desert His standard.

The third thought is this ". . . the Lord fulfil all thy petitions" (Psalms 20:5). If my desire is only His will, His glory, then ". . . if we ask any thing according to his will, he heareth us" (1 John 5:14).

Oh, my JEHOVAH JIREH, "my God who provides," let me walk so in oneness with You that my faith will not tremble.

His Thoughts Toward Me:

147

My Thoughts Toward Him:

April 11

It is evening now. The word has come: surgery tomorrow. So I will write this, and then I will go to bed. My heart is quiet before my Jehovah Shalom; whatever the outcome, my confidence will not be shaken, for in quietness and confidence is my strength.

I have watched in delight today as my father turned to Mother and very clearly said, "Kiss me." I treasure Daddy's words, "You are a precious daughter, too," after I told him what a precious father he was to me. And I delight in the pursed lips underneath that green oxygen mask; it was removed for a minute while I collected my kisses.

Expressions of love are so important. How grateful I am to God for the heritage my mother and father have given me in this respect. My heart, beloved, reaches out to those of you who have not had such a heritage. But listen, listen carefully if this is your case. Weep not for the past, begin, inaugurate expressions of love, give your family this heritage from this day forward. Don't let your awkwardness stop you, reach out, be the aggressor; then, wait patiently for the barriers to come down. No weapon stands against love. Say it, give it, express it. And if you don't know how to begin, remember, God is love and He first loved us and gave Himself. So go to the source, and ask the One who has shed His love abroad in your heart to let it spill out on others.

Daddy rallied awhile yesterday and said to Mother, "You mean all the world to me." Think of what she has to treasure tonight, those precious words.

God says to you, ". . . I have loved thee with an everlasting love . . ." (Jeremiah 31:3). Think of what you have to treasure tonight, those precious words.

His Thoughts Toward Me:

My Thoughts Toward Him:

April 12

The phone rang this morning around 3:00 A.M. I had been asleep for a little over two hours. Now, before I go back to bed (it's 6:30 A.M.) . . . I feel I must share with you.

The hospital called to tell us that Daddy had taken a turn for the worse—his breathing had stopped. The doctor was on his way. As I hung up the phone, I went to get ready to take Mother and Grandmother to the hospital; but I had to pray. I fell to my knees beside the bed to cry out to my God. I can't really describe what was going on in my body, but it was almost like a fire with everything madly rushing around inside. My head was fine; outwardly, I did not tremble, but inside it seemed like everything was boiling. As I sit here and write, I think of "though it (your faith) be tried with fire" (1 Peter 1:7); I am reminded of what I have shared with you in the thoughts of the last three days. "How, God, could I have been so wrong?" I pled with Him according to Psalm 20. I called to my Jehovah Shalom. When I got off my knees, my body felt better. It was 3:46 A.M. As we left the house, the fog was terrible. I prayed for our protection—wouldn't the enemy love to have us panic and be harmed in some way! We crept to the hospital, in my mind were the words, *I was wrong.* I began to pray aloud, "Though He slay me, yet will I trust Him" (Job 13:15). I thought of my poor mother. Had I given her hope that would prove to be false? Yesterday, beside Daddy's bed, I said, "I may be wrong, Mother, but I feel God has given me assurance that Daddy will live."

We stood and waited at the door to the Respiratory Intensive Care Unit. I could see one of the doctors in the door to Daddy's room. We could not go in—we waited. My heart cried out to God; I pled my case before the Righteous Judge of all the earth. I called to Him asking Him to give to Mother that which I could not give. If my body had felt the way it had, what was she feeling? She is one with Daddy. Then, I thought of others, *Now, in some way, I will be able to understand what others have felt physically in times of great emotional stress.* The doctor came in.

Daddy was all right. They had him on a respirator, but he could not breathe on his own. "The hospital shouldn't have called," he said. He would not have called us. The doctor's concern was for Mother, his countenance wrapped a blanket of compassion about us. We told him not to be concerned; it was our doing. We had requested to be called.

Later on today, they will amputate Daddy's leg. I think the doctor felt that they should have done it yesterday. But I know there are no accidents. This was part of the trial of our faith.

This morning, God reminded me of Peter when he walked on the water. Oh the panic, the fear, that came when Peter took his eyes off Jesus and looked at the turbulent waters. "Oh, Peter, I understand how you felt." There was only one thing to do—cry, "Lord, save me." AND HE DID!

His Thoughts Toward Me:

My Thoughts Toward Him:

April 13

"I will bless the Lord at all times: his praise shall continually be in my mouth" (Psalms 34:1).

Praise—that which releases God's power and puts prayer onto its highest plane. Praise takes you above the circumstances and situations upon earth to the Throne of God. And there He sits, the God who is love, who reigns supreme. And as we rehearse His goodness, His attributes, His perfect ways, His promises, there is peace; there is rest; there is comfort; there is confidence. Whatever happens will be right for righteousness, justice, and mercy are His Throne.

I sit in my father's room in the Respiratory Intensive Care Unit and sing, quietly waiting for them to take Daddy to surgery. As I sing, my soulish being comes in tune with my spirit as my physical being utters, confesses, that which my spirit knows to be true. Thus my *whole* being is brought under the control of His blessed Holy Spirit.

As instrument after instrument monitors Daddy's vital signs, praise takes me beyond what my eyes see: the high temperature, the pulse fluctuating around 124, the fluctuating blood pressure, and, at times, a seemingly erratic recording on his cardiogram. My father lies there unable to communicate, intubated with a respirator. My ears hear the rapid, noisy breathing as the accordion-type diaphragm moves up and down monitoring my father's breathing. But I *will* continue singing.

Singing, no matter what the eyes see or the ears hear, singing is the triumph of faith.

F. J. Huegel in his book, *Prayer's Deepest Secrets,* writes, "Saints (referring to Christians as saints) all down the ages have realized that when prayer, conceived as supplication for certain ends, fails, then praise succeeds. When we offer praise in the face of circumstances quite contrary to our happiness we take sides with God who has permitted the circumstance . . . when the dross has been removed from the gold, the refiner will remove the fire."

"O God, how I want to learn to praise You at all times, for there is never any reason not to!"

His Thoughts Toward Me:

My Thoughts Toward Him:

April 14

They have taken my father to surgery. Verbal expressions of love were given—the kiss on the forehead, the whispered, "the Lord bless you and keep you . . . the Lord make His face to shine upon you and grant you peace both now and forevermore." This is a blessing I have heard my father give countless times at the back of the sanctuary at the close of the service. When I was in my twenties, my father left his good position in the business world to serve God as an Episcopal priest. Now, I wanted to give the blessing that means so much to him.

The elevator doors closed. We went to wait and to continue our vigil of praise and supplication.

"Although the fig tree shall not blossom, neither shall fruit be in the vines; the labour of the olive shall fail, and the fields shall yield no meat; the flock shall be cut off from the fold, and there shall be no herd in the stalls: Yet I will rejoice in the Lord, I will joy in the God of my salvation. The Lord God is my strength, and He will make my feet like hinds' feet, and He will make me to walk upon mine high places . . ." (Habakkuk 3:17–19).

Is this not what God wants—lips that will echo the soul's resolve, "though He slay me, yet will I trust Him" (Job 13:15)? Does that not say, "God, You are God, and I rest in all that You are"? It is our way of saying, "God, I love You, worship You, trust You . . . not for Your gifts to me nor for what You can do for me, but because of who You are. I love You for You."

Is this not the unconditional love God expresses toward us? May we give Him the same.

His Thoughts Toward Me:

My Thoughts Toward Him:

April 15

If we would but learn to praise our God in the midst of the fire, it would carry us *through* the "dark night of the soul." Huegel, in *Prayer's Deepest Secrets,* says, "Nothing has such power to turn our seeming defeats into glorious victories, as praise does. It is when the going is unutterably hard that praise carries us through. We naturally would give way to discouragement and fear and doubt. But the triumph of faith comes when we sing in spite of it all."

My dear Christian brother, Paul Billheimer, tells us in his book, *Destined for the Throne* (Christian Literature Crusade), that "the secret of answered prayer is faith without doubt (Mark 11:23). And the secret of faith without doubt is praise, triumphant praise, continuous praise, praise that is a way of life."

Oh, beloved, what is it that you have been praying about for so long? What fire have you been called into for assaying, testing, and refining? Stop now and look unto your God. For what can you praise Him?

Take a moment, quiet your heart before Him, what do you know about God that would enable you to praise Him for your particular trial or testing? List these things and then use them as a guide to praise.

His Thoughts Toward Me:

My Thoughts Toward Him:

April 16

"Mrs. Lee, they have taken your husband back to RICU." Daddy had made it through surgery again. All I could do was walk back and forth in that waiting room and praise the Lord. I looked up to the heavens and thanked God for that Throne of Grace. At the right of that Throne, stands the triumphant Lamb who ever lives to make intercession for us, our Great High Priest who can be touched with the feeling of our infirmities—the Resurrection and the Life.

The doctor's face radiated a quiet joy over the success of the amputation. "The next twenty-four hours are critical. If his temperature comes down my joy will know no bounds. It will be a miracle." The doctor's concern had been an infected graft. Daddy's third emergency surgery was to remove a necrotic colon which then presented the very real possibility of infection to that graft of the abdominal aorta.

How much can a body endure? As much as God says endure. And what do we do? How much can we endure? We can endure whatever comes our way. Our times are in His hands, and His hands are nail-pierced hands, hands that bear eternal witness to His great love wherein He loves us. Since His hands are hands of love, since He holds us in His hands, whatever comes into our lives must be filtered through His fingers of love. Therefore, we can endure, for His grace is sufficient.

How do we endure? We endure as Moses endured. ". . . for he endured, as seeing him who is invisible" (Hebrews 11:27). We are to look not at things which are seen, but at things which are not seen. We are to continue to run with patience the race that is set before us that we might be found unto praise and honor and glory at the appearing of Jesus Christ, whom having not seen, we love. Oh, we love Him. . . .

His Thoughts Toward Me:

My Thoughts Toward Him:

April 17

"But without faith it is impossible to please him; for he that cometh to God must believe that he is, and that he is a rewarder of them that diligently seek him" (Hebrews 11:6).

How grateful I am to the Spirit of God for all that He has taught me from His Word about the sovereignty and the character of my God. It is this knowledge that has sustained me and maintained me in these days of testing.

The knowledge that God is sovereign, that He rules over all, that there are no accidents in a Christian's life—that is peace. The knowledge that our God ". . . doeth according to his will in the army of heaven, and among the inhabitants of the earth: and none can stay his hand, or say unto him, What doest thou" (Daniel 4:35) is the solid anchor that holds in the most fierce of tempests. The knowledge of the character of this One who has supreme reign, the knowledge that the very essence of God's being is love brings unqualified trust.

To live according to all this knowledge, that is faith.

Oh, beloved, how well are you getting to know your God? The prophet Daniel, in warning God's children of stressful times, says,

155

". . . but the people who know their God will display strength and take action" (Daniel 11:32 NAS).

I believe great days of testing are ahead for those who live in the United States of America. Are you prepared, beloved? Are you taking time to get to know your God? You cannot act in faith upon that which you do not know; without faith, it will be impossible to please God.

May we pray for one another, for the whole body of Christ, that we will truly see what is really important and give ourselves diligently to it. What would I do if you did not pray for me?

His Thoughts Toward Me:

My Thoughts Toward Him:

April 18

"He's stopped breathing!" The lab technician at the desk passed the word to the nurse in the other room. "He's stopped breathing." What awful words! Cessation, cessation of life—stopping—quitting—giving up. Don't stop breathing! Do something, hurry!

Then, the nurse comes, walking not running. Why? Because she knows her patient is on a respirator, and when the patient gives up, quits, cannot breathe, the respirator takes over.

For a moment—that seemed more than a moment—Daddy stopped breathing tonight. Then, the respirator took over, and instead of cessation there was life. The breathing was done for my father by the respirator. The respirator will continue to breathe for Daddy until he can breathe on his own; it will work with the body filling his lungs purposefully, perpetually with oxygen.

As I think about it, it seems that praise is to faith and prayer what a respirator is to my father at this time. Our faith grows weak, almost quitting, almost giving up. Hurry, do something, please don't quit believing now—believe, please believe! When faith is about to die, to quit, praise can take over and become its life until once again faith can act on its own. In the front of my Bible, is this statement by my dear brother, Paul Billheimer, from his book, *Destined for the Throne,* "The missing element that is necessary to energize triumphant faith is praise—perpetual, purposeful, aggressive praise. Praise is the highest form of prayer because it combines petition with faith. Praise is the spark plug of faith. It is the one thing needed to get faith airborne, enabling it to soar above the deadly miasma of doubt. Praise is the detergent which purifies faith and purges doubt from the heart."

Oh, beloved, when our faith is about to stop, may we turn to praise, perpetual, purposeful, aggressive praise. Praise is what has sustained my faith; it is what sustains me now as I lay down to sleep.

His Thoughts Toward Me:

My Thoughts Toward Him:

April 19

The phone rang just as we were leaving the house to go to visit my father. It was the doctor. Something was wrong. They would need to operate on my father again, right away. X rays had shown gas in Daddy's abdomen—a pocket of air. The doctor explained that it could be a perforated ulcer; if it were, Daddy might make it. However, it might be more necrotic (dead) intestine; then, he probably would die. Our regular doctor, who had done the other four surgeries in these past sixteen days, was off for the weekend. This doctor was one of his partners. He wanted us to fully understand that Daddy was a candidate for death.

I had to have prayer support. Hurriedly, I called Jack—no answer. Then, I dialed our offices—no answer. On the way to the hospital, I cried out, "God I don't understand. What are You doing? Is Daddy going to die? (Physically . . . I knew he was all right spiritually.) Have I misunderstood Your word to me? How can I minister to Mother? What do I do?"

Praise, I must praise Him. For the first time, I was close to crying. My heart ached as I watched my dear mother and my grandmother. I knew they must be hurting so inside. I began to sing inside, to praise my sovereign God, to look at Him not at the storm. We went in to be with Daddy, talking to him, blessing him, and praying he would hear although he did not respond. His temperature was high. His blood pressure was so dangerously low. His kidneys were still not working on their own.

I had to have specific prayer support. So I called home and Reach Out again—no answer, until I reached Al, one of the men on our staff. When I began to speak to him, I cried for a moment. Then, Al prayed for me; in his prayer, he prayed, "Lord, let Kay walk on the water." He did not know how Mother and I had read last night about Peter walking on the water and faltering when he took his eyes off Jesus to look at the storm tossed sea. That prayer was a confirmation to me from my God, and peace reigned supreme.

I've written too much. I'll write more later on today. It's 3:32 A.M. as I write this. As we have been confronted with death daily these past sixteen days, I've thought, *This is what Easter is all about . . . He is risen . . . the Resurrection and the Life . . . and those that believe shall never die* (John 11:25–26). *I believe this, Lord.*

His Thoughts Toward Me:

My Thoughts Toward Him:

April 20

God says, "Consider it pure joy . . . whenever you face trials of many kinds, because you know that the testing of your faith develops perseverance. Perseverance must finish its work so that you may be mature and complete, not lacking anything" (James 1:2–4 NIV).

We were sitting at the nurses' desk in RICU waiting for Daddy's room to be straightened up. Once again, Mother kissed Daddy good-bye as they took him to surgery. We sat and talked. Mother said, "Maybe the Lord has more yet to do in us . . . more to teach us."

As we held hands and talked, admiration welled in my breast for this precious woman. My father could not have a more perfect wife. How I have admired her down through the years as I watched her so sensitively fulfill her ministry as the wife of a minister. The past trials of her life, which have been many, have wrought that perfecting—that maturing—that has made her one of the kindest people I know.

We talked together about God's command in James to count it all joy in a trial. Why? How? By realizing each trial has a purpose in the life of a Christian, that a trial is not some unfortunate twist of fate, but rather it is part of God's sovereign design for our good. It is to mature us, to bring us to Christ-likeness, so that we will not stand in shame before His Throne when we go home.

The word for endurance or patience (KJV) in the Greek is *hupomeno* which means to abide (meno) under (hupo). In other words, we are not to seek to flee from trials that would test or refine us so that the dross in our lives might be burned out and the silver refined.

Thus it is with joy and trust that Mother, Grandmother, and I wait upon our God.

His Thoughts Toward Me:

My Thoughts Toward Him:

April 21

Once again, my father survived another surgery. Truly, we know our times are in His hands, and it is in this fact that we trust. As the word came to us for the need of another surgery plus the word of how very critical it all was, I once again thought of Job and how tragic news hit him wave after wave; yet the waves of the storm did not cast him down, nor did they cause Job to take his eyes off his God, "The Lord gave and the Lord hath taken away; blessed be the name of the Lord."

Job blessed God, even when God took away the hedge and permitted Satan to attack, touch, and destroy all that Job possessed. Then, Satan saw that Job really loved God, not for what God did for him or for how God blessed and protected him, but rather for God Himself. Oh, we know from reading the Book of Job that he had not yet reached perfection, three trials that were yet to come would be used of God to draw Job into an even more intimate relationship with His God; but Job's walk with God when it all began was mature enough to sustain him.

Praise God for this sure promise: "There hath no temptation [trial, testing] taken you but such as is common to man: but God is faithful, who will not suffer [permit] you to be tempted above that ye are able; but will, with the temptation [trial, testing] also make a way to escape, that ye may be able to bear it" (1 Corinthians 10:13).

We are able, and Daddy is able. Some have said, "How can he take any more?" We can only take anything because God will

160

never permit it to be more than we can bear.

Oh, beloved, I know we are not the only ones going through trials, testings, temptations. My heart goes out to so many of you who are in such great affliction. May God use this to make me more compassionate toward you, more sensitive, more aware of how to minister to you.

His Thoughts Toward Me:

My Thoughts Toward Him:

April 22

What happens when death is so near?

As I've watched my father, I've noticed his eyes open very wide and look up. Another time several days ago before the respirator was put back in (he can't talk with a respirator), there was a purposeful stretching of Daddy's arm straight up, heavenward, with his hand fully opened. I told Mother to ask Daddy what he was reaching for. "Spirit," was his reply. "Holy Spirit, darling, is that it?" His head nodded yes.

I don't know if I can explain what is taking place with me in my spirit right now or not. But I want to try to share it with you. Maybe somehow, someway, someday God will use it in your life.

I am in a state where I don't know what to pray or how to pray. There's no agitation, no turmoil, no doubt within, but there is just a quiet waiting. I am waiting on God, no longer reminding God of what I think He promised me but just abiding, waiting, knowing that God's perfect will shall be done. There is a real peace. I have a feeling Daddy wants us to release him. Daddy has never wanted to be put on life support systems just to keep him existing, and I wonder if this is something going on in his mind. However, at this point the support system means healing not just sustaining life.

One of father's doctors told us that he just "happened to order a chest X ray . . . no specific reason." It was this chest X ray that revealed air in my father's upper abdomen that prompted the surgery which revealed peritonitis. They cleaned out Daddy's abdomen and are now doing all they can to stop the infection with antibiotics. If Daddy lives, there will be no medical explanation. No one doubts it will have to be a miracle.

The doctor just stood at the foot of the bed and said, "Never in all my life have I seen such endurance in a man, to have survived all that he has endured. Keep praying."

In Mother's being and in mine, there is a new depth of peace. "Thank You, precious Prince of Peace. We praise You that the government is upon Your shoulders."

His Thoughts Toward Me:

My Thoughts Toward Him:

April 23

I once heard the story of a dear Christian missionary who ran an orphanage for girls in Japan. She literally lived by Isaiah 9:6, "For unto us a child is born, unto us a son is given: and the government shall be upon his shoulder: and his name shall be called Wonderful, Counseller, The mighty God, The everlasting Father, The Prince of Peace."

God had so quickened this verse to her heart and so enlightened its truths to her that whenever she was confronted with a trial, of any sort, she would simply say to the Lord, "The government is upon Your shoulders." She would rest in that truth. God was in charge; He would have to take over; it was not her responsibility.

One day during the war, she discovered that her orphanage was without soap; it was all but gone, and there was no way to purchase more because of the war. When the "no-soap-news" reached her ears, she immediately turned to her Prince of Peace, her Wonderful Counselor, her eternal Father, her mighty God with, "Lord, the government is upon Your shoulders. We must have soap for Your girls." Upon committing this to the Lord, she then gathered the girls into the chapel to stand before the Lord for soap. As they were waiting upon God in the Chapel, one of her assistants came, bowed before her, and requested her presence in the office. There was a gentleman who wished to see the work being done at the orphanage. As she turned to say she couldn't come, she had a check in her spirit. She would go, leaving the girls in the chapel.

When the Japanese gentleman finished his tour of the orphanage, he was touched by what he saw. He turned to the missionary, "I am so deeply impressed by the work you are doing here. How I desire to help you in some way; but with the war and all, I can't. I have nothing but my soap factory!"

Are you in a no-soap situation? I understand, we are, too! But praise God, rest is ours, "the government is upon His shoulders."

His Thoughts Toward Me:

My Thoughts Toward Him:

April 24

"There remains therefore a Sabbath rest for the people of God. For the one who has entered His rest has himself also rested from his works, as God did from His" (Hebrews 4:9, 10 NAS).

What state am I in now with my father? I believe it would be called the rest of faith. It is not passivity but rather a quietness bathed in peace. It is where all agonizing in prayer ceases and is replaced by an absolute trust and quietness born by total confidence that whatever happens will be fine because God is in absolute control.

It is a rest of faith that I would like to live in at all times. How I would appreciate it if you would pray for me in this respect.

My first awareness of this rest of faith came when I read the book, *Hudson Taylor's Spiritual Secret* (Moody Press). The book is a classic; as far as I am concerned, this biography ought to be required reading for every Christian. In the next few days, I am going to share some precious truths from it which will greatly bless you and encourage you to have a copy of your own. It will help you to learn more of this rest of faith or as it is referred to in the book, "the exchanged life."

Once Hudson Taylor had learned the truth of the exchanged life, he wrote, "It doesn't matter, really, how great the pressure is; it only matters *where the pressure lies.* See that it never comes *between* you and the Lord . . . then, the greater the pressure, the more it presses you to His breast."

That's where I am now, cradled between His shoulders; I can hear the beat of His heart and I'm secure.

His Thoughts Toward Me:

My Thoughts Toward Him:

April 25

Six to eight months before entering this life of rest, "the exchanged life," Hudson Taylor suffered many hours of inward darkness and was very close to despair. As founder of the China Inland Mission, he was pressed upon and sorely tried from many direc-

164

tions. He had covenanted before God never to solicit funds for the support of the work of the mission or its missionaries. A thousand pounds *less* than usual had been contributed during the first half of the financial year, and yet their needs had only increased. There were problems with the government because of a misrepresentation on the part of one outside the work. Then, the public press wrote things that only confused the issue. But the trials without were not as great as those within!

In a letter written to a loved one, Taylor wrote:

"I cannot tell you how I am buffeted sometimes by temptation. I never knew how bad a heart I have. Yet I do know that I love God and love His work, and desire to serve Him only and in all things ... Often I am tempted to think that one so full of sin cannot be a child of God at all ... May God help me to love Him more and serve Him better. Pray that the Lord will keep me from sin, will sanctify me wholly; that He will use me more largely in His service."

As you read excerpts from his letter, does your heart cry out, *Yes, Lord, yes! That is me. That is what I want.*

Do you know the same pressure of trials without, trials within? Do you wonder just how much a body can stand? The trials without we shall all experience. In Philippians 1:29, it is written that we shall suffer. But the trial within, must we live with that also?

Yes, but only until we learn that we cannot be our own Savior either in whole or in part. Think upon it.

His Thoughts Toward Me:

My Thoughts Toward Him:

April 26

Was Hudson Taylor not looking up to the Lord in all these trials? Did he not know the promises of God? Did he not know God's sovereignty, God's provision?

Oh yes, he knew. When you read his book your eyes will be filled with wonder, your heart with admiration; he had already ordered his life according to these thoughts: "When I get out to China, I shall have no claim on anyone for anything. My only claim will be on God. How important to learn, before leaving England, to move man, through God, by prayer alone."

But there was more to learn; this lesson was the life of rest! Oh, beloved, when we hunger and thirst, we shall be filled if we will but go to the source, the fountain of living waters. And if we do not know the way God will see that someone will come to lead us from the desert to the wellspring where we can rest by the still waters. God used several people in Hudson Taylor's life. One was George Mueller. George Mueller had already entered into this life of rest; he was supporting a family of some 2,000 orphans through faith and prayer. This support was without endowments, appeals, or even letting their wants be known. George Mueller's great needs, however, did not keep him from being concerned about others. He knew the greatness of his God and His heart. He not only prayed for funds for his orphans; but he also prayed for money that he might give to further the gospel in foreign lands.

When Hudson Taylor was in the midst of the trials that I shared with you yesterday, God moved Mueller to write a letter to Hudson Taylor and his missionaries that accompanied his gift to the work. These were words that Hudson Taylor sorely needed to hear as he sought for the way out of the desert to the wellspring. "On Him then reckon, to Him look, on Him depend; and be assured that if you walk with Him, look to Him and expect help from Him, He will never fail you. An older brother, who has known the Lord for forty-four years, who writes this, says for your encouragement that He has never failed him. In greatest difficulties, in the heaviest trials, in the deepest poverty and necessities, He has never failed me; but because I was enabled by His grace to trust in Him, He has always appeared for my help. I delight in speaking well of His name."

Oh, beloved, may we look unto Him—there is no other!

His Thoughts Toward Me:

My Thoughts Toward Him:

April 27

There was more to George Mueller's letter to Hudson Taylor than just exhortation! There was a sure and real expression of love.

Those of you who have known me for some time have seen me change. Oh, I have not altered doctrinally nor in adamant feelings for the gospel; these have just grown. But what you say you have seen is a softening, a new gentleness, more love. And I needed it! And I need even more. I believe this trial of my faith will help. God has taught me so much in so many different ways these past twenty-two days. One of the things I asked others to pray for me during this time was that I would be all I should be to my mother and my family. Although I've stumbled at times, I have not gone down. God has answered my prayer; He has held me up. Never have I known such spiritual intimacy with my mother as I have known through this trial. We have entered into a new relationship, and it brings us such great joy.

Before I share with you how Hudson Taylor entered into the life of rest, let me share with you the first part of George Mueller's letter to Hudson Taylor and his missionaries. It reminds me of your many expressions of love shown to me and my family during this trial. How greatly God used the prayers, letters, phone calls, messages, cards, flowers—assurance of your love.

"My chief object is to tell you that I love you in the Lord, that I feel deeply interested about the Lord's work in China, and that I pray daily for you. I thought it might be a little encouragement to you in your difficulties, trials, hardships and disappointments to hear of one more who feels for you and who remembers you before the Lord. But were it otherwise, had you even no one to care for you—or did you at least seem to be in a position as if no one cared for you—you will always have the Lord to be with you. Remember Paul's case at Rome (2 Timothy 4:16–18)."

Pray, beloved, that I will never fail to first give love before I give exhortation, for I'm sure that exhortation without love is nothing!

His Thoughts Toward Me:

My Thoughts Toward Him:

April 28

It was a letter from John McCarthy that God used to bring Hudson Taylor into the victory he so longed for! John had entered into rest and the truth had to be shared to reveal the wellspring of the life of rest to Hudson Taylor. The water of life gushed forth, and Hudson Taylor drank deeply and was satisfied. The wearisome traveler's journey was over. He could rest.

I shall only quote parts of the letter, enough to make you want to read more, enough to make you long, as I long, to fully know this life of rest.

"Holiness . . . it was the subject of all others occupying my thoughts, not from anything I had read . . . so much, as from a consciousness of failure—a constant falling short of that which I felt should be aimed at; an unrest; a perpetual striving to find some way by which one might continually enjoy that communion, that fellowship, at times so real but more often so visionary, so far off.

"Do you know, I now think that this striving, longing, hoping for better days to come is not the true way to holiness, happiness or usefulness. It is better, no doubt than being satisfied with poor attainments, but not the best way after all. I have been struck with a passage from a book . . . entitled, *Christ Is All.* It says,

" 'The Lord Jesus received is holiness began: the Lord Jesus cherished is holiness advancing; the Lord Jesus counted upon as never absent would be holiness complete . . . He is most holy who has most of Christ within and joys most freely in the finished work. It is defective faith which clogs the feet and causes many a fall.'

"Abiding not striving nor struggling; looking unto Him, trusting Him for present power; . . . resting in the love of an almighty Saviour, in the joy of a complete salvation, 'from all sin'—this is not new, and yet 'tis new to me . . . Christ literally all seems to me, now, the power, the only power for service, the only ground for unchanging joy.

"How then to have our faith increased? Only by thinking of all that Jesus is and all He is for us: His life, His death, His work, He, Himself as revealed to us in the Word, to be the subject of our constant thoughts. Not a striving to have faith . . . but a looking off to the Faithful One seems all we need; a resting in the Loved One entirely, for time and eternity."

Hudson Taylor said, "As I read, I saw it all. I looked to Jesus, and when I saw,—oh how joy flowed!"

"God . . . may we see!"

His Thoughts Toward Me:

My Thoughts Toward Him:

April 29

How blessed I was this morning when I knelt beside my bed to pray and to read Psalm 20. "May the Lord answer you in the day of trouble! May the name of the God of Jacob set you securely on high." I saw it in an entirely different light! It was fulfilled; it was done; it was completed. God had spoken, and it was so! This, I believe, is the life of rest—to see all as already accomplished and to rest in the fact of its accomplishment.

Mr. Judd, a fellow worker, wrote of Hudson Taylor:

"He was a joyous man now, a bright happy Christian. He had been a toiling burdened one before, with literally not much rest of soul. It was resting in Jesus now, and letting Him do the work —which makes all the difference. Whenever he spoke in meetings after that, a new power seemed to flow from him and in the practical things of life a new peace possessed him. Troubles did not worry him as before. He cast everything on God in a new way, and gave more time to prayer. Instead of working late at night, he began to go to bed earlier, rising at 5:00 A.M. to give time to Bible study and prayer (often two hours) before the work of the day began.

"Hudson Taylor's life was no longer a life lived by imitating Christ but rather living in the continuous reality of 'Christ liveth in me.' Now, instead of bondage there was liberty; instead of failure, quiet victory within; instead of fear and weakness, a restful sense of sufficiency in another.

"Hudson wrote to his sister, 'As to work—mine was never so plentiful, so responsible or so difficult, but the weight and strain are all gone.' "

This, beloved, is what it is like to enter into rest, no matter what befalls, "even though tested by fire" the weight and strain are gone!

His Thoughts Toward Me:

My Thoughts Toward Him:

April 30

"There hath no temptation taken you but such as is common to man: but God is faithful, who will not suffer you to be tempted above that ye are able; but will with the temptation also make a way to escape, that ye may be able to bear it" (1 Corinthians 10:13).

On March 17, Daddy entered the hospital; now, it is April 22. I have been away from Mother for thirteen days. All this time, I have been unable to write this final day's meditation for this devotional. During these days, the doctors have told Mother of Daddy's diseased liver and of a stroke that has apparently affected a small part of his brain.

Gladly, joyfully, would my mother care for my father for days, months, or years. "But it would be so hard on your father, Kay." This is my mother—a woman who loves deeply, who loves selflessly, who cares for others above herself.

Mother and I have talked much these days of God and His loving ways. How gently God has brought her to this willingness to release the man who has truly become bone of her bone, flesh of her flesh. God has been so gentle in not taking Daddy home through the traumatic shock of dying in surgery but rather has prepared Mother, step by step, bringing her to "a way of escape, that she may be able to bear it" as 1 Corinthians 10:13 promises. How good is our God, how perfect are His ways. He is our ROCK, our SHIELD, our FORTRESS, our very present HELP in the time of trouble—our God of all comfort. Our times are in His hands, and His are hands which, because of love, have offered to the world the gift of His son even to God's own hurt, to God's own loss. They are hands pierced through with love.

On April 22, Jack and I were in Atlanta. I was going to get dressed for our Television Prayer Banquet when the phone rang. It was about 5:00 P.M. "Honey, your father died at four o'clock this

afternoon. It was so peaceful." *But he lives! Praise God . . . he lives!*
   God's timing is perfect. All that He does has a purpose. Never
will I forget April 22, 1980. There is a way of escape in the midst
of all life's trials, temptations, and testings; there is an answer, a
sure answer, to the question, How Can I Live?

His Thoughts Toward Me:

My Thoughts Toward Him:

MAY

May 1

The words are so familiar, "The Lord is my shepherd; I shall not want" (Psalms 23:1). So familiar because we have heard them over and over again, especially if we went to Sunday School as children or if we have attended a lot of funeral services. "The Lord is my shepherd; I shall not want" is the first verse of the Twenty-third Psalm which is probably the most familiar of the Psalms to the world at large. What is the purpose of this Psalm? Is it just meant to be read at funeral services to help the living get through the loss of their loved one or is it more than that? Is it meant to help the living get through life? Is it a Psalm of comfort or a Psalm of life? It is both, it is a Psalm of comfort for life, no matter what life brings.

As a principle of life, its truths are all summed up in the first and glorious verse, "The Lord is my shepherd; I shall not want." It is an unconditional truth for every child of God. Oh, how I long to so walk by it in every circumstance of life, that I would realize that, because I am His, I shall not want. No matter what situation I might find myself in, whether by man's doing or by my own ineptness—I shall not want because the Lord is my Shepherd. If we were to appropriate this truth by faith, what peace, what rest, we would know all the days of our lives! If we were to live by this truth moment by moment, circumstance by circumstance, we would not be moved or shaken by anything that would ever come our way.

Oh, beloved, this promise of God is ours for the believing. May we not be deceived by that age-old whisper of the serpent, the devil, the father of lies who hisses, "Yea, hath God said?" Satan only seeks your destruction. Listen to God, God cannot lie.

God is so precious. As I write this I am in Berchtesgaden, Germany, where I will be for the next two weeks speaking to military wives from all over Europe and Asia. Knowing that I was to write this month's devotional on the Twenty-third Psalm, God, I believe, wanted to prove Himself to me again as the Shepherd who keeps His sheep from the want of any good thing!

I know it sounds unorganized but, in my rush to get away, I forgot to pack my liquid make-up base. For you men, that is the most vital part of a woman's make-up. (Someday you may find out how vital it is when your wife forgets hers, and you have to go shopping at some weird hour!) Because I have skin problems I wear a specific brand and, of course a special color! The color is Warm Beige. My predicament caused me to cry, "O Father, how could I have forgotten something so necessary!" Now, obviously, beloved, this was not a matter of life, death, or souls for the Kingdom, but just a desire to look as good as possible as I communicated woman to woman. Yet, my Shepherd cared—nothing is too small or insignificant if it concerns His sheep.

Upon arriving in Frankfurt I poured out my sad tale of woe to my hostess. With but minutes to spare, we headed for the Post Exchange before it closed. There, of all the stateside cosmetics available, they just happened to carry my particular brand . . . but alas, every box was labeled as carrying the same shade, a shade far too dark for me. Then, on impulse, my hostess opened one of the boxes. You guessed it! It was my shade. Curious now, she opened every box. There was only one bottle of the shade I used. It was all I needed.

Nothing—absolutely nothing—is too small or mundane for the One who has numbered the very hairs on your head. *Whatever* concerns you, beloved, is of the utmost concern to Him. This is the teaching of 1 Peter 5:7 "Casting *all* your care upon him, *for he careth for you*" (italics added).

Let's begin this month by recording our wants or cares and then bringing them before our Shepherd, one by one, in prayer. As you talk with Him regarding each one, record any insights given to you by your Shepherd.

My Wants (cares)	My Shepherd's Insights

May 2

As I write today's devotion, I fear that some of you will not do what I am going to ask you to do. To be honest, I'm afraid you will pass over it, and, for this reason, I have been tempted to pass over it as well. But I can't. So neither can you, dear one. Please do it. I know it will help.

I have written below Psalm 23 in its entirety. Read through the Psalm asking your Shepherd to speak to you in an intimate way. After you prayerfully read it through once, read the Psalm through again. This time note where the pronoun referring to the Lord changes from "He" to "Thou." Mark it in some way. Now read the Psalm again, this time listing below what the Shepherd does for His sheep. Then read it once more, noting what benefits come to the sheep as a result of the Shepherd's care.

The Lord is my shepherd; I shall not want. He maketh me to lie down in green pastures: he leadeth me beside the still waters. He restoreth my soul: he leadeth me in the paths of righteousness for his name's sake. Yea, though I walk through the valley of the shadow of death, I will fear no evil: for thou art with me; thy rod and thy staff they comfort me. Thou preparest a table before me in the presence of mine enemies: thou anointest my head with oil; my cup runneth over. Surely goodness and mercy shall follow me all the days of my life: and I will dwell in the house of the Lord for ever.

The Shepherd's Care	The Sheep's Benefits

Finally, beloved, list below what the sheep has to do.

May 3

If you are ever going to know the Shepherd's care, you must first realize your great need for a shepherd. If any animal God created ever needed a shepherd, it is sheep! And I truly believe that God created sheep so we could see what we are like.

Learning about sheep can be very humbling and very eye-opening! To learn about sheep is to see how greatly we, as sheep, need our Shepherd. It makes you cast yourself on Him in total dependence, and that is where we are meant to live!

Sheep are the dumbest of all animals. Because of this they require constant attention and meticulous care. They are helpless, timid, feeble animals that have little means of self-defense. If they do not have the constant care of a shepherd they will go the wrong way, unaware of the dangers at hand. They have been known to nibble themselves right off a mountain side. If they are not led to proper pastures, they will obliviously eat or drink things that are disastrous to them. Not only that, they will literally live their lives in a rut if the shepherd does not lead them to new pastures. Sheep easily fall prey to other animals, and, when they do, they are virtually defenseless without their shepherd to protect them. Sheep can also become cast down and, in that state, panic and die. And so because sheep are sheep, they need shepherds to care for them.

You, beloved, are the sheep of His pasture. It was for you that God ". . . brought up from the dead the great Shepherd of the sheep through the blood of the eternal covenant, even Jesus our Lord" (Hebrews 13:20 NAS) and through Him, beloved, He will "equip you in every good thing to do His will, working in us that which is pleasing in His sight . . ." (Hebrews 13:21 NAS).

Oh, precious sheep, take a good look at your life. How can you make it on your own? Can you see your need for a Shepherd? In what areas? Write them out below.

May 4

The welfare of sheep depends solely upon the care they get from their shepherd. Therefore, the better the shepherd, the better the sheep. When you see sheep that are weak, sickly, and infested with pests, you can be sure that their shepherd really does not care for them.

What is our Great Shepherd like? Learn that and you will understand why you can confidently say, "The Lord is my shepherd; I shall not want." Believe it and you will know a life of perfect rest. Walk in it, in the obedience of faith, and you will experience contentment no matter what your circumstances of life.

Oh, beloved, how vital it is that we as sheep know our Shepherd! Only then will we know why there is no want for those who are His. There is a marvelous word for us in Daniel 11:32 that will become our theme verse for the next days as we get to know our Lord, our Shepherd. ". . . but the people that do know their God shall be strong, and do exploits."

The Twenty-third Psalm, which shows us the ministry of our *Great* Shepherd, is couched between two other Psalms that show us two other aspects of our Shepherd. Psalm 22 shows us the *Good* Shepherd who lays down His life for His sheep; Psalm 24 shows us our *Chief* Shepherd, the King of Glory, who is to come again as stated in 1 Peter 5:4. Before the Lord can ever function as your Great Shepherd, you must first know Him as your Good Shepherd because it is here that you meet Him as your precious Savior. Listen to His words, "Truly, truly, I say to you, I am the door of the sheep" (John 10:7 NAS). There is no other door, there is no other way to enter in and to become God's sheep, except by Jesus. "All who came before Me are thieves and robbers; but the sheep did not hear them" (John 10:8 NAS). *His sheep hear His voice;* they know truth when they hear it. And once they hear truth, they recognize it for what it is—reality! "I am the door; if anyone enters through Me, he shall be saved [perfect security], and shall go in and out [perfect liberty], and find pasture [perfect sustenance]. . . . I am the good shepherd; the good shepherd lays down His life for the sheep" (John 10:9, 11 NAS).

A shepherd in the east who knew nothing of God's Word was describing his sheepfold to a curious inquirer. As he pointed to the sheepfold, the inquirer said, "But where is the door?"

"I am the door," the shepherd replied. "At night, when the sheep enter the sheepfold, I lie down in the opening. None can enter or leave without going over me, because I am the door."

When did you hear His voice? When did you enter into God's family through Jesus the Christ? When did you begin to follow Him?

May 5

He walked into a nine-foot cell and was immediately imprisoned in darkness. As the bolt slid and the padlock was fastened on the door, he found himself caught in a night of steel, bound in bands of iron. It was October 1950. Geoffrey Bull was a prisoner in China.

"I had no Bible in my hand, no watch on my wrist, no pencil or paper in my pocket. There was no real hope of release. There was no real hope of life. There was no real possibility of reunion with those I loved. The only reality was my Lord and Savior Jesus Christ. Divested of all, He was to become everything to me. He was to break my bars and enlarge my coasts in the narrow room. He was to be my fullest nourishment amidst the meager food. My meat which my captors 'knew not of.' He would make me glad with His countenance. He would let me hear His voice. As in the days of His nativity, Herod may reign and imagine slaughter against the innocent but let me only see His star and I would come to worship Him." (From *God Holds the Key*, Geoffrey Bull: Hodder and Stoughton Publishers.)

What if that had been you, instead, imprisoned in that cell? Would you have known your Shepherd well enough to have been able to say in confident faith, "The Lord is my Shepherd; I shall not want"? In the darkness of the night of imprisonment, would you have known enough to look for His star so that you might worship Him?

What does it take to be able to worship God and confidently proclaim Him as your all-sufficient Shepherd? Worship is based on knowledge—a knowledge that I pray will be wonderfully deepened in the days to come. To worship God is to recognize His worth and bow before Him.

Suppose someone were to ask you, "What is your Shepherd like that He could so provide for you that you would not even want—no matter what—no matter even if you found yourself in a prison cell?" How would you answer, beloved? Write it below.

May 6

When Moses met God at the burning bush, God commissioned him to stand before Pharaoh and say, "God says, 'Let My people go that they may serve Me.' " Moses responded by asking, "Who am I, that I should go to Pharaoh, and that I should bring the sons of Israel out of Egypt?" (Exodus 3:11 NAS). It is interesting that God never answered Moses' question about his personal qualifications for such a task. Rather we find God saying to Moses, "Certainly I will be with you . . ." (Exodus 3:12 NAS). Moses would not want, the Shepherd was his for the task. All Moses had to do was follow.

However Moses did need to know who his God was. He needed to know who was going to separate the children of Israel out of Pharaoh's sheepfold. So Moses asked God His name. "Whom shall

I say sent me?" Oh, how I love God's answer, "I AM WHO I AM . . . Thus you shall say to the sons of Israel, I AM has sent me to you. . . . This is My name forever, and this is My memorial-name to all generations" (Exodus 3:14, 15 NAS).

I AM! I AM what? I AM all that you will ever need. I AM all that you will ever need at any time, in any place, in any situation.

Oh, beloved, your Shepherd is our El Shaddai. This name for God, El Shaddai, comes from the word *breast*—the place for succoring one's child. God is our all-sufficient One whose grace is sufficient for us so that we can be "content with weaknesses, with insults, with distresses, with persecutions, with difficulties, for Christ's sake; for when I am weak, then I am strong" (2 Corinthians 12:10 NAS).

What has God asked you to do? Where has your Shepherd led you? Does it seem too hard, too difficult, impossible because of who you are? Oh my beloved, look to your Shepherd and you shall not want for He is your El Shaddai, your "I AM"—all that you will ever need. That is His memorial-name forever, even to you, to your generation. Where do you feel insufficient? Write this out below. Then meditate on how God can meet those needs.

May 7

Our Shepherd is the Sovereign God. He rules over all. ". . . His dominion is an eternal dominion; his kingdom endures from generation to generation. All the peoples of the earth are regarded as nothing. He does as he pleases with the powers of heaven and the peoples of the earth. No one can hold back his hand or say to him: 'What have you done?' " (Daniel 4:34, 35 NIV.)

If you are going to live a life of peace, a life of rest and contentment no matter what your circumstances, you must be aware of the sovereignty of your Shepherd. When you entered into the sheepfold you saw that the One who laid down His life for you was truly God incarnate, God in the flesh. Now you must know that as

God, your Shepherd is sovereign. To recognize His sovereignty is to worship Him aright.

When one says that God is sovereign, he means that nothing can happen in this universe without God's permission. Oh, man retains his free will and responsibility, but they cannot be executed unless God concurs. Neither necessity, nor chance, nor malice of Satan controls the sequence of events or their causes. God is the supreme Ruler over all, and no one nor any circumstance of life can thwart His desire or His plan. Your Shepherd is the sovereign Ruler of all the universe, beloved, and that is why you shall not want.

Why don't you take a few minutes and meditate upon this truth. Then, write out below exactly what God's sovereignty means to you. You might want to list the particular things in your life over which He has control.

May 8

The baby was choking. Frantic with fear the young mother picked her up and ran to the car. She had to get to the hospital. Hurriedly she backed out of the driveway, only to run over and kill her older daughter.

As this beautiful young mother shared her story with me, my heart wrenched with the horror of it all. I thought, "O Father, how could she handle it if she did not understand Your sovereignty!" But she did know the sovereignty of God. It was horrible, it was painful, but it did not destroy her. She would not live as a demented woman locked up in a padded cell of "what ifs," "whys," and "if onlys." She would not bitterly harangue God, asking Him why He had permitted this. Nor would she refuse the open arms which would draw her to her El Shaddai and His all-sufficient breast. She would be comforted with the comfort which He alone could give. She would bow as Job bowed before his sovereign Father and say, ". . . The Lord gave and the Lord has taken away.

Blessed be the name of the Lord" (Job 1:21 NAS). And I, along with others, would see her peace and realize once again what it means to have the Lord as our Shepherd.

The One who sits upon His throne ruling over all is a God of love (1 John 4:8). Love is the very essence of His being, therefore He can never act apart from love. He loves us with an everlasting love, a love that will not fail, a love that continually seeks our highest good. His sheep are in His hands, and those hands are hands of love. Nothing—not any situation or any person—can snatch us out of His hands (John 10:27). Held tightly in His grip, we are shielded by His fingers of love. Anything that comes into our lives—into yours or mine, beloved—will be filtered through fingers of love. The sovereign God is a God of love. Whatever He does, whatever He permits, is all in love.

Has anything ever happened to you that made you doubt His love?

His Thoughts Toward Me:

May 9

Have you ever felt caught or trapped in a particular situation that seemed absolutely insane, horrid, unbelievable, inconceivable? All of a sudden your plans, dreams, hopes are shattered. You wonder, *How did this happen?* It seems like a nightmare from which you will surely awaken. You think, *This couldn't be happening to me; it will alter the course of my life. It will ruin everything!* You wonder how you can survive. Your mind goes bananas as gloom settles like a fog over the present, and dire forecasts of danger are predicted and transmitted through the night by your imagination.

Then all of a sudden you panic. What should you do? You have to do something, but what?

The clap of thunder causes the little sheep to stop his grazing and look up. The sudden noise and the pelting of the rain have his attention. Panic sets in, where is his shepherd?

Fear not, little flock, your Shepherd is watching over you. "Remember this, and be assured; Recall it to mind, . . . For I am God, and there is no other; I am God, and there is no one like Me, Declaring the end from the beginning And from ancient times things which have not been done, Saying, 'My purpose will be established, And I will accomplish all My good pleasure'; . . . Truly I have spoken; truly I will bring it to pass. I have planned it, surely I will do it" (Isaiah 46:8-11 NAS).

Oh, beloved sheep, whatever happens, you can know that His will shall be accomplished in your life, because you are His. He is the Alpha and the Omega—the Beginning and the End. Your Shepherd has not left you, He is there to complete that which He has begun, to make you into His image. This is His plan for you and it will not be thwarted. All that God inaugurates, He completes. He is the God of the finished work.

So rest, little sheep, your Shepherd is there; He is in control. Whatever comes to you has been filtered through fingers of love, and it will serve to accomplish His purpose.

My Thoughts Toward Him:

May 10

Have you ever become frustrated because you have been suddenly detained, somehow you have been held up or kept from carrying out your plans? Your time has not been used the way you had planned. And so you have become agitated, impatient, irritable, upset, angry. You have kicked yourself for getting into such a situation or have ranted and raved over the incompetence of those who have fouled everything up.

Oh, little sheep, why do you get all upset? The Shepherd is there, did He not lead you, are not the steps of a righteous man ordered by the Lord? (Psalms 37:23.) Man's goings are of the Lord; how can a man then understand His own way? (Proverbs 20:24.) Quit your frustration! You do not need to understand. Walk by faith and know that goodness and mercy are following you because the Lord is your Shepherd. You shall not want. Your times are in His hands (Psalms 31:15). The eternal God is the Author of time, and every moment counts to Him. He will not squander your time. He has a precious blessing, a precious lesson for you at every turn. Rest and in everything give thanks for *this is* the will of God in Christ Jesus concerning you, otherwise it could not happen.

A pastor was headed for a speaking engagement in another part of the United States. He found himself rushing through the airport to make his connection. The rush was needless. The plane was to be delayed for at least an hour. The pastor's smile was refreshing to the airline agent after receiving so many "blessings" from irate travelers. He simply said, "My times are in God's hands, so I don't sweat it!"

With a sure hour to spare and a promise that they would not leave without him, the pastor went to eat. Fifty minutes later when the pastor returned to inquire about the flight, the agent turned ashen.

"You got on the plane ten minutes ago; I saw you. How could you be standing here?"

The pastor smiled, "Obviously that wasn't me, I'm here."

Now a deathly white, the agent said, "But I saw you. I know it was you. I saw your ticket and boarding pass."

The pastor just shook his head, "But I'm here."

Later the news came: The plane had crashed. All were killed.

Your times are in the hands of the sovereign God, dear sheep, so do not fret—rest. If God makes you stand and wait, He sees it not as loss but gain. It all has a purpose—His.

My Thoughts Toward Him:

May 11

Have you ever wondered, *Where is this life of peace that is supposed to belong to the child of God?* Do you ever toss and turn unable to sleep because your mind will not allow your body to rest? Pressures, fears, discontentment, unhappy relationships tramp up and down the corridors of your mind forbidding sleep. The night grows long; you grow weary, and in your weariness you wonder if this is all there is. Are we born for sorrow and trouble, a life of turmoil and turbulence?

No, beloved, this is not to be your style of life if the Lord is your Shepherd. He is to make you lie down in green pastures; He is to lead you beside still waters (Psalms 23:2). This is the Great Shepherd's promise to His sheep—a promise of rest.

Why then is there no rest? It is because, beloved, in some way you have failed to appropriate the grace of God which He says is sufficient for all your needs (2 Corinthians 12:9). For sheep, true rest is to lie down in green pastures. Of all the books I have read on the Twenty-third Psalm, none has blessed me more than Phillip Keller's *A Shepherd Looks at Psalm 23* (Zondervan). I cannot recommend it enough. It was from Keller that I learned that sheep must be free of four things before they can rest. Today I want to make you aware of what these four things are and then in the days to come, we will take them one by one and discuss them in a very practical way. So follow closely, precious sheep, as we pasture at verse two for a while, gleaning all we can.

First, sheep must be free from hunger. They cannot lie down as long as they feel a need for finding food. Yet in this second verse of Psalm 23, we find that the Shepherd has so satisfied the sheep's hunger that they can lie down right in the midst of green pastures.

Second, if sheep are to rest, they must be free from fear. Sheep are helpless, timid animals with little means of self-defense. They are easily frightened. Are you, beloved, beset with fears?

Third, sheep cannot rest unless they are free from friction. Tension with others of their kind keeps them on their feet, they feel they must defend themselves!

And fourth, sheep cannot rest unless they are free from pests. Sheep can be greatly aggravated and driven to distraction by flies, parasites, or other pests which would seek to torment them.

Which of these things holds you prisoner, interrogating you night after night? What fears, what frictions, what aggravations, what hungers? List them below and in the days to come we will take them before the Great Shepherd.

May 12

I'm on a plane, flying home from Germany as I write this. Oh, how I wish I could share with you, face to face, all that God has wrought in these past two weeks. Truly God has been with us and has done a life-changing work in a multitude of lives.

Hours were spent not only in teaching, but in listening, hurting, weeping, praying, and then instructing. Sometimes I just shook my head in disbelief. One precious child shared something that was so horrible that Billie, my traveling companion, couldn't finish her meal. Oh, how our hearts ached. The awful, awful wages of sin! How do people get so messed up? Why are they so restless, so tormented, so anxious about life? It's because they do not know their Shepherd or because they have refused to follow Him. They have not known nor fed upon the green pastures of His Word. And because of hunger they have been constantly foraging for something to satisfy their inner craving. Sheep that are hungry won't lie down. They can't. They lack vigor, vitality, they are weak, malnourished, subject to disease, yet driven, because they are not satisfied. So, untended by the shepherd, they eat anything and everything ofttimes to their own destruction.

This is what had happened to so many with whom we shared. They had not fed upon the Word of God; they had not known the way of truth. They had not desired the sincere milk of the Word that they might grow thereby (1 Peter 2:2), nor had they gone on to strong meat that they might be mature in the faith, able to discern good and evil doctrine (Hebrews 5:14). No, they had been stolen away by the thief who comes only to steal, and kill, and destroy. . . . or a hireling had abandoned them to the wolves (John 10:10, 12 NAS). Over and over again I heard, "Thank you for being so open about your own life, and thank you for feeding us the Word of God without compromise." "It's been so long since I've had meat." One chaplain hugged me and said, "My life has been changed; I'll never be the same. I'm off the fence." All this because they were fed the Word of God. Beloved, what has hunger caused you to do?

May 13

"The Lord has told me I must talk with you. When can we get together?" Oh, how I admired this chaplain. Pride would not keep him from humbling obedience. God had shown him that he had gotten caught up in the "busyness" of being a chaplain and in the vanity of psychology all to the neglect of the Word of God. And so he came to find out how to really dig into God's Word, to study it precept upon precept. He saw that a ministry without the Word of God, as its pivotal point (as its focal point) is not a life-giving nor a life-changing ministry. He saw that he had to saturate himself with the Word of God.

Did not our Shepherd say, ". . . the words that I have spoken to you are spirit and are life"? (John 6:63 NAS.) "Man shall not live by bread alone, but by every word that proceedeth out of the mouth of God" (Matthew 4:4). And so the Shepherd prayed for His sheep, "Sanctify them [make them holy] in the truth; Thy word is truth" (John 17:17 NAS).

But because man has thought he could live by bread alone, because man has been taken captive "through philosophy and empty deception, according to the tradition of men, according to the elementary principles of the world, rather than according to Christ" (Colossians 2:8 NAS), man is anything but holy. Man is all messed up.

As I taught, women would burst out sobbing. Suddenly they saw what they had done. They had gone against God's holy law, they had done those things they ought not to have done and there was no health in them. They were riddled with the seeping, putrifying sores of sin—immorality, incest, abortion, divorce (once, twice, more), wounded children, dominated husbands. They were governed by nagging destructive tongues and hardened hearts that had to be broken with the hammer of God's Word.

Oh, beloved, are you wandering about, foraging, searching, unable to rest, getting all messed up because you won't spend time feeding in the pastures the Shepherd has prepared for you? What will it take to make you get into His Word?

My Thoughts Toward Him:

May 14

After fifteen years, suddenly it was back. It came after she boarded the plane. "It was like something was going to happen, and I had no control over it. I wanted to run, to get away, but I was caught on the plane. Before I was saved, when fear would hit me, I would run, I would get out of the house or wherever I was."

But this time she could not run. The fear that came over my dear friend that day was not the fear of flying but rather a sudden fear for her child whom she had left behind. However, because it happened on a plane, the fear was transferred to flying. What a problem this presented, for every week she had to fly to another state to teach a Bible class.

Sheep have a tendency to run when they are frightened. A sudden noise, a sudden disturbance, can cause panic in the sheepfold. And when fear strikes, the sheep take off, running frantically in any direction, often into danger. There is only one cure for fear as far as sheep are concerned. And it was the only cure for my friend. When sheep are suddenly struck by fear, the shepherd senses it immediately and quietly moves among them reassuring them of his presence. As soon as the sheep become aware that the shepherd is with them, the desire to run vanishes because fear has been replaced by trust. *The Lord is my Shepherd; I shall not want.* He makes me to lie down—rest not panic.

My friend was soon to realize that this fear was a fiery dart from the enemy and that to run would only cause Satan great delight. She learned that she must turn and gaze upon her Shepherd the moment fear struck. "When I am afraid, I will put my trust in Thee. In God, whose word I praise, in God I have put my trust; I shall not be afraid. What can mere man do to me?" (Psalms 56: 3, 4 NAS.) And so she would endure "as seeing Him who is invisible" (Hebrews 11:27). She would be kept in perfect peace by keeping her mind stayed upon her Shepherd, she would trust in Him (Isaiah 26:3). Was she ever again bothered by fear? Yes, we'll talk about it more tomorrow, but today, beloved, why don't you list your fears below and then talk to the Shepherd about them.

May 15

Fear is not from God. God has not given us the spirit of fear, but of power and of love and of a sound mind (2 Timothy 1:7). Therefore when you find yourself the target of the enemy's fiery dart of fear you must have enough presence of mind to raise your shield of faith, with which you will be able to extinguish all the fiery darts of the evil one (Ephesians 6:16). A sound mind is a mind under control, a disciplined mind that does not panic, does not lose touch with reality, does not give way to imagination, does not lose consciousness, does not fall into depression. When fear would catch you in its vise-like grip, you must consciously rehearse the love of God and remember His sovereignty. Remember, whatever would come your way would have to be filtered through God's sovereign fingers of love. Perfect love casts out all fear because fear has torment (1 John 4:18). Recognizing all this and then knowing that fear is from the father of lies (the thief who would kill and destroy) you must then appropriate that power which is given to you by God. Remember, God has not given you the spirit of fear but of power. How do you appropriate this power? Recognize that you are in a warfare. Look to your Shepherd. Submit to God. Tell your Shepherd you are His; He can do anything with you that He wants. This really discombobulates the enemy! Then, ". . . Resist the devil and he will flee from you" (James 4:7 NAS).

A sudden dart of fear is still periodically aimed at my friend, but she does not panic. The moment fear comes, she consciously recognizes that it is from the enemy. She says it is almost as if the enemy says, "Here comes that fear again. You aren't going to be able to handle it. You are going to go into a panic."

"But," she says, "I know it is him, and I do not entertain the thought for a moment. I refuse it and go on with whatever I was doing."

Oh, beloved, this is how you, too, must handle fear. Look to the Shepherd, listen to His Words. List below, step by step, how you will handle fear when it comes.

May 16

Are you tense? Edgy? Discontented? Restless? Irritable? Losing weight? When sheep get this way, they cannot lie down. Rest is impossible! These are sure signs that there is rivalry among the sheep, so the shepherd looks for friction within his flock. People aren't the only ones who get involved in competition for status or who go about asserting themselves. This is also common among sheep. And, oh, how the tension builds!

Authority within the sheepfold is established by a butting order. In Ezekiel 34:20–22 NAS, God says to His wayward people, "Behold, I, even I, will judge between the fat sheep and the lean sheep. Because you push with side and shoulder, and thrust at all the weak with your horns, until you have scattered them abroad, therefore, I will deliver My flock, and they will no longer be a prey; and I will judge between one sheep and another."

Oh, beloved, how it must hurt our Shepherd's heart to see us butt, shove, and push one another just so we can be recognized, elevated, or established in authority over others. Didn't the Good Shepherd come not to be ministered unto, but to minister—to give His life a ransom for many? (Matthew 20:28.) And didn't He tell us that to become great in the Kingdom of God we must become servants?

"Have this attitude in yourselves which was also in Christ Jesus, who, although He existed in the form of God, did not regard equality with God a thing to be grasped, but emptied Himself, taking the form of a bond-servant . . ." (Philippians 2:5–7 NAS).

Jesus who is God did not exalt Himself. He made Himself a servant. How can we help but take this form also!

We are to "do nothing from selfishness or empty conceit, but with humility of mind let each of you regard one another as more important than himself" (Philippians 2:3 NAS).

Are you missing that life of rest which is supposed to be yours because you are trying to assert yourself or because others are butting you out of the way? When you sit in church next Sunday, look around you at the flock. What is your attitude toward them? And what is your attitude toward other groups of Christians who seem to be more successful or as successful as your group? Is there jealousy in your heart or a spirit of rivalry? If so, you will not be able to lie down in the green pastures your Shepherd has prepared for you. If you have been "butting," write out your prayer of confession below.

May 17

Sheep cannot live without water, and yet they can go for months without actually drinking if the weather is not too hot. Sheep usually get their water from three sources: streams or springs, deep wells, or the dew on the grass. It is the dew on the grass that can carry them until their grazing takes them to streams, springs, or wells. The secret is to catch the grass or vegetation while it is still wet with dew.

You've got it! It has to be early in the morning before the sun of the day dries up that clean, pure dew! Thus, the shepherd will rise early in the morning to make sure that his sheep are out and grazing early. Then, when the heat of the day comes, the sheep will have already satisfied their hunger and thirst and can retire to the shade of a tree and lie down to rest. Sheep that are up early, feasting on dewy vegetation, are the most confident, serene, and able to cope.

Can you not see what our Shepherd is seeking to lead us into?

He knows the heat of our day, the pressures that will come as things get hot and busy, and so He bids you to come graze with Him in the early hours of the day:

> The Lord God hath given me the tongue of the learned, that I should know how to speak a word in season to him that is weary: he wakeneth morning by morning, he wakeneth mine ear to hear as the learned (Isaiah 50:4). My voice shalt thou hear in the morning, O Lord; in the morning will I direct my prayer unto thee, and will look up (Psalms 5:3).

Now, beloved, there is no law that says you must meet with God every morning or He will not bless you. Please do not think that! What I am suggesting is this. If you want to remain serene, confident, and able to cope, you need to drink of Jesus. He is the fountain of living waters. He alone can satisfy you in a dry and thirsty land where there is no water. And that is what it is like out there in this world of ours; it is a dry and thirsty land. Therefore you will in all probability find it best to arise a little earlier in order to meet with your Shepherd.

Unless you are getting good Bible study at church or in your community, it can be a long time between springs, streams, or wells. So you must be sustained on your daily dew. I have found that once my day starts, the heat is on—children, home, business, school, sports, meetings, church activities. Then it is difficult to get pure, clean dew, and without it my tongue is thick with thirst and certainly is not the tongue of a disciple!

Why not try it for just *one* month, without fail, and see if that morning dew doesn't make a difference. Will you?

May 18

"He leads me beside quiet waters" (Psalms 23:2 NIV). Sheep are frightened by swiftly moving streams. They are easily carried downstream by the current. Also, if they have on their coats of wool, they can easily become waterlogged and sink. So sheep and rapid water do not mix. And sheep know it! Whenever they have to cross water that has any depth to it at all, there is only one safe place for the sheep and that is next to the shepherd. And so our Shepherd says to us, ". . . Do not fear, for I have redeemed you; I have called you by name; you are Mine! When you pass through the waters, I will be with you; And through the rivers, they will not overflow you. When you walk through the fire, you will not be scorched, Nor will the flame burn you" (Isaiah 43:1, 2 NAS). The Lord is your Shepherd, you shall not want.

Oh, precious one, do you feel like you have been caught, swept away by some sudden, swift current of events? Do you feel that you are being pulled under, absorbing your problems rather than casting them off? Are you weighed down in the waters of trouble? Are you overwhelmed, do you fear for your sanity? Do you feel that you might not make it, that you might drown? Sheep that do not stay close to the Shepherd are the ones that get in trouble. Have you tried to cross the waters alone?

Oh, beloved, do not despair, your Sovereign Shepherd is there. Draw near to Him and listen to His words for He hath said, ". . . I will never desert you, nor will I ever forsake you" (Hebrews 13:5 NAS).

The waters will not overflow you. They cannot overflow you. Call to your Shepherd. When the three Hebrew children were thrown into the furnace of fire, they saw a fourth there, the Son of God (Daniel 3:25). When all deserted the Apostle Paul, the Lord stood with him and strengthened him (2 Timothy 4:16, 17). God has never forsaken His sheep; would He forsake you? Write out a prayer to your Shepherd. Tell Him about the waters.

May 19

What does the Psalmist mean when he says, "He restores my soul" (Psalms 23:3 NAS)? When a sheep becomes "cast down," it needs to be restored.

Have you ever felt so "down" that you wondered if you would

ever get up? Or maybe depression has so settled around you like a morning fog that you have forgotten what it was like to awaken to days of expectation bright with clear blue skies and white cotton-puff clouds. Or perhaps you feel abandoned by God. You know God's Word says He will not forsake you, but for some reason you feel He has. You have called out to Him, even cried for Him but apparently He has not heard. If He had, surely you wouldn't feel so abandoned! So forsaken!

Oh, precious one, if any of this is descriptive of you, it may be that you are a "cast" sheep. I learned from Phillip Keller that a cast sheep is one which has been caught on its back and is unable to get up—it needs to be restored. Oftentimes a sheep will lie down to rest; then, deciding to have a good stretch on its side, it will suddenly become off balance. It may have lain in a hollow or depression in the ground, or it may be heavy with fat or wool or with lamb. At any rate, suddenly its center of gravity shifts and the poor thing finds itself on its back. Sometimes it cries out, but ofttimes it is silenced with fear. Panicked because its feet cannot touch the ground, the sheep flails its legs frantically in the air. As it does so, gases begin to build up in the sheep's rumen. As these gases build, it cuts off circulation, especially to the sheep's legs. The sheep feels paralyzed. On its back, unable to get up, it is utterly cast down.

The shepherd is the only hope for a cast sheep. Unless he finds the sheep, it will die. If the day is sunny and hot the sheep will only last a few hours. On top of that, a cast sheep is easy prey for all sorts of predators.

The shepherd wastes no time. Quickly he scans the horizon looking for buzzards circling in the air. If he sees any, he hurries to that spot to rescue, to restore, his sheep.

Aren't you thankful that the omniscient, omnipresent Lord is your Shepherd! If you are cast down and unable to get up, He knows where you are. He knows that the enemy's predators are all around seeking as a roaring lion to devour you (1 Peter 5:8). But fear not, little sheep, He is on His way to rescue you; He will restore your soul. That is why this book is in your hands. "The Lord sustains all who fall, and raises up all who are bowed down. The eyes of all look to Thee, and Thou dost give them their food in due time. Thou dost open Thy hand and dost satisfy the desire of every living thing. . . . The Lord is near to all who call upon Him, To all who call upon Him in truth . . . He will also hear their cry and will save them" (Psalms 145:14–19 NAS).

Those, beloved, are the words of your Shepherd.

May 20

Are you locked in a situation of despair? Have your tears been your food day and night? Have others said to you, "Where is your God?" (Psalms 42:3 NAS.) Have you cried out to God, "Why hast Thou forgotten me? Why do I go mourning?" (Psalms 42:9 NAS.) Do you wonder why you are where you are or if you will ever change? If the depression will ever go away? Precious sheep, you are *cast* and need to be restored.

What causes a sheep to become cast down? Does it happen only to the weak? Maybe understanding something about how sheep become cast will help you! Let's see. Wouldn't it be wonderful if it did!

Sheep are usually cast for one of four reasons. First, many sheep become cast while looking for a soft spot, a cozy rounded hollow in the ground. It is in these soft hollows that they are more apt to end up on their backs. They want it easy. I have found that people with time on their hands, or people with no outreach or deep concern for others, or people who tend to be introspective and preoccupied with their own problems are susceptible to depression. Because things are easy or soft, they have time to think, to focus on the negatives in their lives. And ofttimes it rolls them right over on their backs. Why do we seek soft living when the Son of Man was so about His Father's business that He allowed Himself no rest, no pillow on which to lay His head!

The second reason many sheep become cast is that they are fat. Overweight sheep are not only the quickest to become cast but they are also the least productive and the least healthy of the sheep. They simply have too much abundance. How like us! Once we have it made, once we get fat with the overabundances of life, we see little need to depend upon our Shepherd.

We lose that joy of dependence, of praying and waiting for God's answer and His provision. We get caught up in "things." What we need we buy. Who needs a Shepherd! And as we get caught up in the luxuries and social pressures of life, we suddenly find ourselves out of vital touch with the Shepherd. Our "busyness," our preoccupation with getting ahead or with keeping up a certain life-style, has landed us flat on our backs. We have forgotten what it is like to walk in dependence upon our Shepherd, we are caught, fat and empty.

Tomorrow we will look at the last two reasons that sheep become cast. But today, let's stop together and take a good honest look at ourselves. Could we become cast sheep? Any sheep can—the largest, the strongest, the fattest, the healthiest. Are you looking for an easy, soft life or are you willing to "endure hardness as a good soldier of Jesus Christ" (2 Timothy 2:3)? Are you getting overly fat living luxuriously on the things of the world? Are you entangling yourself in the affairs of this life rather than pleasing Him who has called you to be a soldier (2 Timothy 2:4)? Take time to think upon these things, beloved.

May 21

The third reason a sheep can become cast and need restoring is that it has too much wool. Its fleece becomes clogged with mud, sticks, burrs, ticks, and manure. Sounds repulsive, doesn't it? Yuk! Who would want to touch it? The wool, laden down with all this, puts so much weight on the sheep that it just cannot get up. What a pitiful sight! You would think the shepherd of such a sheep would just let it go. After all, it was the sheep who made such a mess of itself, just let it stay on its back. But alas, this is impossible for the Great Shepherd. He gave His life for these sheep, they are precious in His sight. He came to seek and to save the lost and to return them unto the Bishop and Guardian of their souls. Did He not say it was the sick who had need of a physician? Even so those cast helplessly upon their backs need their Shepherd no matter how pitiful their plight! And so He goes in search of the one who is missing. And when He finds that one, flat on its back, legs stiff and paralyzed, there is much rejoicing. He has found his sheep who was lost. Tender words of loving rebuke, of admonition, and of instruction spill from the Shepherd's mouth as He reaches down to this sheep which He knows so well. Turning it upon its side, the Shepherd massages its legs restoring the circulation so it can again walk at His side.

If it has become cast because of its wool, He knows that the time has come to shear His sheep. This clogged fleece has to go! Every encumbrance and the sin which does so easily entangle it has got to be laid aside (Hebrews 12:1 NAS). Did you know that God did not allow His priests who were ministering in the tabernacle to wear wool because wool was a picture of the self-life? Thus His sheep with too much wool must be sheared, to be stripped down in order to keep from being cast down! Paul said, "I keep under my body, and bring it into subjection: lest that by any means, when I have preached to others, I myself should be a castaway" (1 Corinthians 9:27). "Therefore let him who thinks he stands take heed lest he fall" (1 Corinthians 10:12 NAS). We must all be careful of that self-life that can be clogged with sins and encumbrances, that would so easily weight us down.

Finally, a ewe heavy with lambs could become cast. Sometimes, beloved, those who are bearing the care of others or those pregnant with a ministry can suddenly find themselves upon their backs, weighted down, unable to get up on their feet. How vital it is that such a one walk continuously at the Shepherd's side, never straying, being careful to rest on solid ground, wary of hollows that would throw him off balance. May we remember that He "shall gently lead those that are with young" (Isaiah 40:11). And may we allow ourselves to be led. He never drives His sheep. He leads them.

May 22

"All we like sheep have gone astray; we have turned every one to his own way . . ." (Isaiah 53:6).

"Before I was afflicted I went astray . . ." (Psalms 119:67).

It is so sad when dependent sheep try to live in an independent manner! Some sheep can be so stubborn; they just don't want to stay with the flock. They want to graze where they want to graze. They don't want to follow the shepherd, they want the shepherd to follow them, or at least be there should they need him. And need him they will, if they keep wandering off. You see, sheep are so dumb they can eat their way right off a cliff!

When a shepherd has a sheep with an independent streak, he often has to take some radical action to keep the sheep from "self-destructing." What the shepherd will do is break the sheep's leg. He'll catch that independent sheep, lay it down, and break its leg with a rock. Now it can't wander. But his purpose is not to cripple the sheep; his goal is much higher. After breaking the sheep's leg, he tenderly binds it in a splint. The shepherd then lifts the helpless sheep to his bosom and enfolds him in his shepherd's robe. Brokenness has brought it to the bosom of the shepherd. There the sheep will feel the tender caresses of his shepherd. There the sheep will feel the beat of his shepherd's heart. There the sheep will hear his shepherd's every word. There the sheep will be fed by his shepherd's hand. There, because of brokenness, the sheep will get to know his shepherd as he never knew him before. When the leg is mended, the sheep, having become accustomed to intimacy with his shepherd, will follow closely at his side.

"The Lord is near to the brokenhearted" (Psalms 34:18 NAS). Usually that is all it takes—that independent spirit is broken and God is well pleased. "The sacrifices of God are a broken spirit; A broken and a contrite heart, O God, Thou wilt not despise" (Psalms 51:17 NAS).

Oh, beloved, have you been prone to wander? Can you not see the love of the Shepherd in breaking you that you might dwell near to Him in safety? Will you not thank Him for breaking you? Do not be bitter; He moved in love with your highest good in mind.

My Thoughts Toward Him:

May 23

Do you feel like you are in a rut? Has your life become a boring, meaningless, routine existence? Are you tired of doing the same old thing day in and day out? Do you feel that were you to die, you would have lived a life that never really had any significant effect upon the lives of others? If you can answer yes to any of these questions, then it is time to follow the Shepherd who will lead you "in the paths of righteousness for His name's sake" (Psalms 23:2). For, beloved, you were chosen by Him that you might go and bear fruit (John 15:16), that you might walk in the good works that He foreordained for you (Ephesians 2:10).

Sheep are creatures of habit. If they are left to themselves, they will graze the same ground over and over again, walking over the same trails until the land becomes waste land and their paths erode into gullies. Ground over grazed by sheep often becomes polluted with parasites and disease. That is why sheep so desperately need a shepherd. They must be managed; they must be led on to new pastures, to prepared tables of land where they can be properly fed.

Our Shepherd has prepared abundant pastures for us. But, alas, how many prefer the contaminated ruts, the barren pastures, to the new and greener grazing grounds He would lead us to if we were only willing to follow.

If you are in a rut or feel that life is meaningless, let me ask you when you last set aside time to diligently seek His face in prayer, asking Him to reveal His will to you? When was the last time you prostrated yourself on the floor in prayer and said, "Use me God or I'll die! I must worship You by serving You." When was the last time you heard of some need or of some opportunity to share the gospel, to counsel a needy one, to visit the sick, to spend time in intercession to those abandoned in nursing homes, to cook a meal for someone, to baby-sit for a young mother, to help younger women become better wives and mothers, to disciple a Timothy, to prepare yourself in God's Word, to encourage some faint-hearted Christian, to come alongside and support someone who is weak, to work at being a better partner or a better parent or a better child, to volunteer in a Christian ministry, to care for the orphans and the widows, to sew for those who are in need, to give to those in want, to share the precious truths of His Word with others?

Are you being led in paths of righteousness *for His name's sake,* or are you living in the rut of self-centeredness? Ask your Shepherd where He would lead you.

My Thoughts Toward Him:

May 24

Every now and then it happens, and yesterday was such a day. It was an unseasonably warm, bright, exquisitely beautiful day— a May day in February. I couldn't bear to drive my car down the hill to our office. I had to walk. As I came down through the grass, I felt like doing "a Julie Andrews"—running, twirling, and singing, "The hills are alive with the sound of music." All I wanted to do was play, to be outside, to soak up the warmth of the sun, and to feast my eyes on the heavens so magnificently adorned in white cottontail clouds. I felt so good, so warm, so alive. My heart was filled with rejoicing. I couldn't thank my Father enough for the beauty and warmth of it all. It felt so good to be alive, to belong to Him. You know, sunny, exquisitely beautiful days have that kind of effect on a person.

In parts of our country where people live for months under overcast skies that are constantly pelting them with rain, you will find people surrounded by clouds of depression. Anger and frustration seem to reign over tongues that cut and destroy. Suicide rates soar. There is something about living in shadows, about living in valleys surrounded by mountains and covered in clouds, that causes an air of depression to settle in upon the souls of men. When the light of the sun is shut out, darkness and all its vain imaginations take over.

Yet every day cannot be sunny; night must follow day. If there are to be mountains there must of necessity be valleys. If there were no sun, there would be no shadows. And if every day were bright and sunny, would we appreciate beautiful days? Where would be the watering, the replenishing of the land, the storing up of waters in the deep parts of the earth so that warm, sunny days would not turn into horrible threatening periods of drought!

"Yea, though I walk through the valley of the shadow of death, I will fear no evil: for thou art with me" (Psalms 23:4). All of a sudden the pronouns in this Psalm change from "He" and "me" to "I" and "Thou." And with the change of pronouns comes a change in atmosphere. All of a sudden you become acutely aware of the intimacy of two walking together. Why?

Because they are in a valley of deep darkness. The light of the sun has been blocked out by a looming mountain. The path that the Shepherd has *chosen* for His sheep is through a valley. It is dark in the valleys, shadows cast frightening images. Wild winds and storms can whip violently through the mountain passes causing one to tremble. Why come this way? Because in the valleys there are more abundant sources of water; there the sheep can drink long and deep. Also, the valleys are the way to the mountaintop's luscious vegetation!

Jesus stood and cried out, saying, ". . . If any man is thirsty, let him come to Me and drink. He who believes in Me, as the Scripture said, 'From his innermost being shall flow rivers of living water' " (John 7:37, 38 NAS).

Valleys are meant, beloved, not to depress or to irritate you, not to make you fear or tremble, but to bring you into hitherto unexperienced intimacy with your Shepherd. Valleys are designed to lead you to the Fountain of Living Water that you might drink deeply and be satisfied. Valleys are designed to show you that, because the Lord is your Shepherd, you need not want or fear for He is with you.

Are you in a valley, is the sun shut out? Do not fear, precious sheep. Your Shepherd, God's Son, is there with you; it is all in His plan. He has an eternal purpose. Drink deeply.

Write out below a description of your valleys. How did God satisfy you or meet your needs when you were in these valleys? What new lessons of intimacy were you taught?

May 25

She had lived for ten years in a dungeon far below the surface of the ground. Her only light came at meal times when she was provided with a candle. Although Louis XIV had condemned her to prison, Madame Guyon knew that, like Paul, she was the Lord's prisoner, not the king's. In her tenth year of imprisonment, taking pen in hand, she wrote by candlelight:

> A little bird I am, shut from the fields of air; yet in my cage I sit and sing to Him who placed me there; well pleased a prisoner to be because, my God, it pleases Thee.
>
> Nought else have I to do, I sing the whole day long; and He whom most I love to please, doth listen to my song. He caught and bound my wandering wing but still He bends to hear me sing.
>
> My cage confines me round; abroad I cannot fly; but though my wing is closely bound, my heart's at liberty. My prison walls cannot control, the flight, the freedom of my soul.
>
> Ah' it is good to soar these bolts and bars above, to Him whose purpose I adore, whose Providence I love; and in Thy mighty will to find the joy, the freedom of the mind.

Oh, beloved, have you ever wondered how people in circumstances such as these "can soar these bolts and bars above"? How can they be imprisoned and still sing? What is it? Are they different than we? Have they been given an extra portion of God, of His grace? Do they have something which you and I could never even dream of attaining? What sustains them?

Remember yesterday, beloved, when we talked about walking through the valley of the shadow of death and fearing no evil because our Shepherd is with us? Well, I didn't finish the fourth verse, there is more. Much more, not in words but in meaning.

The verse goes on to say, "I will fear no evil, for thou art with me; *thy* rod and *thy* staff, they comfort me" (Psalms 23:4).

There is no fear; there is contentment, rest, comfort not only because of the Shepherd, but also because of the Shepherd's rod and His staff. Tomorrow I will tell you about the rod; today let's talk about the staff.

The staff is the extension between the shepherd's hand and his sheep. It is used to rescue and restore sheep when they fall into the water or are caught in a thicket or graze over the side of a cliff. The staff is also used to draw the sheep together and to restore lambs to their ewes. The shepherd will many times guide his sheep with his staff. And last, but most precious, the shepherd uses his staff to touch his sheep so that he can have intimate contact with them while he walks towering above them.

The staff is a picture of the Holy Spirit—the extension between our Shepherd's hand and us. "I will not leave you as orphans; I will come to you." "And I will ask the Father, and He will give you another Helper [Comforter], that He may be with you forever" (John 14:18, 16 NAS). It is the staff which identifies the shepherd. Isn't it beautiful!

So remember, beloved, wherever you are, His staff, His Spirit, is your Comforter.

How familiar are you with the ministry of your Shepherd's staff, the Holy Spirit? Why not take time today to read Romans 5:5 and 8:1–39 and write down all you learn about the Holy Spirit and you, as His sheep.

May 26

Why do some Christians seem to have a much more intimate relationship with the Father than others have?

I think one of the major reasons is that they have come to know the purpose and thus the comfort of their Shepherd's rod. The shepherd's rod is an extension of his right arm, the arm of power. It is the prototype for the sceptre, the symbol of authority of the early kings of the East. The shepherd's rod is a symbol of the Word of God, our authority. By it we live, by it we rule. The shepherd's rod like God's Word, is a weapon of power, of protection or defense.

The shepherd's rod is also used to examine sheep. The shepherd causes his sheep to pass under his rod, and at that time, the shepherd examines each one intimately to determine its need and to lay bare any hidden problems that might cause the sheep to be weak or infirm. "I shall make you pass under the rod . . ." (Ezekiel 20:37 NAS). And so the Great Shepherd watches carefully over us, passing us under His rod, cleansing us by washing us with the water of the Word.

How intimate are you with your Shepherd's rod, beloved? Do you know its power, authority, and protection in warding off the attacks of the enemy just as a shepherd would use it to club the snakes or wolves that would attack his sheep? Do you have the cleansing and thus the protection that the Word of God brings? Are you examined by means of it daily?

Spend your time today looking up the following verses. Next to each reference write down what you learn about the Word.

2 Timothy 3:16, 17

Hebrews 4:12

Ephesians 5:26

Ephesians 6:16, 17

May 27

"Thou preparest a table before me in the presence of mine enemies" (Psalms 23:5).

There has always been many a range war between cattlemen and sheepherders because sheep can literally ruin land by overgrazing. They will actually eat the very root of a plant thus leaving land barren. Sheep must be kept on the move. Therefore, a good shepherd carefully plans his sheep drives, picking out the best of summer ranges for their feeding. Preparation of these ranges is a difficult and laborious task, but it is an essential one. So, many times the shepherd goes before them to prepare a table or mesa for their grazing. The table must be carefully searched because there are certain plants that can poison sheep. All these must be removed beforehand. Plus the shepherd must make sure that there is an adequate supply of water for his sheep. On top of all this, the shepherd must be aware of the various predators that occupy that land. Such knowledge allows him to plan his line of defense. Phillip Keller's book, *A Shepherd Looks at Psalm 23*, tells much of the labors that go into the preparation of the table or mesa. It is an outstanding work and I cannot recommend it highly enough.

When I think of how the Shepherd prepares "a place of feeding" for his sheep even in the midst of its enemies, I cannot help but think of the story of John Sung, a man who was used to awaken multitudes to the reality of a life consecrated to God.

John Sung was a brilliant young Chinese who had come to America to study. While in seminary, of all places, he came under heavy conviction from God that he was not truly saved. Because of this, he fell into a severe depression. The faculty of the school was greatly concerned and was debating what to do with John when his depression suddenly gave way to an unrestrained exuberance! Not realizing John had been saved, they committed him to a mental institution.

Finding himself locked up in a ward of dangerous, fighting maniacs, John tried to escape and failed. Dejected by his failure to escape, dark thoughts of ending his life took form in his mind until the Lord rebuked him. God's Word came, ". . . All things work together for good to them that love God. . ." (Romans 8:28). "If you can endure this trial patiently for 193 days, you will have learned how to bear the cross and walk the Calvary road of unswerving obedience . . ." Little did John realize that his Sovereign Shepherd had gone before and prepared a table for him in the presence of his enemies. God was about to anoint him with oil.

Seeing his ordeal in a new light, John moved under his Shepherd's rod. He devoted almost all his waking hours to reading the Bible through forty times, each time using a different scheme of study. In a mental institution, his valley of the shadow of death, John learned to know his Shepherd and the comfort of His rod and staff. It was this time, shut up with God and His Word, that brought John Sung into an intimate relationship with his Shepherd. And, as a result, he was to become a brilliant flame for God in the East.

What table has God prepared for you, dear sheep?

Now, write out what enemies you are afraid of. Then, list any of the promises of God that cover these enemies. Thank your Shepherd that He is your protection!

May 28

Have you ever gotten a bug up your nose? I have! Don't ask me how! You can be sure that neither one of us planned it . . . neither I nor the bug! Somehow that bug got off course or my sniff had just too much power to it. At any rate, once caught, the poor bug did not know where he was. It felt as if I had inhaled a Mexican jumping bean. The poor thing was darting back and forth, up and down, apparently panicked by my violent shaking, snorting, and blowing. It was found dead in my handkerchief.

When I read, *A Shepherd Looks at Psalm 23*, I discovered just how much I had in common with sheep. Bugs up their noses drive them to distraction too.

Sheep can suffer greatly because of the nose fly. This is a fly that seeks to deposit its eggs on the mucus membrane of the sheep's nose. If this happens the eggs hatch into small wormlike larvae that eventually work their way up the nose into the sheep's head. As these larvae burrow into the sheep's flesh, a tremendous irritation occurs causing the sheep to thrash and beat its head against anything it can find. A sheep can become so driven to distraction by the irritation that it will actually kill itself in a desperate attempt to get rid of the source of aggravation.

As I learned this truth, I could not help but think of so many who are tormented by thoughts that have burrowed their way into their flesh. Eggs have been laid by the enemy and have hatched into repulsive, destructive worms that have worked their way into their heads. Thoughts of fear, rejection, bitterness, hatred, failure, incompetency, sensuality, greed, and more plague God's sheep, tormenting them, driving some even to suicide.

But is this to be the fate of God's sheep? No, the Shepherd does have a way to keep His sheep from such torment: "Thou anointest my head with oil" (Psalms 23:1).

There is an oil that the Shepherd can prepare that will keep the sheep from nose flies and their destructive work. How does it work? We'll see, beloved, in the days ahead. But let me ask you a question today. Is there a bug tormenting you? What is it? Write it down, then ask your Shepherd for His oil.

May 29

Satan is the Christian's nose fly. His target is your mind. He wants to deposit thoughts in your mind that will hatch lies which will burrow their way into your flesh and drive you to distraction. Satan will do anything he can to destroy you. ". . . he is a liar, and the father of lies" (John 8:44 NAS).

"I hate my little boy, but I don't know why. I know it's wrong. I try to love him but I can't."

She had come to my friend, Billie Campbell, for counseling. This feeling of hatred for her son was driving her to distraction. As Billie shared the counseling situation with me, she said, "There's only one thing I learned that might give us a clue to her problem. When her son was little, she had to leave him with a baby-sitter while she worked. One day when she picked him up from the sitter's, the sitter's neighbor commented that she hated screaming children. She couldn't stand them. Ever since then this precious girl has been panicked about her child making a fuss in public."

As Billie and I prayed about the situation, we felt this was our clue from the Lord. Satan had planted a lie in that woman's head through the neighbor's comment.

In the light of this, we felt that God wanted this dear mother to take the Lord Jesus Christ back to that day in her memory and to stand hand in hand with Him and say, "Lord, I refuse this lie from the enemy. You love my son just as he is. He is a gift from You, and I love him and thank You for him."

What joy was Billie's, for as she shared this counsel with this tormented young mother, the mother began to cry as she related another story.

"Soon after I was saved, which wasn't too long ago, I had a dream. You see, I've been rejected most of my life. Anyway, in my dream, Jesus took me by the hand and took me back to my school. One by one, He went up to each of my classmates and my teachers who had been so mean to me and He said, 'This is my child and I love her very much.'"

Satan had planted an egg that had hatched into a destructive lie, a lie that was causing great torment. But the Shepherd had already anointed her head with His protective oil through that dream. She knew where this unreasonable hatred had come from—from the father of lies.

Beloved, has Satan deposited a lie in your mind? Is there some thought that keeps plaguing you? You know it isn't right, but you cannot shake it? Do not despair. We shall seek the Shepherd's care in the days to come.

His Thoughts Toward Me:

May 30

How does the enemy get his wormlike lies burrowed into your head? If you knew the answer to that, you would be on your way to having your problems solved.

When it is the season for nose flies or other pests that afflict sheep, a good shepherd will prepare a special oil that will serve as a protective measure against their tormentors. Then, oil in hand, he will duly smear it over the head and nostrils of each of his sheep.

So now, beloved, since it is always the season for Satan's nose flies, let's get our heads duly treated with the Shepherd's oil. Remember, Satan's target is the mind, and so God tells us in 2 Corinthians 10:5 that we are to destroy speculations and every lofty thing raised up against the knowledge of God. We are to take every thought captive to the obedience of Christ. This, plus Philippians 4:8, is the Shepherd's oil that will protect us from Satan's tormenting lies. But how is it applied? By the raw, naked obedience of faith. When a thought comes to your mind, before you grant it entrance and entertain it within your chambers of reasoning and meditation, you are to "Philippians 4:8" it. Every thought is to be frisked at the door of your mind before you let it in. Check that thought carefully. Is it true? Honorable? Right? Pure? Lovely? Of good report? Excellent? Worthy of praise? If the answer is, "No," to *any* of the above, then you, according to God's Word in Philippians 4:8, are not to think or dwell upon it. It is a speculation or a lofty thing raised up against the knowledge of Jesus Christ. Smear on the oil, take that thought captive to the obedience of Jesus Christ. Remember, as a man thinks in his heart so he is (Proverbs 23:7), so keep your heart with all diligence for out of it are the issues of life (Proverbs 4:23).

Now that is how you protect your head. But what do you do if the lying larvae have already dug into your flesh and set up their irritation? Then you need to do some radical surgery. First, ask

God to search your mind and reveal to you where the enemy has erected his stronghold. What lie or deception has he deposited into your head? When God shows you, then find the truth in the Word of God that refutes what Satan has said. When you find your truth, command Satan to leave you and order the stronghold or fortress torn down by God's Holy Spirit. Tell God you purposefully, willfully choose to believe His Word.

Ask the Lord Jesus Christ, the One who is the Truth to stand there with you against the enemy's stronghold and, by your God's authority, destroy it knowing that "the weapons of our warfare are not of the flesh, but divinely powerful for the destruction of fortresses" (2 Corinthians 10:4 NAS). Then in faith, praise God, for you are more than a conqueror through Him. Should the thought try to come back again, refuse it, over and over again, until it gets weary and flies away exhausted. Then, beloved, your cup will overflow! (Psalms 23:5.)

Write out a prayer of gratitude to your Great Shepherd.

May 31

Beloved, do you ever feel lost in the crowd, as though you are not important or significant? You look at other Christians and feel that they are the superstars, the greats, the ones who are really being used by God, the ones who really mean a lot to the Kingdom of God. And then there is you! You may not even feel bad that you are not noticed or that your name is never mentioned. It would embarrass you anyway, because, after all, you know you're not important. Or maybe it does hurt not to be noticed. Of course you would never let anyone know it, but it would be kind of nice to hear your own name mentioned now and then. It would feel good, at least, to be recognized, at least, just once. But then it will probably never happen. It's just something you will dream of, because you are not *important,* so who would remember your name?

Oh beloved, No, no, no! You are wrong. You are precious. You are important. You are special. You are *His* sheep. Turn around you and look. Goodness and mercy are following you. You are so special that you will dwell in the house of the Lord forever. You are His; He has called you by name. Oh, how I wish I could put my arms around you and tell you this truth in person.

"I am the good shepherd; and I know My own, and My own know Me" (John 10:14 NAS). God knows you, precious one, by name (John 10:3). You are not just one of a flock, but an individual who is very special and very precious to your Shepherd. He knows you, and you are so special to Him that, if He had ninety-nine other sheep and you were lost, He would know that you were the one missing. And He would not stop looking for you, calling you by name, until He had found you (Luke 15:3–6). Sheep are the shepherd's most valuable possession. He is a shepherd because he has sheep. A good shepherd knows each one of his sheep intimately —so intimately in fact that he gives each one a name. And it is by that name that He calls you. Your name is important to your Shepherd. To Him you are very significant, very important. Don't ever forget it, beloved.

Oh, you may not be known by multitudes but what does that matter, for you are known to your Shepherd, the King of Kings. The Chief Shepherd is coming again: to ". . . receive you to Myself; that where I am, there you may be also" (John 14:3 NAS). *You* will dwell in the house of the Lord forever (Psalms 23:6). Hallelujah! The Lord is my Shepherd; I shall not want. Write a love note to your Shepherd—tell Him you will follow Him.

JUNE

June 1

For over 400 years, the heavens had seemed as brass. For 400 years, God had been silent. For years, all Israel had to cling to were the promises of a Messiah. The final words had been those of the prophet, Malachi, " 'Behold, I am going to send My messenger, and he will clear the way before Me. And the Lord, whom you seek, will suddenly come to His temple; and the messenger of the covenant, in whom you delight, behold, He is coming,' says the Lord of hosts" (Malachi 3:1 NAS).

The promise of the New Covenant, the Covenant of Grace, which would supersede the Old Covenant, the Covenant of Law, had first come through the prophet, Jeremiah. It was then confirmed and amplified by Ezekiel. Finally, Malachi recorded his last and wonderful promise . . . the promise of the coming of the Messenger of the Covenant. This Messenger would instate a covenant that would literally change the hearts of men—both Jews and Gentiles. The Law which had been written on tables of stone would now be written on the fleshly tables of their hearts (Jeremiah 31:33). The Covenant of Law from which men continually departed would be replaced by a covenant that would cause them to fear God in such a way that they would not turn away from Him (Jeremiah 31:3, 4). He would be their God, and they would be His people forever and ever. He would put His Spirit within them and cause them to walk in His statutes and to keep His commandments (Ezekiel 36:26–28).

Now there He was before their very eyes. It was the night of the Passover, "And while they were eating, Jesus took some bread, and after a blessing, He broke it and gave it to the disciples, and said, 'Take, eat; this is My body.' And He took a cup and gave

212

thanks, and gave it to them, saying, 'Drink from it, all of you; for this is My blood of the covenant, which is to be shed on behalf of many for forgiveness of sins' " (Matthew 26:26–28 NAS).

And they thought back to that day in the synagogue at Capernaum when so many of His disciples withdrew, to walk with Him no more. They did not want any part of being a covenant partner with this Jesus of Galilee. Little did they know that this was Malachi's Messenger of the Covenant!

My Thoughts Toward Him:

June 2

". . . This is a difficult statement; who can listen to it?" (John 6:60 NAS). And so they grumbled and walked out of the synagogue in Capernaum. Jesus, the Bread of Life! The bread from heaven! Eat His flesh! Drink His blood! Likening Himself to God's manna! Eat and not die! ". . . How can this man give us His flesh to eat?" (John 6:52 NAS). It was too difficult and so "many of His disciples withdrew, and were not walking with Him any more" (John 6:66 NAS).

Did they not understand that Jesus was calling them into a covenant relationship with Himself? In all probability, they understood for He was talking in covenant terms. But eat His flesh—they couldn't quite understand that. At any rate, to enter into covenant with this One who was held in great skepticism by the religious leaders was just too much, too costly. Total commitment was just too much to ask when they weren't really sure who He was. What if He wasn't what He said He was! Working miracles, multiplying loaves and fish was fine, following Jesus that way was great, even exciting. But the binding commitment of covenant? They just weren't ready for that!

I wonder how many of us are ready for it. I wonder how many fully realize what it means to enter into the New Covenant, to become a covenant partner with the Lord Jesus Christ. Oh, beloved, how I have longed to put this teaching into print, to share with you what God has taught me about covenant. It is, to date, the most precious of all the truths I have ever learned. It is a teaching that, once comprehended, takes the veil off of so many Scriptures which at one time were hidden under a cloud of mystery. You have read them, accepted them, quoted them, but still you have felt there had to be more.

Well, here it is, beloved, the "more" of that covenant which was cut for you.

His Thoughts Toward Me:

My Thoughts Toward Him:

June 3

Andrew Murray in his book, *The Two Covenants,* says, "If we were to but grasp the full knowledge of what God desires to do for us and understood the nature of His promise, it would make Covenant the very gate of heaven." And how true his statement is. By the end of this month, by His grace—and through the blessed Spirit's ministry of leading us into His truth—we shall see what it truly means to eat His flesh and drink His blood, to enter into covenant with Him.

It's going to be so good you're hardly going to be able to stand it! But we must take it step by step. So be patient as, under His direction, I lay it down for you precept upon precept. As I write, my earnest prayer is, "O Father, grant by Your Spirit that I might make it as thrilling in print as it is when it is taught face to face." Every time I teach it, beloved, I literally get chill bumps at the awesomeness of it all.

The word *covenant* is used approximately 298 times in the Word of God, if I counted correctly. And if you are really going to appreciate it fully, you must know the Hebrew and Greek words used for covenant. The Old Testament word for covenant is the Hebrew word, *bereeth,* which means "in a sense of cutting, a compact or agreement made by passing through pieces of flesh, a confederacy, a league." Now, hang on to this meaning because, in the days to come, it will throw you into a state of awesome wonder as you walk through the pieces! The New Testament word for covenant is the Greek word, *diatheke. Diatheke* means "a contract, a testament." And thus we see the Word of God divided into the Old Testament or Old Covenant and the New Testament or New Covenant.

Everything that God does for you and me as His children is based on covenant. In biblical times, a covenant was the most solemn, binding agreement that could ever be made. Once two parties entered into covenant, it was understood that all they possessed was henceforth held in common. Although covenants are really not a part of our culture today, they were very common in the lands of the Bible. As a matter of fact, covenants are still entered into in Eastern countries, in Africa, and in various tribes throughout the world. But because we, as a people, are unfamiliar with covenant agreements, I am going to share with you, step by step, how men cut covenant. My information comes from a book, *The Blood Covenant,* by Clay Trumbull. As I studied and meditated upon it and upon Andrew Murray's book, *The Two Covenants,* God, by His precious Spirit, led me, step by step, showing me what it meant to me as His child.

And then came the verse, "The secret of the Lord is for those who fear Him, And He will make them know His covenant" (Psalms 25:14 NAS).

June 4

"Now it came about when he had finished speaking to Saul, that the soul of Jonathan was knit to the soul of David, and Jonathan loved him as himself. . . . Then Jonathan made a covenant with David because he loved him as himself. And Jonathan stripped himself of the robe that was on him and gave it to David, with his armor, including his sword and his bow and his belt" (1 Samuel 18:1, 3, 4 NAS).

When two men entered into a covenant with one another, the first thing they did was to exchange robes. The exchanging of robes symbolized the "putting on of one another." Has anyone ever said to you, "I saw an outfit the other day that looked just like you"? Our clothes are an expression of us, of our tastes, of our preferences. This changing of robes was an act that said, "I am so becoming one with you that I will take on your likeness." This, beloved, is what the New Covenant is all about—our taking on His likeness.

In Romans 13:14 NAS, Paul writes, "But put on the Lord Jesus Christ, and make no provision for the flesh in regard to its lusts." To those in Ephesus, he wrote, "And put on the new self, which in the likeness of God has been created in righteousness and holiness of the truth" (Ephesians 4:24 NAS). Those who would enter into covenant with God must know that they are to bear the image of the heavenly . . . to be holy even as He is holy (1 Peter 1:16).

I'll never forget that day in July 1963, when I fell to my knees and cried out, "O God, You can do anything to me that You want, if You'll only give me Your peace." And He did; He gave me the Prince of Peace, the Lord Jesus Christ. Oh, I didn't understand it all at the time, but that day I partook of the blood of the covenant. The change was instantaneous. When I arose from my knees, I just knew I could no longer dress the way I had dressed. No longer was I to wear the attire of a harlot—I belonged to Him! That was almost eighteen years ago and, since that time, day by day, year by year, as I have beheld His glory, He has been transforming me ". . . into the same image from glory to glory . . ." (2 Corinthians 3:18 NAS). What about you, beloved? Have you put on His robe? It is part of the New Covenant.

My Thoughts Toward Him:

June 5

When a covenant was cut between two parties, *both* partners exchanged robes. And so we see our Covenant Partner, Jesus Christ, who loved us as Himself, putting on our robe of humanity. "Since then the children share in flesh and blood, He Himself likewise also partook of the same . . ." (Hebrews 2:14 NAS). "Although He existed in the form of God" [although Jesus Christ was the perfect expression of the perfect character of God], He "did not regard equality with God a thing to be grasped" [to clutch and hold on to at all costs], "but emptied Himself, taking the form of a bond-servant, And being made in the likeness of men. . . . He humbled Himself by becoming obedient to the point of death, even death on a cross" (Philippians 2:6–8 NAS).

What would cause Jesus, the Son of the Sovereign God, the Ruler of all the universe, to leave the Ivory Palaces, where the heavenly host constantly sang His praises? What would cause Him to come to earth only to confine Himself to our fleshly image and to be despised and rejected of men? Love. Unconditional, unqualified love. Love for you. Because God loved you as Himself, He wanted to enter into a covenant with you. Therefore, He exchanged robes—God put on your humanity.

Oh, beloved, do you realize the practicality of it all? You have a Covenant Partner who can be touched with the feeling of your infirmities, who can sympathize with the weaknesses of your flesh, because He was tempted in all things, just as you are, yet He was without sin (Hebrews 4:15–16). He understands your weaknesses, so why try to hide them or cover them up? Why feel condemned by them, Child of God . . . "Who is the one who condemns? Christ Jesus is He . . . who also intercedes for us" (Romans 8:34 NAS). Your Covenant Partner is your High Priest, so run to Him for help in time of trouble, of need, of failure, of weakness, of temptation. Run! That is what He is there for! He was without sin . . . so He handled the flesh correctly. He will give you His solution. Remember you put on His robe, the Holy Spirit. Jesus, as a man, lived by the Holy Spirit, so walk in His likeness by His Spirit moment by moment and you shall not fulfill the lust of the flesh! And never forget that because He is your Covenant Partner there is no condemnation, ever! (Romans 8:1.)

My Thoughts Toward Him:

June 6

When Jonathan and David made a covenant with one another, they not only exchanged robes but they also exchanged belts or girdles (1 Samuel 18:4). The belt or girdle represented a man's strength. Thus the exchange symbolized the fact that now, as covenant partners, they would compensate for each other's weaknesses. Should one run out of strength, then the other would become his strength. Oh, what a beautiful picture this is for us, for if you are like me, you are so aware of your total inadequacy, your lack of strength, of power, of ability when it comes to living life God's way or ministering to others.

One of my most frequent cries to my Lord is, "O Father . . . I can't. You will have to do it. If You do not do it, Father, it will only be flesh and the flesh profits nothing, and I don't want to waste Your time doing 'nothings.' " I will never forget hearing Stuart Briscoe say, years ago, "God doesn't need your ability, all He needs is your availability." So it's, "I can't. You can. Let's go!" Oh, beloved, this is what your Covenant Partner is for—your weakness, your "I can'ts." So many times we say that we can't serve God because we aren't whatever is needed. We're too weak, too incapable, not talented enough or smart enough or educated enough or whatever. But if you are in covenant with Jesus Christ, He is responsible for covering your weaknesses, for being your strength. He will give you *His* abilities for your disabilities! Really, what our problem is then, is not weakness but independence! We use our weakness as an excuse when in reality it cannot be an excuse because He is our strength. Therefore, if we do not turn and appropriate His strength for our weakness, we are walking independently! And in covenant, you die to independent living. Listen to what God said to Paul, "My grace is sufficient for you, for power is perfected in weakness . . ." (2 Corinthians 12:9 NAS). God's word to Paul is the same word to us because Jesus Christ is also our

Covenant Partner. Therefore, we must say with Paul, ". . . Most gladly, therefore, I will rather boast about my weaknesses, that the power of Christ may dwell in me. Therefore I am well content with weaknesses, with insults, with distresses, with persecutions, with difficulties, for Christ's sake; for when I am weak, then I am strong" (2 Corinthians 12:9, 10 NAS).

Now then, beloved, knowing this truth and not living by it would be failure on our part, wouldn't it? If you excuse yourself from serving God as He has called you to serve Him because of your personal weaknesses or difficulties of any sort, then your problem is not really weakness but independence! Independence because, although you are inadequate, you will not turn to your Covenant Partner and say, "I cannot do it, You will have to!" When you enter into covenant you die to independent living!

We will talk about this more tomorrow, but today why don't you list below ways or occasions in which you have failed to appropriate His strength.

June 7

Are there times when you think you just cannot go on, you cannot take any more? You feel like fainting, just checking out into peaceful oblivion, going to sleep, maybe to wake, maybe not to! Or you feel like walking away. Just how much can a person bear anyway? Or you feel like throwing up your hands—it's impossible! You will never win! What's the use? Or is there so much pressure on you, you wonder how you will ever get it done? Why not give up? (This last one is where I'm hit the most!) Or have you fought and fought—in prayer, in fasting, in labor—and not won yet? Are you about ready to quit, to go AWOL?

Beloved, whatever, whichever, or even if I didn't hit the point where you are out of strength and about ready to quit because the hassle is too much (maybe you are discouraged in your Bible studies or *Precept Upon Precept* courses), have you appropriated your

Covenant Partner's belt? Are you girded with His strength? Listen to His words to you today.

"Hast thou not known? hast thou not heard, that the everlasting God, the Lord, the Creator of the ends of the earth, fainteth not, neither is weary?" (Isaiah 40:28.) (Hallelujah! That is your Covenant Partner!) "He giveth power to the faint [fatigued]; and to them that have no might he increaseth strength" (Isaiah 40:29). Those who have no might, beloved, are those who are tired and weary from the fight! "Even the youths shall faint and be weary, and the young men shall utterly fall: But they that wait upon the Lord shall renew [exchange] their strength; they shall mount up with wings as eagles; they shall run, and not be weary; and they shall walk, and not faint" (Isaiah 40:30, 31).

Our society is filled with runaways, dropouts, and quitters. The epidemic of walking away has hit our land with effects as devastating as the bubonic plague, and it has destroyed millions of effective lives and relationships. We are no longer a people of our word. Personal commitments mean nothing. We are so self-centered that we have ceased to lay down our lives for others. We have seen others faint or walk away and we have followed in their weakness. We have fainted when we could have persevered by exchanging our strength for His! With His strength, not only could we have kept on walking, we could have run! Share below with your Father, tell Him where you have fainted. Then talk to Him about it.

June 8

The third ceremonial act that covenant partners performed was the exchanging of their weapons. This act symbolized the taking on of one another's enemies. "And Jonathan stripped himself of the robe that was on him and gave it to David, with his armor, including his sword and his bow and his belt" (1 Samuel 18:4 NAS).

When two entered into covenant, they understood that now all they had, they held in common—even each other's enemies.

Whenever one was under attack, it was the duty of the covenant partner to come to his aid!

Oh, what light this brought! Now I could understand why I did not have to worry about defending myself against my enemies! My Covenant Partner was my defense. I was to give love. He would deal in justice. "Never take your own revenge, beloved, but leave room for the wrath of God, for it is written, 'Vengeance is Mine, I will repay, says the Lord. But if your enemy is hungry, feed him, and if he is thirsty, give him a drink; for in so doing you will heap burning coals upon his head.' Do not be overcome by evil, but overcome evil with good" (Romans 12:19–21 NAS).

As I meditated upon this, the Lord brought to my mind the Apostle Paul's first face-to-face encounter with the Lord. Paul, then Saul, was on his way to Damascus to root out Christians in order to take them prisoner and thus stamp out Christianity. He had already consented to Stephen's stoning. ". . . suddenly a light from heaven flashed around him; and he fell to the ground, and heard a voice saying to him, 'Saul, Saul, why are you persecuting ME?' " (Acts 9:3, 4 NAS.) Because Christians were in covenant with Christ, Paul was persecuting Jesus! Oh, beloved, how we need to see this truth. When you wound, harm, or persecute another Christian, you are doing it to Christ! In Psalms 105:8–15, God reminds His people of the covenant He had made with them and that He had permitted no man to oppress them and had even reproved kings for their sake saying, "Do not touch my anointed ones, And do My prophets no harm" (Psalms 105:15 NAS).

Has someone come against you as an enemy? Call to your Covenant Partner. In His perfect timing and in His perfect way, He will come to your defense. Let me give you just one example. An escapee from a nearby prison had forced his way into an old couple's home. From the bedroom, the invalid husband heard the rough language as this man threatened and cursed his wife. Holding a gun over her, he ordered her to prepare him a meal, he was starving! Unable to get out of bed to come to his wife's rescue, the dear old man began to cry aloud in prayer to his Covenant Partner. Suddenly, after hearing the crying pleas, the prisoner turned to the woman and said, "Here, I'm leaving." She watched in utter amazement as he laid several dollars on the kitchen table and then walked out of their house.

June 9

When we enter into covenant with Jesus Christ, not only does He take on our enemies, but we are to take on His! It is a mutual agreement to be honored by both parties.

Oh, how our hearts thrill when we hear wonderful stories of the Lord's protection of His people. And there are so many of these stories to be told, one after another. But what about stories of how Christians have stood with the Lord against His enemies? Jehoshaphat, King of Judah, had to be reproved by Jehu: "Should you help the wicked and love those who hate the Lord and so bring wrath on yourself from the Lord?" (2 Chronicles 19:2 NAS.)

How can we, who say we love God, side with those who hate him? How can we love God and walk in the world's ways, join in its activities, and espouse its philosophies when it goes against all for which God and His Kingdom stands? Yet so many side with the world, don't they? John 13–15 records a conversation Jesus had with his disciples right after they partook of their covenant meal.

It was during this time of instruction that Jesus warned them of His enemy, the world. "If the world hates you, you know that it has hated Me before it hated you. If you were of the world, the world would love its own; but because you are not of the world, but I chose you out of the world, therefore the world hates you" (John 15:18, 19 NAS).

The world hates Jesus because He took away their excuse for sin. As a man of like passions as we, He lived and served God as man was created to do. And in so doing, He took away man's cloak, man's covering, man's excuse for sin. And so men hated Him because of His righteous life—a life lived according to God's standards, according to God's wisdom.

The world does not like righteousness! Why? Because the world has set its own standards, it has adopted its own philosophies—standards and philosophies opposed to God.

What about you? Does the world love you or does it hate you? Does your righteous life expose its sin or have you so adopted the world's standards, the world's philosophies, that it has opened up its arms to you in loving welcome? And if so, where does that leave your Covenant Partner?

Take time to meditate on this and then write your thoughts below.

June 10

It happened years ago when I stood in the foyer of Grace Kinser's home in Atlanta preparing to teach our class. Approximately 250 women came to an instant and dead silence when I took the microphone and said, "I am so horribly grieved for I have just heard that someone in this class today is guilty of committing adultery." Faces were like stone; no one moved a muscle. All there was was a horrible, deathly silence. Each wondered who it was. Would I dare say her name aloud? Would the adulteress be thrust forward in the center of the crowd? They waited, and I paused. Adultery—it was too horrible an offense to be named among Christians, and I felt God would have them feel the awfulness of such a sin.

I had prayed much about that class that day. I was teaching the book of James. "Father, O Father, how can I teach it in such a way as to make them see what an abomination it is to be spiritual adulteresses. How can we be friends with the world, Father, when the world hates You and Your Son?" and this was the way that God had given me to get their attention. And it did! We've never forgotten it, have we, girls?

Physical adultery among Christians causes many a head to wag, many an eye to weep, and many a heart to grieve. But what effect does spiritual adultery have upon us when we see or hear it named among the saints?

James wrote, "You adulteresses, do you not know that friendship with the world is hostility toward God? Therefore whoever wishes to be a friend of the world makes himself an enemy of God" (James 4:4 NAS). And who is the prince of this world system that sets itself against God and against His righteous standards? Is it not Satan? So for you to love the world, to befriend the world, to adopt its standards, its code of living, its philosophies is to say to Jesus, "Jesus, I know I belong to You, but before the wedding I want to have an affair with Your arch enemy." And so we crawl into the world, the devil's bed! And our Covenant Partner weeps. His "pure virgin" has been deceived, beguiled, ". . . led astray from the simplicity and purity of devotion to Christ" (2 Corinthians 11:3 NAS). She has not taken on the enemies of her Covenant Partner, but rather has chosen them above the Lover of her soul.

Is someone who is reading this guilty of adultery? Confess it, then ". . . go your way; from now on sin no more" (John 8:11 NAS).

June 11

At the risk of belaboring a point, precious one, I feel that maybe God would have us spend one more day looking at our covenant agreement to stand with our Partner against His enemies. One sees that spiritual adultery is rampant in the churches. And spiritual adultery takes an awful toll upon the next generation of Christians. ". . . a spirit of harlotry has led them astray, And they have played the harlot, departing from their God. . . . Therefore your daughters play the harlot, And your brides commit adultery" (Hosea 4:12, 13 NAS). Spiritual adultery gives birth to physical adultery! This is why, beloved, we are seeing *so much* immorality among those who claim the name of Christ. And they are sinning! They are walking out of marriages! They think they are remarrying without impunity! There is no fear of God before their eyes! Why? Because so many have played the harlot with the world that, rather than expose sin, the church has given men an excuse to sin! We (and I use the term because I am a member of the church) have tolerated sin within the camp. We have overlooked it rather than judging those within the church by not associating "with any so-called brother if he should be an immoral person, or covetous, or an idolater, or a reviler, or a drunkard, or a swindler . . ." we have not removed "the wicked man from among *ourselves*" (1

Corinthians 5:11, 13 NAS). Not to deal with sin in the church is to choose man's reasoning and ways above God's orders. This, then, is to side against God. Only recently I heard of a well-known man of God whose music director asked him for prayer because he had to confront a member of the choir. The choir member was committing adultery. It was a known fact, yet the pastor forbade him to confront the adulterer. "Let it go, maybe it will pass over." This pastor is also encouraging remarriage when there were no biblical grounds for divorce.

Oh, beloved, can you not see that this compromise, this adoption of worldly philosophies, is spiritual adultery? And in our spiritual adultery, we have bred physical adultery.

What are you tolerating or loving that is of the world and thus against Christ? Write it below, then deal with it thoroughly before it destroys you and others.

June 12

A covenant was not entered into lightly. Breaking a covenant commitment was punishable by death.

Now, dear one, what I am about to share with you for the next few days may be hard, very hard, for some of you to handle. But, beloved, I must teach the whole counsel of God's Word. I cannot, before God, leave out that which you may find distasteful, hard to believe, or incompatible with your understanding of God. And I'm sure you appreciate this, knowing that ". . . If I were still trying to please men, I would not be a bond-servant of Christ" (Galatians 1:10 NAS). I fully realize that as a teacher of God's Word I "shall incur a stricter judgment" and that I am to be careful how I build upon the foundation of Jesus Christ in your life (James 3:1 NAS; 1 Corinthians 3:10, 11). And so in godly reverence I share the following.

After robes, belts, and weapons were exchanged, they would then take an animal and split it down the middle, down its back. They would lay the two pieces of the animal on the ground opposite each other. Then the two individuals would stand between these two walls of blood and point to heaven calling out to God. Then, pointing their fingers to the dead animal, they would say, "God, do so to me and more if I break this covenant." In other words, they were saying that this covenant was so binding that to break it would warrant the transgressor's death!

What does this mean to you and to me? It very simply means that if you are not faithful to your covenant with Jesus Christ, He has a right to kill you prematurely (early, before your time) and take you home. If you are His and you break covenant, you will not die and go to hell; you will simply go home early—in embarrassment! Now there are a number of passages that deal with dying before one's time. We will deal with those in the days to come. But for today, meditate upon Ecclesiastes 7:17 NAS, "Do not be a fool. Why should you die before your time?"

My Thoughts Toward Him:

June 13

When David and Jonathan entered into a covenant with one another, that covenant agreement superseded all other relationships, even those of birth. Therefore, when King Saul, Jonathan's father, became jealous of David and sought to take David's life, Jonathan was obligated by virtue of covenant to protect David from his father. Jonathan's love for David was to have preeminence over his love for his father. In 1 Samuel 20:8 NAS, we see David reminding Jonathan of that fact: "Therefore deal kindly with your servant, for you have brought your servant into a covenant of the Lord with you. But if there is iniquity in me, put me to death yourself; for why then should you bring me to your father?" And so Jonathan, having called upon God to deal with him if he did not keep this covenant, swore to protect David. "If it please my father to do you harm, may the Lord do so to Jonathan and more also, if I do not make it known to you and send you away, that you may go in safety . . ." (1 Samuel 20:13 NAS).

But then Jonathan, too, was concerned, for I'm sure he knew that Samuel had anointed David as the next king of Israel. And so Jonathan reminded David of the solemn commitment of covenant: " 'And if I am still alive, will you not show me the lovingkindness of the Lord, that I may not die? And you shall not cut off your lovingkindness from my house forever, not even when the Lord cuts off every one of the enemies of David from the face of the earth?' So Jonathan made a covenant with the house of David, saying, 'May the Lord require it at the hands of David's enemies' " (1 Samuel 20:14–16 NAS). In doing this, Jonathan is calling upon the Lord to kill David by the hands of his enemies if David fails to care for Jonathan's descendants.

Understanding that a covenant relationship superseded all other relationships helps you to understand our Lord's call to those who would enter into covenant with Him. "If anyone comes to Me, and does not hate his own father and mother and wife and children and brothers and sisters, yes, and even his own life, he cannot be My disciple" (Luke 14:26 NAS).

Let me ask you a question. Does Jesus Christ have the preeminence in your life above all other relationships? _____. If the answer is no, then, beloved, there is something very wrong. Deal with it today. Put your excuse in black and white so you *can* deal with it.

June 14

It is kind of hard to believe that God would purposely cause someone to die prematurely, isn't it? And yet it is true, and, as we share today and tomorrow, we will see that it is because of a failure to keep our side of the covenant. This is clearly taught in the eleventh chapter of 1 Corinthians. However, beloved, before we go there let me briefly share some Scriptures with you. Read them carefully, so you hear what God is saying. Hebrews 12:9 NAS implies premature death when it says, ". . . shall we not much rather be subject to the Father of spirits, and live?" James 5:19, 20 NAS says, "My brethren, if any among you strays from the truth, and one turns him back; let him know that he who turns a sinner from the error of his way will save his soul from death, and will cover a multitude of sins." Then 1 John 5:16 NAS says, "If any one sees his brother committing a sin not leading to death, he shall ask and God will for him give life to those who commit sin not leading to death. There is a sin leading to death. . . ."

Now then, let's look at 1 Corinthians. This passage concerns the Lord's Supper or Holy Communion. Remember now, that this meal symbolized entering into a covenant. "And when He had given thanks, He broke it, and said, 'This is My body, which is for you; do this in remembrance of Me.' In the same way He took the cup also, after supper, saying, 'This cup is the new covenant in My blood; do this, as often as you drink it, in remembrance of Me.' For as often as you eat this bread and drink the cup, you proclaim the Lord's death until He comes. Therefore whoever eats the bread or drinks the cup of the Lord in an unworthy manner, shall be guilty of the body and the blood of the Lord. But let a man examine himself, and so let him eat of the bread and drink of the cup. For he who eats and drinks, eats and drinks judgment to himself, if he does not judge the body rightly" (1 Corinthians 11:24–29 NAS).

What is it like when you partake of the Lord's Supper or Holy Communion in your church? Do you go to the altar lightly or routinely? Or as they pass the grape juice and bread do you casually take it, wishing secretly that they would hurry and get it over? As you wait does your mind wander, or do you search your heart?

You may say, what difference does it make? Well, beloved, it could be the difference between strength and weakness, or the difference between sickness and health, or the difference between life and death. It makes a great deal of difference. We'll look at it tomorrow.

My Thoughts Toward Him:

June 15

What is the purpose of the Lord's Supper or, as some call it, Holy Communion? As Paul tells us in 1 Corinthians 11:25, 26, it is done in remembrance of Christ. We are remembering the covenant that was instituted by Jesus, the Messenger of the Covenant. The New Covenant is an agreement, a confederacy by which God and man become one. Wonder of wonders! But it is even more than that; it is also a proclamation of the Lord's death until He comes again. And as we remember the death of our Lord Jesus, the Lamb of God, we must remember that it was because of sin that He died. Your sin, my sin. Therefore, as you take the bread, you are to remember His body broken for you, for your sins which were written in His flesh (1 Peter 2:24). And as you take the wine or grape juice you are to remember that it was His blood that was shed for your sins for without the shedding of blood there is no forgiveness of sins (Hebrews 9:22). Now then, since you, in taking the Lord's Supper, are acknowledging the necessity of Christ's death for your sins, how can you partake without examining yourself and seeing if there be any wicked way in you? Any sin unconfessed? Any sin unforsaken? Any disobedience to God's revealed will? Any bitterness or unforgiveness towards others? How can you partake of this supper which is a symbol of God's forgiveness of man's sins and yet withhold forgiveness from others yourself?

And so God warns us in 1 Corinthians 11:28 to examine ourselves. What happens if we do not examine or judge ourselves and just go ahead and lightly, routinely take communion? God says, "For this reason many among you are weak and sick, and a number sleep" (1 Corinthians 11:30 NAS). Because they would not judge themselves rightly, God had to discipline them (1 Corinthians 11:31, 32). This discipline took three forms according to 1 Corinthians 11:30: weakness, sickness, and death.

Some experienced a bodily weakness. Are you weak, and yet do not know why? Or are you sick, and the doctors cannot find out why? Now listen carefully, beloved, so you do not misquote me. I am *not* saying that *all* weakness and *all* sickness are due to unconfessed, unjudged sin when taking communion. But I am saying that weakness or sickness may be due to that! I read of one woman who was cured of a terminal illness when she confessed

229

her bitterness and made things right with the offended parties. Sin can have an awful toll upon our bodies! As a matter of fact, sin unchecked, sin undealt with, can bring premature death. This is what Paul means when he says, "and a number sleep." Sleep is always the term used to refer to a believer's death. Now, let me clarify one more point. If a person dies at a young age, it does not necessarily mean that God has taken him home early because he has broken covenant. Who can determine then the reason for a person's early death? Only God or the believer who dies. Oh, if you see a person who claims to know God walk in stubborn rebellion and then die, you could probably assume it was a premature death. However, that is not the issue. Rather, this is a warning to you of the seriousness of entering into covenant with the Lord.

Beloved, why not take a few minutes alone with your Lord Jesus Christ and ask Him to reveal to you any ways in which you are failing to honor Him as your Covenant Partner. Write down His thoughts to you that they might be kept as a reminder of His will and His way for you.

June 16

I will never forget that day in a chapel service when we were told about a man of God who had gotten involved in an adulterous affair. I was sick and I was afraid. As soon as I was free, I ran to the prayer room and locked the door. I opened my Bible to 1 John 5:14 NAS, "And this is the confidence which we have before Him, that, if we ask anything according to His will, He hears us." Then I stretched out on the floor of that prayer room, flat on my face, and cried out to God, "O Father, you know that I am capable of doing the same thing that man did. You know the weakness of my flesh. O Father, you have to promise now that, if I ever walk away from you, if I ever say 'Leave me alone, I don't care anymore,' that You will kill me and take me home early rather than let me bring shame to Your name. O Father, do You see this fourteenth verse . . . well, I have asked according to Your will, so You must answer me."

At that time I knew nothing about covenant, I was but a babe in Christ. But God knew my heart, and I knew His holiness. I think sometimes, beloved, many Christians have a warped understanding of God's love. They don't know how to balance or reconcile it with His holiness, justice, and righteousness or with the rest of His character. It is hard for them to conceive of God taking a life prematurely; yet Deuteronomy 32:39 NAS says, ". . . It is I who put to death and give life. . . ."

God is a holy God and His will for His people is holiness. When you came to Him, beloved, it was to make Him Lord, to be conformed into His image. Is there anything stopping you? If there is, forsake it, give it to Him. Whatever it is, it's not worth missing His blessing, His "Well done, my good and faithful servant."

Or possibly you, like me, have a fear of slipping, of falling, of getting caught in a sin. If so, then fall on your face and tell Him all about it. Write your prayer below.

June 17

One day, after I had studied covenant, I nearly came unglued. I was reading through the Old Testament for my quiet time when I came upon Jeremiah 34. But, before we look at what thrilled me so, let me refresh your memory about the Old Testament word for covenant so you can appreciate my excitement. It is the word *bereeth* and it means "a compact or an agreement made by passing through pieces of flesh." Now don't forget that definition because in the next few days it is absolutely going to give you spiritual goose bumps. At least it will if I can capture the thrill and awesomeness of it all on paper!

In Jeremiah 34, the word of the Lord had come to Jeremiah for His people. Remember, Jeremiah prophesied and warned the Southern Kingdom of Judah right up through the time of their captivity. Judah had already seen Israel go into Assyrian captivity because of breaking God's covenant, but that did not seem to deter Judah from her own wicked ways. Oh, why is it that we will not listen to God? Why is it that we think we can sin and get away with it? Why do we go on and on in our rebellion, insisting on walking in our own stubborn, willful way, knowing all along that it is contrary to God's Word?

Judah had done this. Judah had profaned God's name and thus the Word of the Lord came, ". . . 'Behold, I am proclaiming a release to you,' declares the Lord, 'to the sword, to the pestilence, and to the famine; and I will make you a terror to all the kingdoms of the earth. And I will give the men who have transgressed My covenant, who have not fulfilled the words of the covenant which they made before Me, when they cut the calf in two and passed between its parts—the officials of Judah, and the officials of Jerusalem, the court officers, and the priests, and all the people of the land, who passed between the parts of the calf—and I will give them into the hand of their enemies and into the hand of those who seek their life. And their dead bodies shall be food for the birds of the sky and the beasts of the earth' " (Jeremiah 34:17–20 NAS).

I wonder what God will do to America if it does not turn from its wicked ways? Did we not in a sense enter into an agreement with God when we promised religious freedom in our constitution and when we put on our coins, "In God we trust"? How long will it be before we repent or before God brings sword, pestilence, famine, and enemies upon our land? And remember, when or if judgment comes, judgment must begin at the house of God!

My Thoughts Toward Him:

June 18

After robe, belt, and girdle had been exchanged, those entering into covenant then cut an animal in two and laid its parts on the ground. Then, standing between the parts, they vowed, "God do so and more to me if I break this covenant." The next thing they did was to walk through the pieces in the form of a figure eight. This was called a "walk into death" and it signified that they were dying to their rights, to independent living. Now they would no longer live for themselves, for their own pleasure, but they would live for their covenant partner.

Was this not what Christ was calling His disciples to, and was this not why so many walked away? "And He summoned the multitude with His disciples, and said to them, 'If anyone wishes to come after Me, let him deny himself, and take up his cross and follow Me'" (Mark 8:34 NAS). I believe, that what we call the "call to discipleship" is really . . . equally . . . inseparably a call to salvation, a call to enter into the New Covenant. When I deny myself am I not dying to my rights? And when I take up my cross, am I not walking into death? And when I follow Him, am I not walking His way and not mine? Can you see the parallel?

Oh, beloved, do you ever wonder if we are really presenting the gospel as Jesus, our Lord, would have it presented? I think sometimes we are so eager to get decisions, head counts, names on the role, or baptisms for our church records that we present a watered down gospel which in essence is not really the gospel! For when the gospel is truly believed, it is unto salvation not only from sin's penalty but also from sin's power and then someday from sin's presence. True salvation is a walk into death, crucified with Christ so that old things pass away and all things become new! It is saying, "I turn from my old way of life to your way, God . . . to serve You, the true and living God, and to wait for Your Son from heaven" (1 Thessalonians 1:9, 10).

Oh, beloved, when did you walk into death? Have you ever told God that you were willing to deny yourself, to take up your cross, to follow Him, to lose your life for His sake and the gospel's? When?

June 19

Until I understood the customs of covenant, I never fully appreciated or understood what happened to Abraham on the day of his salvation. Remember how, in Genesis 12, God called Abraham out of Ur of the Chaldees and promised to bless him and to make him a great nation? In Abraham (then called Abram) all the families of the earth would be blessed. Abraham was seventy-five at the time and his wife Sarah (then called Sarai) was ten years younger. Well, time passed, year after year, and this man who was to be the father of many was still without a son. Then one day, when the word of the Lord came to Abraham, Abraham asked God about his apparent sterility. Would God have Abraham's servant Eliezer be his heir since Abraham was childless? Is this the way God would do it?

"Then behold, the word of the Lord came to him, saying, 'This man will not be your heir; but one who shall come forth from your own body, he shall be your heir.' And He took him outside and said, 'Now look toward the heavens, and count the stars, if you are able to count them.' And He said to him, 'So shall your descendants [seed] be.' Then he believed in the Lord; and He reckoned it to him as righteousness" (Genesis 15:4–6 NAS).

This was the day of Abraham's salvation, the day according to Romans 4 and Galatians 3 that righteousness was imputed to Abraham's account by faith. When God made the promise of the seed, then Abraham believed God. The word for believe in Genesis 15:6 carries the idea of an unqualified committal of oneself to another. This, beloved, is the belief that saves. It is not just a knowledge, a mental assent or acceptance, but rather a belief by which a person surrenders himself completely, without reservation, without qualification to a truth that he has heard. And what was the truth that God showed Abraham that night? It was the promise of a seed. "Now the promises were spoken to Abraham and to his seed. He does not say, 'And to seeds,' as referring to many, but rather to one, 'And to your seed,' that is, Christ" (Galatians 3:16 NAS). Christ was the seed. It was about Christ that Abraham believed. And so God reckoned him righteous and that very day God made a covenant with Abraham. We'll look at it tomorrow. It's exciting! Oh, dear one, have you really believed in Jesus?

June 20

With the promise of a seed to Abraham also went the promise of a land. So, after God reckoned Abraham as righteous, Abraham had another question for God. What a neat relationship they had! It's the kind you and I are supposed to have, where we talk out everything with God. God loves it. So Abraham said, " 'O Lord God, how may I know that I shall possess it?' So He said to him, 'Bring Me a three year old heifer, and a three year old female goat, and a three year old ram, and a turtledove, and a young pigeon.' Then he brought all these to Him and cut them in two, and laid each half opposite the other; but he did not cut the birds" (Genesis 15:8–10 NAS). *(Now don't ask me why he didn't cut the birds because I do not know.)* "And it came about when the sun had set, that it was very dark, and behold, there appeared a smoking oven and a flaming torch which passed between these pieces. On that day the Lord made a covenant with Abram . . ." (Genesis 15:17, 18 NAS).

Oh, beloved, do you know who that smoking oven and flaming torch was? It was the Lord. God came down in a theophany and by Himself passed through the pieces of flesh. He was making an unconditional covenant with Abraham; a covenant that would stand no matter what, a covenant that could not—would not—be broken because God had walked through the pieces Himself! It was a covenant that guaranteed that one day the Messiah, the Messenger of the Covenant, would come, and, with His coming, all the nations of the earth would be blessed, including the Gentiles. "And if you belong to Christ, then you are Abraham's offspring [seed], heirs according to promise" (Galatians 3:29 NAS).

What a day that was when God passed through the pieces! But in covenant two passed through the pieces. Was man not to walk through the pieces? Oh, beloved, I can hardly wait to share with you tomorrow what God showed me—all by Himself!

His Thoughts Toward Me:

June 21

What I want to share with you next, beloved, is one of the most thrilling insights on the teaching of the covenant given to me by God's Spirit. As I sat and meditated upon this ceremonial custom of cutting covenant, I kept asking, "But, Father, in covenant *both* parties had to walk through the pieces of flesh. You walked through the pieces, but . . ." and then the answer came! It was so beautiful I could hardly contain it! I saw it all, and then "the Lamb of God" took on even a deeper meaning. My body tingled as I saw the awesome intricacy of it. "Oh, the depth of the riches both of the wisdom and knowledge of God" (Romans 11:33 NAS).

It will take me three days to share it with you because I want to take you step by step. So take my hand, precious one, and together we shall, in awesome reverence, walk through the pieces.

The mysteries of the New Covenant were laid out for us thousands of years ago when Moses by God's command erected the tabernacle. To appreciate covenant, you must be aware of how the tabernacle was constructed. So we will begin our walk through the pieces by familiarizing ourselves with the tabernacle. The Book of Hebrews tells us that the earthly tabernacle constructed under Moses' direction was patterned after God's throne in heaven: just as the priests were to serve as "a copy and shadow of the heavenly things," so "Moses was warned by God when he was about to erect the tabernacle; for, 'See,' He says, 'that you make all things according to the pattern which was shown you on the mountain' " (Hebrews 8:5 NAS).

In Hebrews 9:1–5, we find a description of the furniture as it was arranged in the tabernacle. A diagram of this is on page 238. As you look at this diagram, you can see that a veil separated the Holy Place from the Holy of Holies. "Now when these things have been thus prepared, the priests are continually entering the outer tabernacle [the Holy Place on your diagram], performing the divine worship, but into the second [the Holy of Holies on your diagram] only the high priest enters, once a year, not without taking blood, which he offers for himself and for the sins of the people committed in ignorance. The Holy Spirit is signifying this, that *the way into the holy place* [Holy of Holies on your diagram] *has not yet been disclosed . . .*" (Hebrews 9:6–8 NAS, italics added).

The veil in the temple was that which separated the ark of the covenant (a picture of God's throne) from the people. Only once a year, on the Day of Atonement, could the high priest enter beyond the veil to appear in the presence of God for the people. The veil stood between the people and God. And even then, on the Day of Atonement, the people themselves could not enter into God's presence. A priest had to go for them. They were shut out by the veil. And what a veil it was! It was not some gossamer cloth, but was approximately four inches thick. Josephus, the Jewish historian, said it would take two teams of oxen pulling from opposite directions to tear it apart.

The only way then to enter into God's presence was to go through the veil. But alas, man was shut out from direct communion with God!

June 22

Now, what does all this mean to us as regards covenant—walking through the pieces of the flesh of an animal cut in two, the tabernacle, the veil that separated the Holy Place from the Holy of Holies?

"It was now about the sixth hour, and darkness fell over the whole land until the ninth hour" (Luke 23:44 NAS). As Jesus hung on the cross, the Judean Jews filled the temple area. It was the Passover. Family after family was slaying their Passover lamb. Suddenly there was a cry, a cry from Golgotha that reached the portals of heaven and then reverberated through Jerusalem's man-made tabernacle as "the veil of the temple was torn in two

THE TABERNACLE AND THE TRIBES OF ISRAEL

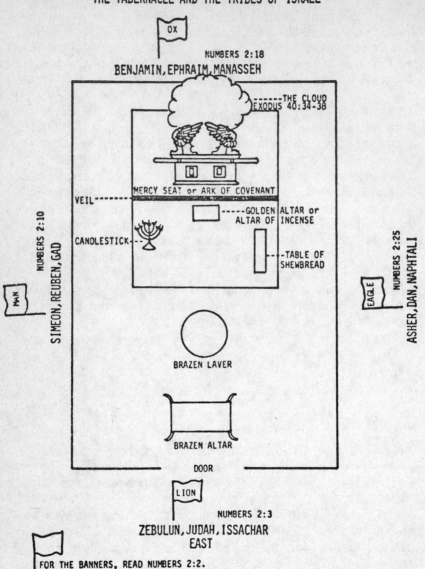

NUMBERS 2:18
BENJAMIN, EPHRAIM, MANASSEH

THE CLOUD
EXODUS 40:34-38

MERCY SEAT or ARK OF COVENANT

VEIL

GOLDEN ALTAR or ALTAR OF INCENSE

CANDLESTICK

TABLE OF SHEWBREAD

NUMBERS 2:10
SIMEON, REUBEN, GAD

NUMBERS 2:25
ASHER, DAN, NAPHTALI

MAN

EAGLE

BRAZEN LAVER

BRAZEN ALTAR

DOOR

LION

NUMBERS 2:3
ZEBULUN, JUDAH, ISSACHAR
EAST

FOR THE BANNERS, READ NUMBERS 2:2.

from top to bottom, and the earth shook; and the rocks were split" (Matthew 27:51 NAS).

There it stood, open to all who would look, never to be hidden from man's sight again—the ark of the covenant! The veil hung limp, ripped in two by some unseen, supernatural hands. What had once been shut to man was now open for the veil that kept man out had been torn in two. "... Therefore, brethren, we have confidence to enter the holy place [the Holy of Holies] by the blood of Jesus, by a new and living way which He inaugurated for us *through the veil, that is, His flesh"* (Hebrews 10:19, 20 NAS, italics added).

Now can you understand the cry of John the Baptist? "Behold, the Lamb of God who takes away the sin of the world!" (John 1:29 NAS.) God had a Passover Lamb—a Lamb found to be without spot or blemish. Now it was the fourteenth day of Nisan, the day to slay the Lamb. The Lamb was slain. There He hung, the covenant sacrifice, the veil of His flesh ripped in two for you and me. God has laid out the pieces. You are no longer separated from the Holy of Holies. Behold the Lamb and walk through the pieces into the very presence of the Almighty God Himself! And cry out, "My Lord and my God!"

His Thoughts Toward Me:

June 23

There He hung, Jesus, the Christ, the Lamb of God, the veil rent in two. Truly He is the Way, and the Truth, and the Life and no one comes to the Father but *through* Him (John 14:6). There is no other way to enter into God's presence except through the rent veil of His flesh. Now, through His death, the way into the Holy of Holies has been disclosed (Hebrews 9:8). Now, by the blood of Jesus, man can enter that place with confidence and without fear of judgment (Hebrews 10:10). The way has been made; now it is up to man to say to God, "By faith I walk into death—death to my old way of life, death to my independent way of life, death to my rights." This, beloved, is the true repentance, the true surrender, that brings genuine salvation. Have you ever walked this way, through the pieces of the Lamb of God?

Not only was Jesus the Way, but He was also the Truth. He spoke the truth, but many did not believe. Instead they believed the devil, the father of lies, who does not stand in the truth because there is no truth in him. Oh, beloved, when you walk through the veil of Christ's flesh, you walk into a whole new realm, the realm of truth, of reality. You leave the darkness of lies and deception and the falsities of life because finally you know what is right— what God says in His Word.

Jesus, the Covenant Lamb of God, the Way, the Truth, and the Life. He is Life, for ". . . unless you eat the flesh of the Son of Man and drink His blood, you have no life in yourselves" (John 6:53 NAS). For His flesh is true food and His blood is true drink; he who eats the bread of life shall live because of Him (John 6:55, 57).

Yes, there He hung, the Way, the Truth, the Life. The Way you should walk; the Truth you should believe; the Life by which you would live. Have you gone His way, believed His truth, lived His life? When did you walk into covenant?

June 24

After having walked into death by passing through the parts of the animal, the two cutting covenant would stand opposite one another and make a cut in their own flesh. Usually they would cut their wrists and then, clasping hands, would mingle their blood to signify that two had become one. No longer were they to live or act independently of one another. What affected one would now affect the other.

Remember the day when a man's word was good, when what was vowed with the lips was as binding as any written contract? Remember when you could ask "Will you shake on it?" and seal an agreement with a handshake? Many feel that the handshake had its origins in the cutting of the wrists and the mingling of the blood.

It was after the Passover that Jesus, having inaugurated the New Covenant, prayed to the Father before He went to the cross. At Calvary the cut of covenant would take place as they pierced His hands and His feet—and two would become one.

Our Lord's prayer to His Father that night was on behalf of those whom God had given Him out of the world. His prayer was that "they may be one, even as We are . . . that they may all be one; even as Thou, Father, art in Me, and I in Thee, that they also may be in Us . . . that the love wherewith Thou didst love Me may be in them, and I in them" (John 17:11, 21, 26 NAS).

What bearing would it have on the body of Jesus Christ if every member were but to realize the full implication of what it means to be one with Christ, to fully realize the import of Paul's words, "Or do you not know that your body is a temple of the Holy Spirit who is in you, whom you have from God, and that you are not your own?" (1 Corinthians 6:19 NAS.)

Do you know, beloved, that if you are His by covenant, you are no longer your own? And knowing that you are not your own, how do you live? What do you do with the members of your body which are now the members of Christ?

June 25

How complete was this oneness between covenant partners? How far did it extend? To what extent am I now one with my Covenant Partner? What, besides myself, is now His? And what, besides Himself, is mine? All—all that we both possess.

After they had passed through the pieces and mingled their blood, the covenant partners would give each other "the blessings." Each would give to the other an accounting of all his resources for these resources were now at the disposal of the covenant partner should they be needed!

And so when we enter into covenant with our Lord and our God, all that is His becomes ours. Thus comes the sure promise of Philippians 4:19, "And my God shall supply all your needs according to His riches in glory in Christ Jesus" (NAS). Because we are in covenant with Him, we are now "heirs; heirs of God, and joint-heirs with Christ" (Romans 8:17). This is why, after the inauguration of the New Covenant at the Last Passover, Jesus told his beloved disciples, ". . . Truly, truly, I say to you, if you shall ask the Father for anything, He will give it to you in My name. Until now you have asked for nothing in My name; ask, and you will receive, that your joy may be made full" (John 16:23, 24 NAS).

Oh, beloved, if you are His, then this is your right, your privilege of covenant, a blessing to be appropriated by faith. What do you need? What do you lack? It is yours for the believing, for the asking, for all that is His is now yours.

If you have not (and you are not asking just to gratify your own lusts) then it is only because you ask not (James 4:2, 3). What is His is yours, because you are His.

My Thoughts Toward Him:

June 26

How well those of Jesus' day understood the principles of covenant! With them it was a full commitment that penetrated every area of their lives. A covenant entered into was a covenant to be kept!

This commitment is so clearly seen as we look at the days of the early church. Being in covenant put the believer into a covenant relationship not only with God but also with the whole family of God! It was a relationship that took on deeper ties than those of flesh and blood.

One day when Jesus was told that His mother and brothers had arrived, "He said, 'Who are My mother and My brothers? . . . Whoever does the will of God, he is My brother and sister and mother" (Mark 3:33, 35 NAS). When we enter into covenant with God, we come into a new family where we are members one of another. It is to be a relationship of such depth that if one member would suffer, we would all suffer and if one would rejoice, we would all rejoice for it is a relationship that puts away independent living (1 Corinthians 12:12–26). The Book of Acts tells us how well the early church understood and lived by this principle. "And all those who had believed were together, and had all things in common; and they began selling their property and possessions, and were sharing them with all, as anyone might have need. And day by day continuing with one mind in the temple, and breaking bread from house to house, they were taking their meals together with gladness and sincerity of heart, praising God, and having favor with all the people. And the Lord was adding to their number day by day those who were being saved" (Acts 2:44–47 NAS). Some have said this was communism, others communal living—but neither are right. It was simply covenant!

Let me give you something to meditate upon, beloved, and as you meditate, why don't you write down your insights for future reference. If you were to live this way, how would it change your relationship with other Christians?

June 27

How committed should we be in our relationship with other members of Christ's body? As we have seen, those in covenant held all things in common so that if one had any need, whatever his covenant partner possessed was at his disposal without question and without reservation.

In Acts 4:32–35 NAS, we see this attitude being lived out in the early church. "And the congregation of those who believed were of *one* heart and soul; and not one of them claimed that anything belonging to him was his own; but all things were common property to them. And with great power the apostles were giving witness to the resurrection of the Lord Jesus, and abundant grace was upon them all. *For there was not a needy person among them,* for all who were owners of lands or houses would sell them and bring the proceeds of the sales, and lay them at the apostles' feet; and they would be distributed to each, as any had need" (italics added).

When Paul wrote those in Corinth, he had to remind the believers that they were to abound in the gracious work of giving. "But just as you abound in everything, in faith and utterance and knowledge and in all earnestness and in the love we inspired in you, see that you abound in this gracious work also. For this is not for the ease of others and for your affliction, but by way of equality—at this present time *your abundance being a supply for their want,* that their abundance also may become a supply for your want, that there may be equality; as it is written, 'He who gathered much did not have too much, and he who gathered little had no lack' " (2 Corinthians 8:7, 13–15 NAS, italics added).

Is it right for us to store our funds for emergencies and in doing so to ignore the immediate needs of our brothers and sisters in Christ? If Christ has promised to supply all our needs because we are in covenant with Him, then do we need to fear that if we meet another's needs, we will have nothing left for ourselves in a day of want? Should any member of the body of Christ ever have to seek financial aid outside the church? For what are we given an abundance? For our own pleasures or rather, that we might supply another's want? Which do you think it is?

Think of what it would mean to the body of Jesus Christ, and to the work of Jesus Christ, if we were but to live in the fullness of covenant!

His Thoughts Toward Me:

My Thoughts Toward Him:

June 28

Have there ever been times when you have wondered if God had forgotten you or abandoned you?

After the covenant parties had made a cut upon their bodies and mingled their blood and after they had shared the blessings with each other, they would then seek a way to seal that covenant cut. They would rub something into the wound in order to cause a permanent scar that would be a constant reminder of the fact that they were now responsible to one another. If the cut had been in the wrist, every movement of the hand—dressing, eating, working —would remind them of their covenant partner and of their obligation to care for him forever.

I am sure there have been times of difficulty, stress, loneliness, and testing in many of your lives when you may have wondered if the Lord had not forsaken you. Possibly you have cried out in need and have not seen help forthcoming immediately. Or maybe you have felt so desperately alone, confused and helpless because the arm of flesh upon which you leaned has been taken away in death. The loving arms of protection are gone, the counsel of another has been silenced and you feel horribly alone needing to lean but with no one to lean upon!

"But Zion said, 'The Lord has forsaken me, And the Lord has forgotten me. Can a woman forget her nursing child, And have no compassion on the son of her womb? Even these may forget, *but I will not forget you*. Behold, I have inscribed you on the palms of My hands . . .'" (Isaiah 49:14–16 NAS, italics added).

Oh, beloved, the next time you feel abandoned, forsaken, or horribly alone, "Reach here your finger, and see My hands; and reach here your hand, and put it into My side; and be not unbelieving, but believing" (John 20:27 NAS). Remember He has engraved you on His palms . . . and ". . . He Himself has said, 'I will never desert you, nor will I ever forsake you,' so that we may confidently say, 'The Lord is my helper, I will not be afraid. What shall man do to me?'" (Hebrews 13:5, 6 NAS). Endure ". . . as seeing Him who is unseen"; overwhelmingly conquer through Him who loved *you* for nothing shall be able to separate *you* from the love of God, which is in Christ Jesus our Lord (Hebrews 11:27; Romans 8:37, 39 NAS).

My Thoughts Toward Him:

June 29

The next thing that took place was the changing of names. To call another's name or to bear his name gave you both the authority that went with that name and authority over the one whom you named. Thus in covenant, you would take on, in addition to your own name, the name of your covenant partner. We see a picture of this in the covenant of marriage where the bride takes the name of her husband.

After God cut covenant with Abram, the Lord appeared to him and said, "As for Me, behold, My covenant is with you, And you shall be the father of a multitude of nations. No longer shall your name be called Abram, But your name shall be Abraham; For I will make you the father of a multitude of nations" (Genesis 17:4, 5 NAS). When God changed Abram's name, He put the breath sound of His own name, "the heth" as it is called, into Abram's name. He also did the same to Sarai's name. "Then God said to Abraham, 'As for Sarai your wife, you shall not call her name Sarai, but Sarah shall be her name" (Genesis 17:15 NAS).

And thus to all Christians comes the promise of a new name, as John records the words of the Lord in Revelation 2:17 NAS, "He who has an ear, let him hear what the Spirit says to the churches. To him who overcomes (see 1 John 5:5), to him will I give some of the hidden manna, and I will give him a white stone, and a new name written on the stone which no one knows but he who receives it."

And even now, do we not bear a new name, the name Christian? Christian means little Christ. Oh, beloved, how well do we carry that name? Can the world see His authority over us and His authority in us? Has He not breathed into us also the breath of life and thus the authority of His name? "'. . . as the Father has sent Me, I also send you.' And when He had said this, He breathed on them, and said to them, 'Receive the Holy Spirit. If you forgive the sins of any, their sins have been forgiven them; if you retain the sins of any, they have been retained' " (John 20:21–23 NAS).

"But Peter said, 'I do not possess silver and gold, but what I do have I give to you: In the name of Jesus Christ the Nazarene— walk!' " (Acts 3:6 NAS).

You have His name—live like it!

My Thoughts Toward Him:

June 30

After all these things had taken place, they sat down to partake of a covenant meal. At this meal they took bread, broke it, and then placed it into the mouth of their covenant partner with these words, "You are eating me." Then a cup of wine was offered to the covenant partner along with the words, "This is my blood; you are drinking me." Often, unless of course they were Jews, they mingled drops of their own blood in with the wine.

Does all this ring a familiar sound? Remember the little ceremony at the wedding reception, remember wondering if you should order the photographer's ridiculous shot of you with your mouth wide open while your mate fed you a piece of wedding cake? Did you ever wonder where that custom came from? Now you know. Isn't it beautiful! It is a picture of giving yourself to another—unconditionally, totally, eternally.

An unqualified committal of oneself to another, this, beloved, is covenant. This is salvation. They are one and the same. This is what God means when He says, "Believe on the Lord Jesus Christ, and thou shalt be saved . . ." (Acts 16:31). It means to give yourself to Christ unconditionally, without qualification; to cease from your independent living; to become one with Christ, bone of His bone and flesh of His flesh.

Oh, there is so much more to share with you on covenant. There are so many rich, precious gems that will so graciously adorn your salvation as their facets brilliantly reflect the light of Truth. How I look forward to sharing them with you in the coming month.

But for today, beloved, let me ask you a question. Have you drunk of His cup? Have you partaken of the Bread of Heaven? Or will you, like so many others, walk away? Many have. Many have walked away after seeing the depth of commitment that Jesus calls for. Many have walked away after realizing that salvation is a denial of self, a taking up of the cross, and a life to be spent following Him. Many have walked away because His words are difficult sayings—too hard for them to believe. Have you believed?

My Thoughts Toward Him:

JULY

July 1

Dare he speak to God? To share so openly? Was he not but dust and ashes? A man born of the earth—a man who would return to the earth! Could man question God? Did he have any right to be so bold, so presumptuous? Oh, Abraham had no trouble in challenging men, but to challenge God!

He felt sick. How could a righteous God do this? It didn't seem fair. What was he to do? Keep silent? Never speak? Just submit? Not question? Suddenly it hurt. This was His God, His Covenant Partner, and he questioned His justice. Should he speak his mind and risk God's anger or keep silent and be disillusioned. What did their relationship permit? Was it all to be one-sided? Was he meant to be just a "yes-man" to God? Was this what God wanted from their friendship?

Slowly, as Abraham walked with his three unexpected guests, he began to reason that these three men had sought him out. He did not seek them. Was it not the Lord who had even broached the subject when He said, " 'Shall I hide from Abraham what I am about to do, since Abraham will surely become a great and mighty nation, and in him all the nations of the earth will be blessed? For I have chosen him, in order that he may command his children and his household after him to keep the way of the Lord by doing righteousness and justice; in order that the Lord may bring upon Abraham what He has spoken about him' " (Genesis 18:17–19 NAS).

Now they stood alone, face to face. The other two had gone. It was just the Lord and himself. The reasoning continued as Abraham talked to himself, "Surely the Lord did not mean for me to be a mere pawn, otherwise why would He even bother to tell me what He was going to do to Sodom and Gomorrah?"

Suddenly it was too much. This was not the God Abraham had worshipped. Something was wrong. He had to speak, at least ask if there was an explanation, Abraham had to know how his God could do such a thing!

". . . Wilt thou also destroy the righteous with the wicked? Peradventure there be fifty righteous within the city: wilt thou also destroy and not spare the place for the fifty righteous that are therein? That be far from thee to do after this manner, to slay the righteous with the wicked: and that the righteous should be as the wicked, that be far from thee: Shall not the Judge of all the earth do right?" (Genesis 18:23–25.)

Now as Abraham rehearsed all that followed after he challenged God with his "Far be it with, Thee," he smiled. So this is what it meant to be the friend of God, instead of being just His slave! "No longer do I call you slaves; for the slave does not know what his master is doing; but I have called you friends, for all things that I have heard from My Father I have made known to you. You did not choose Me, but I chose you, and appointed you, that you should go and bear fruit, and that your fruit should remain, that whatever you ask of the Father in My name, He may give to you" (John 15:15, 16 NAS). Those chosen by God—those in covenant with God—had recourse with God. They did not have to fear God's anger or suppress their questions about the justice of His ways. They could talk to God. They could reason with Him. They were God's friends!

His Thoughts Toward Me:

My Thoughts Toward Him:

July 2

Friend—we say it so casually, so loosely. How far we have digressed from the original meaning of the word! Friend was the term used to describe those who had become partners through a blood covenant, and it was really quite a costly title.

As we studied last month, we saw that the final step in entering into covenant was to partake of a covenant meal. During this meal, the partners would feed each other a piece of bread and say, "This is my flesh. You are eating me." Then, as they offered each other a cup, they said, "This is my blood. You are drinking me." After having performed the rites of the covenant ceremony, they were known as "blood brothers" and from then on they would call each other "friend." The word friend was synonymous with blood brother. There was no other relationship in the East stronger or more binding than that of friend, blood brother.

In the East today, Abraham is known as Ibraheen el Khaleel, Abraham the friend, or as Khaleel Allah, the friend of God. And so he was! For in the Old Testament Abraham is the *only* one called "the friend of God." Exodus 33:11 NAS tells us that God spoke "to Moses face to face, just as a man speaks to his friend . . ." but the word for friend in this verse means companion or neighbor. It is not the same word for friend used to describe God's relationship with Abraham. Why? Because God had entered into a covenant with Abraham as we saw in Genesis 15, when He appeared as ". . . a smoking oven and a flaming torch which passed between" the pieces of the flesh of the animals. "On that day the Lord made a covenant with Abram . . ." (Genesis 15:17, 18 NAS).

All the world over, men who were friends because of a blood covenant were to be ready to give their very lives for one another or even to give for each other that which was dearer than life itself —their sons.

Can you see now how far we have departed from the true meaning of the word *friend?*

His Thoughts Toward Me:

My Thoughts Toward Him:

July 3

"Friend," the term of covenant. Remember what I said about this friendship? Those who were in covenant with one another were to be ready to lay down their very lives for each other. When they had entered into their covenant relationship, they had cut their flesh, mingled the blood from their wounds, and then rubbed a substance into their cuts in order to leave permanent scars on their bodies. These scars, usually in their hands or wrists, would then serve as a constant reminder of their commitment and obligations to their covenant partner.

For all eternity our Christ shall bear in His body the brand marks of covenant, marks made that day when they pierced His hands and His feet and put a spear into His side. The piercing was a demonstration of that covenant love Jesus had spoken about when He said, "Greater love has no one than this, that one lay down his life for his friends" (John 15:13 NAS). His resurrected body would eternally bear those marks of covenant. Did not Thomas testify of this when, doubting the Lord's resurrection, he said, ". . . Unless I shall see in His hands the imprint of the nails, and put my finger into the place of the nails, and put my hand into His side, I will not believe" (John 20:25 NAS)? It would take the wounds of covenant to convince Thomas! Then one day, there He stood before him saying, "Reach here your finger, and see My hands; and reach here your hand, and put it into My side; and be not unbelieving, but believing" And Thomas answered, "My Lord and my God!" (John 20:27, 28 NAS).

I wonder, in a way, if Thomas' doubt was not sort of a picture of Israel's! How awesome are the words of Zechariah's prophecy regarding the second coming of the Messiah, Jesus the Christ. "And I will pour out on the house of David and on the inhabitants of Jerusalem, the Spirit of grace and of supplication, so that they will look on Me whom they have pierced . . ." (Zechariah 12:10 NAS).

"And one will say to him, 'What are these wounds between your hands?' Then he will say, 'Those with which I was wounded in the house of my *friends'* " (*see* Zechariah 13:6 NAS).

God's covenant with Abraham was a covenant with Israel. He was wounded by His friends for His friends! What love! What a Blood Brother! Someday Israel will realize it and weep! Have you realized it yet? Stretch forth your hand and put it into His wounds, before it's too late and you weep in the shame of doubt!

My Thoughts Toward Him:

July 4

A covenant friend was willing to give his all, there was nothing too great to ask of him: ". . . There is a friend that sticketh closer than a brother" (Proverbs 18:24). Covenant commitment was unconditional. It was so deep that a friend would lay down his life for his blood brother or would go even further than that if necessary. A covenant friend would give that which was even dearer than his own life; he would give his son. To a man of the East, there was nothing more precious than his seed, his son, the one who would carry his name and his life into the next generation.

God had cut covenant with Abraham and He had passed through the pieces. They had taken on one another's name. Abram became Abraham as God put the "heth" from His name into Abra-h-am. And then God had taken on Abraham's name by calling Himself "The God of Abraham."

Then the day came. The day when God tested the strength of Abraham's covenant commitment to Him! "And it came to pass after these things, that God did tempt Abraham, and said unto him, 'Abraham': and he said, 'Behold, here I am.' And he said,

'Take now thy son, thine only son Isaac, whom thou lovest, and get thee into the land of Moriah; and offer him there for a burnt offering upon one of the mountains which I will tell thee of.' And Abraham rose up early in the morning, and saddled his ass, and took two of his young men with him, and Isaac his son, and clave the wood for the burnt offering, and rose up, and went unto the place of which God had told him. . . . And Abraham took the wood of the burnt offering, and laid it upon Isaac his son; and he took the fire in his hand, and a knife; and they went both of them together. . . . And they came to the place which God had told him of; and Abraham built an altar there, and laid the wood in order, and bound Isaac his son, and laid him on the altar upon the wood. And Abraham stretched forth his hand, and took the knife to slay his son. And the angel of the Lord called unto him out of heaven, and said, 'Abraham, Abraham:' and he said, 'Here am I.' *And he said, 'Lay not thine hand upon the lad, neither do thou any thing unto him: for now I know that thou fearest God, seeing thou hast not withheld thy son, thine only son from me"* (Genesis 22:1-3, 6, 9-12 quotes and italics added).

Has the day ever come, beloved, when God has tested you to see if you were willing to put on the altar that which is as dear as life itself? And how did you respond? Were you willing? Why not? Why don't you write your thoughts below. It is good to acknowledge them. It causes you to be honest and open with your Friend.

July 5

Many times covenant agreements were extended beyond individuals to their families. The men entering into covenant with one another wanted that compact to include their seed, their descendants, and so they would enter into covenant as the representative head of a family.

This was the covenant that God made with Abraham. It was not to be just a compact between the two of them, but was to extend beyond Abraham to his seed. God would become not only the God of Abraham, but also of Isaac and of Jacob. Those then who were of Abraham's seed would know the benefits of God's covenant with Abraham. And to them would be extended the lovingkindness of covenant. Have you ever thought about that term used so often throughout God's Word, the term *lovingkindness?* It is a covenant term. Listen to these precious words of David, "But the lovingkindness of the Lord is from everlasting to everlasting on those who fear Him, And His righteousness [faithfulness to His gracious promises] to children's children, to those who keep His covenant, And who remember His precepts *to do* them" (Psalms 103:17, 18 NAS, italics added). Lovingkindness—the pledge of the promises and benefits of covenant not only to Abraham, but just as surely to Abraham's seed.

Jehoshaphat, King of Judah, knew that, because of God's covenant with Abraham and his seed, lovingkindness was also his. And how he needed it! Word had just come that a great multitude was coming from beyond the sea. The sons of Moab and of Ammon and some Meunites had massed together to war against him. "And Jehoshaphat was afraid and turned his attention to seek the Lord; and proclaimed a fast throughout all Judah. So Judah gathered together to seek help from the Lord . . ." (2 Chronicles 20:3, 4 NAS). And when they were all gathered together, what did Jehoshaphat do but remind God of His covenant relationship with Abraham and thus with him because he was part of Abraham's seed. Listen to his words of covenant faith, " 'Didst Thou not, O *our* God, drive out the inhabitants of this land before Thy people Israel, and give it to the descendants of Abraham Thy *friend* forever?' " (2 Chronicles 20:7 NAS, italics added).

Oh, how God loves to extend the lovingkindness of His covenant promises to Abraham's descendants. "And if you belong to Christ, then you are Abraham's offspring [descendants, seed], heirs according to promise" (Galatians 3:29 NAS).

Where do you run in your time of need? Why not, like Jehoshaphat, cry out to your covenant-keeping God? He heard Jehoshaphat, will He not hear you?

My Thoughts Toward Him:

July 6

Have you ever wondered why on earth God chose circumcision to be a sign of His covenant with Abraham? I know that to some it has been a matter of whispering, an embarrassment. Something that was decently avoided in discussion. I have even had precious women come to me and ask in a whisper, "What did Jewish women do? They couldn't be circumcised! How, then, could they be included in the covenant promise? Or weren't they included?"

The word of God to Abraham had been, " 'Now as for you, you shall keep My covenant, you and your descendants after you throughout their generations. This is My covenant, which you shall keep, between Me and you and your descendants after you: every male among you shall be circumcised. And you shall be circumcised in the flesh of your foreskin; and it shall be the sign of the covenant between Me and you. . . . But an uncircumcised male who is not circumcised in the flesh of his foreskin, that person shall be cut off from his people; he has broken My covenant' " (Genesis 17:9–11, 14 NAS).

There it was, ordered by God—every male circumcised in the flesh of his foreskin. But why there? And why did God make it such a cut that women could not participate in it? These are probably questions that many have had in their heart but never verbalized. Well, I can relate to those, dear ones, because I wondered the same thing.

How beautiful it was for me to see God's answer. Let me share it with you, for I know it will thrill you. But first let's talk a moment about these bodies that God created for us. You know, when God made man, He said, "And it was good." He made every part of us —body, soul, and spirit. Our bodies are His precious design. In light of this, I wonder why we often look upon them with disgust or shame. Surely that is not from God, nor is it spiritual even though we would prudishly consider it to be.

Why circumcision? Well, when two men wanted to show that they were extending the covenant to their descendants, to their seed, they made a cut on their bodies *closest to the site of paternity.* And so God required a cut in the foreskin as a reminder that when a man's seed came forth, be it a sperm that would produce a male or one that would produce a female, that child was under the protection and bonds of covenant. Isn't that beautiful? It was God's good, perfect, beautiful, holy design.

My Thoughts Toward Him:

July 7

One of the most beautiful illustrations in all of Scripture regarding covenants between families is found in the story of Mephibosheth, Jonathan's son. Oh, how it will minister security to your soul. I can hardly wait to share it with you in the days to come! You are going to be so excited. I know you will probably cheat and read ahead! Don't worry, I love it! Just make sure you go back and meditate on these truths so you will reap the full benefit of this book . . . and so His work will be able to go forth in the strength of prayer.

In 1 Samuel 18 we have the first account of the covenant made between David and Jonathan. After that covenant was made, King Saul, Jonathan's father, would not permit David to return to his home. David now became one of Saul's men of war called upon to defend the nation of Israel. Remember now that Saul was Israel's King by the people's choice. Israel was tired of not having a king to rule over them like other people so they pled for a King and got Saul.

David's victories at war brought him great acclaim from the people, and jealousy reared its ugly head. Saul began to look upon David with great suspicion. "Now Saul was afraid of David, for the Lord was with him but had departed from Saul" (1 Samuel 18:12 NAS). From that time on Saul could not rest. "Now Saul told Jonathan his son and all his servants to put David to death. But Jona-

257

than, Saul's son, greatly delighted in David" (1 Samuel 19:1 NAS).

Now remember, David and Jonathan were in covenant together. They had exchanged robes, swords, and belts. They had made an agreement to protect one another, to take on one another's enemies. Where would Jonathan's loyalty lie? It had to be with David, even above his natural loyalty to his father. This was covenant—a relationship that superseded all others.

"So Jonathan told David, saying 'Saul my father is seeking to put you to death. Now therefore, please be on guard in the morning, and stay in a secret place and hide yourself. And I will go out and stand beside my father in the field where you are, and I will speak with my father about you; if I find out anything, then I shall tell you" (1 Samuel 19:2, 3 NAS).

Oh, beloved, before we go any further, let me ask you, does your covenant with Christ have preeminence over all other relationships? "He who loves father or mother *more than* Me is not worthy of Me; and he who loves son or daughter *more than* Me is not worthy of Me" (Matthew 10:37 NAS, italics added). You are to live "so that He Himself might come to have first place in everything" (Colossians 1:18 NAS). Anything less is disloyalty
   disobedience
   idolatry.

July 8

Tension hovers in the air like an early morning fog giving a haziness to the covenant bond made in days gone by. As so often happens, the pressure of untoward circumstances causes one to forget the surety of promises made long ago. David, fully aware of Saul's intentions and knowing ". . . there is hardly a step between me and death" (1 Samuel 20:3 NAS), pleads the promises of the covenant made with Jonathan. "Therefore deal kindly with your servant, for you have brought your servant into a covenant of the Lord with you. But if there is iniquity in me, put me to death yourself; for why then should you bring me to your father?" (1 Samuel 20:8 NAS.) But if David is apprehensive, so is Jonathan! Jonathan is torn, not by the conflict between his father and David for Jonathan knows where his loyalty lies, but rather he is torn because he has an inkling about the future. He knows God has left his father. He knows the Lord is with David. He knows that Israel is David's, not Saul's. But what about him? Will David, as King, remember his covenant with him? And what if Jonathan dies? What will happen to Jonathan's seed should God grant him a son? And so Jonathan reassures David, but, needing assurance himself, he also pleads for another covenant—a covenant between the two houses, the house of David and the house of Jonathan.

" 'If it please my father to do you harm, may the Lord do so to Jonathan and more also, if I do not make it known to you and send you away, that you may go in safety. And may the Lord be with you as He has been with my father. And if I am still alive, will you not show me the lovingkindness of the Lord, that I may not die? And you shall not cut off your lovingkindness from my house forever, not even when the Lord cuts off every one of the enemies of David from the face of the earth.' So Jonathan made a covenant with the house of David, saying, 'May the Lord require it at the hands of David's enemies.' And Jonathan made David vow again because of his love for him, because he loved him as he loved his own life" (1 Samuel 20:13–17 NAS). Now, the covenant between their houses having been confirmed, Jonathan helps plan David's escape should Saul become set on killing David. That night Saul's anger at Jonathan's allegiance to David throws him into a rage. When "Saul hurled his spear at him to strike him down . . . Jonathan knew that his father had decided to put David to death" (1 Samuel 20:33 NAS). Jonathan went out to warn David. He must flee. As they kissed each other and wept, Jonathan said to David, " 'Go in safety, inasmuch as we have sworn to each other in the name of the Lord, saying, "The Lord will be between me and you, and between my descendants and your descendants forever" ' " (1 Samuel 20:42 NAS).

And so they departed, in grief but in assurance. The covenant promises stood no matter what the future held.

And so it is with you, beloved, no matter what your current trials, the covenant promise holds for you because when "you belong to Christ, then you are Abraham's offspring [seed], heirs according to promise" (Galatians 3:29 NAS).

July 9

So the days turn into weeks, the weeks into months, and time goes on with no letup as David continues to flee and Saul pursues determined to destroy him. Saul in bitterness continues to belch, fouling the air as he lashes out, "For all of you have conspired against me so that there is no one who discloses to me *when my son makes a covenant with the son of Jesse* [David], and there is none of you who is sorry for me or discloses to me that my son has stirred up my servant against me to lie in ambush, as it is this day" (1 Samuel 22:8 NAS, italics added). And even though ". . . Saul sought him every day . . . God did not deliver him into his hand" (1 Samuel 23:14 NAS).

And what about David? How did he handle it all? When opportunity came for David to kill Saul, he knew that he could not stretch out his hand against him because Saul was the *Lord's anointed* (1 Samuel 24:6, 10). David rested in God's sovereignty. David knew that God had anointed him rather than Saul to be king over Israel. But he also knew that he had to wait for God's timing. So when an opportunity came to kill Saul, David refused to do so, saying to him, "May the Lord judge between you and me, and may the Lord avenge me on you; but my hand shall not be against you" (1 Samuel 24:12 NAS).

Oh, there were days of doubt as well as days of trust. The clouds of circumstances at times obliterated the reality of the presence of God's promises. David even said to himself, " 'Now I will perish one day by the hand of Saul . . .' " (1 Samuel 27:1 NAS). And yet the promise of God stood sure whether David *felt* the reality of it or not. "If we are faithless, He remains faithful; for He cannot deny Himself" (2 Timothy 2:13 NAS).

The days of testing were coming to an end; it was just that David did not know when! But God did!

What about you, beloved? As I write this I cannot help but feel that we all need this message. Too often the clouds of circumstances or feelings obscure the reality of the sun. The warmth, brightness, and resultant joy of clear sunny days are replaced by a dismal dreariness that seems to have come to stay, and eventually you forget what those bright sunny days were like. Forgetting that beyond those clouds the sun still shines in all its joyous warmth, you don your apparel of depression. But the clouds will pass, the sun remains steadfast, shining daily whether we see it or not, as sure as the promises of God. May we learn to remember that, beyond the clouds, the promises of God do not fail to shine. The clouds will eventually be lifted; so let us daily put on ". . . the oil of gladness instead of mourning, The mantle of praise instead of a spirit of fainting" (Isaiah 61:3 NAS).

July 10

"Saul and Jonathan are dead." The words, delivered in breathless excitement, did not have the effect that the Amalekite expected. Had not Saul sought to kill David? Would this not give David the throne? For not only was Saul dead, but also all of his sons but one! It was true that Ish-bosheth still remained, but what would he be against David?

Why his words had struck a cord of grief beginning a wait of mourning rather than a cord of joy resounding an anthem of praise, he did not know. What was wrong? Why did David tear his clothes and weep?

The Amalekite did not understand. He did not know the heart of David. Saul was his King before he was his enemy. Saul was God's anointed. And his son Jonathan was David's blood brother!

Instead of being the hero who had delivered the final death blow to the already wounded body of Saul, instead of being the bearer of good news to David, the Amalekite became the enemy.

Suddenly he was made aware of the grievousness of his act as David asked, "How is it you were not afraid to stretch out your hand to destroy the Lord's anointed?" (2 Samuel 1:14 NAS).

It was over just like that! "David called one of the young men and said, 'Go, cut him down.' So he struck him and he died. And David said to him, 'Your blood is on your head, for your mouth has testified against you, saying, "I have killed the Lord's anointed." ' Then David chanted with this lament over Saul and Jonathan his son and he told them to teach the sons of Judah the song of the bow . . ." (2 Samuel 1:15–18 NAS).

It was a song sung in Judah, but apparently it never reached the ears of the one who so desperately needed to hear it—Mephibosheth, Jonathan's son. Or if he did hear it over the next bitter years of his life, he did not believe it. Part of the lament went this way . . . "How have the mighty fallen in the midst of battle! Jonathan is slain on your high places. I am distressed for you, my brother Jonathan; You have been very pleasant to me. Your love to me was more wonderful than the love of women. How have the mighty fallen, And the weapons of war perished!" (2 Samuel 1: 25–27 NAS.)

Oh, what a difference it would have made if only Mephibosheth, Jonathan's seed, had known of the covenant cut for him when he was still in the loins of his father! But ignorance crippled him.

And it is the same today, beloved. Multitudes have been crippled because of ignorance of the New Covenant, cut for us in the body of Jesus Christ.

"Crippled? Crippled, you say? I don't understand it?"

You will, beloved, in the days ahead. Bow today and ask God to prepare your heart for His message.

July 11

When the Amalekite fled to tell David what he thought was good news, another message went out from Jezreel that was to strike a cord of terror in the hearts of another group of people.

Can you imagine what it must have been like that day? Maybe there was a sense, a premonition, of something being . . . No! Ridiculous! Saul and Jonathan would be fine! After all they were mighty warriors. And Jehovah was on their side. Troubling thoughts had to be dismissed; they were silly.

And then ". . . the report of Saul and Jonathan came from Jezreel . . ." (2 Samuel 4:4 NAS).

"Saul is dead."

"Jonathan . . . what about Jonathan?"

"Jonathan is dead. And so are Abinadab and Malchishua. You must flee!"

Flee! Why would they have to flee? Possibly because of the Philistines. Or maybe it was because only Saul's son, Ish-bosheth, was left. That meant that after Ish-bosheth, Mephibosheth was now second in line for the throne. What if David ever found out? Would he not kill Mephibosheth so he could have the throne of Israel?

It was enough, no more need be heard. With that, Mephibosheth's "nurse took him up and fled. And it happened that in her hurry to flee, he fell and became lame" . . . "crippled in his feet" (2 Samuel 4:4 NAS).

He was five years old. Old enough to remember. Old enough to grow up in bitterness. Old enough to sense that David was his foe. His mother had been taken in death, then his father. And here he was a prince, a prince without hope of a throne. What was a prince doing living in Lo-debar! He belonged in a palace with servants not in these mountains of Gilead being raised by Machir, son of Ammiel.

As the years lengthened, so, I imagine, did his bitterness as he watched the other children run and play. Sometimes it must have seemed unbearable. Crippled! Crippled! Nothing but a piece of garbage, a dog, and dead at that! Worthless! And then to top it all off, there was the growing fear of David! What if David ever found out about his existence, his whereabouts? Would David's men kill him as they had killed his uncle, Ish-bosheth? (2 Samuel 4:5–12.)

Even his inheritance was gone! David had it! David was ruling Israel when *he* should have been! And so the years passed in bitterness, in fear, in disgust, in disappointment, in relative poverty. And it was all because Mephibosheth was ignorant of the covenant cut for him. He was crippled because of ignorance, because he fled when he did not have to!

What about you, precious one? Are you crippled in both feet because you have run away from God in fear, ignorant of the covenant cut for you? Has your ignorance of God's love, of His covenant, caused you great bitterness of soul? Have you been living in the poverty of Lo-debar rather than in the riches of the inheritance which belongs to those of covenant? Do you sometimes feel worthless, like a piece of garbage? Is there any hope for you? Oh, yes, you'll see in the days to come.

His Thoughts Toward Me:

My Thoughts Toward Him:

July 12

When Mephibosheth was summoned by King David he apparently knew nothing of the conversation between David and Ziba, Saul's former servant. Nor did he know what David's reaction would be to him because he was lame. Nor did he really understand David's heart. Instead he was overcome by a fear and a bitterness born of prejudice and of rumor—rumor which spreads like dandelion seeds caught and carried every which way by the winds of "have you heard," taking root wherever they land, marring the otherwise beautiful meadows of truth.

David had been thirty when he was anointed king over Israel at Hebron (2 Samuel 5:3, 4). When he captured the stronghold of Zion, the City of David, he had said, " 'Whoever would strike the Jebusites, let him reach the lame and the blind, who are hated by David's soul, through the water tunnel.' Therefore they say, 'The blind or the lame shall not come into the house' " (2 Samuel 5:8 NAS). The word apparently spread among the people that their

King despised the lame and the blind and therefore they would never be allowed in the City of David. In all probability this rumor only added to Mephibosheth's bitterness and fear.

Now that the long war between the house of Saul and the house of David had ended, "David reigned over all Israel; and David administered justice and righteousness for all his people" (2 Samuel 8:15 NAS); ". . . and the Lord helped David wherever he went" (2 Samuel 8:14 NAS). "Then David said, 'Is there yet anyone left of the house of Saul, that I may show him kindness for Jonathan's sake?' Now there was a servant of the house of Saul whose name was Ziba, and they called him to David; and the king said to him, 'Are you Ziba?' And he said, 'I am your servant.' And the king said, 'Is there not yet anyone of the house of Saul to whom I may show the kindness of God?' And Ziba said to the king, 'There is still a son of Jonathan who is crippled in both feet.' So the king said to him, 'Where is he?' And Ziba said to the king, 'Behold, he is in the house of Machir the son of Ammiel in Lo-debar.' Then King David sent and brought him from the house of Machir the son of Ammiel, from Lo-debar" (2 Samuel 9:1–5 NAS).

And Mephibosheth came into the City of David lame in both feet.

Beloved, let me ask you a question for meditation. How well do you know the One who sits upon the throne? Are you fully aware of the fact that He administers justice and righteousness for all His people or are you the victim of rumors about God? Do you feel that God would never find you acceptable, fit to enter His city because you are lame?

My Thoughts Toward Him:

July 13

Mephibosheth limped into David's presence. His body shook. He couldn't keep it under control. The fear that had begun to rumble, seethe, and foam in the very core of his being was now about to erupt. Just as gases build in a volcano until the pressure becomes so great that the magma blasts its way to the surface venting itself in the weakened rock, so Mephibosheth's fear could no longer be contained. The pressure was too great; the rock was weak. Maybe relief would come when he prostrated himself on the floor before David's throne. Maybe that would silence the tremors.

Suddenly it was as if he were five again. The frantic shouts and orders given on that fateful day along with the pain seemed almost too much to bear. "Saul and Jonathan are dead . . . killed in battle." His five-year-old mind was confused. "Dead? What does dead mean? Why are they grabbing me? Why are we running away?" And then it came, that awful excruciating pain. His feet dangled. He wanted his daddy. "Hush, child, Daddy's gone and so is Granddaddy. Hush! There's no sense crying, you'll never see them again." It was the extreme heat of that day that caused the magma to form that would one day erupt like a volcano. Oh, the pressure had built with time, as Mephibosheth was warned over and over again that David would surely kill him if he ever found him. Over and over he heard about the inheritance that was rightly his as Saul's grandson. Over and over he had to deal with the shame and inconvenience of being lame in both feet. Now he was prostrating before a throne that was seemingly occupied by an usurper.

It was too much. At least Mephibosheth thought it was. The fear showed. David saw it.

Compassion and lovingkindness flowed from the throne, but Mephibosheth was totally ignorant of it. Why? Because he did not have the facts straight. *He had never had them straight.* He was ignorant. All he knew was what had been told him from childhood by people who were prejudiced, people who only had Saul's point of view. Mephibosheth's mind had been steeped over the years in the family's thinking, the family's tradition. He had lived for years in utter ignorance of the covenant that had been cut for him, cut for just this time, cut for just this occasion. He was ignorant of the time when his father, Jonathan, had taken a precaution against this day and had said to David, "And you shall not cut off your lovingkindness *from my house forever,* not even when the Lord cuts off every one of the enemies of David from the face of the earth" (1 Samuel 20:15 NAS, italics added).

And so Mephibosheth trembled in fear before the throne.

And what about you, precious one? Have you lived in ignorance and in fear of God? Have you been taught that you were the one

266

who was heir to the throne of your life? Did you ever fear that if you ever gave your life to God, He would do something terrible to you like send you to Africa, or give you cancer, or kill your loved ones?

Quit shaking. You have heard lies. Those who told you such things knew nothing about the covenant cut for you when you were still in the loins of God yet to be brought forth by incorruptible seed! (James 1:18; 1 Peter 1:23).

His Thoughts Toward Me:

My Thoughts Toward Him:

July 14

"And Mephibosheth, the son of Jonathan the son of Saul, came to David and fell on his face and prostrated himself. And David said, 'Mephibosheth.' And he said, 'Here is your servant!' And David said to him, 'Do not fear, for I will surely show kindness to you for the sake of your father Jonathan, and will restore to you all the land of your grandfather Saul; and you shall eat at my table regularly.' Again he prostrated himself and said, 'What is your servant, that you should regard a dead dog like me?' Then the king called Saul's servant Ziba, and said to him, 'All that belonged to Saul and to all his house I have given to your master's grandson. And you and your sons and your servants shall cultivate the land for him, and you shall bring in the produce so that your master's grandson may have food; nevertheless Mephibosheth your master's grandson shall eat at my table regularly.' Now Ziba had fifteen sons and twenty servants. Then Ziba said to the king, 'According to all that my lord the king commands his servant so your servant will do.' So Mephibosheth ate at David's table as one of the king's sons. . . . So Mephibosheth lived in Jerusalem, for he ate at the king's table regularly. Now he was lame in both feet" (2 Samuel 9:6–11, 13 NAS).

Come and dine? Dine at the King's table? Incredible! A dead dog eating at the King's table regularly! The term *dead dog* was a Hebraism for an embarrassing piece of garbage. And yet here was Mephibosheth—an enemy of David's by his choosing, not by David's—a man lame in both feet, crippled from fleeing from David, a man worthless and embarrassing in his own eyes being bidden by the King to come and dine! Why? What did Mephibosheth do to deserve this honor? Nothing. What was there about him that he should have this honor? Nothing. Then why? It was because of Jonathan. "... for I will surely show kindness to you for the sake of your father Jonathan" (2 Samuel 9:7 NAS).

It was because of covenant. Mephibosheth was set apart, sanctified because of covenant.

"But we see Jesus, who was made a little lower than the angels for the suffering of death, crowned with glory and honour; that he by the grace of God should taste death for every man. For it became him, for whom are all things, and by whom are all things, in bringing many sons unto glory, to make the captain of their salvation perfect through sufferings. For both he that sanctifieth and they who are sanctified are all of one: for which cause he is not ashamed to call them brethren" (Hebrews 2:9–11). He is not ashamed to call you brethren. Can't you hear Him?

"Come and dine, the Master calleth, 'Come and Dine.' You can feast at Jesus' table anytime. He who fed the multitude, turned the water into wine, bids His hungry children, 'Come and Dine.' "

Oh, beloved, have you eaten His flesh? Have you drunk His blood? Have you entered into covenant with Him?

July 15

Most of us live the better part of our lives with the subconscious dread that someday we will be caught, found out, exposed for what we *really* are. The mask will be taken off! All that we have hidden behind, all we have covered ourselves with—be it a certain personality, an image, power, success, obscurity, illness, whatever—will suddenly be taken away. We will be exposed. And we tremble. What will be the verdict?

There are so many things with which people cover themselves—wisdom, might, affluence, influence. And those who are foolish, weak, poor, and despised look at them and think, "Man, those people have it made!" But do they? Are these the things that really make a person? According to man they are. But not according to God for His ways are not our ways, His thoughts are not our thoughts (Isaiah 55:8).

As a matter of fact, I believe that many times these things—wisdom, might, affluence, and influence—are what keep us from being all that we were created to be. They keep us from the inheritance that we could have in Jesus Christ if we were but to see that apart from Him we are truly nothing but "dead dogs, crippled in both feet." We are so content with our humanistic "dining with distinction" that we won't come and dine at the King's table. We don't see that, compared with the Lord's table, our pretentious trappings look like two-bit hash and potato joints.

Mephibosheth, having been summoned before the king, could not help but notice the difference between David's house and Machir's of Lo-debar! And it is the same today, when you come into the King's presence, suddenly all you thought was so great fades into pale insignificance. And so does all you were once impressed with, for now you have an extended vision. As you prostrate yourself before the throne, under the King's gaze, suddenly everything is stripped away. You see yourself as nothing but a piece of garbage, a dead dog. Crippled! Crippled because you ran away!

But when the King looks at you He sees you from an entirely different perspective—the perspective of the throne! Compassion pours from His heart of love. Dead dog? Nonsense! This is Jonathan's seed! Why should I regard you, you ask? Why, don't you know that a covenant was cut for you? I have need of you. I have searched for you, found you, and chosen that you shall dine with me regularly!

Oh, beloved, with God it does not matter what the "real you" is like. "For consider your calling, brethren, that there were not many wise according to the flesh, not many mighty, not many noble; but God has chosen the foolish things of the world to shame the wise, and God has chosen the weak things of the world to shame the things which are strong, and the base things of the world and the despised, God has chosen, the things that are not, that He might nullify the things that are, that no man should boast before God. But by His doing you are in Christ Jesus, who became to us wisdom from God, and righteousness and sanctification, and redemption" (1 Corinthians 1:26–30 NAS).

You are not a piece of garbage; rather you are precious in His sight. God cut a covenant for you with His Son. "And if you belong to Christ, then you are Abraham's offspring [seed], heirs according to promise" (Galatians 3:29 NAS).

His Thoughts Toward Me:

My Thoughts Toward Him:

July 16

Dining at the king's table was not the only privilege given to Mephibosheth! He was also to receive an inheritance, an inheritance that was lost through his grandfather Saul's death. And with that inheritance came Saul's servant Ziba with his sons and his servants. ". . . 'All that belonged to Saul and to all his house I have given to your master's grandson. And you and your sons and your servants shall cultivate the land for him, and you shall bring in the produce so that your master's grandson may have food; nevertheless Mephibosheth your master's grandson shall eat at my table regularly.' Now Ziba had fifteen sons and twenty servants" (Samuel 9:9, 10 NAS).

Thirty-six people would serve Mephibosheth. They would cultivate his grandfather Saul's land and bring in its fruit. How good this was for, even with his inheritance and his privilege of dining at the King's table regularly, Mephibosheth still remained lame in both feet.

As I meditated upon all this, I began to see even more parallels between Mephibosheth and me. I feel that God would have me share these with you for the next couple of days. Not because they are pretty but because God might use them to help some of you to identify and have hope.

If you would trace my bloodline way, way back, as far back as one can go, you would find that my great (multiplied hundreds of times) grandfather was Adam. The one married to Eve. He had an inheritance of land—the earth—over which he was to have dominion as a vice-regent under God. He lost the inheritance and eventually died because he turned from God's way to his way and ate of the tree of the knowledge of good and evil. Because of Adam's sin, I lost my inheritance. As I grew up, my concept of the King of Kings was twisted, distorted, marred by my ignorance of truth. The winds of "have you heard" blew seeds of lies that took root in my mind. One day because of the heat of disappointment, pain, frustration, I ran away leaving behind the little bit of truth I possessed. I thought, "I should be sitting on the throne calling the shots, running my own life." So I shook my fist at God and went my own way. In the process of running downhill, I was crippled. I hobbled in darkness growing more and more disillusioned, more and more dissatisfied. I was an embarrassment to my family, to my Creator, and finally, one day, even to myself. I looked at my life—it was garbage and so was I. Then fear began to nibble at what was hidden in the dirty alleys of my life. What if I were to die? What if I were to stand before God? Surely He would have to condemn me to hell. Oh, I tried to clean up my act, to wear masks of respectability. At times I would even don my religious garb and model it before my friends lest they suspect my harlotries. The apron of motherhood was tied around my waist regularly, many times out of guilt and to cover my Dr. Jekyll-and-Mr. Hyde transformations as I desperately sought for love. I became whatever the occasion required just so that someone would want me. I compromised what I thought I believed because, who knew, maybe I was

271

wrong. Yet underneath it all, naked before the mirror of myself, it began to hit me, "You aren't what you thought you were. This is the real you. You can't change; you can't walk straight anymore; you are deformed for life." Try as I would, I couldn't stop being what underneath it all I really was. I would regurgitate what I had done because it was nauseating, but eventually I would go back and partake of what I had vomited. Just like a dog.

Do you in any way relate?

July 17

Was there no hope? Was this to be my character for life? Was I only to get worse and worse until I could not bear to live? Was I to despise myself, my life, and thus others for the rest of my days?

The fear grew. The fear of being found out. The fear of it all catching up with me. The fear of self-destructing. The fear of God's just—I knew it would be just—judgment.

Then one day the summons came to appear before the King. Someone said, "Kay, why don't you quit telling God what *you* want and tell Him that Christ is *all* you need."

But Christ was not all I needed, I needed a husband. I had divorced mine. If I were to be happy, I had to have a husband. And I needed other things. So I replied curtly to this rude, inappropriate challenge, *"Christ is not all I need.* I need a husband, a. . . ." And I went home.

The next morning when I awoke I needed peace. I was sick. Sick with a sickness no doctor could cure. I was a nurse. I knew. That day I just couldn't go to work. I couldn't handle it. I called Johns Hopkins and told my doctor I wouldn't be in.

The summons came within several hours. I turned to my son, Mark, and said, "Mommy has to be alone for a few minutes. I'll be right back." I ran up the stairs and prostrated myself beside my bed, and cried, "O God, I don't care if I never see another man as long as I live, I don't care if You paralyze me from the neck down, I don't care what You do to my boys—if You'll just give me peace." And He gave me peace, the Prince of Peace, the Lord Jesus Christ. "Come now, and let us reason together, . . . Though your sins are as scarlet, They will be as white as snow" (Isaiah 1:18 NAS).

"This is the covenant that I will make with them after those days, says the Lord: I will put My laws upon their heart, and upon their mind I will write them, . . . and their sins and their lawless deeds I will remember no more" (Hebrews 10:16, 17 NAS).

The fear was gone. The condemnation was gone. I had lain there, naked in His sight with naught to cover my sin, and He had called me "Beloved" when there was nothing lovely about me (Romans 9:25).

When I got up, I did not know "what" had happened to me, I only knew that now I belonged to Him and that He was by my side. For me, at the time, it was enough. Little did I realize the inheritance that was mine. The inheritance that I would begin to hear about the next day! All I knew then was that everything was all right. The fear was gone. But the lameness wasn't.

July 18

"Come and dine," the Master called. "I have food to eat that you know nothing about" (John 4:32 NIV). God sent a young man for me to date. Dave brought the food. It was a Phillip's translation of the New Testament. I devoured it. I couldn't get enough. I saw things I had never seen when I had read the Bible before. How could I ever have thought this Book was boring? It was alive. One night, as I lay on the living room floor reading Philippians 4:19 it suddenly dawned on me, "I'm wealthy! I'm wealthy! My God shall supply all my needs according to His riches in glory through Christ Jesus my Lord." I just rolled over to my back and grinned at the ceiling. The King had begun to reveal to me the inheritance that was lost through grandfather Adam but restored through covenant. "The earth is the Lord's, and the fulness thereof" and I was an heir of God, a joint heir with Jesus, the last Adam! (Psalms 24:1).

As I dined at the King's table regularly, I learned more and more about my inheritance. And yet, transformed though I was, I saw that I was still lame in both feet! Lame but changed! What was it? How could it be?

Let me show it to you in our story of Mephibosheth. But as I do, I want you to know that I am simply using the story as an illustration. It is not to be carried any further theologically. It is simply that I saw myself in Mephibosheth as God emphasized his lameness by repeatedly referring to it. Apart from Jesus I am nothing, I can do nothing. I need a helper, a servant, because I am lame in my flesh. And so, just as Ziba and company served Mephibosheth, I have the Holy Spirit to give me the aid, the help I so desperately need. "By His doing [through the Holy Spirit] you are in Christ Jesus [baptized into His body], who became to us wisdom from God, and righteousness and sanctification, and redemption, that, just as it is written, 'Let him who boasts, boast in the Lord' " (1 Corinthians 1:30, 31 NAS).

When our grandfather Adam sinned in the garden of Eden and died, he lost the Spirit of God. But when God saves us there is a renewing of the Holy Spirit. The Holy Spirit then becomes our enabler and overrides the lameness of our flesh. This, beloved, is what the New Covenant is all about as we shall see in the wonderful days to come.

His Thoughts Toward Me:

My Thoughts Toward Him:

July 19

Do you know what I find as I speak in various parts of our country? Ignorance. And apathy. The apathy excuses the ignorance. People do not really know their God. Nor do they know His Word. As a matter of fact, if you were to ask the majority of those who *profess* Christ to explain to you what is theirs by virtue of the blood of the New Covenant, many could not tell you. Yet their whole life in Christ is based on the facts, the truths of this covenant.

As a matter of fact, to prove it, let's do a little experiment today. Today, I want you—now don't squirm or put this book down or read on. Be a good trooper, even if it hurts. It will do you good! I want you to list below all that you know about the New Covenant. Do not consult any books, not even your Bible. Pretend that you have been caught without your Bible and that you have to explain to another what God promised His people through the New Covenant.

Oh, precious one, listen to me. This is not to embarrass you, but rather to help rescue you from any apathy or complaining that has mired you down into the quicksand of God's disapproval. It is to keep you from being ashamed when you see Him face to face and have to give an account at His judgment seat (2 Timothy 2:15, 2 Corinthians 5:10). This is to help you gird up the loins of your mind that you might run the race that is set before you. Get out of the grandstands of criticism and get on the track and run where you belong. Sweat—go ahead, it is all right. It's natural for those that run! And it is good. It gets rid of the impurities, the body wastes. Don't let this be said of you: "For though by this time you ought to be teachers, you have need again for some one to teach you the elementary principles of the oracles of God, and you have come to need milk and not solid food" (Hebrews 5:12 NAS).

What I Know About The New Covenant:

When And Where I Learned It:

July 20

Now, let's learn all we can about what I call "The Three Covenants of Salvation." We only have a *few* days, which isn't much, but it will be enough to enrich your life immeasurably and to enable you to share His gospel more effectively. By the way, have I told you that there burns within my heart a love for you, though many of you are unseen and thus unknown to me? It's the love of the Lord, and this is why I discipline myself to write. I write for you, at His bidding, because you truly are precious, beloved of God, and He and I want you to know that!

There are three covenants that God uses to bring a person to Christ: the Abrahamic Covenant, the Old Covenant, and the New Covenant. When I teach this, I like to diagram them as I have done on page 277.

Let me give you a brief synopsis of each covenant, and then tomorrow we will begin looking at each one separately. Now, beloved, what I am going to do is give you some good solid teaching, so hangeth Thou in there! It will get very practical, very livable, but *first* you must have an understanding of the truth of it all. Deity is always based on doctrine. Share with me how you live, and I will tell you what you really believe.

The Abrahamic Covenant is the covenant that gives us the promise of the seed, the Lord Jesus Christ. The Old Covenant is the law which came by Moses, and, believe it or not, it plays a vital role in bringing a man to Christ. If we would use it more, we would probably not have so many *false* professions of salvation! The New Covenant is the Covenant of Grace which comes by Jesus Christ and makes us children of God. "For the law was given by Moses, but grace and truth came by Jesus Christ" (John 1:17).

Now, as you learn more about each covenant in the days to come, record the essentials on the diagram below. If you write big, use a separate piece of paper because there is much to learn. God is going to give you truth by which you can not only live but also disciple others.

THE ABRAHAMIC COVENANT	
THE OLD COVENANT	THE NEW COVENANT
(LAW)	(GRACE)

July 21

The future seemed so dark, so final. Why? Why hadn't they listened! How could she have been so deceived? Now everything was ruined. "It was that serpent's fault. He lied to me! He deceived me! Who wants to be as gods knowing good and evil if it means this? What if God sees us?"

Frantically they wove their fig leaves. They finished just in time. But their hiding had been in vain. Suddenly they were face-to-face with God. They were afraid. They should have been. They had sinned.

Then the word of the Lord came. Eve could scarcely believe her ears. Hope dawned, like the brilliance of the morning sun as it pushes away the burden of darkness from earth's shoulders. She would have a seed, a seed that would bruise Satan's head! Hallelujah! That old deceiver, that horrible serpent, would not triumph after all.

There it was, the first promise of the coming of the Messiah through the seed of the woman. It had been spoken . . . sealed by the lips of God. It would come to pass. There was hope.

Hundreds of years would pass and then the promise of the seed would be spoken again, this time to a man named Abram. "Now the promises were spoken to Abraham and to his seed. He does not say, 'And to seeds,' as referring to many, but rather to one, 'And to your seed,' that is, Christ" (Galatians 3:16 NAS). The Messiah, the Christ, would come forth from the loins of Abraham. "In hope against hope he believed, in order that he might become a father of many nations, according to that which had been spoken, 'So shall your descendants [*seed*] be.' And without becoming weak in faith he contemplated his own body, now as good as dead since he was about a hundred years old, and the deadness of Sarah's womb; yet, with respect to the promise of God, he did not waver in unbelief, but grew strong in faith, giving glory to God, and being fully assured that what He had promised, He was able also to perform. Therefore also it was reckoned to him as righteousness" (Romans 4:18–22 NAS).

"On that day the Lord made a covenant with Abram" (Genesis 15:18 NAS), and God, in the form of a smoking oven and a flaming torch passed through the pieces of the sacrifice (Genesis 15:17). Because God *alone* passed through the pieces of flesh, it was a covenant that depended on the faithfulness of God alone.

The Abrahamic Covenant was made and ratified by God—the seed as promised to Eve and then to Abraham would come and take away our sins.

And what, with regard to the Abrahamic Covenant, is God's promise to you and to me? It is this, recorded for us in Galatians 3:29, "And if you belong to Christ, then you are Abraham's offspring [seed], heirs according to promise" (NAS). Do you belong to Christ? How do you know?

July 22

Has there ever been a time when you took a good honest look at your life? I mean when you really sat down and evaluated the way you were living in the light of what you knew or had heard was right or wrong?

Has there ever been a time when you realized that your life did not measure up to God's commandments? A time when you realized that, were you to stand before God, you would stand guilty because you had not obeyed His commandments? Maybe you had put others or your profession before God—idolatry. Maybe you had lingered around some married friends looking, wondering what it would be like to be married to him or her, even flirting a little—coveting. Maybe, because you were hurt or jealous, you implied, said, or led others to believe wrong things about another person—bearing false witness. Maybe you did not give your parents the obedience, the respect due them—not honoring father and mother. Maybe you copied an answer or a paper that was not yours or took too much change at the store or even took some things that did not belong to you—stealing. Maybe you satisfied your physical desires outside of marriage or thought about seducing someone—adultery.

Let me ask you a question. How do you feel about your life? Are you pleased with it? And how do you think God would evaluate your life? Do you think He would be pleased with it? Why don't you meditate on this for a few minutes and then jot down your thoughts below.

Now, what do you think you could do that would make your life more acceptable to God? Think about it; write it down; and we'll talk more tomorrow.

July 23

Four hundred and thirty years had passed since God had cut covenant with Abraham. Now Moses stood at Mount Sinai bearing the message of another covenant as he "recounted to the people all the words of the Lord and all the ordinances . . ." (Exodus 24:3 NAS). God had given Moses the Law. Now Moses was imparting that Law with all of its precepts and ordinances to God's chosen people. As they stood to hear these laws of God, they knew that they were good. The Law was right! Man should abide by it! After all God should be first. Idolatry was wrong. Parents should be honored. Coveting and stealing were bad. And murder, God forbid! And who would want his wife to lie with another? The Sabbath—man needed rest; it should be holy. Yes, these were fine laws; laws that would benefit them as a people, for surely those who would abide by these would live righteous lives pleasing to God and to man. So ". . . all the people answered with one voice, and said, 'All the words which the Lord has spoken we will do!' " (Exodus 24:3 NAS.) There it was, a covenant acceptable to both parties. The order was given. Moses "sent young men of the sons of Israel, and they offered burnt offerings and sacrificed young bulls as peace offerings to the Lord. And Moses took half of the blood and put it in basins, and the other half of the blood he sprinkled on the altar. Then he took the book of the covenant and read it in the hearing of the people; and they said, *'All* that the Lord has spoken *we will do, and we will be obedient!'* " (Exodus 24:5–7 NAS, italics added.) The Covenant of Law was made. So Moses, Aaron, Nadab, Abihu, and seventy of the elders of Israel went up on Mount Sinai to partake of the covenant meal, and they beheld God, and they ate and drank (Exodus 24:9–11).

The Law was established; now it was to be obeyed to the letter, without fail! "For whoever keeps the whole law and yet stumbles in one point, he has become guilty of all" (James 2:10 NAS). It was right. It was good. It was holy. They were to keep it—but they didn't! They couldn't. They thought they could, but they couldn't because they were sinners. Sin . . . indwelling sin! They had not recognized it, and, try as hard as they could, desire as much as they did, they still broke the Law. That old man, that old self born of Adam's sin, ruled their flesh causing the members of their bodies to be slaves to sin (Romans 6:6).

Oh, what wretched men they were! The good that they wanted to do, they could not do. They knew the Law was holy, good, just, and yet indwelling sin kept them in bondage (Romans 7:12, 14, 23). They did the very things they hated! There was no use, who could ever free them from these bodies of death (Romans 7:24)?

The Law that they thought would bring righteousness and life only brought death. Why had God given the Law if it couldn't make a man righteous? Good question, isn't it? Have you ever tried to keep the Law or do what was right and found out that, no matter how hard you tried, you failed? Frustrating wasn't it?

What's the answer? We'll see in the days to come. How precious and liberating it will be!

July 24

If the Law can't shape us up, if it can't change us and make us righteous, then why on earth did God give it?

Let's review for a minute before we answer that question. Remember when Moses shared God's Law with the people? What was their response when it was read to them? Right, "all that the Lord says, we will do." They heard the Law, saw that it was right and good, and decided that they would live by it, keeping its commands and precepts. *They thought they could do it,* but they did not reckon with the fact that they were sinners just like every Gentile. For "by one man sin entered into the world, and death by sin; and so death passed upon all men, for that *all* have sinned" (Romans 5:12, italics added). "For all have sinned, and come short of the glory of God" (Romans 3:23). ". . . Both Jews and Greeks are all under sin . . . There is none righteous, not even one" (Romans 3:9, 10 NAS).

The Law was given by God for two reasons. It was given first to show us our sin and second to keep us in custody until the day when we would believe in the Lord Jesus Christ. Now, beloved, let me urge you not to rush through these devotionals because what I have to share with you is so absolutely essential. It may seem a little heavy to some of you. Heavy it may be, but it is essential. You must understand it, so persevere. You see, beloved, most of our problems have come because of ignorance of God's Word and His ways. If it was not ignorance, then it was disobedience.

God gave the Law because man needed to see his sin. He needed to see that in his flesh dwelt no good thing . . . and thus by the works of the Law no flesh would be justified in God's sight (Romans 3:20). The only way man would ever recognize his sin was through seeing God's holy, righteous, just Law ". . . for through the

Law comes the knowledge of sin" (Romans 3:20, NAS). And so Paul wrote in Romans, ". . . I would not have come to know sin *except through* the Law; for I would not have known about coveting if the Law had not said, 'You shall not covet' " (Romans 7:7 NAS, italics added).

Oh, beloved, how my heart aches for our world today for we live in a society that has heard so little of God's Law, God's Word, God's way. And as a result multitudes have sown an awful crop of corruption in their flesh. Their lives, along with relationships that were designed to sustain them as a whole person, have become as bitter as gall so that, when they come to talk to me bent over in pain, they can hardly speak for the retching nausea of their sin. How I hurt when I hear them say, "Why didn't I hear these truths before? Maybe I wouldn't have gotten so messed up. Oh, if only I had heard!" And my heart aches. Where were those who were supposed to proclaim God's Law so that man, at least, might have recognized sin for what it was?

By the way, as I write this tonight my heart is so filled with love for you that it spills over into my eyes!

July 25

"I would not have come to know sin except through the Law; for I would not have known about coveting if the Law had not said, 'You shall not covet' " (Romans 7:7 NAS).

What part has God's holy Law played in your life? How many of its just and righteous Law ordinances have you known? Have you realized just exactly what sin is? When you sinned, did you know that you were going directly, purposefully, and willfully against His holy commandments? Or did you tremble, just as I did as a child because of exposure to God's Law—tremble for fear of God's judgment and thus walk in outward conformity to His do's and don'ts?

As I grew up, there were things that were definitely wrong and things that were definitely right. There were clear-cut absolutes

—most of life was either black or white with very little gray. And these absolutes kept me in check as far as my external behavior was concerned. I considered myself to be a pretty good girl. I really did not see myself as an awful sinner until I reached my twenties. For although I knew the commandments, I do not remember sitting under any really convicting teaching or preaching that pointed out the exceeding sinfulness of my flesh. Thus, I did not see my desperate need for change, my desperate need for Jesus Christ to rescue me by His Spirit from my sinful old nature of self. I do not remember any preaching or teaching that broke up the hard, dry, fallow ground of my heart. As a child I had to work in our World War II Victory Gardens and help dig flower beds. Many times those gardens had to be edged with a spade. Sometimes, when the ground was particularly hard for lack of rain, I would have to jump up on the spade with both feet in order to get it to penetrate that hard earth. That was the kind of teaching and preaching I needed. I needed to hear a word from the Lord as "the preaching went to meddlin' " in the thoughts and intents of my heart!

Oh, how the complacent, dead church needs to see Mount Sinai all in smoke because the Lord descended upon it in fire; and its smoke ascending like the smoke of a furnace, and the whole mountain quaking violently (Exodus 19:18 NAS). God needs to answer man's sin with thunder and warn the people (Exodus 19:19, 23). But to do so, He needs men who will proclaim God's holy Law without fear, without compromise. He needs men like the Jeremiahs, the Isaiahs, the prophets of old who will gird up their "loins, and arise, and speak to them all which" He commands them—men who will not be dismayed by their faces (Jeremiah 1:17).

It takes the Law to show us our sin and God's just displeasure and rightful judgment upon those who trangress His holy commandments. It is the preaching of the Law that prepares the way for the message of grace. It is the proclamation of the Law that brings men to repentance, and except we repent we shall all likewise perish (Luke 13:3).

How does your life measure up to the Law, the Old Covenant? "But," you may say, "I'm not under the Old Covenant, I've been saved!"

Good. How does your life measure up to the Law? Does grace make you lawless? Can it? No, for the righteousness of the Law is fulfilled in us who walk not after the flesh, but after the Spirit (Romans 8:4).

His Thoughts Toward Me:

My Thoughts Toward Him:

July 26

You . . . Church . . . lay down that wedding garment. It is not time yet for the bride to put on white. Rather clothe yourself in black sackcloth. Put on the garments of mourning. Put a cloth to your nose and mouth and step out into the neighborhoods of the world. Don't stop up your ears. Listen to their wailing, to the cry of mourners. Families weeping for their dead. As you walk through the streets, doesn't the stench of death seep through that cloth you hold over your nose and mouth? Is that why you are convulsing in retching nausea? No, don't turn away. Don't run back to the security of your sanctuaries and sing your hymns. Quit shutting your eyes. Open them. Let them see for a moment the horror, the tragedy of the wages of sin! Look for a minute at the children of those who have never heard the gospel, let alone the just commandments of God's holy Law. Quit running, quit hiding in the niceties of life for a moment. Please, just for a moment leave the Temple and the Pharisees and go eat dinner with Jesus as He sits with tax collectors and prostitutes, with sinners, with those who need a physician. For a moment gaze fully on death, the awful wages of sin, and then you will see more clearly why God gave men the Law even when He knew that they could never keep it. Even when He knew that it could never make them righteous. Even when He knew that it would only expose their sin for what it was—sin, a very real condition of their heart, theirs because they belonged to the human race, theirs because they were born of Adam.

God's second purpose in giving the Law was to restrain men from drinking the dregs of sin's chalice, from tasting in full the bitter gall that lay at the bottom of the cup—gall that would convulse their beings until they withered up into greyish black, cold, twisted forms of human beings. The Law was given to keep men in custody from sin's awful wages until they could come to faith in the Lord Jesus Christ. Listen carefully, beloved, to God's Word. "But before faith came, we were kept in custody under the law, being shut up to the faith which was later to be revealed. Therefore, the Law has become our tutor to lead us to Christ, that we may be justified by faith" (Galatians 3:23, 24 NAS).

Now, beloved, since I am almost out of writing space for today, let me leave you with a question, and we will complete this tomorrow. How would the Law be an asset rather than a detriment in the life of an unbeliever? Write out your answer. Put it in black and white as there are many humanistic voices that say hearing God's commandments only causes men to go on an awful guilt trip and therefore messes them up psychologically for life.

July 27

Could the knowledge of God's holy Law mess a person up psychologically and produce guilt and a sense of condemnation that will damage them for life? Yes, I think it could in a way, *if all* a man ever heard was the Law *and* he *never* heard of Jesus Christ who was the fulfillment of that Law. So as we reason together today, it is important that you remember that, ever since the day sin entered into the world through Adam and Eve, there has *always* been the promise of the seed, the One who would come and crush Satan's head and set men free from sin. Before God ever gave the Law, the Old Covenant, there stood the Abrahamic Covenant promising a Savior for man's sin, the Lord Jesus Christ. Thus we must remember that when we share the Law, when we tell men of its holy and just requirements, we must always tell them of the way of escape, the grace of God that is every man's through belief in the Lord Jesus Christ.

Now then, let's take one last look at the Law before we proceed to the New Covenant. The Law, as we have seen, served two purposes. First, it was given to reveal man's sin so that man, having seen clearly his sin, might then see his need of a savior. The Law shows a man his inability to attain righteousness on his own. Galatians 3:19 says, "Why the Law then? It was added because of transgressions, having been ordained through angels by the agency of a mediator, until the seed should come to whom the promise had been made" (NAS). The Scripture has shut up all men under sin, that the promise by faith in Jesus Christ might be given to those who believe.

The second purpose of the Law was to restrain men from sin, to keep them in custody so they would not drink of the dregs of sin's poisonous chalice and thus bear the awful, ugly scars of sin's death for "when lust has conceived, it gives birth to sin; and when sin is accomplished, it brings forth death" (James 1:15 NAS). The law of the harvest stands even in the fields of grace, "Do not be deceived, God is not mocked; for whatever a man sows, this he will also reap. For the one who sows to his own flesh shall from the flesh reap corruption, but the one who sows to the Spirit shall from the Spirit reap eternal life" (Galatians 6:7, 8 NAS). Thus Galatians 3:23 tells us we are kept in custody under the Law. The Law becomes our tutor, our child attendant who watches our behavior and who serves to lead us to Christ. The Greek word for "kept in custody" is *phroureo,* a military term that meant to guard as a garrison or to block the way of escape. The Law served to keep the Jews—and us—from the contamination of the world's vices; to keep men locked up within its restrictions and thus out of trouble.

That is why, beloved, I wanted you to take a walk through the world's streets of death, to smell its stench, to see its awful wages. I wanted you to be convinced of the place of the Law so you will teach it to your children and thus keep them from the world's contamination. I want you to see it so you won't be taken "captive through philosophy and empty deception, according to the tradition of men, according to the elementary principles of the world"

(Colossians 2:8 NAS). I want you to see it so that you might go into the world and preach the *whole* counsel of God—which includes all three covenants. Don't leave out the Law!

July 28

As the armies of Babylon lay siege against Jerusalem, as the word of the Lord warning of famine, of fighting, of fire, of destruction was about to come to pass, there came a new word from God. A word of promise. A word of hope. A new covenant. Oh, it was yet for days to come but it was a promise to remember, to cling to, to believe in, to wait for!

What was this new covenant like? What did it promise? What would it do for man? Let me share it with you a little bit at a time, explaining it step by step. Oh, beloved, how liberating are the truths! So many are deceived regarding the grace of God because they do not understand the New Covenant, the Covenant of Grace which came by Jesus Christ. Oh, stop for a minute and ask God to open the eyes of your understanding and to lead you into all truth by His Spirit.

" 'Behold, days are coming,' declares the Lord, 'when I will make a new covenant with the house of Israel and with the house of Judah, not like the covenant which I made with their fathers in the day I took them by the hand to bring them out of the land of Egypt, My covenant which they broke, although I was a husband to them,' declares the Lord. 'But this is the covenant which I will make with the house of Israel after those days,' declares the Lord, 'I will put My law within them, and on their heart I will write it; and I will be their God, and they shall be My people. And they shall not teach again, each man his neighbor and each man his brother saying, "Know the Lord," for they shall all know Me, from the least of them to the greatest of them,' declares the Lord, 'for I will forgive their iniquity, and their sin I will remember no more' " (Jeremiah 31:31–34 NAS).

The New Covenant is so different from the Old Covenant that

it seems at times a study in contrasts. Whereas the Old Covenant was God's law written on tables of stone, the New Covenant was God's law written within, upon man's heart.

There would now be an inner knowing of what was righteous and what was unrighteous, of that which pleased God and that which offended Him. This New Covenant would not kill a man, slay him in his sin, but would bring life—life from the Spirit. It would not be like the Law, a ministry of condemnation, but its ministry would be to produce the righteousness that the Law could not produce, "weak as it was through the flesh" (Romans 8:3, 4 NAS).

Tomorrow, I will explain Jeremiah 31:33, 34 to you. For now, listen to these words from 2 Corinthians 3:5–9 NAS and then meditate upon them. Paul is writing as a servant of the gospel, of the New Covenant:

". . . Our adequacy is from God, who also made us adequate as servants of a new covenant, not of the letter, but of the Spirit; for the letter kills, but the Spirit gives life. But if the ministry of death, in letters engraved on stones, came with glory, so that the sons of Israel could not look intently at the face of Moses because of the glory of his face, fading as it was, how shall the ministry of the Spirit fail to be even more with glory? For if the ministry of condemnation has glory, much more does the ministry of righteousness abound in glory."

Why don't you go back to July 20 and put down these contrasts on your chart on the three covenants. Then list those things you also learned about the New Covenant from Jeremiah 31:33, 34, and ask God to show you what it means to you. As you begin to understand what it means to you, write it all out below.

July 29

Have you ever had anyone say to you, "I'd become a Christian, but I just couldn't live the life? If I were ever going to make a commitment to God, I'd want to keep it, and, you see, I know I just couldn't be what I'm supposed to be for God. I just couldn't; so I might as well forget it." Have you ever had anyone say these words to you? I heard them several weeks ago as I witnessed to a young man. (When you're forty-seven everyone is young—even you!)

A person like this knows at least one thing—the Christian life is to be a life lived on a higher plane. The one thing, however, that they do not realize is that, when you truly believe on the Lord Jesus Christ and are saved, God causes certain definite changes to take place within you. This is the difference between the Old and the New Covenant. In the Old Covenant, the responsibility for keeping the Law rested totally upon man and, because of his flesh, he just couldn't handle it! However in the New Covenant, the Spirit of God comes in and does what the flesh cannot do: He changes man! Let's look at it step by step. Let's go back to Jeremiah 31:33, 34.

In the New Covenant, God not only writes His law upon the fleshly tables of a man's heart, as we saw yesterday, but He also says that He becomes your God and you become His people. Can you imagine! You become His. What a privilege! "See how great a love the Father has bestowed upon us, that we should be called children of God; and such we are" (1 John 3:1 NAS). ". . . You have received a spirit of adoption as sons by which we cry out, 'Abba! Father!'" (Romans 8:15 NAS).

In the New Covenant, God says that "they shall not teach again, each man his neighbor and each man his brother, saying, 'Know the Lord,' for they shall all know Me. . . ." (Jeremiah 31:34 NAS). What does this mean? I believe it means that, when you have really entered into the New Covenant, you know God from an inner experience, witness, or teaching by His Spirit rather than only knowing about God from what you hear from others! You see, beloved, when you are born again you get a new "resident" Teacher. First Corinthians 2:12 NAS says, "Now we have received, not the spirit of the world, but the Spirit who is from God, that we might know the things freely given to us by God." ". . . He will guide you into all the truth . . ." (John 16:13 NAS).

While the Old Covenant could only reveal our sin and expose it for what it is, the New Covenant takes our sin away for under this covenant the Lord declares ". . . I will forgive their iniquity, and their sin I will remember no more" (Jeremiah 31:34 NAS). Under the New Covenant all sins are gone! ". . . Having our hearts sprinkled clean from an evil conscience and our bodies washed with pure water" (Hebrews 10:22 NAS), we are now under no condemnation for sin for our sins are buried in the deepest ocean (Micah 7:19). And, as dear Corrie ten Boom would say, "God has put up a sign . . . 'No Fishing Allowed.' " Hallelujah, what a covenant!

You become His, He becomes yours. You know Him now, not because of the external witness of others, but by revelation. Your sins are gone forever, never to be remembered by God. They are forgiven and forgotten!

But is this all? Oh no, beloved, there is more. There is the Enabler who so transforms you that you can live the life God requires. We'll see that truth tomorrow. Today, meditate upon these things and listen to what your Teacher, the Holy Spirit, has to say.

His Thoughts Toward Me:

My Thoughts Toward Him:

July 30

Have you ever been afraid that you might turn your back on God and walk away, never to return? It's a devastating thought, isn't it? What torment to think that one day you might do that. You read about certain kings in the Old Testament who turned their back on God and you shudder. Could that happen to you as a child of God?

Beloved, I know that many have been taught differing theologies on the eternal security of a believer, but what does God's

Word say regarding this? What does it say about those who enter into the New Covenant, the Covenant of Grace? Listen to God's Word in Jeremiah 32:39, 40 NAS as we look at still another aspect of the New or Everlasting Covenant. "And I will give them one heart and one way, that they may fear Me always, for their own good, and for the good of their children after them. And I will make an everlasting covenant with them that I will not turn away from them, to do them good; and I will put the fear of Me in their hearts so that they will not turn away from Me."

God promises that *He will put the fear of Himself into our hearts.* God Himself will do it *so that* we will not turn away from Him! This, beloved, is the keeping power of God that causes us to fear Him always. This, beloved, is the Father's answer to the prayer of His Son on our behalf. "Holy Father, keep them in Thy name, the name which Thou hast given Me, that they may be one, even as We are" (John 17:11 NAS). And so those of the New Covenant, in the confidence of faith in God's Word, can join with Paul as he says, ". . . I know whom I have believed and I am convinced that He is able to guard what I have entrusted to Him until that day" (Timothy 1:12 NAS).

Did not your Shepherd say, "I am the good shepherd; and I know My own, and My own know Me. . . . But you do not believe, because you are not of My sheep. My sheep hear My voice, and I know them, and they follow Me; and I give eternal life to them, and they shall never perish; and no one shall snatch them out of My hand. My Father, who has given them to Me, is greater than all; and no one is able to snatch them out of the Father's hand" (John 10:14, 26–29 NAS).

We are kept by Jesus, held in the hand of God, *never to perish* for He hath said, "I will never leave thee, nor forsake thee (Hebrews 13:5) for "He predestined us to adoption as sons through Jesus Christ to Himself . . ." (Ephesians 1:5 NAS). ". . . Having also believed, you were sealed in Him *with the Holy Spirit of promise,* who is given as a pledge of our inheritance, with a view to the redemption of God's own possession, to the praise of His glory" (Ephesians 1:13, 14 NAS, italics added), "for the gifts and the calling of God are irrevocable" (Romans 11:29 NAS).

"Now to Him who is able to keep you from stumbling, and to make you stand in the presence of His glory blameless with great joy, to the only God our Savior, through Jesus Christ our Lord, be glory, majesty, dominion and authority, before all time and now and forever. Amen" (Jude 24, 25 NAS).

Stop, beloved. Read this once more, meditating upon it, and then ask God to speak a word to your heart. What are His thoughts toward you?

July 31

How can you live the Christian life? How can you serve your God? Only one way—by the Spirit. None but the Spirit of God can effect the holiness of God and without holiness no one will see the Lord (Hebrews 12:14). And so only the One who said, "Be ye holy even as I am Holy" (1 Peter 1:16) can give you His purity of life. And only the Spirit of God can endue you with power for service. This, beloved, is what the New Covenant brings—holiness and power by the indwelling of the *Holy* Spirit. "A new heart also will I give you, and a new spirit will I put within you: and I will take away the stony heart out of your flesh, and I will give you an heart of flesh. *And I will put my spirit within you, and cause you to walk in my statutes, and ye shall keep my judgments*" (Ezekiel 36:26, 27, italics added).

Jesus said that unless you eat His flesh and drink His blood—the blood of the New Covenant—you would not have eternal life. This eating symbolized the partaking of the person of Jesus Christ. And so in the New Covenant, you are given the Holy Spirit of promise, "Another Helper, that He may be with you forever . . ." He "will be in you" (John 14:16, 17 NAS). And when the Spirit comes to live in you, what will He do? Well, according to the promise of Ezekiel 36:27, *He will cause you* to walk in His statutes and you will be careful to observe His ordinances.

Oh, beloved, do you not see that what the Old Covenant, the Law, justly demanded, the New Covenant, Grace, provided! "For what the Law could not do, weak as it was through the flesh, God did: sending His own Son in the likeness of sinful flesh and as an offering for sin, He condemned sin in the flesh, in order that the requirement of the Law might be fulfilled in us, who do not walk according to the flesh, but according to the Spirit" (Romans 8:3, 4 NAS).

How could His disciples ever live the life? How could they ever carry on His work? How could they ever convince the world that Jesus had come in the flesh? It would not be by might, nor by power, but by His Spirit (Zechariah 4:6). This was His promise to those of the New Covenant, to those whom He would send into the world—to be in the world but not of the world so that the world might believe in Him through their Word (John 17:18, 16, 20). Those who believed in Him would do the works that He had done . . . and even greater because He was going to the Father (John 14:12).

Oh, Jesus has left us here but He has not left us without a comforter, without a guide, without an enabler because He is our Friend. "And I will ask the Father, and He will give you another Helper, that He may be with you *forever;* that is the Spirit of truth, whom the world cannot receive, because it does not behold Him or know Him, but you know Him because He abides with you, and will be in you" (John 14:16, 17 NAS, italics added).

This is the New Covenant! Live in the light of it, beloved, by His Spirit!

AUGUST

August 1

"The steps of a good man are ordered by the Lord . . ." (Psalms 37:23). "Man's goings are of the Lord; how can a man then understand his own way?" (Proverbs 20:24.)

One of the keys that unlocks the door to a life of usefulness, power, and blessing is the key of obedience. If you and I are to know a fulfilled life, we must learn to know God's voice and to heed His instructions.

Bahkt Singh is a man from India who has been greatly used of God to establish many indigenous works in his country. He is a man who truly walks with God because he takes time to talk to God. One day as he was preparing to go to a conference in India, the Lord spoke these instructions into his ear, "There is a brother who wants to go to the conference also, but he does not have a blanket." Bahkt Singh was taken back, "But, Lord, this is my only blanket. You know that we must have two things to go to the conference, money for the train and a blanket! You have provided both for me. If I give away my blanket, I will not have one for the conference. Besides, Lord, it is a brand-new blanket; it doesn't even have a hole in it!" The voice persisted, and Bahkt Singh obeyed. When he arrived at the dwelling of the blanketless man to give him his blanket, the man's joy knew no bounds. "I have been praying. I knew I was to go to the conference, but I told God that I had no blanket." Bahkt Singh returned home knowing that his steps had been ordered by the Lord.

Upon entering into prayer, another conversation took place within his soul. "There is another man who is to go to the conference, but he has no money. Go and give him your money." Bahkt Singh went. It was hard because now it seemed that he could not go to the conference; but obedience was better than weeping, than regretting, than missing God's will. The money was given; another brother could go to the conference.

Then, the word of the Lord came to Bahkt Singh a third time. "Go to the conference." "But, Lord, I have no money. You had me give it away." The still, small voice said, "What would you do if you had the money?" "I would go to buy my train ticket." "Go." When Bahkt Singh arrived at the station he found the longest line that he could stand in so that the Lord would have more time to supply the money. But, alas, the line moved quickly. The ticket agent asked, "Round trip or one way?" Bahkt Singh hesitated. Then, sensing the man's impatience, he said, "Round trip." "That will be thirty-seven, twenty-five." Then, all of a sudden, there was a great commotion as a man burst in, "O Bahkt Singh, how glad I am to see you. Take this quickly. I was told to get it to you. I must rush, or I'll miss my train." Bahkt Singh opened the envelope; a note was inside, "The Lord told me to enclose the following and to send it to you. I can understand the thirty-seven, yet why the twenty-five . . . I do not know!"

His Thoughts Toward Me:

My Thoughts Toward Him:

August 2

"Survivalists" are being interviewed on television talk shows and are gaining national attention as we seem to be hurtling more and more rapidly toward a chaotic national disaster. Survivalists are people who make elaborate preparation for themselves and their families in order to survive any circumstance, natural or man-made, that would create shortages of food, fuel, and other of life's necessities. The survivalists are trusting in their own capacity to protect themselves.

The Christian has the promise of God Himself, the place of refuge. The decisions that Christians make regarding preparation for days of famine and national upheaval must be based on individual conviction, but a careful consideration of God's promises to His children is worthy of note:

But thou, O Lord, art a shield for me; my glory, and the lifter up of mine head (Psalms 3:3).

Now know I that the Lord saveth his anointed; he will hear him from his holy heaven with the saving strength of his right hand. Some trust in chariots, and some in horses; but we will remember the name of the Lord our God (Psalms 20:6, 7).

Though an host should encamp against me, my heart shall not fear: though war should rise against me, in this will I be confident (Psalms 27:3).

My times are in thy hand: deliver me from the hand of mine enemies, and from them that persecute me (Psalms 31:15).

Behold, the eye of the Lord is upon them that fear him, upon them that hope in his mercy; To deliver their soul from death, and to keep them alive in famine (Pslms 33:18, 19).

. . . but the Lord upholdeth the righteous. . . . They shall not be ashamed in the evil time: and in the days of famine they shall be satisfied (Psalms 37:17, 19).

God is our refuge and strength, a very present help in trouble. Therefore will not we fear, though the earth be removed, and though the mountains be carried into the midst of the sea (Psalms 46:1, 2).

Survivalists? Not really. They have only themselves. At best, they'll hold on for a few terror-filled days. But as for the Christian, his dwelling is the secret place of the most High. There, he abides, forever, under the shadow of the Almighty. What a difference!

His Thoughts Toward Me:

My Thoughts Toward Him:

August 3

"He that dwelleth in the secret place of the most High shall abide under the shadow of the Almighty. I will say of the Lord. He is my refuge and my fortress: my God; in him will I trust. Surely he shall deliver thee from the snare of the fowler, and from the noisome pestilence. He shall cover thee with his feathers, and under his wings shalt thou trust: his truth shall be thy shield and buckler" (Psalms 91:1–4).

She had stopped at the red light. Before she even realized the car door had opened, a man had a gun stuck in her side. He demanded, "Lady, just drive. Don't do anything dumb!" She had just heard a message on Psalm 91. This Psalm told her that God was her refuge, that He was her fortress, that He would deliver her from the snare of the fowler, that He covered her with His feathers, that He was her shield and buckler. But in this instant, at the red light with a gun in her side and her mind in a whirl, she could not think of the exact words of the Scripture. Thus, in desperation, all she could come up with and exclaim was, "Feathers! Feathers! Feathers!" The invader panicked! He shouted, "Lady, you are crazy!" As quickly as he had appeared, he disappeared!

Oh, how precious to know that when we can't think of a promise word for word or when we don't have time to quote a promise for the situation in which we find ourselves, God knows His promises, and He knows our heart. How important it is for you to hide His promises in your heart so that you will be ready to claim them at any moment!

His Thoughts Toward Me:

My Thoughts Toward Him:

August 4

What do you do when you find yourself in need? Where do you turn? What is your first impulse? Is it to turn to man, or is it to turn to God?

Sometimes, I think we, in the United States, are plagued by having too much—so much that we see no need to call upon God. Why should we call to God? We seem to have all the answers—computers, libraries, universities, television—these tell us the answers. Stores, factories, credit unions, doctors, psychologists, they are all there, easily accessible, to meet all of our needs. Is it no wonder that we see no need to run to the promise of Jeremiah 33:3, "Call unto me, and I will answer thee, and shew thee great and mighty things, which thou knowest not." Oh, for that childlike faith and trust that would flee to the Throne of Grace crying, "Abba, Abba, Father, I need you!" Oh, for that faith that would turn to God before it ever turned to man and that would turn to man *only* because it had been directed to do so.

Let me tell you a true story that will thrill your heart. It was told to me by Leonard Ravenhill. It's a story of childlike faith amongst a group of natives who had received the gospel from a young man who vividly opened to them the life and ministry of Jesus Christ. They listened to story after story with rapt attention, believing, receiving, wanting more. Finally, the missionary moved on; but he would be back!

Soon after he left, one of the natives fell from a tree and broke his leg. The distortion of the bones could not be hidden beneath the unbroken skin; movement was excruciating. Immediately, in one accord, the natives began to call upon God. "O Jesus, when You walked upon earth, You healed the lame man. Our brother is lame, he cannot walk. So, Jesus, You heal him, too." The man was healed! Some time later, one of the believers suddenly died. Again, they called, "Father! God! Call Jesus! Jesus, come quickly this man is dead like that man Lazarus that You brought to life. Bring him to life." The man lived!

Oh, for that faith as a grain of mustard seed that would call unto Him so that He might answer you and show you great and mighty things! What will your prayer be today? I pray that it will be, "Father, teach me to run to You in childlike faith . . . to call for You."

His Thoughts Toward Me:

My Thoughts Toward Him:

August 5

"Cast thy burden upon the Lord, and he shall sustain thee: he shall never suffer the righteous to be moved" (Psalms 55:22).

Sometimes, God gives us promises with conditions; this is one of them. Holding on to burdens too heavy to bear will only cause you to stumble as you struggle to maintain your stance. Peter narrows down the conditions of the promise when he tells you to cast all your care upon Him for He cares for you (1 Peter 5:7). There's the problem. Our anxieties or cares throw us off balance. Anxiety, care, worry is a bump in the road that causes many Christians to stumble. Yet God has promised that He will never allow the righteous to be shaken. The condition? Cast your burden upon the Lord.

The Greek word for anxiety or care means "to divide, to rip or tear apart." That's what worry does to you. When you hold on to your anxiety, when you refuse to cast it on the Lord, the result in your life is a dividing, a ripping, a tearing apart. The man who says with his mouth, "I am a Christian," says, "I trust, I rely on, I have confidence in the Lord Jesus Christ." The same man, then, denies this trust, this reliance, this confidence when he confesses worry, care, or anxiety. The circle becomes a vicious one until the reality of God's simple truth sinks in: If you will cast your burden on the Lord, then you will not be shaken.

Jay Adams, in his booklet, *What To Do About Worry,* notes three questions that are helpful in getting your worries sorted out, collected in a bag, and ready to be cast on the Lord. These are good to apply when anxiety comes in like a black cloud. Ask yourself the following questions. Then, act!

1. What is my problem?
2. What does God want me to do about it?
3. When, where, and how should I begin?

If your desire is to be sustained, to be immovable, the Lord promises He will sustain you, He will make you immovable.

His Thoughts Toward Me:

My Thoughts Toward Him:

August 6

Once again, Vanya had been summoned to the major's office. Vanya assumed that the summons meant more questions, more warnings, more discipline; but he loved his God, and he would stand up for Him even in the Russian army!

As he walked to Major Gidenko's office, suddenly, ". . . something flashed and glittered in the sky overhead. . . . The light was dazzling, like sunlight on a mirror. He lifted his eyes upward at the same instant that he heard a voice, 'Vanya. Vanya.' " There was an angel above him. The words spoken were ". . . unmistakable, clear . . . 'Do not be afraid. . . . Do not be afraid. Go. I am with you' . . . His joy was like a fire within him. . . . He made his way to the major's office and knocked quietly on the door."

When Vanya was inside and seated, he found that his assumption regarding the purpose of the summons was correct. There awaited more questions, more warnings, and, this time, severe discipline!

As the interrogation session ended, Vanya received the orders which Major Gidenko felt would deter, once and for all, Vanya's absurd claim that he knew the living God! "I am going to order you to stand in the street tonight after taps are played until you are willing to come to me and apologize for the nonsense you have been circulating around the base about yourself and your so-called experiences with God. Since the temperature is likely to be some twenty-five degrees below zero, for your sake, I hope you quickly agree to behave sensibly . . . you will obey my instructions in summer uniform. That is all."

At first, the cold wind slamming against him was painful. He began to wonder, "How long can I stand here? . . . What if I freeze to death?" . . . Then, the glory of the morning revisited him. . . . "Do not be afraid. I am with you!" The angel's words! They had been for tonight! When the officers came out at twelve-thirty to check on him, they offered to let him in *if he would deny his God.* He refused! "By three o'clock in the morning, he was dozing on his feet. . . . He had sung. . . . He had prayed for every officer. . . . He had cried out to God for the men in his unit." Suddenly, a voice startled him, "You are to come inside."

When inside, the officer questioned him, "What kind of a person are you that the cold does not bother you?" Vanya answered quietly, "Oh, comrade, I am a person just like you, but I prayed to God and was warm." (From *Vanya,* Myrna Grant: Creation House.)

"The angel of the Lord encampeth round about them that fear him, and delivereth them" (Psalms 34:7). Yes, an angel ministered to Vanya! And isn't it a great consolation to know that the angel of the Lord encamps around you to deliver you! Oh, how this promise, this sure Word of God, frees you to go where He calls you to go, to be what He calls you to be, to do what He calls you to do!

Beloved, if you have not read the book *Vanya* by Myrna Grant, you must. Order it immediately. How it will bless your life! Also you will want to purchase her *Ivan* series (Tyndale House) for your children.

His Thoughts Toward Me:

My Thoughts Toward Him:

August 7

Are you exhausted? Is life wearing you out? To use an old expression, do you feel like you are "spinning your wheels"? Are you very busy? When you slow down and take stock, do you find life rather routine, rather empty? Have you even set certain goals for yourself? Do you find that when these are attained, they don't seem worth the price? Or you may even become weary in trying to meet your goals.

There is a familiar promise in the Word of God that has taken me through many a "wearying situation" so that I have not lost my strength in the task, but rather I have renewed it. Before we share any further, let me quote this promise for you.

"He gives strength to the weary, And to him who lacks might He increases power. Though youths grow weary and tired, And vigorous young men stumble badly, Yet those who wait for the Lord Will gain new strength; They will mount up with wings like eagles, They will run and not get tired, They will walk and not become weary" (Isaiah 40:29–31 NAS).

Here is God's promise to those who become weary, to those who lack might, to those who would faint. It is yours, it is mine to claim, and I can tell you that it is true! It has never failed. However, before you run with this promise, let me share with you the condition that accompanies it.

Those who gain new strength, who mount up with wings like eagles, who run and do not get tired, who walk and do not become weary are those who *wait for the Lord,* who *hope in the Lord.* In wearying situations, there must be a turning to the Lord, a looking to Him who is the Lord of your life. Are your tasks, your goals under His Lordship? Maybe your strength is gone because you have not waited before God or sought His face, His will in your undertaking. Maybe God can't give you strength because you are expending it on things that are dissipating your energies which should be used for Him, for His glory. So when you are weary and no strength comes, be still, get alone with God, wait upon Him to see what He would say to you.

If you are walking under God's leadership, if you are in the place or task of God's appointment and you find yourself weary, needing strength, go to the Father, hope in Him, claim His promise, and soar above all those difficulties with your eagle's wings.

His Thoughts Toward Me:

My Thoughts Toward Him:

August 8

You know the feeling—your heart races, your chest tightens, and panic paralyzes your mind. It comes on you suddenly and unpredictably. It may take a moment for you to realize what has gripped you in its vise, but soon you know that it is fear!

Fear hits all of us at different times. The phone rings in the middle of the night. The doctor says the lump is malignant. Your child runs away from home. All of these, and a thousand other situations, are all fear-producing. They bring on panic. But God's Word states, over and over, that God is the answer for fear. "The Lord is my light and my salvation; Whom shall I fear? The Lord is the defense of my life; Whom shall I dread?" (Psalms 27:1 NAS.)

Practically speaking, how do you cope? How do you handle it

303

all? How do you conquer that paralyzing fear that seems to strike at your most vulnerable point?

The first step to conquering fear is to recognize from where it comes. Second Timothy 1:7 says, "For God hath not given us the spirit of fear; but of power, and of love, and of a sound mind." When fear strikes and you find yourself lacking in power, failing in love, and thinking irrationally, you can be sure the fear is not from God.

The second step, in dealing with fear, is to rid your life of it. As a conscious act of your will, you can deal with that fear. First John 4:18 states, "There is no fear in love; but perfect love casteth out fear. . . ." How does perfect love act? Perfect love has come to know and has believed the love which God has, for God is love and the one who abides in love abides in God, and God abides in him (1 John 4:16). When faced with fear, there must be a conscious turning from the irrational to the rational. You must say, "I know and believe that God loves me and that He is sovereign. Nothing can happen without His permission. This fear is not from God who abides in me. I will not be overwhelmed by paralyzing thoughts. I will put my trust in God." The consequence of this choice is the "casting out," the hurling away of the dread, of the torment of fear. This is the sound mind, a mind under control, that God promises us. This mind is yours for the claiming, for the obedience. Then, with your mind under control, you will be able to act, to react, to move in power, in love in every fear-producing situation. It is a fact. Believe it, act on it, and you'll see results!

I'll share a fantastic, true account of some people who claimed and acted upon this promise in tomorrow's devotion.

His Thoughts Toward Me:

My Thoughts Toward Him:

August 9

The night that the dam broke at Toccoa Falls, Georgia, was a night when fear could have prevailed. The testimony to the world would have been different had not the Word of God been planted earlier in the hearts of those who would be leading characters in the tragic drama that claimed the lives of thirty-nine people, most of them children.

One man's story illustrates the reality of God's Word on fear. "We had less than five minutes' warning before the water struck our trailer. I ran to help get the children together. My wife had already gone to the bedrooms and pulled the sleeping children out of bed. We huddled together in the hall and prayed as the water picked up the trailer and started hurtling it and us down the current. The trailer broke apart and as I tried to pull the children out and put them into a clump of trees that we had bumped into, one of the walls collapsed and I knew my wife and two youngest children were gone. My three oldest children and I were finally able to get out of the flood and to be reunited. Later, while I was sitting by a fireplace in a neighbor's house, I thanked God for His grace and His presence for I felt a deep sense of His nearness to me. I remembered that my wife had spent some time telling the kids to be ready to meet Jesus when they were riding the flood out. I knew the children were ready because they did not scream in panic but each time they were scared by some new thing, they yelled, 'Jesus, Jesus!' " (From *TFC Today*, Evangelical Press Association.)

When you are afraid, what can you do? You can panic, lose control, become paralyzed, or you can say, "What time I am afraid, I will trust in thee" (Psalms 56:3).

When fear comes, where can you run? You can run to the Rock that is higher than you, the One who promised you a refuge in the midst of storms.

Oh, His child, learn well, His promise to you, then run and hide in its folds, "God is our refuge and strength, a very present help in trouble" (Psalms 46:1).

His Thoughts Toward Me:

My Thoughts Toward Him:

August 10

In the midst of great hurt or grievous tragedy, the almost too glibly quoted, "And we know that all things work together for good . . ." becomes a promise that, in our pain, we might tend to deny. Yet, when thoughtfully compared with the sovereign love that spills out of similar promises, we know that the Word of God is true. His promises are yea and amen!

" 'For I know the plans that I have for you,' declares the Lord, 'plans for welfare and not for calamity to give you a future and a hope' " (Jeremiah 29:11 NAS). If we could only see that God does not design our ruin but rather our refinement, we could fall back on this great promise which would become a bed of comfort. Again, from Toccoa Falls, a lesson in trust, in reliance on God's promise is learned.

The sounds of the dam break awoke the Kemp family from their sleep. Thurman Kemp grabbed his nine-year-old son, Morgan, and Dixie, his wife, grabbed seven-year-old Chris. Dixie shares her story. "In an instant, tons of water came hurtling down on us, shattering the roof. The floor beneath us gave way and something hit Chris under his chin. He was pulled away from me but I grabbed him back by the sleeve. Then there was such a force of water that it ripped him out of my grasp and he was gone. . . . I know I won't see Chris again until I reach heaven, and I will never get over missing him . . . but I will not

306

mourn, because I am content to know that God has a plan and my son was part of that plan. Because of his death, others have already found life in Jesus Christ. This is my comfort." (From *TFC Today,* "Beauty for Ashes," Dixie Kemp: Evangelical Press Association.)

Painful? Yes. Hard to handle? Yes. But God has promised, "And we know that all things work together for good to them that love God, to them who are the called according to His purpose" (Romans 8:28). And God's Word is true! You can rest in it. You can rely on it.

His Thoughts Toward Me:

My Thoughts Toward Him:

August 11

Have you ever been in a large house alone at night? Have you ever experienced that sick feeling deep down inside when you believed that you heard footsteps in the hall?

Have you ever been the only one at home over a period of time and received obscene telephone calls late each night? Have you experienced the gut-level panic each time the phone rang after eleven—you knew it would be that voice again!

Recently, the reality of one of our Father's promises to us really struck me as I listened to a tape of Darlene Rose's testimony. Darlene was the first non-native woman into New Guinea. There, she lived among the Boogus People. These were a brutal lot of bandits and pirates who looted the villages and killed at will.

Darlene tells of a time when the Boogus People stabbed to death four of her near neighbors. "Shortly after this event," Darlene says, "I was lying in bed one night half awake, half asleep; I was very aware of noise in the house. I sat up in bed, then I grabbed Mrs. Jaffrey and shook her until she was awake. 'We need to get up and chase the rats out again,' I told her. I moved quickly toward the door. As I opened it into the hall, I saw a man pass by. I stepped into the hall. Next, I realized it was one of the Boogus men. He stopped and raised his black robe to pull out his large knife. Although I do not know why, I began to chase this man down our long hall, through the bathroom, off the back porch, and down the mountainside. When he was joined by other Boogus People, I stopped dead still and thought of what a foolish thing I had just done. But the Lord comforted me and assured me of His protection.

"For the next several nights, we could hear the Boogus People outside of our house. But never again did they try to break into the house!

"After the war was over and I went back into New Guinea, I talked with one of the boys from the Boogus People. I asked him if he had been with them the night that they robbed our house. He dropped his head and answered, 'Yes, and we came back several nights after that, but you always had all those people in white on guard out there.' "

What is the promise that has taken on new meaning and depth for me? It is Psalms 91:10, 11. "There shall no evil befall thee, neither shall any plague come nigh thy dwelling. For he shall give his angels charge over thee, to keep thee in all thy ways." How blessed it is to know that He has given His angels charge over me —over you!

Just think, the next time you are alone at home and hear footsteps in the hall, the next time the phone rings late and that voice comes on the line, you can rest for no evil will befall you, the Lord has given his angels charge over you!

His Thoughts Toward Me:

My Thoughts Toward Him:

August 12

What will it be like when you see Jesus face to face? Suppose God were to take you home today and your labors for Him were ended. Do you know what follows death for the Christian? It is the Judgment Seat of Christ. There, "... 'As I live, says the Lord, every knee shall bow to Me, And every tongue shall give praise to God. So then each one of us shall give account of himself to God' ... For we shall all stand before the judgment-seat of God" (Romans 14:11, 12, 10 NAS).

Did you know this, beloved? I didn't! For several years, I lived as a Christian, thinking that heaven was heaven, that heaven would be the same for all. I had not yet seen that God, in His righteousness, had to distinguish faithfulness and reward it ... for in all ways, He is a just God. His warning to us is, "Watch yourselves, that you might not lose what we have accomplished, but that you may receive a full reward" (2 John 8 NAS). God's promise, on the other hand, is, "Blessed is a man who perseveres under trial; for once he has been approved, he will receive the crown of life, which the Lord has promised to those who love Him" (James 1:12 NAS).

God has promised crowns! Crowns for you, crowns for me! Rewards—not loss, not shame, not embarrassment—but, "Well done, my good and faithful servant, enter thou into the joy of the Lord."

It is yours, it is mine, a promise for the taking if we will only love Him with a love that will *persevere* no matter what the trial, the testing, the temptation.

One day, I had the privilege of talking with Harlan Popov, the author of *Tortured for His Faith.* This precious saint of God lived in man's hell as a prisoner of the Communists for thirteen years. I asked him that day, "What kept you faithful? Was it your knowledge of God's Word? What was it?" He looked at me in the sweetest way, and in his broken English, said, "When you love someone, you'll do anything for him."

Popov's love for his God shall, someday, be rewarded with a crown of life for he persevered under trial. That is God's promise. That is His reward.

Will you so love Him—no matter what?

His Thoughts Toward Me:

My Thoughts Toward Him:

August 13

Ravensbruck! In 1945, when one spoke that word, it was always in a whisper. The horror, the terror, the anguish, the dread it conveyed to so many when spoken aloud was just too much to bear. Ravensbruck was the notorious women's extermination camp of World War II. It was this much-dreaded prison in which Corrie and Betsie ten Boom found themselves.

The women were awakened at 4:00 A.M. They had to line up for roll call at 4:40 A.M. Next, they received their breakfast of a liquid about the color of coffee and a dark slice of bread. Then, the work crews were dispensed for their eleven-hour work day. At the end of their long day, they walked back to the main camp on swollen, aching legs only to stand in line for an hour or longer to get dinner, turnip soup. The women slept on wooden platforms designed for four; they slept with nine or ten on each platform. To add to their discomfort, there were lice and fleas in abundance!

As the two sisters looked about them at their circumstances: the hunger, the cold, the lack of privacy, the brutality of the enemy, the loneliness for home, the sickness, they realized why God had placed them there. There were thousands of terrified, tortured, battered women who desperately needed to be ministered to. God had even preserved their Bible through the inspections! They soon realized, too, that as the world in which they were being engulfed grew stranger and darker, one fact grew increasingly clearer, brighter, truer, and more beautiful; this fact was the truth of the promise of God: "Who shall separate us from the love of Christ? shall tribulation, or distress, or persecution, or famine, or nakedness, or peril, or sword? . . . Nay, in all these things we are more than conquerors through him that loved us" (Romans 8:35, 37).

Corrie relates, ". . . It was not a wish. It was a fact. We knew it, we experienced it minute by minute—poor, hated, hungry. We are more than conquerors! Not 'we shall be.' We are! Life in Ravensbruck took place on two separate levels, mutually impossible. One, the observable, external life, grew every day more horrible. The other, the life we lived with God, grew daily better, truth upon truth, glory upon glory." (From *The Hiding Place,* Corrie ten Boom: Chosen Books.)

Do you find yourself, even now, in a hard situation, a difficult circumstance? Is your walk with your Father growing better daily, truth upon truth, glory upon glory, as a result of your difficulty? Have you stopped and considered His love for you, His child? Have you meditated upon this, His promise to *you?* "Who shall separate us from the love of Christ? shall tribulation, or distress, or persecution, or famine, or nakedness, or peril, or sword? . . . Nay, in all these things we are more than conquerors through Him that loved us." You are more than a conqueror! He has promised it! Will you live in the light of it?

His Thoughts Toward Me:

311

My Thoughts Toward Him:

August 14

" 'And he who overcomes, and he who keeps My deeds until the end, to him I will give authority over the nations; And he shall rule them with a rod of iron, as the vessels of the potter are broken to pieces, as I also have received authority from My Father; and I will give him the morning star' " (Revelation 2:26–28 NAS).

What an awesome promise! Those who overcome, those who keep Christ's deeds until the end will be those who shall, someday, have authority over the nations, actually ruling them with a rod of iron. Can you imagine, we shall rule with Christ over this earth when He returns as King of kings and sets up His kingdom here on earth?

But this is another promise that must be examined carefully for it is directed to those who overcome and to those who keep His deeds. Who are overcomers? The author of Revelation is also the author of 1 John, and it is he who defines overcomers. "For whatsoever is born of God overcometh the world: and this is the victory that overcometh the world, even our faith. Who is he that overcometh the world, but he that believeth that Jesus is the Son of God?" (I John 5:4, 5.)

Overcomers, then, are all believers. They overcome by their faith, by believing God, by taking Him at His Word. Can you imagine someone ruling with Christ who does not believe the Word of God? No! Can you imagine someone ruling apart from the Word of God? Of course, you can! We have seen it in nation after nation! Horrible, isn't it! No absolutes—inconsistencies, vacillation, inequities—man, in his finite, limited wisdom, ruling according to his own convictions and desires.

The second condition for ruling over the nations is that we must keep His deeds, we must do His works. Can you imagine God allowing someone to rule in His Kingdom who refused to do God's deeds, God's works? How inconsistent!

What is God trying to show us? Would you someday rule with Christ? Then, you, as I, must learn to walk in faith, to take God at His Word, to trust in Him. We must learn to persevere, to keep His deeds, to do His works until the end, to not quit, to not faint! God is training you and me, in this life, for the Throne!

His Thoughts Toward Me:

My Thoughts Toward Him:

August 15

When you are caught between a rock and a hard place because of a need in your life, what do you do? Do you try to figure out how you can change things around in order to meet your need? Do you go to a friend and ask for his help? Or do you just tell everyone about your need because you know if you tell enough people that someone will meet your need?

Recently, I heard a godly, godly man tell a story of how he ran to his Father with a need! Dr. P. N. Kurien relates the following story: "I was preaching in the Boston area, and there came a call from Los Angeles to come immediately. I went to the airport to purchase my ticket. I asked the ticket agent for a ticket to Los Angeles. The ticket's price was one hundred and eighty dollars. I pulled out my wallet and counted out ninety dollars. Ninety dollars was all I had! I knew God had called me to go to Los Angeles; I knew God was faithful; I knew He had provided for me to go to Los Angeles before He had ever called me to go. So I asked for a ticket to get me as close to Los Angeles as possible for ninety dollars. I was headed to Kansas City. I got on the airplane. At once, the devil began, 'You are so foolish! You are in a land that flows with milk and honey. You could have asked someone for your fare!'

313

I said, 'Devil, you are a liar; God is faithful!' I opened my Bible at Genesis, and I began to claim the promises of God; I went all the way to Revelation. While I was in Revelation, the plane landed. I got my baggage and went to the lobby to wait on God. I said, 'God, I don't even have money to buy a Coke, but I have enough food on my body to live for a week. When You provide the money I need, I will go to Los Angeles.' As I closed my eyes to continue in prayer, someone touched my shoulder. She said, 'Are you a minister?' 'Yes,' I replied. 'Are you from India?' she questioned. 'Yes,' I answered. 'What are you doing here?' she continued. 'I am ministering the Word of God. I am a pilgrim, a traveler for Jesus,' I said. She said that she had watched me on the plane as I had opened and closed my Bible; God had shown her that I had a need. She handed me one hundred and fifty dollars. It was plenty to get to Los Angeles."

The next time that you are caught "between a rock and a hard place" because of a need in your life, what are you going to do? What would God have you do? Is He not your Father? Then, go to Him and give Him an opportunity to fulfill His promise, ". . . my God shall supply all your need according to his riches in glory by Christ Jesus" (Philippians 4:19).

His Thoughts Toward Me:

My Thoughts Toward Him:

August 16

The professor was so late for class that the men decided he wasn't coming. Since they could not leave the classroom without the order from their officer, one of the men proposed a debate. "We shall debate the question: What is the difference between

Vanya's God and our god (which he claims is the state)?"

The debate was begun by asking Vanya who his God was. His reply came, "My God is almighty and all-powerful—." Before he could continue, a sergeant in the room demanded, "If your God is all-powerful and can do anything, prove it. Let Him get me a leave tomorrow to go home. Then I'll believe in Him."

Vanya prayed in his spirit, "Lord! Can this be from you? Will You be tempted by men? What they ask, is this right, Lord?" Then, the answer of the Lord came to Vanya, "Tell them I will do this." Vanya boldly announced before the entire group, "Tomorrow the Lord says you will go home on leave."

That night, Vanya found the sergeant lying on his bunk wide awake. The officer could not sleep; it all seemed absurd to him; he half-believed that he might get a leave! Vanya whispered to the sergeant, "There is much to talk to you about. Since you will become a believer tomorrow, there are many things I must tell you." As the morning broke, they discovered they had talked all night. Sergeant Prokhorov could only say, "My head is so full of ideas, I may never sleep again."

At the sound of the bugle, Vanya found out that the night delivery of bread had not arrived; he had to leave for Kerch right away in order to get bread for breakfast. He was disappointed; he had wanted to be around when Prokhorov got his leave!

When Vanya pulled back into the camp about an hour later, truck loaded with bread, he was surprised that there was a small commotion near the garages where the truck was to be parked. As he jumped down from the truck, excited shouts pierced the air, "Comrade Prokhorov has left on leave! Prokhorov has gone! We have been waiting to tell you!"(From *Vanya*.)

"And this is the confidence that we have in him, that, if we ask any thing according to his will, he heareth us: And if we know that he hear us, whatsoever we ask, we know that we have the petitions that we desired of him" (1 John 5:14, 15). What a promise! If we ask anything according to His will. He will grant it! May you, may I, learn to hear His voice and to pray according to His will!

His Thoughts Toward Me:

My Thoughts Toward Him:

August 17

Do your past sins stalk the corridors of your mind? When night falls and all is quiet, do their creaking memories cause you to toss and turn? Do you cry, "My sins are ever before me"? "That's all under the blood; I am a new creation in Christ Jesus now, it has been forgiven, forgotten." These are the truths you rehearse, the promises of God. Yet still the thoughts come again and again. Are these things to torment you all the days of your life?

Ezekiel 33:16 says, "None of his sins that he hath committed shall be mentioned unto him: he hath done that which is lawful and right; he shall surely live." If your sins are forgiven—if God remembers them no more—then, why are they being mentioned to you? That is a good question and one that you need an answer to if you are being tormented by past sins and failures. Either you are not believing God's promises, or you have not fulfilled the conditions of this promise in Ezekiel, or the devil is attacking you. Let's take it one step at a time. If God says you are forgiven and tells you what He has done with your sins, then your response must be one of faith—taking God at His Word and walking in the light of it. However, there could be a possibility that you have not fulfilled God's conditions in Ezekiel 33 and, therefore, your sins are being mentioned to you to get you to deal with them properly. Listen to the conditions of Ezekiel 33:14, 15, "Again, when I say unto the wicked, Thou shalt surely die; if he turn from his sin, and do that which is lawful and right; If the wicked restore the pledge, give again that he had robbed, walk in the statutes of life, without committing iniquity; he shall surely live, he shall not die." If your sins are not to be mentioned to you, then you must make full restitution, even though your sins are confessed and are under the blood. You must pay back what you have stolen; you must return what you have taken as earnest money (restore the pledge); you must walk according to God's statutes and flee from sin. If you do not make restitution to the one you have offended, how can you expect him to receive you as forgiven by God when you have not made things right with him? Does he know that you have confessed your sin to God, bringing it under the blood as promised in 1 John 1:9, "If we confess our sins, he is faithful and just to forgive us our sins, and to cleanse us from all unrighteousness"? No! And even if you tell him that you are right with God, does that make you right with him whom you have offended? Of course not! It is for this reason that God, in Leviticus, as He instructs His people about their trespass offerings, also instructs them to make full restitution (Leviticus 6).

When you are right with man and right with God, then your sins shall not be mentioned to you! If they are, it will be the enemy and you can tell the liar to leave!

His Thoughts Toward Me:

My Thoughts Toward Him:

August 18

"The Lord is near to the brokenhearted, And saves those who are crushed in spirit" (Psalms 34:18 NAS).

What a glorious principle and promise we see repeated over and over throughout Scripture. David, the man after God's own heart, knew the agony of the brokenhearted and the inner pain of the

317

crushed in spirit. Yet, David could affirm with his whole being, "It is good for me that I have been afflicted. . . ."

A. W. Tozer has said, "It is doubtful whether God can bless a man greatly until He has hurt him deeply." Abraham could never have known the depths of God's feeling until he was asked to slay his son, his only son. Moses, called to lead the Jews out of Egypt, was only useable after he had been exiled, crushed, and broken on the backside of the desert. In the crushing, in the breaking, there was God.

Saints, throughout the ages, have repeated the same story, "When I was at my lowest, when I thought my heart would literally break, there was God. I wouldn't take anything for that communion."

Algerius was a young man who lived and died as a Christian during the dark days of the Inquisition. This young man, only a teenager, was imprisoned. He was, eventually, burned at the stake for his faith in Jesus Christ. His words from prison indicate that he knew the reality of the promise, "The Lord is near to the broken-hearted, And saves those who are crushed in spirit."

Algerius wrote, "In a state of misery I have had very great delight. In a lonely corner I have had most glorious company, and in the severest bond, great rest. All these things, my fellow brethren in Jesus Christ, the gracious hand of God has given me. Behold, he who at first was far from me is now with me, and the one I knew but a little, I now see clearly. . . . He comforts me, he fills me with joy, he drives from me bitterness and renews within me strength and sweetness. . . ." (From *Faithful Unto Death*, Myron S. Augsburger: Word Books.)

How is it with you? Is your heart broken? Is your spirit crushed? Do you find reality in the promises of God?

His Thoughts Toward Me:

My Thoughts Toward Him:

August 19

What is it that will hold you, that will keep you, that will sustain you, that will maintain you when you could let your mind go, when you feel like you could literally burst at the seams?

Roger Ingvalson, who was an American pilot during the Vietnam War, was flying his plane one day at 500 miles an hour when he had to bail out over Communist-held territory. Two miracles occurred at this point. First, he had no broken bones. Secondly, he was captured immediately by the Viet Cong soldiers which prevented the furious natives from killing him.

Roger was kept in a bamboo-cage prison until he could be taken to a prison camp. Once he arrived at the prison, ". . . he was put into a cell four feet wide for twenty months of solitary confinement. During these months, he saw no one except the guard. He was given a toothbrush and every forty-five days he was given a bar of soap. Despite the cold winter, he was not given socks to go with his sandal-type shoes (made of tire casings). He had mosquito netting to place over his wooden-board bed, but he could have no paper and pen and no books except those containing Communist propaganda."

You might ask, "How could he survive? Who could endure living in a box alone? Is he sane today?"

Roger says, "Actually, I kept from going crazy by knowing that God was with me. I wasn't alone. I had a cellmate named Jesus Christ." (From *The Inside Story,* Nell Mohney: The Upper Room.)

"Thou wilt keep him in perfect peace, whose mind is stayed on thee: because he trusteth in thee" (Isaiah 26:3).

It is a promise, a surety that you can have His peace no matter what—if you meet His condition. This promise will hold you, will keep you, will sustain you, will maintain you *if* you will keep your mind stayed upon Him.

His Thoughts Toward Me:

My Thoughts Toward Him:

August 20

It was 1947, and Corrie ten Boom had come from Holland to defeated Germany with the message that God forgives. She had just related to a group of desperate, despairing people the truth that when a man confesses his sins, God removes them as far as the east is from the west and that He remembers them no more! She so wanted the truth of forgiveness to become *reality* to this embittered people. As she finished her message, she looked up and saw him walking toward her. It all came rushing back! She could see him in uniform standing in the large, stark room where the women's dresses and shoes were in a pile on the floor. She could vividly recall the utter disgrace of walking naked past this very man. She could see, in her mind's eye, the frail, pain-riddled form ahead of her in the line of naked women; it was her dear sister, Betsie.

Her thoughts were shattered by his voice, "A fine message. How good it is to know that *all* of my sins are forgiven." He could not be saying that to her! Maybe he did not remember that she was at Ravensbruck where he had been her guard. But he continued, "I was a guard at Ravensbruck, but since then I have become a Christian." She did not want to hear what the man was saying. Yet, he continued, "I know God has forgiven me, and I want to hear from your own lips that you, too, forgive me." Then, he extended his hand to her. Her mind raced, "Does he not remember that Betsie died in that place? How does he expect me to erase her slow, terrible death simply by his asking me to do so?"

Then, in the midst of her inner battle, the Lord reminded her that He, every day, had to forgive her of her sin. She knew that the promise that God would forgive her sin was conditional. The condition for her sins to continually be forgiven by her heavenly Father was that she, too, must continually forgive others. She knew this truth; she had just taught it! Now, could she handle the *reality* of the truth which she knew so well, which she had just taught? She knew that forgiveness was an act of the will, and she knew her will could function regardless of her feelings.

Mechanically, she held her hand out toward her prison guard. Their hands met. "I forgive you, brother, with all of my heart." She could truly say that to this man. The former guard and the former prisoner stood for a moment, hands clasped. Corrie ten Boom says of that moment, "I had never known God's love so deeply as I did then."

"For if ye forgive men their trespasses, your heavenly Father will also forgive you: But if ye forgive not men their trespasses, neither will your Father forgive your trespasses" (Matthew 6:14, 15). God has promised His children forgiveness of sin, but it is a conditional promise. Is forgiveness a truth you know in your head, or is it a *reality* in your life? Is there anyone you need to forgive? Remember, your Father forgives your sins—*if* you forgive the sins of others.

His Thoughts Toward Me:

My Thoughts Toward Him:

August 21

"Let us hold fast the confession of our hope without wavering, for He who promised is faithful; ... Therefore, do not throw away your confidence, which has a great reward. For you have need of endurance, so that when you have done the will of God, you may receive what was promised" (Hebrews 10:23, 35, 36 NAS).

It is tempting sometimes to pick a promise out of the Word and to run with it. We claim it. We declare it to be "a word from the Lord." We stand on it. Yet, we fail to read the "fine print." And when the promise does not come to pass in our life, we feel that God has failed. What is the problem? Is it the Word of God? No! God, who promises, is always faithful; "If we believe not, yet he abideth faithful: he cannot deny himself" (2 Timothy 2:13). The most practical illustration of this truth hits home with all of us when we consider the common problem of dieting! We pray, "Lord, I want to lose weight. I know that undisciplined eating does not glorify You as Lord of this temple. Just fill me with Your Holy Spirit, and I will have the fruit of the Spirit which is love, joy, peace, longsuffering, meekness, self-control. Ah, self-control." The next day, you still weigh two hundred pounds, and the next, and the next. And you continue to eat according to your appetite, your desires, your rationalizations. Then, you go back to the Lord, "But, Lord, You said I have self-control. Why haven't I lost weight?"

The Lord answers in that still, small, easy-to-recognize voice, "My child, have you done My will? Have you exercised that self-control? Have you worked out that which I have worked in (Philippians 2:12, 13)? Have you dieted?"

You see, the Lord is faithful. The promise has not failed. You, beloved, must do the will of God. Then, you will receive the promise!

For the past two weeks, I have been on a very restricted diet. For the last three days, I have been sorely tempted not to endure. When I got on the scales today, I received the promise! I had endured! I had done the will of God. I had lost eight pounds.

Our God is so practical. His promises are so real! If we cannot appropriate His promises now, what will it take to teach us to endure that we might receive His promise?

Our problem is that we do not see that we have need of endurance so that *when we have done the will of God* we may receive the promise.

His Thoughts Toward Me:

My Thoughts Toward Him:

August 22

"... Resist the devil, and he will flee from you" (James 4:7). This is such a powerful promise! But you will notice that it involves a direct act of the will on your part. Resist, literally stand against, the devil—it's a call for action on your part.

"The incident happened on a warm Saturday afternoon in a downtown women's dress shop. In the fitting room, Carol was glancing in the mirror at the first dress she had tried on. Suddenly, the curtains opened and a tall man stood in the doorway. Just a few minutes earlier he had taken money from the store's cash register and prevented the salesladies from running to the street for help by demanding that they remove their clothes and lie under the counter.... 'Take off your clothes and lie on the floor,' he shouted. Assuming that this meant he intended to rape her, she replied, 'No. I will not.'

" 'In that moment,' says Carol, 'he looked like the personification of Satan himself. His eyes were filled with anger, hatred, and fear, as he pushed me to the floor and kicked me several times. As I struggled to get up, he brandished a pocket knife, saying, 'Either you do what I say or I'll kill you.' Instantly, Carol was aware that the power within her (Jesus Christ) was far greater than the power of evil which she faced. So, in a calm, clear voice she said, 'In the name of Jesus Christ, I command that you leave me alone.'

"Immediately the man's hand, holding the knife, dropped to his side. The look of anger and hatred changed to one of bewilderment as he backed toward the door. Carol was able then to run past him. . . ."

Carol was ready to act upon the promise that she knew her Father had given to her. She did resist the devil who was driving this poor, lost soul to destruction. How exciting to see the power of a promise when it is proclaimed!

Thomas Mitchell, the man who had invaded Carol's dressing room that day, in a letter to her, says of that moment when Carol confronted him with this promise of God, ". . . when I was attempting to rob that dress shop, you made a statement to me that literally, physically sent chills down my back. You said, 'In the name of Jesus Christ, I command you to leave me alone.' At that very moment, Mrs. Clark, I felt the presence of something very strong and powerful. My physical being was unable to function temporarily.

"For months on end, after the incident, I would lay awake at night and would not be able to sleep for thinking of the statement you made to me while looking me right in my eyes, and the 'feeling' that came over me at that time. At times I would even get cold chills thinking of it." (From *The Inside Story*, by Nell Mohney.)

Oh, how you should praise your Father for the potency of His promise that will protect you from the evil one—if you will act!

His Thoughts Toward Me:

My Thoughts Toward Him:

August 23

Have you ever been really burdened to pray for someone? You may have prayed for several weeks or maybe even a month. Then, because you had not seen any concrete results, you may have just stopped praying.

God tells us, ". . . The effectual fervent prayer of a righteous man availeth much" (James 5:16).

After Carol Clark's experience with Thomas Mitchell, she began to pray for him daily. Carol continued to pray for Thomas until the night I called her. Then, the dam gave way; the strain of laboring prayer caused tears of release to pour forth. A few days later, Thomas Mitchell's letter arrived. In his letter to Carol, after his salvation, Thomas said, "After I escaped from jail last August, my life was so messed up and I had so little hope for the future, I took a loaded pistol and almost took my life. After I was recaptured, I was placed in an isolation cell by myself. Nothing was in that cell except a small New Testament, and once again, Mrs. Clark, I would find myself thinking of you and also the feeling I had at that time. I don't remember what day or night it was, but I started to read that New Testament.

"In the second week of January of this year, I was saved by the Lord, and dedicated the remainder of my life to Jesus Christ to do with as He sees fit.

". . . I realize that I may never again be a free man for the rest of my life, in a physical sense, but my soul will forever be free."

Praise God that His promises are yea and amen and that the effectual fervent prayer of a righteous man does avail much!

Because Carol was willing to fervently pray for Thomas Mitchell, he is, in actuality, a free man! He will never again be driven by the enemy of his soul. He is free to serve Jesus Christ!

Is there one for whom you have prayed, yet you have stopped because of discouragement?

Oh, you must cling to that promise; don't faint; confess your unbelief; it is the *effectual fervent* prayer of a righteous man that availeth much!

Remember, beloved, there is a condition to this promise. It is the righteous man that God hears. The righteous are those who are walking "rightly," in accordance with the truths of God's Word and in accordance with God's will.

His Thoughts Toward Me:

My Thoughts Toward Him:

August 24

Have you ever heard someone say, "God told me . . ."? Did you want to ask them, "But how did God tell you? How did you know it was God speaking to you?" You wanted to ask, but like me, in times past, you did not want them to know that you were not familiar with the voice of the Lord. To ask such a question, you felt, would make you look less spiritual. So, you kept your mouth shut, all the while longing to know how to have such an intimate relationship with God as to have Him speak to you. I understand! I have been there!

Now, here is a promise from God, not just for the Israelites but for every child of God: "And your ears will hear a word behind you, 'This is the way, walk in it . . .' " (Isaiah 30:21 NAS). If you are like me, you want to know His will; you long to walk in His way; but you need to know His way. That is the question! "How can I know that this is God's way?"

Knowing God's way, dear one, takes time. It takes practice to learn to distinguish the voice of God. Oh, it would be so easy if God would always speak in big, dramatic, hard-to-miss ways, wouldn't it? But that is not God's usual, normal way of speaking.

Elijah wanted to hear what God had to say to him. He was depressed, afraid for his life and, apparently, exhausted. As he sought to hear God's Word, ". . . a great and powerful wind tore the mountains apart and shattered the rocks before the Lord, but the Lord was not in the wind. After the wind there was an earthquake, but the Lord was not in the earthquake. After the earthquake came a fire, but the Lord was not in the fire. And after the fire came a gentle whisper. When Elijah heard it, he pulled his cloak over his face and went out and stood at the mouth of the cave. Then a voice said to him . . ." (1 Kings 19: 11–13 NIV).

God usually speaks in a still, small voice, in words not audible but in conversations of the soul, in word-thoughts. The secret of hearing God's voice is getting to know God's voice. Then, when conversations of the soul take place, you will soon learn to distinguish His voice from your voice or the voice of the enemy. How can you learn to distinguish God's voice?

First, you need to take time to be still before Him, to know that He is God. Then, tell God you want to be led by His Spirit, to commune with Him, to hear so that you might obey. Beloved, we have you write down **His Thoughts Toward Me** so that you might learn the habit of meditating on His truth and then hearing what God wants to say to you personally. When God speaks, He will *never* speak contrary to His written Word. "And your ears will hear a word behind you, 'This is the way, walk in it. . . .' "

His Thoughts Toward Me:

My Thoughts Toward Him:

August 25

"The guard shoved me with the end of his gun through the first cell block and across the courtyard to the next cell block. Then, I saw that they were opening a door in this cell block for me. As I looked above the door, some person had written there, 'This Person Must Die.' I was in death row!

"I was pushed into a six-by-six-foot cell. I dropped to my knees. I was watching the end of the key. I thought, 'When that key turns a complete revolution, I am locked in death row.' I sat there on the cell floor. Suddenly, I realized I was singing. It was a song I had learned as a little girl in Sunday school: 'Fear not little flock whatever your lot, He enters all rooms the doors being shut. He never forsakes. He's never gone. So count on His presence from darkness to dawn.' They locked me in death row, but they could not lock my Lord out! He was there with me! Sometimes, the glory of His presence filled that cell, and I would open my eyes and think I must be in glory."

How would you react if you were locked in death row? Would you panic? Would you cry out to God, "Where are You? Have You forsaken me?" What was it about Darlene Rose that assured her of His presence there with her in that cell?

There *were* times in Darlene's life when she cried out to God thinking that He had forsaken her. But, in all of those times, her Father would gently remind her of His promise to her, ". . . I will never leave thee, nor forsake thee. So that we may boldly say, The Lord is my helper, and I will not fear what man shall do unto me" (Hebrews 13:5, 6).

Do you feel that the Lord has forsaken you, abandoned you in your time of need? Are you His child? Would God abandon His child? No! As the perfect Father, He cannot—He will not. "But Zion said, The Lord hath forsaken me, and my Lord hath forgotten me. Can a woman forget her sucking child, that she should not have compassion on the son of her womb? yea, they may forget, yet will I not forget thee. Behold, I have graven thee upon the palms of my hands; . . ." (Isaiah 49:14–16). Quit pouting; run back to Him; fling yourself into your Father's arms; ask to see His hands.

His Thoughts Toward Me:

My Thoughts Toward Him:

August 26

Sometimes, promises of God don't seem like promises at all for they do not bring blessing but rather judgment! Listen, carefully, to the Word of the Lord, those of you who have declared Christ as your Savior and Lord.

" 'You have today declared the Lord to be your God, and that you would walk in His ways and keep His statutes, His commandments and His ordinances, and listen to His voice. And the Lord has today declared you to be His people, a treasured possession, as He promised you, and that you should keep all His commandments; and that He shall set you high above all nations which He has made, for praise, fame, and honor; and that you shall be a consecrated people to the Lord your God, as He has spoken' " (Deuteronomy 26:17–19 NAS).

" 'Now it shall be, if you will diligently obey the Lord your God, being careful to do all His commandments which I command you today, the Lord your God will set you high above all the nations of the earth. And all these blessings shall come upon you and overtake you, if you will obey the Lord your God. . . . And the Lord shall make you the head and not the tail, and you only shall be above, and you shall not be underneath, if you will listen to the commandments of the Lord your God, which I charge you today, to observe them carefully, and do not turn aside from any of the words which I command you today, to the right or to the left, to go after other gods to serve them. But it shall come about, if you will not obey the Lord your God, to observe to do all His commandments and His statutes which I charge you today, that all these curses shall come upon you and overtake you'" (Deuteronomy 28:1, 2, 13–15 NAS).

God's promise is nothing short of blessing for obedience, cursing for disobedience. Somehow, Christians have been greatly deceived; we think that as long as we are saved it really doesn't matter if we disobey: Christ will forgive us, all we have to do is confess our sin. But, beloved, that is not true! ". . . it is time for judgment to begin with the household of God . . ." (1 Peter 4:17 NAS). ". . . when we are judged, we are disciplined by the Lord in order that we may not be condemned along with the world" (1 Corinthians 11:32 NAS).

Why do I stress the "cursing" aspect of this promise rather than blessing? Look around you at the typical Christian. Is he holy? Is he careful to keep God's commandments with *all* of his heart and *all* of his soul?

As you meditate on God's thoughts toward you today, ask Him to show you any way in which you have turned aside from His words. Remember—blessing for obedience, cursing for disobedience.

His Thoughts Toward Me:

My Thoughts Toward Him:

August 27

"And every one that hath forsaken houses, or brethren, or sisters, or father, or mother, or wife, or children, or lands, for my name's sake, shall receive an hundredfold, and shall inherit everlasting life" (Matthew 19:29).

Rees Howells relates the following story, "The Holy Ghost said to us, 'You must prove to me that you love the souls of the Africans who are to live for eternity, more than you love your own son.'" God said to the Howells as they prayed about taking their son with them to the mission field, 'If you give Samuel up, you can never claim him again.'

"A few weeks before the time for us to leave I was sent for by my uncle. . . . He asked if we were taking Samuel with us. I said, 'No.' 'Where is he going to?' I said I don't know. 'Well,' he said, 'he is to come here.'

"Although we had given him up in our hearts, when the Lord actually opened a door for him, it was like pulling one's heart to pieces. . . . When I arrived at home, my wife was playing with him. . . . for a time I could not break the news; but I took courage and told her. The scene that followed can better be imagined than described, and we were glad we only had to go through it once in a lifetime.

"The morning came when my sister arrived to fetch him. . . . The devil was not quiet. . . . He said I was the hardest man in the world to give my little child up. . . . Samuel's going out was more than emptying the house; he emptied our hearts, too. When I came home that night, I asked my wife, 'How did you get through?' She said she went out into the garden and wept, and thought to herself, 'I have been singing that hymn many a time: But we never can prove the delights of His love, until all on the altar we lay; and this morning I have to prove it.' But then the Lord told me, 'Measure it with Calvary.' And with those words she came through. In praying together afterwards, the Lord showed me the reward. He said to us, 'For everything you give up for Me, there is the hundredfold; and on this you claim 10,000 souls in Africa,' and we believed it."

God gave Rees and his wife their ten thousand souls! But God rewarded their obedience in still a far greater way. One day, Rees met a ship from America that had docked. Off of that ship, stepped Samuel Rees Howells. He had come to labor with his father in Africa. (From *Rees Howells Intercessor,* Norman Grubb: Christian Literature Crusade.)

Has God called you to forsake your home, your brother, your

sister, your father, your mother, your wife, your child, your land? Will you go? Will you obey? Will you prove the delights of His love by laying all on the altar, even those dearest to you? God has promised you a hundredfold in return.

His Thoughts Toward Me:

My Thoughts Toward Him:

August 28

"If I have to put up with this another day, I think I'll scream!" Does this sound familiar? You may have phrased it differently, but still the sentiment was the same. Self-pity, disbelief, murmuring, and complaining are all reflected in an attitude of, "I'm the only one who has ever had to endure this kind of trial."

When the tension builds and panic rises in your heart, God has a word to cool and to calm. He gently whispers that you are experiencing only those trials and temptations to which mankind is continually subjected. He then reassures that, although your temptation may seem heavy, it will not break you; you will be able to cope; there will be a way to escape.

What is your trial? What testing or temptation looms as a spector over your sanity and threatens your peace?

Are you in a marriage that keeps you in a daily hell? Do you have a rebellious child for whom you have despaired? Is your body decaying with an unconquerable disease? Beloved, these trials are common to man; they are normal, but the sovereign God of the Universe has a promise for you in the midst of it all: "No temptation has overtaken you but such as is common to man: and God is faithful, who will not allow you to be tempted beyond what you

332

are able; but with the temptation will provide the way to escape also, that you may be able to endure it" (1 Corinthians 10:13 NAS).

Don't defeat yourself by entertaining self-pity and indulging in murmuring and complaining, rather take God at His Word. You're in a normal situation; you can endure; you will escape! Act, walk, and speak in the light of this promise!

His Thoughts Toward Me:

My Thoughts Toward Him:

August 29

"If you abide in Me, and My words abide in you, ask whatever you wish, and it shall be done for you" (John 15:7 NAS).

The Christian life is to be a life of total dependence, a life cast upon God. We should go to Him for *all* that we need. "For from Him and through Him and to Him are all things . . ." (Romans 11:36 NAS). And He has told us that ". . . apart from Me you can do nothing" (John 15:5 NAS). God must be the supplier of all. What we need, we must seek from Him. We are to ask, God is to answer. That is His promise.

But this promise is another that is conditional. If we expect to receive the promise, we must meet the conditions. The condition of asking and receiving is abiding. That abiding is twofold. We are to abide in Him; His words are to abide in us. Oh, beloved, how often do we violate the Word of God by taking His Word and prostituting it for our own sensual desires never considering that we are to preserve its purity? We are so guilty of wanting what we can get from God without considering that which God desires. Ours is to be a life of abiding, of dwelling in Him, in His presence, in His life until we become so one with Him that His life fills and permeates every cell of our being. Abiding not only is defined as "dwelling in" but, also, "remaining in," to be "at home in." If we are to ask with the expectation of receiving, we must abide in Him. When we do abide, we will ask in accordance with God's will, God's desire, God's character.

The second condition for asking and receiving is that God's Word would abide *in* us, dwell *in* us, remain *in* us, be at home *in* us. God's Word is a revelation of Himself, His ways, His will, His purpose. To miss part of His Word, to neglect the whole counsel of God, is to be deficient or lacking in a complete knowledge of all that God esteems needful for man. What we need to know in order to be perfect unto every good work of life is set down for us in His Word. His Word has been inspired (God-breathed), set down on paper, and carefully guarded so that "no jot or tittle" has been altered. These are words of life; ". . . the words that I have spoken to you are spirit and are life" (John 6:63 NAS).

Therefore, if we expect to have the blessed privilege of asking and receiving, we must see that His words abide in us. We must esteem His words more precious than our necessary food.

How does the Word of God fare with you, dear child of God? Is it important enough that it takes the place of priority in your life? If not, then how can you expect to run to God and ask for whatever you wish?

His Thoughts Toward Me:

My Thoughts Toward Him:

August 30

After being transported to Ravensbruck, they slept in an open field for three nights until they were processed. Then, the prisoners were herded into barracks.

As Betsie and Corrie were looking over their new surroundings, suddenly, something pinched Corrie's leg. "Fleas!" she cried. "Betsie, the place is swarming with them! . . . How can we live in such a place!"

Betsie's calm, quiet reply was not directed to Corrie but to her heavenly Father, "Show us. Show us." Her voice held excitement as she now addressed her sister, "He's given us the answer before we asked, as He always does! In the Bible this morning. Where was it? Read that part again!"

Corrie slipped the Bible from its hiding place and turned to that morning's devotional passage, "Rejoice always, pray constantly, give thanks in all circumstances; for this is the will of God in Christ Jesus."

"That is it Corrie! That's His answer. 'Give thanks in all circumstances!' That's what we can do. We can start right now to thank God for every single thing about this new barracks."

"Such as?" Corrie questioned.

"Such as being assigned here together. Such as what you're holding in your hands (their Bible) . . ." And on and on Betsie went enumerating every detail of their circumstances. But, then, Betsie came to the fleas!

Corrie's immediate response escaped her lips, "Betsie, there's no way even God can make me grateful for a flea."

Weeks later, they were to discover that the fleas had been the only reason that their barracks was not checked or supervised at night! This lack of supervision had lent itself to the nightly Bible studies and prayer meetings in which God allowed Betsie and Corrie to minister to the women. (From *The Hiding Place*.)

God had it planned all the time. All they had to do was to look beyond the fleas to the promises of God. You can never get around it, " . . . God causes all things to work together for good to those who love God, to those who are called according to His purpose. For whom He foreknew, He also predestined to become conformed to the image of His Son . . ." (Romans 8:28, 29 NAS).

Not only did God use the fleas to keep out the guards, He also used them to conform Corrie into His image. That is why so many love her, they see Jesus! Was it worth it?

His Thoughts Toward Me:

My Thoughts Toward Him:

August 31

"If you have run with footmen and they have tired you out, Then how can you compete with horses? If you fall down in a land of peace, How will you do in the thicket of the Jordan?" (Jeremiah 12:5 NAS.)

If you have trouble trusting or believing God in the good times, what will it be like for you in the hard times?

Darlene Rose, a missionary to New Guinea for forty-two years, was able to stand and to withstand physical and emotional abuse that broke other godly people. Before the age of twenty-six, she had been a missionary, a prisoner of war, and a widow. She had been accosted by bandits, deprived of food, and beaten black and blue by the Japanese. When her prison ordeal was over, she weighed sixty pounds, had a head full of lice, and came back to the states with absolutely nothing. Yet, she had competed with horsemen, and she had won! The source of her strength was the Word of God.

As a child, Darlene had memorized volumes of Scripture. When she became a missionary, in the midst of great testing, the Holy Spirit brought those verses to her remembrance. "In the thicket of Jordan," she did well.

In a voice, sweetened by suffering and still tender with tears thirty-six years after the fact, Darlene Rose tells how it was when she received the news that her pioneer-missionary husband had died three months earlier in a prison camp to the north of where she was interred.

"I walked away. I turned to the only One I know to turn to, and I said, 'God.' He answered me immediately, 'My child, did I not tell you that when you pass through the waters, I will be with you, and through the rivers, they will not overflow you, that when you walk through the fire, you will not be scorched, nor will the flame burn you?' " (Isaiah 43:2.)

She was in her early twenties. She was in prison. She was alone. She had lost the husband she loved so dearly, yet she had the promise of God that when she passed through the waters He would be there.

Beloved, are you running with footmen and fainting? Are you passing through waters and drowning? There is a day coming when the competition will be with horses. The race will be faster. The waters will be deeper. The promises of God will be what will hold you. Do you know them? Could God speak to you in the still small voice of His Word?

His Thoughts Toward Me:

My Thoughts Toward Him:

SEPTEMBER

September 1

There are 4 billion people in this world that God created; 3 billion of them are without the gospel. Without the gospel, these people will perish; without the gospel, these 3 billion will spend eternity in the lake of fire where the worm dies not and the fire is not quenched. This is the truth that God's Word teaches. Yet, do you think we Christians really believe that all men without Christ, who have never heard of Jesus, will really perish without a second chance? Does that not seem too hard, too difficult to believe? So what have we done? In some way or another, we have rationalized it away—"God is a God of love," "God just wouldn't do that. He couldn't." "God would never send a man to hell when there has been no way for him to know, to hear." "Surely. . . ."

And so what do we do? Instead of believing God, we try to rationalize away the veracity, the truth of God's Word. We want to get rid of our responsibility, yet there resounds in the chambers of our heart that incessant echo of the voice of God, "Go ye into all the world . . . you shall be witnesses of me . . . whatever you ask shall be given unto you."

Look at your legs, look at your feet, they were given to you that you might go. If you cannot go on your feet, go on your knees. Where your feet cannot take you, let your knees take you.

Listen to yourself as you talk to your friends, to your family, on the telephone, in the world. *Shall your lips speak to man of everything, of everyone, of anything, of anyone, but God? Shall they speak to everyone all day long but not to God?* Why have a mouth? So that you might speak to men of God and to God of men. Then, speak, witness, pray, intercede.

Intercede? How? About what? A world of 4 billion people! How can I go to God for them on my knees when I know nothing about them? How can I speak to God about them except in general, vague terms, in boring, insipid prayers?

Oh, beloved, there is a way, if you will only avail yourself of it, if you will only make the effort. God has made a way through one of His servants who has written the book, *Operation World*. This magnificent piece of work will take you to every country in the world; there it will lay before you the needs of the people; it will provide you with specific needs of real people; your prayers shall become more than hollow words. Will you not take it and go? There are 3 billion *real* people that need you in order that they might know Him. Why don't you order the book and use it as your prayer guides: *Operation World* by P. J. Johnstone, STL Publications, P. O. Box 148, Midland Park, New Jersey 07432.

His Thoughts Toward Me:

My Thoughts Toward Him:

September 2

Go. This is the command of the Lord. Where? To the world, for it is the world that is on God's heart. There are others besides you and me, there are multitudes for whom Christ died. The minute you and I receive the light of the gospel is the minute that you and I become responsible for those who are still in darkness.

Oh, beloved, granted, we cannot all go physically, but we can go *on our knees.* Let me tell you a true story that will woo you to your knees. It is a story told by Dr. P. N. Kurien of India.

An American girl by the name of Eleanor was ministering the gospel in a village in Nepal with an Indian girl. All of a sudden, she was taken captive by the wicked chief of the village. He dragged her away and imprisoned her in the basement of his house. Normally, the basements of homes in Nepal were for the cattle, but even they were gone. The empty hole became her prison. Only the four walls heard her cry, "O God, help me!" It was 9 o'clock in the morning.

Seven or eight hundred miles away, Dr. Kurien's sister, Mary, came flying into his room at 9 o'clock in the morning. "Oh, brother, come and pray . . . Eleanor needs me . . . she is crying . . . come down from your chair . . . kneel down . . . pray . . . Eleanor is crying in Nepal, and she needs help."

After several hours of prayer, they rose from their knees; but still the burden was not lifted. Mary said, "I am going home and pray some more."

And pray she did until 10 o'clock that night! Soon after 10 o'clock, Mary joyously returned to her brother's home. "Eleanor is free now; she is safe." How did Mary know? The burden was gone!

One week later, a letter came from Eleanor telling the story of God's deliverance. The wicked village chief had returned that night to the basement of his home, drunk, intent on raping Eleanor. As he entered the basement, he was stopped by a strong man, a man who threatened his life. The chief turned to Eleanor, "I would show you what I can do to you, but this strong man standing here says he will kill me if I touch you. Get out from here!"

As she groped her way out of the dark basement and walked along the streets of Nepal, she knew she had been saved by the angel of the Lord.

Go? What if we do not go, at least on our knees? What will happen to the Eleanors who are ministering in the most difficult of circumstances?

"O God, teach me this ministry of intercession."

His Thoughts Toward Me:

My Thoughts Toward Him:

September 3

Have you ever knelt to pray and had the fleeting thought, "Why should I pray; God is going to do what He wants to do anyway?" Maybe you have never voiced it, but it is an interesting thought. Why does God, who is sovereign, who by His very word can speak worlds into being, depend on little, finite, frail humans to release His power in this world? We see all through Scripture that He waits on man. He pleads with man; He urges man to exercise the privilege that he has as a believer, the privilege to pray.

In Ezekiel 22:30, 31, when Israel was in as sad a state as the United States is today, God said, "And I sought for a man among them, that should make up the hedge, and stand in the gap before me for the land, that I should not destroy it: but I found none. Therefore have I poured out my indignation upon them; I have consumed them with the fire of my wrath: their own way have I recompensed upon their heads." Picture it, beloved: God looking, searching, seeking for one man to pray, to intercede so that He wouldn't have to carry out the just judgment of His wrath on the nation. It boggles the mind, doesn't it? If the principle of this lesson were ever seared upon our hearts, just think of its ramifications, not only for the nation of Israel but for the world today!

Have you ever thought of the great needs of a vast land like India, for instance, and wondered why God didn't raise up more missionaries and support workers to go in and meet the needs of those people? To understand this perplexing question, we must consider Matthew 9:38, "Pray ye therefore the Lord of the harvest, that he will send forth labourers into his harvest." Strange, isn't it? He is the Lord of the harvest; He is the Source behind the harvest; any laborers that would go out to the harvest would be His laborers; yet He tells us to pray—to ask Him, the Lord God of the universe, to send His laborers into His own harvest.

What a powerful principle, if we would only believe it, apply it,

341

and do it. If it is important enough that God will not move in His own fields until we ask Him, then it must be important enough for us to take Him at His Word and to pray. Will you covenant before God this month, to pray for His world?

Could it be that God is waiting for you, for me, to pray before He sends His laborers to India or any place else to reap the fields that are overripe for harvest? It seems like it, doesn't it? Otherwise, if God were going to do it anyway, why would He tell us to pray?

His Thoughts Toward Me:

My Thoughts Toward Him:

September 4

Watchman Nee, in his outstanding book, *The Prayer Ministry of the Church* (Christian Fellowship Publishers, Inc.), makes a statement that has been rich food for thought for me as I've been learning more about prayer.

"God will not execute anything independently; whatever He does today He does with the cooperation of the church. She is that through which God manifests Himself. . . .

"This whole matter can be likened to the flow of water in one's house. Though the water tank of the Water Supply Company is huge, its flow is limited to the diameter of the water pipe in one's house. If a person wishes to have more flow of water, he will need to enlarge his water pipe."

You know, beloved, it may well be that we are a constricted water pipe. When God's desire is for His power to come forth like a flood, our fragile, half-faith prayers have been holding back His life-giving power to a mere trickle, which is insufficient to truly water a parched land.

When I see the bones of a small child protruding through leathery, malnourished skin, with his abdomen distended to the size of a volleyball; when I see a mother hold that child, rock him, and kiss him as I have my own; when I realize that the little one will probably die shortly, never having known the sweet peace of sleep with a full tummy, my heart is wrenched within me. But, for the grace of God, that could be me holding my son, without God, without hope, knowing nothing of the Bread of Heaven, knowing nothing of the God who will care for His own. It could be me, sitting in darkness never having seen the great Light.

Something deep within me says, *Why, Lord? Why are people sitting in darkness?* And if I am honest and if I listen carefully, I'll receive the answer I don't really want to hear: "Because you, the church, have not obeyed my command to go and to make disciples. Because you have not prayed; you have not interceded; you have not sacrificed your time, your interest, your comfort, your money, or yourself to work My work!"

As one translator has paraphrased Matthew 7:7, "Ask, I ask you to ask; seek, I entreat you to seek; knock, I urge you to knock."

The Lord is limited to our obedience and to our prayers. He cannot move through one who will not obey, through one who will not pray. He has made you in His image; He has given you a free will. Therefore, the choice is yours; yet, the consequence is God's. Never forget that truth, beloved.

So what will you do? Will you obey? Will you pray?

His Thoughts Toward Me:

My Thoughts Toward Him:

September 5

If you and I are going to pray effectively for God's world, we must have fuel for prayer. How can we pray for lands, for people that we do not even know exist? Well, my cry has been, "God, show me how to pray, what to pray. Let me know their burdens, their needs."

An outstanding book, *Operation World,* has been part of God's answer to my cry. I have never seen such a comprehensive work on the peoples of the world and their needs. The author, P. J. Johnstone, has been so led of God in this book that the countries come alive; the needs he shares are current needs; the information he provides is up-to-date. When you use this excellent tool and its data in prayer, you truly feel that you have been used of God in ministering to that particular country for which you prayed. The country and its people become real. This awareness is then used of God to provoke you to intercede at other times. For example, I never even knew the Kurdish people existed. If I had ever heard of their existence, believe me, it didn't even register! But while using *Operation World* in praying for Iran, I learned of the Kurds. The Kurds live in the northwest section of Iran; they are, for the most part, a people forgotten in missionary efforts. One night as I was watching a news special on the crisis in Iran, they mentioned the Kurds; I saw the faces of those for whom I had prayed! I knew them; I knew their awful plight; I understood a little of why they live in darkness.

The prophet Ezekiel, was commissioned by God to go to the children of Israel, a nation that had rebelled against God, that had transgressed His covenant. But before Ezekiel could go and be an adequate spokesman for God, he had to sit where they sat; he did not have to partake of their rebellion, but he needed to be fully informed of their state. Thus we read that the Spirit of the Lord, ". . . lifted me up, and took me away, and I went in bitterness, in the heat of my spirit; but the hand of the Lord was strong upon me. Then I came to them of the captivity . . . and I sat where they sat, and remained there astonished among them seven days" (Ezekiel 3:14, 15). It was at this time that God showed Ezekiel his responsibility as a watchman on the tower.

Oh, beloved, let us pray today for one another. Pray that God will so speak to us through this devotional and through the book *Operation World,* that we might sit where others sit and be astonished to the point of intercession. Pray that we might see our responsibility and that we will not turn from our responsibility to become watchmen in prayer.

His Thoughts Toward Me:

My Thoughts Toward Him:

September 6

Looking at a spinning globe of this world doesn't do a great deal to provoke my interest. It's all too big, too massive, too far beyond my comprehension and experience. Introduce me to the people of a country! Tell me how they live, where they hurt, and what their dreams are, then you have me. People respond to people. I am convinced that until we really see the world as people, we will never really have a true burden to pray.

In his book, *The Prayer Ministry of the Church,* Watchman Nee says, "Whenever God wishes to do a thing He will place a burden upon a brother, a sister, or the whole church." The prayer ministry of the church "is God telling the church what He wishes to do so that the church on earth can then pray it out. Such prayer is not asking God to do what we want to do, but asking Him to do what He wants to do. Oh, let us see that the church is to declare on earth the will of God in heaven." The Scripture says in Romans 8:26, 27 that "we know not what we should pray for as we ought: but the Spirit itself maketh intercession . . . for the saints according to the will of God."

As you pray this month, including this devotional guide in your prayer time, ask God to show you His will and to lay His burden upon your heart for individuals of countries who desperately need prayer. I'll be sharing with you several individuals' experiences, and I'll give you various needs of countries as I know them. But God is waiting for you to ask Him what you should pray, what you should do. The Spirit is waiting to intercede through you on the behalf of those who are perishing and those who are laboring for their salvation. As you finish reading each day's devotional, ask God to lay His burden upon your heart. Then, record that burden under **His Thoughts Toward Me.** How will God speak to you? He will impress upon your mind a certain thought or a certain need. As that thought or need comes to your mind, pray it back to God. But you may say, "How do I know it is not the devil speaking to me or just a thought of my own?" That's a good question. As you get ready to seek to know God's burden, rebuke the enemy; ". . . resist the devil and he will flee from you" (James 4:7). Claim the covering of Jesus' blood that is yours as a believer and ask God to guide you into all truth. Tell God you will do His will. Ask God for His wisdom, then believe that He will give it to you. Then, pray that God will work. He has to move in response to prayer; He said He would. "And this is the confidence that we have in him, that, if we ask any thing according to his will, he heareth us: And if we know that he hear us, whatsoever we ask, we know that we have the petitions that we desired of him" (1 John 5:14, 15).

His Thoughts Toward Me:

My Thoughts Toward Him:

September 7

In early February of 1973, there was a new wave of killings in Kampala. Idi Amin and his advisors had drawn up a list of two thousand prominent Ugandans and scheduled them for execution.

"The pattern of arrests was almost always the same. The Nubian assassins, dressed in their 'uniform' of sunglasses, flowered shirts and bell-bottom trousers, entered an office or home in broad daylight. They called out the name of their victim and humiliated him in front of employees and family members. The terrified man was then tied up and dragged away to the trunk of a waiting automobile. His screams for help meant nothing. No one dared to lend a hand.

"Only a few victims were killed immediately. The rest were taken to prison and tortured to death by the most sadistic methods. Some were cut with bayonets and made to eat their own flesh. Some were thrown into deep pits of freezing water and fed only enough for a slow, agonizing death. Others had arms, legs, or genitals cut off and were left in the dirt to bleed to death. Women were raped and their reproductive organs set on fire. In one prison, Naguru College, men were tricked into killing each other. A prisoner was given a heavy hammer and promised freedom if he would smash in the head of another. When after many blows his fellow prisoner died, another prisoner was brought to the courtyard, with the same promise of freedom, to kill the 'executioner' with the same hammer. The chain went on for hours. Soldiers and Nubians gathered in the courtyard to watch the bloody spectacle. They drank gin, and laughed and joked. When the killings were quick and merciful, they cursed in anger. When they were slow and torturous, they rejoiced. Their hearts were knit together in a terrible celebration of death and suffering." (From *A Distant Grief*, F. Kefa Sempangi: Regal [GL] Publications.)

Where was the church in the midst of all this? What meetings of prayer were called? What tears were shed in God's stead as those created in His image desecrated that which God had made (Genesis 9:5, 6)? What days and nights were spent in fasting on behalf of those living under Idi Amin's regime?

I hang my head in shame for I heard about Amin's reign

of terror, but not once did I talk to God about it. Oh, beloved, may I, may you, learn to go to our knees with the burdens of others! May we learn to take our eyes off of ourselves and to put them upon those who are truly suffering for the sake of the gospel!

His Thoughts Toward Me:

My Thoughts Toward Him:

September 8

"But my God shall supply all your need according to His riches in glory by Christ Jesus" (Philippians 4:19).

Why do people turn to witchcraft, to chants, to ceremonies, to witchdoctors? The gods they worship seem so mean, so hard to please, so easily angered. Why do they allow witchdoctors to mutilate their bodies? Why do they give their very best to their gods? Can they not see the deception of it all? Why is it so hard for those caught in this darkness to turn to the Light of the world? What does it take to make men see that light is better than darkness? They must see a Christianity that works! They must see Christianity work, not just in church but in the nitty-gritty of life, where "the rubber meets the road."

Kefa Sempangi's compelling, absorbing, and gripping book, *A Distant Grief,* so clearly shows us the need for a wholistic gospel, a gospel that meets the needs of the whole man. Christianity involves the body, soul, and spirit of a man, and it will minister to all of man's needs (1 Thessalonians 5:23).

In the midst of all of Amin's atrocities, Kefa realized that Christ's redemption was wholistic; therefore, the message he preached must speak to the whole of human existence. The people had to see that in every point where Satan was strong the redemptive power of Jesus Christ was stronger. If the devil could supply their needs, could not God? This truth was brought home to Kefa in a number of ways. One means was through a vono bed.

The elders of the church were meeting; all of a sudden they heard her insistent knock. There she stood. "She was barefoot and her hair was not properly combed, but she seemed totally unashamed in our presence. I could see in her face the erosions of extreme poverty and I also saw that while she was almost defeated, she had not yet given up." She had come to ask them to pray. "I am so much in need of a vono bed and there is no way I can get one. God has to provide for me." A vono bed was nothing but a mattress with springs. The request seemed "especially strange now, when our whole country was in serious trouble. Surely we had more pressing things to think about. One of the elders promised that we would pray for the bed and, after many reassurances, the woman left the room. I immediately forgot her request and was surprised when, during our prayer time, several elders remembered the woman's mattress."

The following Sunday there was a great commotion in the church. "Her face was shining and she was almost dancing with excitement. 'The Kingdom of God has come! Jesus has given me a vono bed.'"

Oh, beloved, when you pray, pray for the whole person.

His Thoughts Toward Me:

My Thoughts Toward Him:

September 9

After the Easter service, Kefa pushed his way through the crowd to the vestry. He was too tired to notice that five men followed him, until he heard the door close behind him. He turned to see five rifles pointed at his face. Kefa relates the following story. "Although I had never seen any of them before, I recognized them immediately. They were the secret police of the State Research Bureau—Amin's Nubian Assassins.

"For a long moment no one said anything. Then the tallest man, obviously the leader, spoke, 'We are going to kill you,' he said. 'If you have something to say, say it before you die.' He spoke quietly but his face was twisted with hatred.

"I could only stare at him . . . My mouth felt heavy and my limbs began to shake.

"From far away I heard a voice, and I was astonished to realize that it was my own. 'I do not need to plead my own cause,' I heard myself saying. 'I am a dead man already. My life is dead and hidden in Christ. It is your lives that are in danger, you are dead in your sins. I will pray to God that after you have killed me, He will spare you from eternal destruction.' "

The tall one took a step toward Kefa and then stepped back. His face was changed. He lowered his weapon and motioned the others to do the same.

" 'Will you pray for us now?' " The gunman spoke loudly and impatiently. Kefa had them bow their heads and close their eyes. He still did not trust them, so he prayed with his eyes open expecting to be killed any minute.

In deep fear and with great simplicity, he prayed that the men would be forgiven and would not perish in their sin.

As the prayer ended, the tall one spoke first. " 'You have helped us,' he said, 'and we will help you. We will speak to the rest of our company and they will leave you alone.' "

Too shocked to reply, Kefa watched as they filed out of the room. The tall one started to go but turned to ask, " 'I saw widows and orphans in your congregation,' he said. 'I saw them singing and giving praise. Why are they happy when death is so near?' " It was difficult for Kefa to speak but he answered him, " 'Because they are loved by God. He has given them life, and will give life to those they loved, because they died in Him.' " The tall one shook his head in perplexity and walked out the door.

Oh, beloved, let us pray for all those under persecution in the world. Pray that they will stand firm in one spirit, with one mind striving together for the faith of the gospel and that they will in no way be alarmed by their opponents, which is a sign of destruction to others but of salvation to those who believe (Philippians 1:27, 28).

His Thoughts Toward Me:

My Thoughts Toward Him:

September 10

What breaks the power of the enemy in lands where men are caught in the web of fear to be devoured piecemeal by Satan and all his demonic host? Kefa, in his book, *A Distant Grief,* speaks to this question so well. I believe that as we read his insights, we will get new light into prayer for those in darkness.

"I began to listen with new ears to the prayers of petitions and thanksgiving coming from members of the congregation. We had a long sharing-time before each service . . . In both verbal and written testimonies, the same message was repeated over and over again. God was meeting the needs of His children. He was blessing them not only with spiritual gifts and physical healings but with increased crops, fair prices, reconciled relationships, and pregnancies.

"These testimonies caused me to read again the story of Jesus' earthly ministry. The more I read and reflected on His life, the more I saw the naked inadequacy of my own approach to the gospel. I met people at my point of expertise, my knowledge of the Scripture. Christ met people at their point of need. . . .

"This realization brought with it a new understanding of the importance of witchcraft among my people. We were, I knew, a needy people. We could not afford to be answered in abstractions. We could not afford to separate doctrine and life. . . .

"A religion is true if it works, if it meets all the needs of the people. A religion that speaks only to man's soul and not to his body is not true. Africans make no distinction between the spiritual and the physical. The spiritual is not a category among categories but the lens through which all of life is viewed. A tribesman from my village knows that cutting a tree, climbing a mountain, making a fire, planting a garden and bowing before the gods are all religious acts. He lives in the presence of the gods, and he knows that without intervention from them, without baraka, a blessing, there is nothing. There is no coffee harvest, no wood for the fire, no wife, no children.

"For such people, people who live their lives in daily hardship at the edge of nothingness, witchcraft is not a set of beliefs. It is a way of life. I have never heard a poor or needy person discuss the philosophy of witchcraft. Their only concern is what it does, that it works . . . They were not looking for a world view but for a power to transform their lives. If Christianity could not help them, the witch doctor could."

Oh, beloved, let us pray diligently for those who know Christ, that their lives would be constant testimonies to the power of the gospel so that those in darkness might see that ". . . greater is He (Christ) that is in you (Christian) than he (Satan) that is in the world" (1 John 4:4).

His Thoughts Toward Me:

My Thoughts Toward Him:

September 11

The needs around the world are so different and yet so similar. If you could fly from country to country, you would find people in every imaginable state of need. The physical needs of people are of as much importance to the Father as their spiritual needs. While believers in Russia may have sufficient food, they must contend with the satanic oppression of a Communist government. While believers in Guatemala have more freedom to worship, they must concentrate on how to obtain every morsel of food their family eats. A tremendous little book recently published in Guatemala is entitled *Unto the Least of These* (Guatemala Evangelical Ministries). It is written by two missionaries who work in different sections of Guatemala, David Beam and Frank Waggoner. I cannot tell you how my heart was gripped for the people and their great need as I read their book. I want to take two days and share with you some of their stories; I know that these will draw you to your knees.

His world was an apple box in a doorway. His name was Rene, and he was only two years old. Rene lived in Guatemala with his poor, illiterate, nineteen-year-old mother who tried desperately to earn enough money to feed him. Little Rene was so quiet, so weak that no one ever noticed him. No one seemed to know that the baby in the box was starving to death.

A young missionary from the United States finally saw Rene and tried, in his inexperience, to do something to help him and his mother. But help came too late. The day he arrived with a check for them, the mother met him at the door with tear-stained cheeks, " 'You came too late,' she said. 'We buried Rene yesterday.' "

As I was reading about Rene, my spirit groaned within me; tears welled up in my eyes; then I was stopped short with the words, "Rene was born in Guatemala. He lived in darkness. He died in despairing hunger. Will he meet you at the judgment?"

I was moved to pray, "O God, move on our fattened, sluggish hearts to reach out to people in the world. The wasted food in our garbage cans could feed so many Renes in countries all over the globe. But, Father, please don't give us the burden without showing us the way. Teach us to pray for these people, but may we never fall into the 'bless-you-brother-and-be-warmed' syndrome. Show us, burden us, break us until we give, until we go, until their children become as our children in our compassion and in our love. O God, forgive us, teach us, touch us—for Jesus' sake.''

His Thoughts Toward Me:

My Thoughts Toward Him:

September 12

" 'Mister, can you help me?'

" 'Maybe some other time.'

"We kept walking. Finally, we came to the church site and we set the lumber down. Then I turned around. I stared into the stubbly face of the drunken man. He reeked of liquor.

" 'Mister, I want to show you something.'

"Before I could say anything, he began to peel his shirt off over his head. I stood watching a scant three feet away. Around his midriff he had wrapped a cloth of sorts, which he began to untie with unsteady hands. As he weaved, the cloth fell, so did drops of awful, green liquid.

"My eyes grew large as I watched the trembling hands remove the packed newspapers from his midriff. The children, too, were silent and absorbed in the real-life drama. Finally, he removed the third paper pack, and, to my horror, I watched a green part of his intestines plop out of a gaping hole and into his cracked and dirty hand . . .

"I looked at the tears forming in the corners of his reddened eyes.

"Now, it was my own voice that shook. All I could think to say was, 'You need Jesus. He's the only one that can help you.'

"He lowered his head and said, 'I know.'

"Suddenly, it seemed the man was no longer a drunken bum. Rather, he was my brother, and my heart went out to him. No longer was he sick and repulsive. He was one of God's children . . . one whom God was not willing should perish.

"I held my Bible open and read John 3:16.

" 'Do you want to believe in Jesus?'

"He nodded his head and we prayed.

" 'My doctor friend is coming tomorrow. Will you return?' I asked.

"He said, 'Yes.'

"He didn't . . .

"Until almost a year later, he was still drunk. He still wore a dirty bandage. WHY? He was injured in the earthquake. His wound never healed. He took to drinking. He makes money by revealing his entrails and begging.

"Jesus still loves him." (From *Unto the Least of These*.)

Jesus still loves him, but how discouraging it is to see those who will never heal because they turn away from the Source of all life.

David Beam and Frank Waggoner are missionaries in Guatemala who, faced with great needs and provided with little help, "keep on keeping on" despite the failures. Beloved, pray that their hearts might be refreshed in Christ as they labor in the vineyard to which God has called them.

His Thoughts Toward Me:

My Thoughts Toward Him:

September 13

In *Operation World,* P. J. Johnstone says that Germany's "spiritual decline has been one of the tragedies of history. The rise of humanism and destructive criticism of the Bible enfeebled the churches, and opened the door to militarism and Hitler's Nazi tyranny with its war and massacres."

O America, may we take note! Beware! Have we not, too, been enfeebled in the church by the rise of humanism and destructive criticism? Are we not in our selfish, hedonistic, self-centered pursuits opening the door to government control?

Where was the church in Germany when all this began to happen? Did they not see the storm clouds forming? Did they stand in the gap, did they intercede? Or did they sleep? Did they think that God would never let anyone like Hitler take over? Many read *Mein Kampf* and said, "Insane . . . impossible." But did they go to their knees and ask God how to pray? And when they saw some of Hitler's tactics as laid out in *Mein Kampf* come to pass, did they besiege God's throne? Did they carry on with business as usual, or did they call the church to weep, fast, and pray?

"In 1945 the survivors of the German resistance met at Stuttgart with representatives from sister churches in other countries which had suffered mightily at the hands of the Nazis, to proclaim a 'confession of guilt.' They implored God's forgiveness that they had not prayed more faithfully, believed more intensely, witnessed more courageously, and loved more devotedly. The Germans, as new leaders of the Evangelical Church in Germany, confessed their solidarity with the guilt of the German nation for crimes against humanity." (From *By Their Blood,* James and Marti Hefley: Mott Media.)

Apparently, they realized that because they had not been true to God and to His commandments, they could not say with Paul, "Therefore I testify to you this day, that I am innocent of the blood of all men" (Acts 20:26 NAS).

Beloved, pray for those in Germany who truly know the Lord Jesus Christ. "The Theological Seminaries in the universities teach the humanistic neo-orthodox theology that cripples any evangelistic urge, or cultivation of a simple child-like faith in the Lord Jesus and His Word." (From *Operation World,* P. J. Johnstone: STL Publications.)

As God once ignited the souls of John Huss, Martin Luther, and others, ask Him to ignite the souls of today's believers that they would go forth proclaiming the gospel in all boldness and without compromise. Then, pray that a great sense of emptiness will come upon the German people, and that they will, in turn, be more receptive to the gospel.

And, beloved, when you pray, pray that the Christians in America will awaken lest they, too, have to sign a confession of guilt with bloody hands.

His Thoughts Toward Me:

My Thoughts Toward Him:

September 14

If you are like me, when you think of mission fields, you immediately envision huts and savages; or you may think of people bowing down to foreign, weird-looking gods with several extra arms or legs or a big, fat tummy; maybe you see people walking on fire, casting spells, or climbing a tower of sharp swords.

When we think of the more Christian countries, our minds will usually take us to Europe, that civilized continent that multitudes long to visit. There, they desire to parade through galleries that house the art treasures of the world, to sit at sidewalk cafes and hear the latest gossip of the jet set sunning in Cannes, to stand in awe as their eyes caress the magnificent altars and domes of great cathedrals bearing images of the Christian saints of the ages.

But is Europe as Christian as it seems? Free Europe is a continent that is, for the most part, bereft of true Christianity. For instance, there is France.

France is one of the world's more important mission fields today. It is reckoned that over 40 million French people have no real understanding of the true gospel and no connection with a church though most are baptized Roman Catholics. The powerful influence of the Communist party and the dabbling of many in occult practices are symptomatic of the need. We need to pray that the present freedom to evangelize may be used to the full to bring many to a saving knowledge of Jesus Christ. There are many unreached peoples and areas in France. Only about 1,500 of France's 38,000 communes (towns, villages, etc.) have a permanent evangelical witness. There is a great need for Christian workers. There are estimated to be 1,360 full-time evangelical Christian workers in the country, one worker for every 40,000 people. Pray for the raising up of spiritual men of God for the ministry.

Oh, beloved, pray especially for those in France who think they are all right because of their church membership, for those who have a showing of zeal for God but who know nothing of the power of His presence. Surely, these are a stumbling block to those who have fully shed any covering of a religious nature and who openly and blatantly deny the existence of God, heaven, or hell. A church that professes to know God but denies His reality by ungodly living becomes an object of scorn rather than a thorn of conviction. Pray for those who "in vain . . . worship me, teaching for doctrines the commandments of men. For laying aside the commandment of God, ye hold the tradition of men . . ." (Mark 7:7, 8). When you pray, pray for the state of our churches in America also! (The points for prayer are from *Operation World.*)

His Thoughts Toward Me:

My Thoughts Toward Him:

September 15

Can you imagine standing in your city and watching men and women being killed by having nails driven into their eyes? This is what happened in the village of Ba-Jeuba when the Chinese became enraged at twenty-four parents who would not send their children to their Chinese Communist schools. The same inhabitants of that village were also forced to witness the crucifixion of twenty-five of the village's wealthy people. This is Chinese Communism.

In 1951, the Bamboo Curtain fell shutting out the world and shutting in the Christians. "It is estimated that fifty million people were liquidated by the Communists after they took power . . . many Christians would have been in that number. There were very few Bibles left in China as many were destroyed by the Red Guards in the cultural revolution."

Now, the closed door to China has been opened. This open door is an answer to prayer. Now, how are we to intercede for the work in China?

First, we must intercede for Trans World Radio, OMS (Oriental Missionary Society) and other sound missionary endeavors as they go, once again, through God's open door into China. Pray that God will greatly anoint these works and provide the funds and workers necessary to do this work.

Secondly, we must pray that the church will learn a great lesson from their predecessor's work in that land. At one time, the gospel had been preached in nearly every part of China. As a result, there were many churches. However, although a great missionary work had been done in that land, there were weaknesses. There were too many non-evangelical works. There was too much emphasis put on institutional work and not enough on evangelism; nor was there enough emphasis on the training of leaders or the teaching of believers. As a result, the church was not adequately prepared for the Communist holocaust that swept over them. Therefore, we need to ask God to cause His people to thoroughly equip and train believers in the Word of God.

Thirdly, we need to pray for the people of China. Nearly 600 million Chinese have never known anything but Communistic Atheism. For nearly all, life is a drab and purposeless struggle, a constant revolution, and it holds much fear and insecurity and no hope for the future. More and more young people are looking for a deeper meaning to life than Communism offers. Pray that believers in China will lose their fear of Communism that would keep them from preaching the gospel. Pray that they will ". . . fear not them which kill the body, but are not able to kill the soul; but rather fear him which is able to destroy both soul and body . . ." (Matthew 10:28). (The quotation and the points for prayer are from *Operation World.*)

His Thoughts Toward Me:

My Thoughts Toward Him:

September 16

Stories coming out of China about the Christian church are just beginning to surface. Although silenced and kept away from the gaze of the world for over thirty years, the hearty seed of the church planted by the likes of Hudson Taylor and John and Betty Stam continue to grow and even to flourish.

No other word than *delightful* can describe this incident that has occurred in the last few months in China.

The two Americans looked strangely big and out of place in the small worship service that was being held in a dark, back room in China. All through the service, as the two men listened to the wizened, little, old pastor, a man behind them kept poking them and lightly pulling at their shirts.

The two Americans were with a mission organization, and they had traveled worldwide. They were recent arrivals in China, and they had managed to smuggle in 150 Bibles. Caught up with the sights and sounds of the recently unveiled jewel of the China mainland, they had given little thought as to how they would distribute the Bibles.

As the service came to a close, the poking and pulling became more intense. At the last "Amen," the Americans turned to see what their "assailant" wanted. A small Chinese man bowed politely and told them, "I live 400 miles inland. I have come here today because the Lord told me that I would receive Bibles. Are you the ones who have the Bibles?"

Springs of joy flowed in their breasts as the Americans were able to say, "Yes, we have brought your Bibles. . . ."

Have you ever noticed, beloved, how precious the Word becomes in lands where persecution and tyranny reign? Can you say that the Word of God is priceless to you, so priceless that you would go 400 miles to receive a copy? Are you esteeming the words of the Book more precious than your necessary food?

In our land of freedom and plenty, there is an abundance of Bibles. If our land becomes a land dominated by a godless, persecuting government, how dear will a Bible be to you then?

I thank God, and I never want to become ungrateful, for His ready supply of His Word and for the freedom with which we may read and study it. As you wait on the Lord today, pray for Bible couriers to be raised up to take the Word into mainland China. Also, thank God for His good hand which has so freely provided us with His Word.

His Thoughts Toward Me:

My Thoughts Toward Him:

September 17

As the world seems to shrink, we become more and more aware that what touches the other side of the world will eventually touch us. The following story is a true account of a Cambodian family who managed to escape the holocaust in their country. This is just a very small part of the whole tragic saga of their lives.

The two small Cambodian children clung to each other and began to pull back. Urged by their teacher to catch up with the other children who were taking a hike in the Tennessee woods, the two who lagged behind began to cry. At first, they whimpered; soon their whines turned to hysteria; they fell to the ground screaming and holding on to the underbrush. Their teacher, in dismay, called off the hike and returned the children to their home where she found out the reason for the hysterical response of the two. Their father had owned his own business in Cambodia. Because he was a member of the working middle-class, their family had been forced to escape from the Khemer Rouge, the revolutionary Communist government which took over the once peaceful nation. To reach safety, the family was forced to survive a horrifying ordeal in the forests along the border between Cambodia and Thailand. Walking by night to evade detection and surviving on berries, leaves, and pond water, they had known ultimate horror. When overcome by thirst, they had discovered a pond; as they stooped to drink, they saw the putrid flesh and smelled the foul odor of rotting corpses in the water. To the small children, the forest, any forest, held terror.

Beloved, can you possibly imagine an entire country being forced into slave labor—a country with no money, no private possessions, no private property? And can you imagine a land where all of the educated, the military, the teachers, and the professing Christians have been killed? It is unthinkable, isn't it? Well, it has happened in Cambodia in the last five years. One million Cambodian people have been murdered by the government, and 60,000 have gratefully escaped, leaving all that they possessed behind them. Today, a few Christians are scattered throughout the country, but they have no fellowship, no Bibles, and no leadership from older believers in the faith. I can't begin to think how horribly lonesome that would be.

This is much like the holocaust of the Jews that Hitler so methodically carried out forty years ago. The outcry from Americans and Christians was weak then. Again, today, the outcry and aid offered to Cambodia is weak. Aid is coming, for the most part, through organizations with Socialists at the helm. The Socialists are concerned! Where are the Christians? Are you concerned? Will you do what you can? Will you pray? God forgive us for letting others show more concern than we.

His Thoughts Toward Me:

My Thoughts Toward Him:

September 18

Jeannie and David are friends of ours who spent last summer as missionaries in eastern Europe. When they returned to us last fall, they were excited as they related the story of a man named Hans who is from an eastern European country. They had only been in the country a few short hours when the strangeness of it all struck them; they had seen no one smiling. As they had walked down the village streets and sat in the cafe, there were no smiles anywhere.

And then Hans came "accidentally" into their lives. He, too, wore the same, tired, sad expression that all the other eastern Europeans had worn on their pale, lifeless faces. Hans had been a college professor; but when he could no longer support the

Communist regime, he was fired. Now, dressed in shabby clothing, he was open to the gospel they had come to deliver. They moved from place to place as they walked with him; their every move was watched. Finally, in his apartment, as the two Americans led him step by step, Hans was born again. Later, as they drove away, he leaned out over his small balcony waving *... and smiling.* He had found the Source of all joy, the Lord Jesus Christ.

During the months since they left him, each letter they have received from him has been increasingly open, increasingly free, as Hans has affirmed his faith and has made written confessions of the work which the Lord has begun in him. At first, he wrote in "code," but as his faith has grown, his boldness has grown. Truly, the Lord has a witness in that darkened land.

Six centuries ago, John Huss became the first of a long line of believers persecuted and martyred for their faith in eastern Europe. Hans is just one of many who have come to know the Lord Jesus in a personal way since the persecutions intensified in 1973. I am always bowed low when I hear of believers springing from fertile fields made red with the blood of martyrs. While the harvest of believers has been good, there are so many Christian leaders and pastors who are imprisoned and persecuted for their faith. Paul, at least, was able to preach while he was imprisoned. These precious brothers are forbidden to even speak of the things of Christ, and they suffer constant harassment and intimidation. I believe, my precious prayer partners, that we need, above all, to stand, in prayer, against discouragement in the lives of these dear brothers. Our united prayer for them today should be that the God of all grace, who has called them unto His eternal glory by Christ Jesus, after they have suffered awhile, would make them perfect, established, strengthened, and settled (1 Peter 5:10). I pray that for them. I pray that for me. How about you?

His Thoughts Toward Me:

My Thoughts Toward Him:

September 19

Great Britain—the home of Wycliffe, Whitfield, Wesley, Carey, Hudson Taylor, George Mueller, and many others who were used of God to awaken the hearts of men and nations to the reality of the Lord Jesus Christ.

Great Britain, a land of great spiritual need, a land that is being enveloped in the darkness of its own sin. "The nation has lost the sense of mission that made it one of the greatest moral and spiritual forces in modern history. The decline of true Christianity and the rise of the permissive society are characteristic of the age. There are now laws that permit homosexuality, witchcraft and abortion. The rise in the crime rate, immorality and the use of drugs is alarming."

What is the problem? How can we pray for England? I believe that the moral barometer of a country clearly indicates the pressure brought to bear by the Christian community. Are we not the salt of the earth, that which stops the spread of corruption? "... but if the salt have lost his savour, wherewith shall it be salted? it is thenceforth good for nothing, but to be cast out, and to be trodden under foot of men" (Matthew 5:13).

Pray for the church in Great Britain; despite growth, there are serious weaknesses found among Evangelicals. One major weakness is that there exists a lack of Bible teaching and personal study of the Scriptures which has resulted in the average believer being hazy on doctrine, shallow in evangelism, and undiscerning of error among those who claim to base their teaching on God's Word. Also, there is an increase in worldliness and, therefore, little real concern for world evangelism or the support of the missionary enterprise in prayer and giving. Another weakness found among the Evangelicals is that they are allowing divisions among themselves. They are being divided by denominational loyalty, ecumenism, neo-Pentecostalism, action on social issues, and the bitter

Calvinist-Arminian dispute; all of these "issues" damage the unity of believers and hinder their witness to the world outside.

Oh, beloved, pray much for these, your brothers and sisters. Ask God to give them a hunger and thirst for righteousness' sake; ask Him to set their hearts ablaze for those who are perishing; ask our Father to unite them and cause them to march across their land as a mighty army for His glory!

And, as you pray for these, meditate upon these weaknesses of the church in Great Britain. Do these weaknesses bring to your mind, to your heart, another part of the body of Christ which suffers from the same ills? Yes, pray for us; pray for His body in America. Ask God to work in our lives as He works in the lives of the saints in Great Britain! (The quotation and the points for prayer are from *Operation World*.)

His Thoughts Toward Me:

My Thoughts Toward Him:

September 20

"How then shall they call on him in whom they have not believed? and how shall they believe in him of whom they have not heard? and how shall they hear without a preacher" (Romans 10:14)?

The word came; for over two weeks, our trainees at Reach Out prayed that God would protect the Bibles and carry them into the country. Bibles were being floated down a river into the country of Albania. Albania is Europe's most closed and least evangelized land. Apart from floating Bibles downriver, Christian radio broadcasts are the only way, at present, to get the gospel into the land. How we need to pray that God will raise up more believers in the

West who are fluent in Albanian and who can help the brother who prepares programs for Trans World Radio for transmission from Monaco. There are five programs beamed into Albania each week. Pray that these messages will go into the land under the protection and anointing of God's Spirit.

Extraordinary measures have been taken in this land to suppress every vestige of religion. On every tombstone in the land, a red star has been painted over the cross. Over 2,000 churches, convents, mosques, and other religious institutions have been utterly destroyed. When people in Albania speak of time, they refer to the "second century before our era," never the "second century before Christ."

In the book, *Tomorrow You Die*, Reona Peterson tells of how God called her to Albania. When all was said, it was impossible; God could not have called her to go to Albania. There was no way to enter the country but God showed her how to go into Albania! She went in with tour groups. She had been duly warned to remain with the group at all times. She tells of how she escaped from her group one day to sit and talk with the children. "I began to mention names they would know: Lenin, Marx, Hoxha, Scanderberg. Then, pointing to the heavens, I said, 'Jesus.' There was no recognition, just a puzzled look on their faces as they shook their heads. It was hard to keep back the tears; 65 percent of the present population know nothing other than communism."

". . . faith comes from hearing, and hearing by the word of Christ" (Romans 10:17 NAS). Oh, beloved, pray that those in Albania might hear!

His Thoughts Toward Me:

My Thoughts Toward Him:

September 21

When we pray, we must keep in mind that, many times, God does permit His saints to suffer. Romans 8:35–39, however, assures us that whatever befalls us, we are more than conquerors. No calamity will ever separate us from His love!

"Who shall separate us from the love of Christ? shall tribulation, or distress, or persecution, or famine, or nakedness, or peril, or sword? As it is written, For thy sake we are killed all the day long; we are accounted as sheep for the slaughter. Nay, in all these things we are more than conquerors through him that loved us. For I am persuaded, that neither death, nor life, nor angels, nor principalities, nor powers, nor things present, nor things to come, Nor height, nor depth, nor any other creature, shall be able to separate us from the love of God, which is in Christ Jesus our Lord" (Romans 8:35–39).

Have you ever been tempted just to give up, to throw in the towel? Through gritted teeth, discouraged by circumstances, have you snapped, "That's it, I quit"? Discouragement desires to be our constant companion whether in prayer or in service. Let me share a story I heard about a man from India who had every reason to be discouraged. This story so well illustrates the truths of Romans 8:35–39.

His white teeth glistened with a glowing radiance as he related the goodness of the Lord Jesus. He had just been thrown out of jail. His clothes were not elegant, but he bore the marks of a man with a mission—a mission for his King.

He was an Indian man who had been preaching the gospel to his fellow countrymen. He had been arrested, put in jail for several days, taken out of jail, and driven twenty-five miles down the road. As he related his story, he told of his witness to every man in the jail, of his use of the jailor's bathtub to baptize all the men who believed, and of the meals and clean bedding that he enjoyed while a prisoner. Having preached the gospel with great success inside the prison, the officials felt they were doing this dear Christian brother too much good; so they took him twenty-five miles down the road to get him away from the men in the jail. Little did they know that their aid had brought him twenty-five miles closer to a town which he had planned to reach on foot—a town where he would proclaim the gospel of the living Lord Jesus Christ.

Oh, beloved, how we need to pray for Christians around the world! We must pray that whatever comes their way that they will see it as an opportunity to show those around them the reality of Jesus Christ. Pray that Christians will cease murmuring and learn in everything to give thanks, knowing that this is the will of God in Christ Jesus concerning them (1 Thessalonians 5:18).

His Thoughts Toward Me:

My Thoughts Toward Him:

September 22

When they knew God, they glorified Him not as God, neither were thankful; but they became vain in their imaginations, and their foolish heart was darkened . . . and so God gave them up . . . to these things . . . immorality, perversion, and a reprobate mind . . . a mind without absolutes (Romans 1:21–32).

National revival is Sweden's greatest need. Great revivals have swept over the land in past years. Now, the country is well known for its welfare state, wealth, materialism, permissive society, suicides, immorality, and drunkenness (42 percent increase in the last ten years). Yet, there are signs of new interest in spiritual things among young people during the last seven years. The new government needs prayer; the damage of years of permissive legislation and erosion of respect for the things of God by those in high authority must be rectified. Young people have been very adversely affected by the permissive society and a recent survey indicates that 41 percent do not believe that there is a God. This is Sweden!

Now, listen to what it is like in Denmark. Denmark is a Protestant nation far away from God. Few Danes have ever really heard the gospel. There are no Evangelical Bible schools or seminaries in the country. The church is supported by out-of-state funds and is almost a government department.

Denmark, like Sweden, is reaping the harvest of the seed of permissiveness. Denmark is reputed to be the pornographic capital of the world. Liberal laws have legalized many social sins, and there is no longer any censorship of literature, films, etc. The moral degradation of a permissive society has brought no peace or happiness to the people.

Both of these countries are open to the gospel. How this religious freedom needs to be taken advantage of! Pray that God will raise up men and women who will go forth in the calling and anointing of a Jeremiah to pluck up and to break down, to destroy and to overthrow, to build and to plant. Pray that a great spirit of conviction will sweep these lands and bring the people to their knees weeping, crying out for forgiveness.

His Thoughts Toward Me:

My Thoughts Toward Him:

September 23

It happened two years ago in Kiev, Russia. Because so many young people were expressing an interest in the Capitalists' religion, even brazenly wearing Jesus T-shirts, the central government thought it wise to hold a huge conference proving there was no God. The format they chose was a debate between the top Russian scientists and one of the less educated, "deluded" Christians. The air was electric with expectancy as 20,000 people took their seats and as 25,000 people jammed the aisles and doorways on a standing-room-only basis. The Christians throughout the vast conference hall prayed silently as the debate began. As one of the great Russian scientists began to speak, pointing to his model of the universe, his comrade, another noted scientist, began to argue with him. Soon the debate became mass confusion; the people became angry; some, in their disgust, charged the stage, tearing up the scientist's model. As the great government debaters were ushered away by the security police, the lone Christian, anointed by the Spirit, spoke, simply giving the gospel to the quieted crowd. When he was finished, the sweet silence was splintered as 25,000 Russians passionately gave a standing ovation to the small Christian who had spoken at the great conference which had been held to prove, once and for all, that there was no God.

God forbid that we should sin in failing to pray for our brothers and sisters in Russia. The individual Christian faces many terrible forms of persecution; pray for him. There is constant propaganda and crude attempts at conversion to Communism at work and in the home. Discrimination in job opportunities and in education result in the believers being condemned to a life of poverty and deprivation even greater than average; heavy fines are levied for attending "illegal" meetings; imprisonment and deportation to Siberia are among the punishments. There are many refined methods of torture and "treatment" used in mental institutions for those who obstinately persist in believing.

The Lord has quickened to my heart that we should especially pray for those who are brought before courts and tribunals that they would be comforted with the truth of the Scripture that "when they deliver you up, do not become anxious about how or what you will speak; for it shall be given you in that hour what you are to speak. For it is not you who speak but the Spirit of your Father who speaks in you" (Matthew 10:19, 20 NAS).

His Thoughts Toward Me:

My Thoughts Toward Him:

September 24

When you hear the word *Russia* do you automatically think, "enemy"? What comes to your mind when you think of the Russian people? Do you consider them to be sinister, maybe not quite human? I'm not speaking of the beloved church in Russia but rather the average man on the street, the man who works and lives under the communist rule. During the Winter Olympics, my awareness of the people of the world became more sensitive. One fleeting moment during the telecast of the couples' skating finals made me acutely aware of being responsive when God touches your heart with a prayer burden.

The couple was Russian. Their performance had been flawless. They had skated on the ice as a matching pair; now, they stood to have the gold medal placed around their necks. As the stanzas of their national anthem began, the red flag with the hammer and sickle was raised amid great honor and solemnity. The cameras zoomed in for a tight shot of the pretty, delicate, Russian skating star who gazed at the flag of her homeland. Tears welled up in her eyes and spilled down her face. In that moment, she became a real person to me, a person for whom Christ died. Until that moment, she had been a professional skater, a Russian athlete, not really important to me personally; but when I saw her weep with the emotion that women share universally, she became something

372

more; she became an object of prayer. My heart was moved, and my spirit was quickened to pray for her—to ask God to make Himself known in her life, to draw her to Himself.

Since that day, from time to time, God has laid that skating star on my heart to have me pray for her. God is longing to move on the hearts of men, but He will not move until we release Him in prayer. Oh, how my joy would be full to someday see that Russian skater standing in adoration of her Savior at the judgment seat of Christ. Is that an impossible dream? I don't think so. Has God laid someone on your heart for whom you should pray? Beloved, have you been praying for them?

His Thoughts Toward Me:

My Thoughts Toward Him:

September 25

What is your church life like? How do you and the other members of your church family get along? What are your prayer meetings like? Do you think these are strange questions to be asking in a devotional on prayer? Well, perhaps they are; but I have recently been reading *A Song in Siberia* (Anita and Peter Deyneka, Jr.: David C. Cook Publishing Co.), and it has provoked these questions. This book is "the true story of a Russian church that could not be silenced."

You know, beloved, I have become righteously envious of the true church in Russia. Their worship and prayer times make anything we know in America seem pale. They have kept their relationships pure because they have to trust each other with their very lives.

Russia, today, is a fertile field for the gospel. The church has always grown best and strongest where the ground has been soaked with the blood of martyrs. In Russia, martyrs' blood not only soaks the ground, but it stands in pools where the blood has flowed so freely that it has saturated the ground to the point that it can hold no more. It is in those places that the church is truly the church "triumphant."

What we know about the state of the church in Russia is very moving. Think about the questions I asked you at the beginning of today's devotional. What is your church like?

"In the crowded houses where they met, the congregation frequently stood during the entire service—two to four hours." If there were places to sit, the women were given the first choice. "During the service, the worshippers who were sitting changed places quietly with those who stood.

"But during prayer the Christians always stood or knelt. 'For a human ruler we show respect,' an old woman who has been a Christian since the days of the Czar explained. 'When we talk to the King of the universe, we must stand or kneel.' "

When the church prayed as a body, everyone had an opportunity to pray. Inevitably, there would be mothers praying for their children who faced atheistic hostility in schools. Some would pray for their Christian brothers who had been imprisoned for the sake of Christ. Beloved, think of it and weep. Prayer was offered, too, for the church in the West that we might be purified and strengthened. "While one person prays aloud, a sea of prayer surges through the room as other believers whisper their petitions and praise, 'Da Gospodi—yes, Lord,' hear our prayer."

What is it like when your church meets to pray?

His Thoughts Toward Me:

My Thoughts Toward Him:

September 26

Recently, I had a guest at the lunch table who had just left a mission organization in Europe to come home to the States prior to reassignment. Prompted by a mutual friend who was eating with us, she began to share recent testimonies that have come out of Afghanistan. If you're like me, Afghanistan had been a rare word in your vocabulary until the Russians invaded it in 1980. Suddenly, the Afghans have become a people of great interest. My heart was captured with the courage of these people as this missionary related story after story. For the next two days, I'm going to be sharing these stories with you. I'm asking God to burden us, to show us how, to show us what to pray, then to show us His glory manifested in Afghanistan.

A father was standing outside a prison window in a small town on the mountainous outskirts of Kabul, Afghanistan. He was looking through iron bars at the tender face of his eighteen-year-old son. The boy's piercing black eyes filled with tears as the father confessed, "My son, I have been a believer in Jesus Christ for two and a half years. Today, I publicly declare this to you and to anyone else who wants to know it."

The young man had been to Kabul where he had heard of the Saviour. He had believed with his whole being, and he had been bold in his witness when he had returned to his mountain village. As the boy had told friend after friend of his new-found faith, his father had not stopped him. Not many days passed, however, until the boy was seized and thrown into jail. Now, in unbelief, the young man sat listening to his father's testimony. Fear had shut the father's mouth before, but now the courage of his son had caused him to speak and to stand. Fifteen people in that tiny village were born again because of the testimony of one courageous eighteen-year-old boy and his father. Today, God has a powerful evangelistic team in these two Afghan men.

Many believers, in foreign countries, face disinheritance if they confess Jesus Christ. Beloved, how many of us can even think of paying such a cost for becoming a Christian? Have you ever thought what your stand would be like if the personal cost to you were greater than it is?

Ask our God to strengthen and encourage the hearts of the Afghan believers. Ask the Lord to compel them to share the light in the darkness which has engulfed their land. And, as you pray for them, ask your Father to burden *your* heart to share His life with those in *your* world who are groping in darkness!

His Thoughts Toward Me:

My Thoughts Toward Him:

September 27

What if you were in the army in a country that wasn't really your own and you were sent to the front lines to fight with other soldiers of your nationality, while soldiers who were natives stayed behind? It would make you feel strange, wouldn't it? That's what happened in Afghanistan. Germans and their children who were caught living behind Russian borders when the borders were changed after World War II were under obligation to the Russian army. Notorious for getting others to do their fighting for them, the Russians sent many of these German soldiers into Afghanistan; however many of these Germans were not Communists, but Christians!

A missionary couple who lives in Afghanistan received a large box of Russian Bibles several months ago before the Russian invasion. Although they knew no Russians, they did know that "As for God, his way is perfect" (Psalms 18:30). The couple carefully stored the Bibles under some other belongings in the back of their garage. Soon, news reports, though sparse, began to crackle, ". . . the Russians are invading Afghanistan." Boxes were shifted around, the big box of Bibles was dusted, and plans were made to clandestinely distribute them among the Russian troops. The soldiers received the Bibles with a holy joy and great reverence. Many of the men had been praying that they would somehow receive a Bible; they were so hungry for the Word of God.

Beloved, although these German soldiers may seem to be Russian pawns, they abide under the shadow of the Almighty. In your prayer times today, pray specifically for the men in the Russian military who, as Christians, must serve and stand.

His Thoughts Toward Me:

My Thoughts Toward Him:

September 28

His name is T—. He is totally blind. He is a Christian. Due to the extreme persecution in his homeland of Afghanistan, T— had been wavering in his testimony for the Lord Jesus. Not long ago, T— entered a barbershop in Kabul. Although the air was ominously silent, he could feel the presence of many people in the shop. As he entered, he asked the barber, "What are all of these people doing here?" Roughly denying the presence of any other people, the barber rudely led him to the chair. As T— uneasily sat down, he suddenly felt the barber's razor held tight against his throat and heard the hateful words, "Are you one of those Christian infidels?" At that moment, the man who had been wavering in conviction, the man who now had a knife at his throat, made a courageous decision; he began to testify mightily of the Lord

377

Jesus Christ and of His power to save. Barely had his last words escaped his gasping lips, when the Muslim barber ruthlessly slit T—'s throat. He barely missed the jugular vein. Crawling, with the blood dripping from his near fatal wound, T— made it to the home of some believers who took him in and ministered to his wounds.

While he recuperated, five different men, secretly and separately, came to see him; they were the five men who had been sitting in that barber shop, who had witnessed the testimony of T—. They had come to learn more about this Jesus for whom he was willing to die.

Beloved, Afghanistan is a land dominated by Muslims and invaded by Russians. The conflict is fierce; the believers are caught in the middle of it all. Think of what it would be like—virtually alone in the middle of a war . . . a war for the possession of your land. As you pray for T— and the believers in Afghanistan, pray that they would be "steadfast, immovable, always abounding in the work of the Lord" despite their circumstances (1 Corinthians 15:58 NAS). Also, don't fail to pray for the believers in America. Ask God to grant us real conviction and real courage to uphold that conviction!

His Thoughts Toward Me:

My Thoughts Toward Him:

September 29

"If any man come to me, and hate not his father, and mother, and wife, and children, and brethren, and sisters, yea, and his own life also, he cannot be my disciple . . . So likewise, whosoever he be of you that forsaketh not all that he hath, he cannot be my disciple" (Luke 14:26, 33).

I have just read a newsletter from Dr. Clyde Narramore in which he relates the experiences of a young missionary couple who had just put their screaming seven-year-old, Jimmy, on a small plane to go to a mission school. Dr. Narramore described the poignant scene in these words. "In a moment, the plane was just a tiny speck in the distant sky, and then it was gone completely. On the ground the atmosphere was tense. Then, in a moment or two, after the plane had disappeared from sight, Jimmy's parents embraced each other and wept bitterly."

That is a heart-rending scene, isn't it? It is especially hard to think of for those of us who have children. However, separation is not the only problem that missionary children face. Many times, in the midst of great urgency and the intensity of unending work, the sons and daughters of missionaries feel neglected, left out, and, sometimes, unloved. Their hearts and minds, if unprotected, become fertile ground for the enemy's seed. Because so many of these young people go through sometimes harsh experiences, they can grow up with real resentment and insecurities unless they are bathed in prayer.

According to an article written by Elsie Purnell and quoted in *Prayer Power Unlimited* by J. Oswald Sanders (Moody Press), the missionary mother has as difficult a time sometimes as the children. "Many a missionary mother is frustrated over the conflict in her mind between her duties to her family and to 'the work.' She can find a multitude of Scriptures about her duties as wife and mother, but none specifically about a mother involved in missionary work. What priorities is she to observe? Must one be sacrificed for the other?"

Missionary families are just like yours, but they live under the constant pressures of scrutiny by the nationals and isolation from the comforts of home and relatives. Loneliness for the wives and children is often a difficult matter, but separation from children is probably the most traumatic of all the testing experiences that come to missionary mothers. If ever they need prayer support, it's when the parting day comes.

Oh, beloved, we must pray for those who have literally gone to the uttermost parts of the earth. We must pray for our missionaries, people like you and me with the same emotions, desires, and needs. One way to pray for the missionary families that you know

379

is to ask God to put a hedge about them, thereby, protecting them from the enemy who would desire to destroy the family.

His Thoughts Toward Me:

My Thoughts Toward Him:

September 30

J. Oswald Sanders in his excellent book, *Prayer Power Unlimited,* relates this story. "One night at midnight Mrs. Ed Spahr was awakened and burdened for missionary friends, Rev. Jerry and Mrs. Rose, in Dutch New Guinea working among stone-age culture people. She was so burdened for him, she prayed and next morning wrote a letter telling of it. Later it was learned that he received prayer letters from five prayer partners in five continents saying they prayed for him on that specific occasion.

"By adjusting the dateline and time span, it was seen that they all prayed at the same time; at that very time, Mr. Rose was standing with his arms tied behind his back and a huge 'stone-age' savage standing before him with a spear ready to pin him to the ground."

As five prayer partners on five continents prayed, another man in the tribe (there were no Christians in the tribe at that time) spoke to the savage, and he walked away. Dr. Spahr asks, "Could God have made him walk away without the prayer partners? God can do anything He wills, but would He? I don't think He would have. I think it was His desire and will to continue the life of Jerry Rose on earth as a witness through his prayer partners."

Beloved, the responsibility is awesome, isn't it? God has called His laborers to the harvest in response to someone's prayer; now, He is calling us to intercede on behalf of His servants.

As a young child at camp, I remember a missionary doctor, who was home on furlough, speaking to a whole group of us wiggly little girls. I don't remember much that she said, but I do remember that she looked very, very serious. Her words were filled with urgency as she begged us never to just pray, "God bless the missionaries on the foreign fields." She tearfully entreated us to find out what their needs were and to pray specifically for them by name. That was years ago, but it made an impact.

Oh, beloved, to be led in prayer, in specific prayer for specific situations, we must be in communion with God. We must constantly be looking to the hand of our Master; we must keep our eyes upon Him so that we, as His servants, might anticipate His every desire.

May this be our testimony: ". . . He awakens me morning by morning. He awakens my ear to listen as a disciple. The Lord God has opened My ear; and I was not disobedient, Nor did I turn back" (Isaiah 50:4, 5 NAS).

His Thoughts Toward Me:

My Thoughts Toward Him:

OCTOBER

October 1

You pick up the phone and you hear the words, "He is dead." The first time I heard it, I was a senior in High School. He was a young man whom I had dated. Spinal meningitis had taken him in a matter of hours. When I cried, I screamed. I did not know God. The second time, the first words were much the same. "Tom is dead." The next words made the pain even worse. "He hung himself." My husband had committed suicide. I hung up the phone and fell to my knees. I now knew God. The third time, I heard Mother's voice saying, "Your father slipped away quietly this afternoon." Jack held me, and we prayed. Someday, in all probability, my children will be told that I have died, and they will weep and pray. Death is inevitable. *"What man is he that liveth, and shall not see death?"* (Psalms 89:48). Yes, death is inevitable. Even so it is usually a shock when it comes.

When it does come, how will you handle it? If you are like most individuals, it is a thought too unpleasant to deal with. For most of us, unless we are past threescore and ten, death hardly seems a reality, much less a possibility. Somehow, those who have never experienced the death of one dear to them have a hard time conceiving of the fact that death could come to them or to their loved ones. Life is our concern. We are born to live, not to die. And for most of us, no matter how hard or how horrible life is, our goal, our ambition, our desire is to live, to survive. Man will usually hope against hope, rather than welcome death.

Why is this so? I believe there are several reasons. We will explore some of them in the days to come, but today I want to touch on what I believe is one of our greatest reasons for pushing death out of our minds. We do not understand death. We are not certain what lies beyond this life, so we cling to the things that we are certain of, the things we can feel, the things we can touch, the things we have experienced. We are afraid of the unknown. That is why it is always hardest to do something for the first time, like going down a high slide, or jumping off a high diving board, or flying in a plane. But once we have done it successfully, then we say to others, "Come on, it's great! Don't be afraid; you'll love it."

Oh, beloved, there is One who has conquered death. He has come back. He has told us about it. He has gone to prepare a place for us on the other side of death. He is the Resurrection and the Life. And because He conquered death, because He lives, we shall also . . . if we believe in Him.

This month we are going on a journey together to learn all we can about death. So that, when death comes, however it comes, you will be able to handle it in God's way.

Today, write out your fears or questions about death.

October 2

Death is so hard because it separates. One is taken, the other is left.

When death comes, the finality of it all suddenly hits you. There is nothing more. No more touching, loving, caressing, holding. No more talking, no more sharing. No more laughing together or crying together. No longer can you run to that special person for advice, wisdom, insight, guidance, help, comfort, or understanding. Your loved one is gone.

He comes to your mind over and over again and you involuntarily reach out to him, but he is not there. You think, *If only . . . Why did I? . . . I should have . . .* , but all your thinking, all your hindsight is in vain because he is gone. There is no more communication of any kind whatsoever.

You shake your head in disbelief. It is so hard to comprehend, so hard to adjust to, especially when you've lost a wife, a husband, a child, a sister or brother, a mother, or a father and death came prematurely or unexpectedly.

If you are like me, you find the mention of his name or the

thought of him causes your eyes to brim with tears, tears of loneliness, tears of hurt, tears of longing. You brush them away for the sake of those around you and you wish you could just walk away, that you could be alone and let the floodgates succumb to the pressure of your pent-up emotions. But then you look at those around you, apologize, wipe at your eyes, brace yourself, and go on with the process of living. Living—but living with the loneliness of your loved one's absence.

Unless you have experienced it, beloved, it is hard to imagine it, try though you may! When you haven't experienced the death of someone very dear to you, all you can do is say what you think is appropriate to say and do what you feel you should do. But when you have experienced it, then you can really hurt with those who hurt because you understand their pain. You can weep with those who weep.

"When Jesus therefore saw her weeping, and the Jews who came with her, also weeping, He was deeply moved in spirit, and was troubled, and said, 'Where have you laid him?' They said to Him, 'Lord, come and see.' Jesus wept" (John 11:33–35 NAS).

Prayer: O Father, thank you for the One who could be touched with the feeling of my infirmities. Teach me, now, to be touched with the feelings of others that I might rejoice with those who rejoice and weep with those who weep.

My Thoughts Toward Him:

October 3

It's the finality of the separation of death that causes us to weep, to hurt, to mourn, and even to wonder at times if life without the one we love is really worth living.

But is death really as final as it seems or as final as it feels? For some it is. For others it is not. It all depends.

Depends? Depends on what?

It all depends on your relationship to the Lord Jesus Christ. For only in Christ is there life—eternal life that will take you beyond death's door into the presence of God where you will experience life as God meant it to be, life without sin, thus without any mourning, or crying, or pain, life in which there shall no longer be any death (Revelation 21:4 NAS).

For those who have repented of their sins, for those who have turned from their own way to God's way through Jesus Christ, there is life beyond death. But for those who have not repented, who have not turned from their own way to the Lordship of Jesus Christ, death waits beyond death, and this death is called the second death. Listen, dear one, to the Word of God, listen carefully and ask God to circumcise your ears that you might clearly hear:

"And I saw a great white throne and Him who sat upon it, from whose presence earth and heaven fled away, and no place was found for them. And I saw the dead, the great and the small, standing before the throne, and books were opened; and another book was opened, which is the book of life; and the dead were judged from the things which were written in the books, according to their deeds. And the sea gave up the dead which were in it, and death and Hades gave up the dead which were in them; and they were judged, every one of them according to their deeds. And death and Hades were thrown into the lake of fire. This is the second death, the lake of fire. And if anyone's name was not found written in the book of life, he was thrown into the lake of fire" (Revelation 20:11–15 NAS).

If you were to die right now, what would be waiting beyond death's door? Would it be eternal life or would it be the second death? Are you certain? Write out your answer below along with your reason for your answer.

October 4

What happens when a person dies? For a long time that has remained a mystery. All we have had, and all we have needed, is the Word of God. In His Word, God has given us what we need to know to carry us through death into His presence. He has also given men enough truth so that those who refuse the life that is in His Son can know for a certainty the unchangeable fate that awaits anyone who rejects the Lordship of Jesus Christ. Those who refuse to turn from their own way (Isaiah 53:6), who refuse to repent, shall all likewise perish (Luke 13:3).

Yet many of us resist God's Word. We hear it, but we don't hear it. In other words, we listen to the truth and we know it, but it never takes root in our hearts. It might be intellectually acknowledged but it is not really received, believed, trusted, or followed. We give it mental recognition but do not allow it any life-changing power.

This is why so many people believe that they are saved, that they will "make it to heaven," when in reality they are as lost as lost can be and are certain to end up in hell. They know the truth about Jesus Christ, about His death, burial, and resurrection, but this truth has never changed their life. They may say that they believe, but their lives are the same as they were before they were "saved." Yet God says if any man is saved, he is in Christ, and ". . . if any man is in Christ, he is a new creature; the old things passed away; behold, new things have come" (2 Corinthians 5:17 NAS).

Dr. Maurice Rawlings was just such a man. Maurice said he "believed," but he certainly was not a new creature. His walk and his talk were contrary to the One he claimed as his Saviour. I know. I worked for him. He went to church and basically he knew the right answers. When I witnessed to him, he claimed to be saved, but then he would harass me and make fun of Christianity. I found out later that he hated me. I was a thorn in his flesh. (Bless his heart, I had a lot of zeal without the graciousness of Jesus. It's a wonder he didn't fire me!)

Maurice was a brilliant cardiologist who needed a "heart" transplant. Several years later, it happened, he got a new heart. Now we are dear friends. What brought Maurice to Christ? The plea of a man who had died and had been resuscitated. Maurice wouldn't believe God's Word, so God graciously confirmed it through this patient who cried out, "Don't stop, I'm in hell!"

I'll tell you about it tomorrow. But today, let me ask you again, "Do you really believe God's Word? Are you a new creature?"

Don't wait for an experience like Dr. Rawlings'. God won't give all of us the experience that Dr. Rawlings had. I believe God graciously allowed Maurice to have his experience with life after death to prepare him for a very special ministry.

October 5

Dr. Rawlings' experience caused him to reevaluate his relationship with the Lord Jesus Christ in the light of God's Word. He saw, then, that he had never been truly born again. After studying God's Word and being saved and after having the experience resuscitating his patient who was in hell, Maurice became interested in what others were saying about "after death experiences." Something was not ringing true! All of the reports being given were of good experiences, yet God's Word clearly teaches the reality of hell where the rich man was in flames and torment! Something was wrong and it was not the Word of God. There was a hell, the wrath of God awaiting every human being who refused to believe on the Lord Jesus Christ (John 3:36 NAS).

Who would want to cover up the reality of hell and the lake of fire? Who would want to delude men into thinking that death would bring only pleasant experiences? Who would want to cover up the fact that it is appointed unto man once to die and after that the judgment? Would it not be Satan, that deceiver who goes about as an angel of light gathering to himself false apostles to propagate his lies? Listen carefully to God's Word to us in 2 Corinthians 11:13, 14, "For such men are false apostles, deceitful workers, disguising themselves as apostles of Christ. And no wonder, for even Satan disguises himself as an angel of light" (NAS).

Beloved, anyone who ever has an experience contrary to what the Word of God states as true or anyone who ever teaches that which is clearly contrary to God's Word is a person who has been deceived by the father of lies. Satan "was a murderer from the beginning" (John 8:44 NAS) and does not stand in the truth because there is no truth in him. Whenever he speaks a lie, he speaks from his own nature; for he is a liar, and the father of lies.

Therefore, many "after death experiences" as they are erroneously referred to, for true death is final, are the work of the devil. The same is true for many "out of the body" experiences. So remember, as we spend our time looking at death, that truth is found in the Word of God for "Thy Word is Truth" (John 17:17 NAS). The Word of God is our plumb line and if what we hear or experience does not match up with the plumb line, then it's a lie, a deception from the deceiver. May we always be careful to "believe not every spirit, but try the spirits (to see) whether they are of God: because many false prophets are gone out into the world" (1 John 4:1).

October 6

I will never forget the night Maurice brought me his first manuscript. He wanted me to read it and to see whether he was "on target" scripturally. What a privilege. I had been Dr. Rawlings' nurse and had witnessed to him many times. Though I may have botched it in my overzealous witnessing. God knew that I really wanted to see this man saved!

Now here he was holding my hand and getting ready to pray. I sat there with my eyes tightly closed but he didn't say anything. Curiously, I peeked. There was Maurice looking at me and shaking his head. When he caught my eye, he said, "Who would have thought I would be here holding your hand and praying?"

Whoever would have thought it! Certainly not I! And yet, here he was. Once a brash, crude doctor, now he was humbly seeking God's will and thanking Him for the privilege of writing this book. Asking God in some small way to use it for His glory.

As I read the manuscript, I suggested that he open his book with a whopper of an attention-getter. "Tell them what happened, Maurice, the day you resuscitated the man who was in hell. That will get their attention."

The first chapter of his book, *Beyond Death's Door* (Thomas

Nelson Publishers) is entitled "To Hell and Back." Let me share part of it with you:

"More and more of my patients who are recovering from serious illnesses tell me there is a life after death. There is a heaven and a hell. I had always thought of death as painless extinction. I had bet my life on it. Now I have had to reconsider my own destiny, and what I have found isn't good. I have found it really may not be safe to die!"

The turning point in Dr. Rawlings' thinking came when a forty-eight-year-old mail carrier dropped dead of a cardiac arrest during a "stress test" in his office. The other six doctors that worked at The Diagnostic Clinic had left. Only the nurses were there. But they knew what to do. Each began their particular task until finally a pacemaker could be inserted into the large vein beneath the collarbone. During this procedure, the patient began "coming to."

"But whenever I would reach for instruments or otherwise interrupt my compression of his chest, the patient would again lose consciousness, roll his eyes upward, arch his back in mild convulsion, stop breathing, and die once more.

"Each time he regained heartbeat and respiration, the patient screamed, 'I am in hell!' He was terrified and pleaded with me to help him. I was scared to death."

Luke tells of another man who died, and was in hell. Begging for relief, he, too, lifted up his eyes and cried, "I am in agony in this flame" (Luke 16:24 NAS). But for this man, there was no resuscitation. He cried for relief but there was no relief. There was no coming back from death. His destination was set, for ". . . it is appointed for men to die once, and after this comes judgment" (Hebrews 9:27 NAS).

His Thoughts Toward Me:

My Thoughts Toward Him:

October 7

Let me continue the story of Dr. Rawlings' experience—an experience that he said "literally scared the hell out of me." *(I bet you have cheated and have just kept on reading. Oh, well I don't mind. I kinda like it.)*

" 'I am in hell!'

"He then issued a very strange plea: 'Don't stop!'

"I noticed a genuinely alarmed look on his face. He had a terrified look *worse* than the expression seen in death! This patient had a grotesque grimace expressing sheer horror! His pupils were dilated, and he was perspiring and trembling—he looked as if his hair was 'on end.'

"Then still another strange thing happened. He said, 'Don't you understand? I am in hell. Each time you quit I go back to hell! Don't let me go back to hell!'

"Being accustomed to patients under this kind of emotional stress, I dismissed his complaint and told him to keep his 'hell' to himself. I remember telling him, 'I'm busy. Don't bother me about your hell until I finish getting this pacemaker into place.'

"But the man was serious, and it finally occurred to me that he was *indeed* in trouble. He was in a panic like I had never seen before. As a result, I started working feverishly and rapidly. By this time the patient had experienced three or four episodes of complete unconsciousness and clinical death from cessation of both heartbeat and breathing.

"After several death episodes he finally asked me, 'How do I stay out of hell?' I told him I guessed it was the same principle learned in Sunday school—that I guessed Jesus Christ would be the one whom you would ask to save you.

"Then he said, 'I don't know how. Pray for me.'

"Pray for him! What *nerve!* I told him I was a doctor, not a preacher.

" 'Pray for me!' he repeated.

"I knew I had no choice. It was a dying man's request. So I had him repeat the words after me as we worked—right there on the floor. It was a very simple prayer because I did not know much about praying. It went something like this:

> Lord Jesus, I ask you to keep me out of hell.
> Forgive my sins.
> I turn my life over to you.
> If I die, I want to go to heaven.
> If I live, I'll be 'on the hook' forever.

"The patient's condition finally stabilized, and he was transported to a hospital. I went home, dusted off the Bible, and started reading it. I had to find out exactly what hell was supposed to be like. I had always dealt with death as a routine occurrence in my medical practice, regarding it as an extinction with no need for remorse or apprehension. Now I was convinced there was something about this life after death business after all. All of my concepts needed revision. I needed to find out more. It was like finding another piece in the puzzle that supports the truth of the Scriptures. I was discovering that the Bible was not merely a history book. Every word was turning out to be true. I decided I had better start reading it very closely."

His Thoughts Toward Me:

My Thoughts Toward Him:

October 8

Hell. How do I know, how do you know, it exists? Because of testimonies like this? No.

You or I or anyone knows for certain that there is a hell because God, in His infallible Word says "there is a hell." Do you realize that Jesus Christ said as much if not more about hell than He did about heaven? Why? Because many were going there and there would be no way of escape. It is a place prepared by God for the devil and his angels (Matthew 25:41), but it will also become the eternal abode of all those who would not believe on the Lord Jesus Christ in order that they might be saved. It is a place of weeping and gnashing of teeth where the worm dies not and the fire is not quenched (Matthew 13:49, 50; Mark 9:48). It is a place of eternal punishment (Matthew 25:46). A punishment so horrible that Jesus said a man was better off to maim himself in this life than to spend eternity with a whole body that would feel the flames of this eternal fire licking, leaping, and burning but never destroying the members of his body that had served as instruments of ungodliness and unrighteousness. Jesus said, "And if thy hand offend thee, cut it off: it is better for thee to enter into life maimed, than having two hands to go into hell, into the fire that never shall be quenched . . . And if thy foot offend thee, cut it off: it is better for thee to enter halt into life, than having two feet to be cast into hell, into the fire that never shall be quenched . . . And if thine eye offend thee, pluck it out: it is better for thee to enter into the kingdom of God with one eye, than having two eyes to be cast into hell fire: Where their worm dieth not, and the fire is not quenched" (Mark 9:43, 45, 47, 48).

Do you believe Jesus said this? Is God's Word true? Absolutely. To deny it is to believe Satan's lie (John 8:44). Is the Word of God true? *(Answer these questions, beloved; don't avoid them. Commit yourself on paper.)*

Then what do testimonies like the one you read yesterday mean? If they agree with God's Word, they are valid. If they do not agree they fail to confirm the truth and are invalid testimonies. "Thy Word is truth" (John 17:17). So let me ask you again, Is God's

Word true? Do you believe in a literal hell? Why? Write out your answer below.

October 9

Lest you are one of those who finds it hard to believe in a literal hell or wonders how a loving God could ever let men go to a place like that or lest you have read books that only tell you of pleasant death experiences, let me share with you another experience Dr. Rawlings relates in his latest book, *Before Death Comes* (Thomas Nelson Publishers).

" 'The alarms went off, and I felt myself fainting. I knew my heart had stopped. I just knew it had. I felt it! I saw the nurse run into the room where I was located and fool around with the gadgetry to which I was attached to see if it was working properly. Then she thought that I was dead because she yelled "code 99," and then the other nurse came in. The first nurse started breathing into my mouth and then used this black mask over my face, a big black thing that looked like a football with a mask on it. It made my chest rise, and I would breathe.

" 'I had to walk around past this first nurse to see the other nurse who was pushing on my chest. It made the whole bed shake, and she kept mumbling some numbers to herself, maybe to make the rhythm go right. During all this time, my chest pain had gone, and I was really feeling good.

" 'Then I smiled to myself because I began to realize that I had someway floated up to the ceiling of the room and I was looking down on them from up there, sort of floating around. But I never felt better! It seemed strange, seeing me on that bed, but I could see it was my face. Gee, I felt funny! I knew I was dead, but I didn't seem to care!

" 'Then things suddenly started getting dark, and I found myself spiralling through space into another sort of world; I was traveling very fast. It was some sort of tube that ended in a black nothing.

I felt like I was being sucked into a big, black void. I was getting hotter and hotter as I was approaching a light coming from a side-entrance or a side-hole which led to another tunnel which contained long rows of benches with people sitting on them.

" 'They made me sit at the end of one long bench which seemed to stretch for a long distance and angle into another opening or tunnel which was illuminated by a light brighter than this one. I couldn't see where the light was coming from or what was in the tunnel; so I asked a fellow next to me, but he didn't seem to know either. He was also waiting his turn. Then I noticed a grimy looking guard standing near the entrance, his arms crossed. As another batch of people left the bench in our room to go into the next room, the figure ordered all of us to 'move up.' Two of the people I saw on the bench I had known in high school. I'm sure of it.

" 'As we moved down the bench, I was close enough to see around into the next passageway, and there in the walls were large doors with iron gratings containing huge fires behind them. Overseers that seemed to have absolute command were rapidly pushing people into these ovens or fires. As one group of people entered, others were moved up by drivers in the rear passageways.

" 'I prayed and prayed, "God help me! God save me!" In some way my name was called out from far above the passageways, vibrating all the way down to where I was sitting. I heard the voice say, "I have called you back. I have need of you!"

" 'The next thing I knew I was back in my body and looking up into the face of the doctor who was making an awful thrust into my chest that made me feel like my ribs were broken. I really didn't care if he broke all of my ribs! I was just glad to be back. I never want to go back to that place! It opened my eyes about how I was living my own life. I've since made a great change. It has made a believer out of me!'

"For the first two weeks following this event, this patient was withdrawn and didn't try to communicate with his family, his friends, his doctors—or anyone for that matter. He seemed tense, frightened, and not at all eager to relate the story to me the next day after it happened. When I accidentally noticed he had a Bible under the bedcovers, he admitted that he had started reading it. Then he asked me to sit and talk. I learned that he was no longer

394

afraid of the death experience itself. However, he was convinced there was life after death, and he wanted to be sure he would never go back to the 'hot-box.' Live or die, he said he was going to bet his future life on Jesus Christ. He said he wanted to know he couldn't lose."

"Truly, truly, I say to you, he who hears My word, and believes Him who sent Me, has eternal life, and does not come into judgment, but has passed out of death into life" (Job 5:24 NAS).

His Thoughts Toward Me:

My Thoughts Toward Him:

October 10

". . . it is appointed for men to die once, and after this comes judgment." If this Scripture is true, and it is, then how do we explain the fact that *Beyond Death's Door* and other books tell of many people who have had "out-of-body experiences?" Physicians have declared them "dead," yet they have been brought back to life through various resuscitation methods.

I believe a fuller understanding of these extraordinary experiences will come in the days ahead as we look at what the Scriptures have to say about death. However, in the meantime, let's reason together. Paul wrote that for him to be absent from the body would be to be present with the Lord (2 Corinthians 5:8). *So it would seem that death is absence from the body, but not a temporary absence.* It is a permanent absence from this temporal, mortal, earthly tent in which we now dwell. *Death is not the temporary out-of-body experiences we read of today.*

The rich man that Jesus tells us of in Luke 16:19–31 died and was buried. His spirit did not return to his body but rather went to hell

(Hades, really). And we read that, from that place, there was no returning; there was no escape.

"And in hell he lift up his eyes, being in torments, and seeth Abraham afar off, and Lazarus in his bosom. And he cried and said, Father Abraham, have mercy on me, and send Lazarus, that he may dip the tip of his finger in water, and cool my tongue; for I am tormented in this flame. But Abraham said, Son, remember that thou in thy lifetime receivedst thy good things, and likewise Lazarus evil things: but now he is comforted, and thou art tormented. And beside all this, between us and you there is a great gulf fixed: so that they which would pass from hence to you cannot; neither can they pass to us, that would come from thence."

All that awaited the rich man was the day of judgment when Hades would deliver up the dead, small and great. Then he would stand before God and His great white throne and be judged according to his deeds. Because his name was not written in the book of life, he would suffer the second death, the lake of fire (Revelation 20:11–15). And there he would suffer eternal punishment (Matthew 25:41, 46).

Experiences of men who have died and come back do not negate the fact that men die once, but rather they apparently show that irreversible death has not yet taken place. True death is irreversible.

My Thoughts Toward Him:

October 11

Does death seem like an enemy? Why should it if it means going home, being with Jesus, seeing God face to face, and being with our loved ones again? To those who do not know Jesus Christ as their Lord and Savior, death certainly is an enemy. But why should death be unwelcome to those of us whose bodies have become the dwelling place of the Spirit of God? Why should we try to hold on to our loved ones if they are going to be with Him?

Do you think it could be because of the separation that death brings? I do. Death does cause sorrow for the Christian . . . but not the same kind of sorrow that comes to those who have no hope (1 Thessalonians 4:13). Instead there is the sorrow, the grief, the adjustment of separation. But you know, beloved, I believe God permits this sorrow that He might use it to wean us from earth. We are so earth-bound, aren't we? And, if we do not saturate our mind with the precious eternal truths of His Word, it is easy to get caught up in the temporal things of this life. It is so easy to look at the things which are seen rather than at the things which are not seen. So what does God do?

I believe He gently, patiently weans us through sufferings, trials, testings, through situations that cause us to abhor our flesh and its weaknesses, through old age and its infirmities, and through the deaths of loved ones who have gone on before us. And with the tears and aches of the weaning process, He draws us into His everlasting arms. There He succours us as He holds us close to His all-sufficient breast—our El Shaddai. And there, as we dwell between His shoulders in times of need, our ears hear the beat of His heart. And as we snuggle even closer we don't want to move . . . to leave the peace, the contentment, the love that shelters us in His arms.

O Father, the weaning has begun and it's all right for I'm beginning to see what it means to be with Thee. "Therefore we do not lose heart, but though our outer man is decaying, yet our inner man is being renewed day by day. For momentary, light affliction is producing for us an eternal weight of glory far beyond all comparison, while we look not at the things which are seen, but at the things which are not seen; for the things which are seen are temporal, but the things which are not seen are eternal" (2 Corinthians 4:16–18 NAS). What are your thoughts toward Him today?

My Thoughts Toward Him:

October 12

It was April 1980. The doctors did not understand how my daddy could possibly be living. In twelve days he had undergone five major surgeries. Because of the respirator he could not talk with us, but we communicated anyway. At times, when I talked to him about life, he seemed distressed, as a matter of fact, disgusted. Then he lifted his hand upward as if reaching for something. It wasn't the usual purposeless flailing of an incoherent patient but a direct and purposeful reach.

"Mother, ask him what he sees."

"I think he's saying, 'Spirit.' Is it the Holy Spirit, Jack?"

The nod came.

Oh, how I long to talk with Daddy, to find out what happened those last days before he left us. When they rushed him into surgery for the second time that day, I saw the horrible agony on his face. It was a look of desperation. I remember going to the waiting room and crying out to God in my spirit. I really thought God had told me that my daddy would live. The doctors thought he would probably die. I sat there with my New Testament on my lap opened to the Psalm God had given me the morning of Daddy's surgery. As I read Psalm 20 once again, verse six leaped off the page as God quickened it to my heart. "Now know I that the Lord saveth his anointed; he will hear him from his holy heaven with the saving strength of his right hand." All of a sudden the pronouns in Psalm 20 changed in verse 6. It was no longer "thee" and "we" but "he" and "him"—and only in verse six. God assured me that He had met with Daddy in a special way in that operating room. And when he came out, fully awake, peace covered his face. Six weeks later, Daddy would go to be with the Lord, and I would be weaned a little more. Through this I would understand the comfort of the Lord in a new way, and because of this trial would be better able to comfort others in the same need.

For those who know God, there is His grace that is sufficient, even for death. "But in all these things we overwhelmingly conquer through Him who loved us. For I am convinced that neither death, nor life, nor angels, nor principalities, nor things present, nor things to come, nor powers, nor height, nor depth, nor any other created thing, shall be able to separate us from the love of God, which is in Christ Jesus our Lord" (Romans 8:37–39 NAS).

His Thoughts Toward Me:

My Thoughts Toward Him:

October 13

Death. When does it come? It comes for the child of God when our purpose on earth has been fulfilled. The only exception is when a Christian dies prematurely because of sin he has let go unjudged in his body (1 Corinthians 11:27–31; Ecclesiastes 7:17).

"See now that I, I am He, and there is no god besides Me; it is I who put to death and give life. I have wounded, and it is I who heal; and there is no one who can deliver from My hand" (Deuteronomy 32:39 NAS). Jesus has the keys of death and of Hades (Revelation 1:18 NAS) and no one can die until He unlocks death's door.

A minister reports the following case: "I was called in the middle of the night by the hospital nurse who informed me that Mrs. D., one of the parishioners at my little church, was dying. She asked me if I wanted to be present at her bedside. I dressed hastily and went to the hospital as quickly as I could. When I stepped off the elevator, the nurse told me, 'I am sorry I called you out of bed. Mrs. D. is dead.' She then took me into the room where Mrs. D., a little frail, silverhaired lady, had died from a terminal cancer. I was told that all vital signs had ceased. I prayed, simply talking out loud to God, saying that Mrs. D. had insisted on my coming for a purpose and I asked the Lord to let that purpose come to pass if it be His will.

"I then saw Mrs. D.'s eyelid fluttering and then some rustling occurred and then commotion in the room. Mrs. D. opened her eyes wide and stared straight at me. She spoke in a whisper, 'I thank you, Pastor Grogan, for your prayer. I was just talking with

Jesus and He was telling me to come back and do something for Him. I also saw Jim (her husband who had died a short time before).' She turned on her side and drew her knees up almost to her chin, breathing softly and slept.

"As I walked down the corridor to the elevator, I heard the sounds of running feet. The nurse who had witnessed it all from the beginning overtook me and said, 'I'm afraid! What did you do? That woman was dead and she came back to life! I have been nursing for many years and I never saw that happen before. I've always been an atheist.'

"Mrs. D., after she had recovered, had many conversations in which she described to others what she saw during her death: Jesus in His shining brightness and her departed husband Jim. She wanted to stay in heaven but Jesus had ordered her back to talk to others.

"Then one day she called me to her home to tell me that she was going again to the hospital that very day—this time to go to heaven and stay. 'Do not pray for me to live this time.' " (From *Beyond Death's Door*)

You, beloved, are still living. What's your purpose? Have you ever asked God?

October 14

What happens when you die if you are a Christian? Let's look at what God's Word has to tell us and see if we can fit the pieces of the puzzle together so we can get a clearer picture of death. I want to make sure you see these truths from the Word of God for yourself. This is so important because each one of you will have to deal with death. Therefore we need to be as clear and as accurate as we can be in discussing it. We must know what saith the Lord and then live in the light of it. Knowing these truths will help us prepare not only for our own death, but also for the death of others. Therefore, I am going to take several days to cover this topic. I pray that you will be a diligent student.

In 2 Corinthians, Paul refers to our earthly bodies as a tent ... a house in which we dwell. This earthly tent is contrasted with a heavenly house. Peter also refers to his body as his earthly dwelling. Read the following Scriptures carefully and then answer the following questions.

"For we know that if the earthly tent which is our house is torn down, we have a building from God, a house not made with hands, eternal in the heavens. For indeed in this house we groan, longing to be clothed with our dwelling from heaven; inasmuch as we, having put it on, shall not be found naked. For indeed while we are in this tent, we groan, being burdened, because we do not want to be unclothed, but to be clothed, in order that what is mortal may be swallowed up by life. Now He who prepared us for this very purpose is God, who gave to us the Spirit as a pledge. Therefore, being always of good courage, and knowing that while we are at home in the body we are absent from the Lord—for we walk by faith, not by sight—we are of good courage, I say, and prefer rather to be absent from the body and to be at home with the Lord. Therefore also we have as our ambition, whether at home or absent, to be pleasing to Him. For we must all appear before the judgment-seat of Christ, that each one may be recompensed for his deeds in the body, according to what he has done, whether good or bad" (2 Corinthians 5:1–10 NAS).

"And I consider it right, as long as I am in this earthly dwelling, to stir you up by way of reminder, knowing that the laying aside of my earthly dwelling is imminent, as also our Lord Jesus Christ has made clear to me. And I will also be diligent that at any time after my departure you may be able to call these things to mind" (2 Peter 1:13–15 NAS).

1. List what you learned about the earthly tent and about the heavenly house. Compare the two.

THE EARTHLY TENT	THE HEAVENLY HOUSE

2. According to 2 Corinthians 5:6–8, if a Christian is present in his body then he is absent_____. Or to reverse this, if he is absent from the body, he is_____.

3. What is your pledge (down payment) that guarantees you a heavenly building, house, or body?

4. Whether in your earthly body or absent from it, what should be your ambition?

What is your ambition?

October 15

Physical death. What takes place when a Christian dies? According to 2 Corinthians 5:1–9, man's spirit leaves his body and goes to be with the Lord. Remember, we saw yesterday that to be absent from the body is to be with the Lord. But has it been this way for believers since the beginning? No.

Until the Lord Jesus Christ died, was buried, and rose again from the dead, no man could enter the portals of heaven when he died. He went instead to Abraham's bosom or to paradise where he awaited the birth and death of the only begotten Son of the Father who would be the firstborn from the dead (Colossians 1:18), the Lord Jesus Christ.

It seems from Christ's word to us in Luke 16, that before Christ's crucifixion, paradise was also referred to as Abraham's bosom and was considered part of Hades or Sheol. Hades apparently had two compartments that were separated from one another by a great gulf. Stop and take a few minutes to read Luke 16:19–31 carefully and then answer the questions that follow. If you read this in the KJV, the word hell should have been translated Hades. Hell is the final abode of the dead and is the same as the lake of fire. Hades is the temporal abode of the wicked dead and will be thrown into the lake of fire (Revelation 20:13, 14). As you read consult the chart on the next page. *Please stop and do it now—don't skip over this part and keep on reading. You will never learn or grow that way! If you are going to speak with authority you have to first see truth for yourself.*

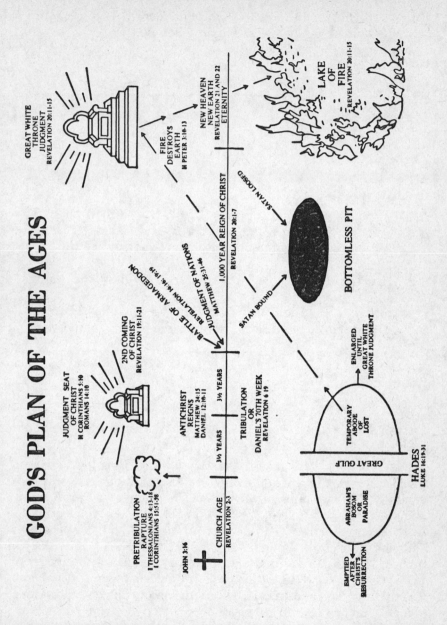

GOD'S PLAN OF THE AGES

GREAT WHITE
THRONE
JUDGMENT
REVELATION 20:11-15

LAKE
OF
FIRE
REVELATION 20:11-15

FIRE
DESTROYS
EARTH
II PETER 3:10-13

NEW HEAVEN
NEW EARTH
REVELATION 21 AND 22
ETERNITY

SATAN LOOSED

1,000 YEAR REIGN OF CHRIST
REVELATION 20:1-7

JUDGMENT OF NATIONS
MATTHEW 25:31-46

BATTLE OF ARMAGEDDON
REVELATION 16:16; 19:1-9

BOTTOMLESS PIT

2ND COMING
OF CHRIST
REVELATION 19:11-21

SATAN BOUND

JUDGMENT SEAT
OF CHRIST
II CORINTHIANS 5:10
ROMANS 14:10

ANTICHRIST
REIGNS
MATTHEW 24:15
DANIEL 12:1-11

ENLARGED
UNTIL
GREAT WHITE
THRONE JUDGMENT

3½ YEARS

3½ YEARS

TEMPORARY
ABODE
OF LOST

PRETRIBULATION
RAPTURE
I THESSALONIANS 4:13-18
I CORINTHIANS 15:51-58

CHURCH AGE
REVELATION 2,3

TRIBULATION
OR
DANIEL'S 70TH WEEK
REVELATION 6-19

GREAT GULF

HADES
LUKE 16:19-31

JOHN 3:16

ABRAHAM'S
BOSOM
OR
PARADISE

EMPTIED
AFTER
CHRIST'S
RESURRECTION

1. What happened to Lazarus when he died?
2. What happened to the rich man when he died?
3. List what you learn about:

ABRAHAM'S BOSOM	HADES

4. What was between Abraham's bosom and Hades?

Let me ask you two more questions, then tomorrow we will look at paradise.

5. What was the rich man's concern once he knew the reality of Hades?

6. How concerned are you about others and their eternal future? Are you concerned enough to share the Gospel even though it's hard for you?

October 16

Today we will look at what our Lord Jesus Christ said about paradise. When He was being crucified, one of the thieves on the cross said, "Jesus, remember me when You come into Your Kingdom." And He said to him, "Truly, I say to you, today you shall be with Me in paradise." Paradise, or Abraham's bosom, was the "holding place of the righteous dead until Christ's death and resurrection. No one could enter heaven before Jesus, so apparently the thief was being told he would go to Abraham's bosom.

Until Jesus died and shed His blood, there could be no remission of man's sins for ". . . without shedding of blood there is no forgiveness" (Hebrews 9:22 NAS). The blood of bulls and of goats which had been sacrificed to God could never take away sin (Hebrews

10:4), and, until sin was paid for and God's righteousness was propitiated (satisfied), man could not enter heaven. So God held those who had faith in the Redeemer who was to come in paradise, Abraham's bosom, until Jesus Christ became the propitiation for their sins and for the sins of the whole world (1 John 2:2).

With His resurrection, Christ then became the first-born from the dead (Colossians 1:18).

After Christ's ascension, paradise was relocated in the third heaven! This insight is given to us from the other two New Testament Scriptures that refer to paradise. The first reference is in 2 Corinthians 12:2, 4 when Paul says that he was "caught up to the third heaven . . . caught up into paradise." Paul confirms that paradise is in the third heaven. Then in Revelation 2:7 (NAS), we read ". . . To him who overcomes, I will grant to eat of the tree of life, which is in the Paradise of God." Since paradise is now in heaven, we know that when a Christian dies his spirit leaves his body and immediately goes to heaven to be with Christ forevermore. This is why Paul wrote, "For to me to live is Christ, and to die is gain. But if I live in the flesh, this is the fruit of my labour: yet what I shall choose I wot not. For I am in a strait betwixt two, having a desire to depart, and to be with Christ; which is far better: Nevertheless to abide in the flesh is more needful for you" (Philippians 1:21–24).

Because Paul understood what death meant for the Christian, he could welcome death and know that to be with Christ was "very much better." What about you, precious one, where would you go should you die?

Are you finding it easier now to think about death? Why not write out your thoughts about death at this point. It will help to verbalize them.

October 17

When will I die? It's a question I'm not sure we would like to have answered. So let's approach it from a more positive perspective.

Who determines when I die? Is there a time for each of us to die? The Book of Ecclesiastes and the Book of Job have much to say about death. Ecclesiastes was a Book written by a man who experienced the vanity of life, so naturally he would have much to say about death. Job is the account of a man who came face to face with death. In one day all his children were killed, and all that he owned was wiped out by one tragic event after another. Then Job was physically attacked by Satan. Job longed for death and talked much with God about it.

Ecclesiastes says, "There is an appointed time for everything. And there is a time for every event under heaven—A time to give birth, and a time to die . . ." (Ecclesiastes 3:1, 2 NAS).

When the time of our death comes, no one can stop it but God. "No man has authority to restrain the wind with the wind, or authority over the day of death . . ." (Ecclesiastes 8:8 NAS).

Job wrote, "In whose hand is the life of every living thing, And the breath of all mankind?" (Job 12:10 NAS.) Our life is in God's hands; He holds or withholds our breath. Man's ". . . days are determined. The number of his months is with Thee, and his limits Thou hast set so that he cannot pass" (Job 14:5 NAS).

"Thine eyes have seen my unformed substance; And in Thy book they were all written, The days that were ordained for me, When as yet there was not one of them" (Psalms 139:16 NAS).

When will I die? Not until God is ready to take me home . . . and then we will see that His time was right. "How precious also are Thy thoughts to me, O God! How vast is the sum of them! If I should count them, they would outnumber the sand. When I awake, I am still with Thee" (Psalms 139:17, 18 NAS).

His Thoughts Toward Me:

My Thoughts Toward Him:

October 18

Will we know people in heaven? Will we recognize them? What will they be like? Will we just be spirits floating around? What about our bodies?

These are questions that we all have. We want to know about our bodies for they are the "tents," as Paul puts it in 2 Corinthians 5, in which we dwell. Several days ago you read that Paul longed to put off his earthly tent, but he did not want to be unclothed, without a tent. Paul rather longed for the day when he would be clothed with his heavenly dwelling or, to say it another way, when that which is mortal would be swallowed up by life.

I want to make sure that you understand it completely, so let's follow step by step the process our body goes through at death. Remember, death is different for a Christian than it is for a non-Christian because the Christian has the promise of an immortal, incorruptible body. I want you to hold on to this truth as we follow the process of a Christian's death.

When God calls one of His children to be with Him, that person's spirit departs from his body. The earthly tent or dwelling place has been abandoned. The breath of life has departed from the body that was made from the dust of the ground (Genesis 2:7). "Then shall the dust return to the earth as it was: and the spirit shall return unto God who gave it" (Ecclesiastes 12:7).

When man's spirit goes to be with the Lord, apparently it has the shape or form of that particular individual's body, which distinguishes it from others in heaven. At the Transfiguration Moses and Elijah were recognized for who they were. It seems from reading Luke 16 that, although we are separated from our mortal bodies, still we feel and operate as if we have all our members. The rich man wanted Lazarus to dip his finger into water and touch the tip of his tongue. Yet, with all this consciousness of body, those in heaven now remain in a sense unclothed or naked, as Paul says in 2 Corinthians 5.

When do we receive our new bodies, what will they be like? First Corinthians 15, the Resurrection chapter, tells us of a wonderful mystery, and we will look at that tomorrow. But for today, beloved, let me share with you two wonderful verses that are referred to as "the purifying hope." They speak of the time when we shall see the Father face to face:

"Beloved, now we are children of God, and it has not appeared as yet that we shall be. We know that, if He should appear, we shall be like Him, because we shall see Him just as He is. And every one who has this hope fixed on Him purifies himself, just as He is pure" (1 John 3:2, 3 NAS).

Are you purifying yourself for that day?

October 19

Have you ever wondered why these physical bodies of ours have to die? If we receive the Lord Jesus Christ as our Savior and Lord and if our bodies become the temple of the Holy Spirit, why then do we have to die? Why could we not live in these bodies forever?

It is because of the awful wages of sin, beloved. Because Adam and Eve's bodies participated in sin and their members became instruments of unrighteousness, the body needs redeeming just as man's spirit and soul need redeeming.

Therefore, God has a plan for the redemption of our bodies. He not only plans to redeem our bodies, but He promises to redeem them. The pledge of this promise is the Holy Spirit. "In Him, you also, after listening to the message of truth, the gospel of your salvation—having also believed, you were sealed in Him with the Holy Spirit of promise, who is given as a pledge of our inheritance, with a view to the redemption of God's own possession, to the praise of His glory" (Ephesians 1:13, 14 NAS). To *redeem* means to "buy and set free," and that is exactly what God does for your body. He buys it with the precious blood of the Lord Jesus Christ, and then He sets it free from its slavery to sin and gives us the promise of its eventual redemption at His appearing. That is why Paul longed to be clothed with his heavenly dwelling. In Romans 8:23 (NAS), he writes, ". . . we ourselves, having the first fruits of the Spirit, even we ourselves groan within ourselves, waiting eagerly for our adoption as sons, the redemption of our body."

When will this redemption of our bodies take place, and what will it be like? In 1 Corinthians 15, Paul tells us how God is going to execute our body's redemption since flesh and blood cannot inherit the Kingdom of God, nor can corruption inherit incorruption: "Behold, I shew you a mystery; We shall not all sleep, but we shall all be changed, In a moment, in the twinkling of an eye, at the last trump: for the trumpet shall sound, and the dead shall be raised incorruptible, and we shall be changed. For this corruptible must put on incorruption, and this mortal must put on immortality. So when this corruptible shall have put on incorruption, and this mortal shall have put on immortality, then shall be brought to pass the saying that is written, Death is swallowed up in victory" (1 Corinthians 15:51–54).

The children of God are going to get brand new incorruptible, immortal bodies when the Lord Jesus Christ comes the "second time . . . to those who eagerly await Him" (Hebrews 9:28 NAS).

"For if we believe that Jesus died and rose again, even so God will bring with Him those who have fallen asleep in Jesus. For this we say to you by the word of the Lord, that we who are alive, and remain until the coming of the Lord, shall not precede those who have fallen asleep. For the Lord Himself will descend from heaven with a shout, with the voice of the archangel, and with the trumpet of God; and the dead in Christ shall rise first. Then we who are alive and remain shall be caught up together with them in the clouds to meet the Lord in the air, and thus we shall always be with the Lord" (1 Thessalonians 4:14–17 NAS).

When Christ comes at His Second Coming there will be a great catching up, or "rapture," of all believers. He will bring the spirits of those who have already died and gone to be with Him in heaven. They shall leave heaven with Christ, coming in the clouds. Then their dead bodies will be raised and will put on incorruption and immortality. Finally, they will experience the glorious redemption of their bodies. Those believers that are alive on earth at that time will then be caught up together with these resurrection bodies of the saints and all shall meet the Lord in the air! Hallelujah!

"Therefore comfort one another with these words" (1 Thessalonians 4:18 NAS). This is why we do not sorrow over death as do those lost ones who have no hope (1 Thessalonians 4:13).

His Thoughts Toward Me:

My Thoughts Toward Him:

October 20

The call came on April 22, 1980. Jack and I were at Grace Kinser's house in Atlanta. I had been sitting beside the pool, reading and praying, preparing for our television prayer banquet that night.

Grace's voice came over the intercom, "Kay, it's your mother." It was such a warm sunny spring day, a day that seemed at the moment incongruous with the words that came so gently over the phone. "Honey, Daddy died at four o'clock this afternoon. He went so peacefully." Jack held me and we prayed. I thanked God for His sovereignty. I knew the Scripture "The Lord kills and makes alive; He brings down to Sheol and raises up" (1 Samuel 2:6 NAS). I believed that the Lord had given and the Lord had taken away, and I blessed the name of the Lord (Job 1:21). I knew God had numbered my father's years to sixty-eight. I would have liked at least threescore and ten, but I knew it was in God's hands, not man's, and I did not blame God. How could I, for, because of the great love with which He loved us, I would see my daddy again.

O Father dear, where would I go, what would I do, how could I survive if I did not know that You were sovereign and that our times are in Your hands. I know the thoughts that You have of me are not thoughts of evil but thoughts of good to bring me to an expected end. As for the Lord, His ways are past finding out, but His way is perfect. You are the Lord, there is no other, the One forming light and creating darkness, causing well-being and creating adversity; You are the Lord who does all these things. And for this trial I have Jesus. Thank You, Father, for letting your Son die that Daddy might live. I thank You that Jesus is the Resurrection and the Life and that he who believes in Him shall live even if he dies. Now let me walk in Your strength, live in Your hope, serve by Your Spirit, and glorify You in this arena in which I am made a spectacle of Your sufficiency. In this, in death, may I overwhelmingly conquer through my Jesus who loves me.

His Thoughts Toward Me:

October 21

It is so strange to walk down streets, to watch life being lived, after the death of a loved one. You feel that everyone should stop smiling, laughing, talking, singing. How can the sun shine, the birds sing, the soft breezes play with the trees when my loved one has died? How can I smile and talk, be kind and sweet, act normally, laugh, and then remember and cry? How can life go on when my loved one has died? How can my children still play and talk about Grandpa so casually . . . it's my daddy that has died! But they can't understand because their daddy is alive. How can life go on?

Suddenly I remembered all my friends who had lost loved ones the year before. When I had consoled them, I had not known how they felt! I had not understood their hurt! Now, I wanted to run, to find them, to put my arms around them to ask them to forgive me. To tell them I had not understood. They did not need to be reminded of what Jesus had said. They needed His arms to hold them in quietness, His eyes to weep for them, His ears to listen to them. They needed one who would stop and be touched with the feeling of their infirmities. They needed the freedom to cry, to hurt, to talk.

And they needed time to adjust, for life does go on. And because we have been left here, on this earth that is not our home, we must go on. We have been left by God to live, to walk in the good works He has foreordained for us, to finish the course that is set before us—redeeming the time because the days are evil—knowing that, when the days He has ordained for us are completed, we too shall die. But until then, we are to live. Life must go on.

O Father, in the days I have left, let me be sensitive, let me comfort your people with the comfort which I received from You —comfort I knew nothing of until I was afflicted.

If you knew you had but a short time to live, what would you do? Write out your thoughts.

You don't know how long you have, so if there is something you should do for God, do it.

October 22

"From that time Jesus Christ began to show His disciples that He must go to Jerusalem, and suffer many things from the elders and chief priests and scribes, and be killed, and be raised up on the third day. And Peter took Him aside and began to rebuke Him, saying, 'God forbid it, Lord! This shall never happen to You'" (Matthew 16:21, 22 NAS). They didn't want to hear it. He wasn't going to die! How could He die? What would they do? How could they go on without Him? Die—it was an absurdity! They wouldn't let it happen! His disciples were so alarmed at Jesus' talk about death that apparently they never heard His Words about His resurrection. Because they would not face the issue, they completely missed out on the joyous hope and certainty of His life after death.

Death is hard to face, isn't it? Especially if you are not ancient and riddled with infirmities. Especially if your loved ones are not senile, if they are not invalids that are merely existing. And, if you find out that someone is close to death, it's hard to tell him that he's going to die, isn't it? It's easier to say, "Oh, you're going to make it. You're gonna be all right." Or to joke, "You're too mean to die. They wouldn't have you."

We do everything else but talk about death. Sometimes you wonder if the person has considered the fact that he might die, that he might not make it through surgery. You wonder, but you don't talk about it. I guess we are afraid that, if we bring up the subject of death, it will throw everyone into a tizzy. So we avoid it. And if death does come, you wish that you had talked about it. Death, except for the return of Jesus, is inevitable and yet we will not prepare ourselves for it; nor do we prepare our loved ones.

It is my prayer for you, beloved, that God will use these next days to encourage you to prepare yourselves and your loved ones for death. Then, when the time and opportunity come, you can minister to the dying or to those facing the possibility of death rather than ignore them or deny that which God may bring to pass.

What would you have to do to prepare to meet thy God? Write it out, look at it in black and white. Face it. Deal with it now.

October 23

We are so consumed with living that we do not give adequate time and attention to dying. Death is distasteful to us. It is an enemy. Therefore, we do not want to acknowledge its possibility, let alone deal with it when it comes.

By some quirk of our thinking, we feel that, if we ignore death or pretend that it does not exist, we will not have to deal with it. But then unexpectedly death enters our lives as an intruder, uninvited and unwelcome, yet unwilling to leave empty-handed. Suddenly, we realize that our death or the death of a loved one is inevitable. Then what do we do?

Most people, when faced with the reality of death, tend to deny it. *It can't be! It can't happen to me! They've got the wrong person! The diagnosis must be wrong! God won't let it happen! I'll believe,*

I'll pray, I'll have faith. God will heal. I just know He'll heal! Somehow, for some reason, we just cannot conceive of death as a reality in our lives. So often there is denial.

Many times the grim announcement of death, whether it has actually occurred or is expected, causes us to cry out in anger, *Why! Why? Why, why me? Why them? Why has God allowed this to happen? What have I done to deserve this? Why now?* We are angry because it does not seem fair. The person facing death is too young, too talented, too good, too needed. Or our cries of "why?" turn into screams of torment because the dying one does not know Jesus. After the "whys," if we have not already questioned the reality of God, we begin to wonder about His existence and about life after death. Then, if we acknowledge God, in all probability there will be a time of bargaining or pleading with Him. Usually we will plead for life or at least for an extension of time. We may make various promises or vows at this time. Even for those who know Christ this is understandable, for death is not easy. Oftentimes depression will set in. For the one who is dying, depression usually comes as a morbid resignation to death that settles in and hovers over him or her like a black cloud. How does one handle the anger and the depression that so often accompany the announcement of death? How can we help the dying deal with these emotions? Are they inevitable? Maybe! But they can be dealt with so that one does not have to be depressed over dying. We will discuss this in the days to come. But for today it suffices to say that it is possible to face death with a healthy resignation that can make it a blessing. Oh, the blessing will not exempt you from realistic, God-given tears of sorrow and loneliness at the thought or reality of separation, but it will keep you from rejecting death as an unconquerable enemy.

"Precious in the sight of the Lord is the death of his saints" (Psalms 116:15).

414

October 24

The thought of death often causes us to bargain with God. We bargain for life, for time. We plead, we beg, we promise. "Anything, God, just let me live," or "Just let my loved one live." We try to reason with God, to make Him understand why it is more important for us or for them to live than to die. And many times, because the thought of death seems so unbearable, we will plead to have our loved ones any way we can—crippled, maimed, comatose, "Please, God, just don't let him die!"

How does God feel about all of this bargaining? To be honest, beloved, I do not know. However, I feel I can tell you for certain that He does understand. Because He became a man Himself, our God can be touched with the feeling of our infirmities (Hebrews 4:15). When He saw Mary and her friends weeping over Lazarus' death, Jesus wept also. He was the Resurrection and the Life, and yet Jesus was deeply moved in spirit and troubled by death! (John 11:30–38.) When news of the beheading of John the Baptist reached Jesus, He had to be alone. Man had been created to live, not to die. But then sin came and spoiled life, and death was the awful wage of man's sin. Jesus hated sin. Now the Christ had come to remove death's stinger, to conquer sin by paying its horrible wages, to ". . . deliver those who through fear of death were subject to slavery all their lives" (Hebrews 2:15 NAS).

Can Jesus understand your fleshly bargaining for life? Yes, He can. Did not Jesus cry out to God, "My Father, if it is possible, let this cup pass from Me; yet not as I will, but as Thou wilt" (Matthew 26:39 NAS). The cup was the cup of death. After Jesus had prayed this prayer and was arrested, He said to Peter, "Put the sword into the sheath; the cup which the Father has given Me, shall I not drink it?" (John 18:11 NAS). And drink it He did, beloved—the full dregs of sin, held in death's cup, as He who knew no sin was made to be sin for us that we might be made the righteousness of God in Him (2 Corinthians 5:21).

If you want to bargain with God, bargain with Him. Do not seek to keep your thoughts, fears, frustrations or anger from God. Talk to Him about it. Tell Him what is bottled up inside. He understands, precious one, He understands. He was a human being made just like you in the flesh (Philippians 2:7) (except, of course,

He was without sin [Hebrews 4:15]) and there is not anything you cannot tell Him. So bargain, if that is in your heart. Question Him if you need to know why. He is your Father, or if He is not, He longs to be; so run to Him and talk freely with Him about it all.

When you have finished bargaining, ask your Father, your Savior, to give you the faith to pray "Nevertheless, not my will but thine be done." Remember that Jesus holds the keys to death and Hades (Revelation 1:18); your times, our times, are in His hands (Psalms 31:15). Then rest in the absolute certainty of the fact that as for God, His way is perfect.

October 25

Anger: It is a very real emotion. And though some may say so, anger is not always a sin. God tells us in Ephesians 4:26 (NAS), "Be angry, and yet do not sin. . . ."

When news of impending death comes, anger oftentimes follows. To deny this anger or to hide it is ridiculous. Anger needs to be recognized and dealt with, because it is a very real emotion of the human part of every man. Even though our bodies are the temples of the Holy Spirit, we still need to realize that our temples are made of flesh, flesh that can become angry. Jesus became angry, and so did God. The problem lies in how we handle our anger.

C. S. Lewis in his book *A Grief Observed* explained anger by describing the two parts of our being! There is a God-aimed, spirit part of us and there is a human, earthly part of us that is greatly affected by death's separation. The God-aimed, spirit part of us responds to God's touch, to the comfort that comes because we know deep down that He loves us and that we can trust Him. But the earthly part of us deals in human relationships and that part hurts and deeply feels the pain of death. As a wife or a mother or a daughter or a friend we feel the awful separation of death. And this is where anger can come in!

We are angry because death is severing a relationship; it is taking us away, separating us from our loved one or, in the event of our own death, from life itself. We are angry at death's apparent victory, but death will someday be swallowed up. When ". . . this mortal will have put on immortality, then will come about the saying that is written, 'Death is swallowed up in victory' " (1 Corinthians 15:54 NAS).

But until death is swallowed up in victory, how do we handle our anger and how do we help others who feel guilty because they became angry—even angry with God? We will talk about it tomorrow, beloved, but what can you do for today? Talk to your Father. Write Him a note telling Him what is on your heart. He wants you to consciously share it with Him. It will help.

October 26

Expressing anger over death can be healing. Bottling it up can be destructive. Joyce Landorf deals with this so beautifully in her outstanding book, *Mourning Song* (Fleming H. Revell Co.). In the chapter entitled "A Time for Anger," she writes:

"How dearly we need to have someone be patient with our doubts, to let us vent our anger, and to understand our frustrations. We need someone not to condemn, challenge, or lecture, but to lovingly help us to wait it out. Someone to turn our eyes on Jesus.

"Many months before her death, my mother slipped out of denial into anger. . . .

"I knew she was moving from, 'Oh, no—not me. I don't have cancer,' to, 'Oh, dear—*it is me.*' Since God had been a part of her life-style so long, I wondered if her anger would be directed toward Him. I didn't have long to wait. . . .

"There she was in bed, leaning back on the pillows. She had her eyes closed, a smile on her face, and her hands were folded on top of an overturned book. . . .

" 'Oh, honey, I've had the most wonderful experience.'

"She had been reading a book about Dr. Paul Carlson, who was a medical missionary to the Republic of Congo (now Zaire).

"She told me she had just gotten to the place where he was running toward the safety of a stone wall when Congolese rebels shot him to death. The area was liberated later, but for him it was just fifteen minutes too late. Mother sat straight up in bed in order to tell it better. She said she had put the book down and felt absolutely furious at God for allowing Dr. Carlson's death, 'After all,' she told God, 'he was only in his thirties—he was a doctor—hard at work for Your cause and for medicine. Why did You do that to him?' she had angrily shouted out to God. 'Why did You cut him down in the prime of his life and ministry? What mean joke were You playing on him—to let him go to Africa, be useful, and then have him get shot just as he was about to be safe?'

"As I looked at her, she lay back against the pillows and said, with a trace of sweet sorrow touching her voice, 'Of course, honey, what I was really downright mad about was why had God allowed me to have such a ministry—and one that was so blessed by His touch—and why was He taking me? Why now?'

"It was the first time that I had heard her, in her own words, admit that she was terminally ill. The moment tore me tenderly apart.

"'Don't cry, honey,' she said. 'Do you know what the Lord answered me about my questions on Dr. Carlson?' (I should have known *He'd* answer her!)

"'No—what?' I asked.

"'Well, He said, "Marion, you think Dr. Carlson was busy and effective for Me and My work there in the Congo? Oh, Marion, you should see him *now!*" Then . . . (my mother's eyes were glistening with tears) then, Joyce, the Lord said, "Marion, my dear child, you think you're busy there? Just wait till you get here! . . ."

"She had vocalized her outcry of anger at the Lord. She had recognized it and dealt with it head-on. Though it had taken time, the wounds of anger were clean cuts. The cuts were well on their way to healing because they were not infected with the pus of bitterness or self-pity.

"God had not been shocked at her outbursts, nor did He punish her for her resentment. He used her anger as an opportunity to give her a hope-filled message. Her past work was not finished, as she thought, but just about to really begin. She could lose her anger within the confines of God's loving message.

"She spent her anger that day and I was never to see, hear, or feel anger in her again.

"I am so glad our Lord understands our anger at death and dying. . . ."

His Thoughts Toward Me:

My Thoughts Toward Him:

October 27

". . . The righteous hath hope in his death" (Proverbs 14:32). Because of this promise, beloved, we can face death rather than deny it. We can resign ourselves to the inevitable. We can accept it, deal with it, and gracefully meet it when it comes. And if God grants us the knowledge of death's impending visit, we can deal responsibly with that knowledge. We can, to a degree, plan our last days together and make them treasured times of love, of assurance, of sharing; and if need be, times of preparation for meeting our God.

Because many are ignorant of death's process or because they refuse to face death, they find themselves unprepared to deal with it when it comes. As a result, grief is only compounded, and when it's all over, they wish they "had known better or done things differently." Even as I write all this, I realize that, had I known what I know now, I could have been more sensitive to the needs of my family when my father died. And because of this, precious ones, I want to share with you what I am learning so that we might learn together. Then we will be able to meet death graciously and victoriously whenever it comes, for even in this we can ". . . overwhelmingly conquer through Him who loved us" (Romans 8:37 NAS). When I say "victoriously," please know that I do *not* mean that we shall not shed tears or feel the ache of loneliness. No, beloved, I have shed so many tears as I've written this month's prayer guide . . . I've hurt for my precious, precious mother, for my sister and my brother, and I've missed my daddy. If I had realized I would not see him again, I would have had one last good-bye, one last long-lingering look. If I had realized that he was going to die, I would have begged the doctors to postpone the surgery. If . . . I have a list of *ifs*. And yet, because I know and believe in the sovereignty of my God of love, I do not dwell on the *ifs*; I cannot dwell on the *ifs*. To do so would mire me down in the quicksand of depression, and I would drown in the futility of what might have been. No, instead I cling in peace of mind to the promises of God which are "yea and amen," knowing that all things keep on working together ". . . for good to those who love God, to those who are called according to His purpose. For whom He foreknew, He also predestined to become conformed to the image of His Son . . ." (Romans 8:28, 29 NAS).

And as I cling to these promises, I thank God for the time He did give me with my father and my mother during those last few weeks of his life.

I do not know how people can survive who do not know God's sovereignty.

His Thoughts Toward Me:

October 28

If you know death is near, what can you do before it comes? How can you make those last days together precious and significant? How can you live them so they can be remembered without regret?

They need to be days of tenderness, of love, and, if possible, of sharing. If death is coming, denial or rejection will not delay its arrival. There is a time to die. God has set that time. "Since his days are determined, The number of his months is with Thee, And his limits Thou hast set so that he cannot pass" (Job 14:5 NAS).

When death is imminent, you need to talk about it. Avoiding the subject will only make it worse. Yet those who are healthy and well are afraid to talk to the dying about death because they don't know what the response will be. And the one facing death wonders how his loved ones are handling the fact that he is dying, but he won't ask. It's a lonely, awkward, silent, unending circle. One of you has to break it, but how?

If you know the Lord, you can seek His guidance. You might ask the sick person, "What has the doctor said about your illness?" Or you could ask, "Has the doctor given you any indication of your prognosis?" (*Prognosis* means the outcome of an illness: whether one will recover or not and, if so, how long recovery will take.) Beloved, as you ask these questions you need to remember that many times doctors have a problem dealing with death themselves, and sometimes they will avoid telling a patient the truth. Many doctors deny death just as their patients do. They do not want to face it because then they have to admit they are not immortal, or they do not want to face it because losing a patient makes them feel that they have failed as doctors. Therefore, you need to let the doctors know that we want the truth and that it is their responsibility to be honest with you.

When the dying one begins to share the ramifications of his illness, the lines of communication will be opened up. Even if he does not mention the possibility of his death, you will have begun to talk, to deal with the reality of his situation. From this beginning, with God's guidance, you eventually can ask him what his thoughts are about life after death. With his answer, whatever it may be, will come your opportunity to share what lies beyond death's door.

One of the reasons God has led me to write this is to give you these truths to share with others so that they might be prepared for death whenever it comes.

My Thoughts Toward Him:

October 29

"Who among all these does not know That the hand of the Lord has done this, In whose hand is the life of every living thing, And the breath of all mankind?" (Job 12:9, 10 NAS.) "So teach us to number our days, that we may apply our hearts unto wisdom" (Psalms 90:12).

The days of the dying are such important days; therefore I want to share some insights the Holy Spirit has helped me glean from experience, from Dr. Maurice Rawlings, and from Joyce Landorf's book, *Mourning Song*. (You must read, *Mourning Song!*)

If your loved one is conscious and able to communicate then spending time together talking is so important. Unsaid things need to be said. Talk about love. Let those precious, treasured "I love you's" pass between you often. When Daddy could not talk he still formed the words "I love you" with his lips. He said it over and over again. Talk about death. Let him share with you how he wants to die. Listen to him. Do not say, "Let's not talk about such gloomy things." If you say that, beloved, you put a dark cloud around death when in reality death for the Christian is stepping into the glory of heaven where the Lamb is the light.

One of the things your loved one may want to talk about is the pain connected with death. Is it painful to die? From all that I have read and heard, it seems that the actual process of death frees you from all pain, because it separates you from the body. Pain would only follow if you were to go to Hades. In *Before Death Comes,* Dr. Rawlings gives a patient's account: "Then I felt my heart stop. It actually stopped! Everything went black, and I knew then what it felt like to die! I was amazed that it was painless—like I had lost my breath, and then I wondered, *Is that all there is?*

"The pain miraculously had gone! I was at peace! It felt like a 'cloud nine' sensation, and the next thing I knew I sat up, got out of my body, and walked on air around the room, it was a floating sensation. I noticed that I could even walk through people! I had to walk around the nurses to see who it was they were really working on. As I looked around them, I was surprised to see myself! It was my face! And yet, here I was over here, feeling great! *That really can't be me, I thought, because the real me is over here!* I tried to tell them, 'I'm over here. Look here.' No one looked. No one seemed to hear me, and yet there were the two nurses over there, yelling out another 'code 99' through the curtain . . . I hated to come back to all this pain when I was having such a good time in this other world."

October 30

Hospitals, especially intensive care units, are hard places in which to die. I will be eternally grateful to the nurses in RICU at Venice Hospital in Florida. As I shared with them my mother's great need to be at my father's side, I reassured them of her stability and loving submission to authority. They realized that caring for a patient goes far beyond meeting his physical needs, and so they allowed my mother to sit at Daddy's bedside by the hour. They truly ministered to the whole man, as several of them even shared spiritual truths with us in Daddy's room. Daddy could not leave the RICU. He died there. However, if it is at all possible, the place to die is at home in your own surroundings, tended by your loved ones. How my heart aches for those abandoned in nursing homes, left to die because they have become a problem or an inconvenience to the living. We have lost the spirit of Christ who came not to be ministered unto but to minister, to lay down His life for others. And when the living neglect the dying, it will be the living who will suffer for it. God has much to teach us through sacrificial service to others, but many are missing it because they are so wrapped up in their own lives. How ashamed they will be when they see Jesus! We need to remember, too, that if we fail to do all we can do now, later we will probably have to deal with the pain and the problem of guilt.

In those precious remaining days, help your loved one keep his mind active. Read to him. Even if he is comatose or unable to respond, you need to remember that hearing is the last sense to go. Comatose patients, upon recovery, have told of things that were discussed in their presence. Since this is true, you need to help the patient feed mentally on things that will minister to him.

Read him Scripture above all else. Use a translation like the New International Version, unless of course he has his own favorite translation. And when you talk to him, do not talk in baby talk or in a condescending way. Talk as you usually talk. Keep your sense of humor. Do not put on a thespian mask of grimness. Be yourself, the person he knows.

Whether your loved one is at home or in the hospital, he needs to know what is going on medically. So often nurses, therapists, and even doctors come in and do their thing without a reasonable word of explanation to the patient. And it can be frightening—the unknown usually is! So see that procedures are explained. Reassure him of the life-saving and monitoring equipment that is there to help him should he need oxygen and so on. Tell him how his medicine will make him feel, what it will do to his body. And reassure him that it is fine to take medication for pain. Let him know that you want to know if he is hurting, that he need not hesitate to ask for relief from pain.

Bright colors are such a help as they break up the sterility of many a hospital room or intensive-care unit, so wear his favorite colors.

Oftentimes dying patients need a lot of sleep, so take full advantage of the precious moments between. Your loved one will enjoy waking and seeing you there, feeling your loving touch, and hearing you say, "I love you." It doesn't matter, precious one, if he sees the tears in your eyes; he will just want you there.

Many times the dying will express great concern over the medical expenses. Tell him not to worry, beloved, and don't you worry either if you are a child of God. God promises to supply all of your needs. It hurts God when we do not trust Him. God does not lie, so commit your way unto Him and watch Him bring it to pass. He is the Lord, the God of all flesh. There is nothing too hard for Him! (Jeremiah 32:27).

His Thoughts Toward Me:

My Thoughts Toward Him:

October 31

There is a time to weep, even for the Christian. There is a time to mourn, although we do not mourn as those who have no hope.

Weeping, mourning, time, these are gifts from God that if handled properly, will lead to healing. Oh, how we need to realize that tears, loneliness, and aching are not a sign of a lack of faith in our God, in His ways, or in His Word. To totally despair of life, to give up, to refuse to be comforted, to become bitter, to become self-centered, to stay angry at God, these would show a lack of faith in God, but not tears or mourning!

In *Mourning Song,* Joyce Landorf shares so well the needs of those who are "left behind to pick up the fragmented pieces of our broken lives." She writes, "Will there ever be a time when our hearts do not feel the tearing and ripping apart that continues to splinter and smash them? Will we ever respond to others and to our daily routines in what we once knew as a normal way? Since the experience of losing to death is so devastating, the immediate answers to these questions seem to be no—unequivocally no.

"Yet at the same instant we shout the answer, 'No,' there is a spontaneous, almost involuntary motion of hope deep within us and somewhere we hear someone say, 'Wait a minute, aren't you God's child? If you are, then hang on to this and grab hold of God's words. He said, 'I'll not leave you comfortless.' Didn't He promise to help us walk this dark valley? Of course He did and now He has given His Word for our safe return to life and normalcy."

What do we, those who are left behind, need when our loved one is taken from us in death? We need to cry, to weep, to be able to open the flood gates when the pressure mounts. Sometimes we will sob, almost bitterly, and at other times the tears will trickle through the cracks of our brave armor. Whatever, it is all right. Jesus wept. And what about those who come to console you, who feel awkward and don't know what to say? Let them weep with you. At times like these, the most comforting words are simply, "I understand." Now is a time for weeping, caring, sharing, holding, not for lectures or platitudes. God's Word to us, as members one of another is to weep with those who weep (Romans 12:15).

Not only do we weep, but we need to know that the ache of separation will linger for a while, maybe even for a year or two. And even then, at times, we will suddenly be hit by a stabbing pain of memory. There are still times when I am suddenly struck by a thought about Tom, my first husband, and his suicide. How important it is during this period of grief to let God be God in our lives, and thus receive Him as "the God of all comfort." Evening and night are times that are especially hard. Ask Him to hold you close. This would be a good time for you to call or to visit your bereaved friends. Houses can be so lonely at night.

Joyce Landorf also shares that we need to accept the apathy of grief. It's hard to go at your usual pace. The listlessness of grief sets in, and we need to expect it. It won't last forever. My dear mother is so very capable and yet she has told me how difficult it was to make even routine decisions after Daddy died. Packing the car to come and visit us was a nerve-wracking experience. This is where friends can come in and rescue those who are grieving. Don't try to get them to pick up their pace, but rather ask God to show you what needs you can meet. My sister, Judy, provided such beautiful support for my mother as she stayed with her after Daddy's death and helped her straighten out a seemingly unending list of insurance forms, papers, and so on that must be taken care of at death. Anything we can do, from cleaning to washing to cooking, will help. In addition, our continued support in the months to come will help fill the void left by death.

Grief brings us into acute awareness of the needs of others. Suddenly we become more sensitive to their hurts. The comfort that we receive from God in times of sorrow is not a comfort to be hoarded but rather to be shared (2 Corinthians 1:3–7). And the more we give, the more we'll find left in the bottom of the barrel. It will become an unending wellspring from the Father. When sorrow causes us to sit where others have sat, we learn about their needs. Illness, dying, and grief have a way of humbling us, of stripping off our cocky self-confidence, our critical if-that-were-me analysis, and our holier-than-thou theologies. Grief leaves us naked and vulnerable. In grief, we can begin to learn the character of love.

Death—how is it conquered? By love, for "God so loved the world, that he gave his only begotten Son, [to die so] that whosoever believeth in him should not perish, but have everlasting life" (John 3:16). Jesus Christ is the Resurrection and the Life, believeth thou this? Then you can be sure, beloved, that when death calls, when your loved one dies, or when you die, the cry will go out, "He is not here. He is risen!"

To be absent from the body is to be present with the Lord. Therefore may our prayer be that ". . . Christ shall even now, as always, be exalted in our bodies, whether by life or by death" (*see* Philippians 1:20 NAS).

Amen and Amen.

My Thoughts Toward Him:

NOVEMBER

November 1

Sometimes, when you are still and quiet with nothing pressing on you, does your mind wander back into the past, where you think of what might have been, if only . . .

I was lying in bed this morning, all snugly and comfortable, enjoying not having to get up. Jack and I are on vacation staying with dear friends in Seattle. David is away at camp. I was thinking about our family and how eager I was for us all to be together again.

Then, my mind began to wander back into the past—way back —and I started thinking about my first marriage, about Tom, about how he was voted the most likely to succeed, and about how he hanged himself! Then, I went back, further still, and I thought of how he would come to pick up our sons, Tommy and Mark, for a weekend; he would bring his date with him, and I would have my date with me. It is painful to write this, to share it with you, but I feel God would have me share. Maybe you can learn from my mistakes; maybe you will be smart enough to listen so that tears of regret will not mark the memories of your past. Then, I began to wonder how much the boys have missed not having their own, their real, father to wrestle with them on the floor after dinner or being able to say, "My mom and my dad and I went . . ."

Why did I do it? Why was I so selfish? Why didn't I think of my sons? Why didn't I think of Tom? Why didn't I think of God and His way? Why didn't I work at keeping my family a family instead of thinking of *my own happiness,* what I needed or thought I needed, what I wanted or thought I wanted?

I wonder if I will ever really know what went through those two little boys' minds—the longing, the hurt, the confusion. Oh, they have survived, but what would it have been if . . . ?

I couldn't let my mind wander anymore; it was too painful. It is done. I am to forget those things which are behind (Philippians 3:13).

Yes, Lord, it is done, and I am so sorry. O Father, how thankful I am that with You it is never *too* late to start from where we are, to stop tearing down, to press on to the prize of the goal of godly living, living the way I am supposed to live.

"The wise woman builds her house, But the foolish tears it down with her own hands" (Proverbs 14:1 NAS).

Get up. The past is past. There is a future and a hope with God. Let us arise and build.

November 2

Building takes time; it takes planning! And that is where most of us have failed so miserably as parents. We have never really stopped to consider where we are going as far as our family is concerned—where we are going, and how are we going to get there!

We are so busy, so caught up in so many activities of life. Busy making a living, busy at church, busy in clubs and organizations of every variety and sort. And, for the most part, it is all worthwhile, and much of it is needful.

We come home; we are tired; we need a break; we just need to relax and have some *time to ourselves.* So we do. We read the paper or we watch television or we putter at whatever we like to putter at or we take a nap. Then, even at rest or play, pressure stands waiting offstage, pressing us to hurry on with our part so that we can get on with the show. The show must go on!

As the light goes out, possibly, you suddenly remember that you meant to do something with or for your son or your daughter. The twinge of guilt is quieted with, "I'll do it tomorrow"; then, you begin to think of tomorrow! It will be the same as today!

The days will roll on into months; then it will be, "I can't believe a year has already gone by! Well, this year, we are going to . . ." But then the year is gone and another and another.

Your children's toys change and so do their bodies. All of a sudden, they are teens! And what you thought about doing, what you would have liked to have done, what you should have done, is now impossible to do! Time is gone.

What kind of a relationship do you have to show for the time? What kind of a child have you raised? What are their memories of childhood things, of relationships?

Children, family, marriage—these are the bedrock of our society! Not money, professions, possessions, inventions, achievements, education, et cetera. Why? Because children, family, and marriage are people! The home is the means *of* or the reason *for* money, professions, possessions, inventions, achievements, education, et cetera! And, yet, we give ourselves to the et ceteras of life!

Have you planned for your child, your family, your marriage? What are your goals for them? How are you going to achieve these goals? What things *must* be done? What time will they take?

Take time; it is vital. Get alone with God and ask God to show you what your family needs. Then, write these needs under **His Thoughts Toward Me.**

His Thoughts Toward Me:

My Thoughts Toward Him:

November 3

Someday, you and I will stand before God and give an account of the way we have lived. " '. . . As surely as I live,' says the Lord, 'Every knee will bow before me; every tongue will confess to God.' So then, each of us will give an account of himself to God" (Romans 14:11, 12 NIV).

And in that time of accounting, we will account for the way we have handled our responsibility as parents and as husbands or as wives. And I believe, also, that we will be accountable for our behavior as children. If God gives commands within any of these areas or relationships of life, we become accountable to God for that command. God has given commands to husbands, to wives, and to children. We shall look at these commands later on this month, but know for now, beloved, that we are accountable for these relationships.

So far this week we have seen that the marriage, the home, and the family need to be built. They just don't happen, although we treat them as if they do. Families, good families, like good marriages, come as a result of careful planning; they just do not happen overnight! They take time and effort—time to develop, time to grow. They take a willful doing of whatever is needful!

So you must make some decisions, and that will take some time. When will you begin? The best time to begin is immediately. If you don't begin now, you will put it off; and, once again, you will be caught in the same old rut of living that you have been walking in all of this time. So determine that, today, you are going to start, no matter what, to make some decisions. After all, what is really important—not urgent, but important, of eternal value? For what are you accountable to God?

Well, begin. Gather your family together sometime today for a family powwow! (1) Tell them that God has shown you how special and how precious they are to you and to Him. (2) Tell them that you want them really to know joy and fulfillment as individuals and as a family. Explain to them that God wants *us* to have a happy home, one filled with love, joy, laughter, peace. A home that is fun to be a part of! (3) If, at this point, you know you have failed your family in the past, ask them to forgive you for failing to put them first. *Do not defend or excuse yourself in any way.* If you do, it will spoil it. (4) Then, tell them that if you are going to have this kind of a home, plans will have to be made on how this can be done. (5) Tell them that, during this month of November, this will be *our* family project and that they will be having some good times of talking, sharing, and planning together in the days to come. Then, by Thanksgiving, your family will have a very special thing for which to be thankful. *(If for some reason, beloved, another family member does not catch your joy, hope, optimism, don't scold or show any anger or disappointment. Ask God to show you why they are reacting this way; just persevere in faith and prayer!)* (6) Have each member of the family write out, on his own piece of paper, what he thinks could be done to make the following two things happen:

(a) to make him happier, and

(b) to make your family life a more happy family life.

Tell them you will discuss their suggestions tomorrow at the family powwow. (If you have little ones that can't write, you write for them; but there must be *no* rebuttals on your part.)

If you are a single parent, don't despair! Begin to build with what you have. Cry to your God, He always hears. He will give you hope. If you have no children, write out what you can do for your marriage and begin planning before your children come. If your children are grown and gone, plan how you can still minister to one another and to them. It is never too late. Or if you live with a roommate, you can have family powwows together!

Now, write out a prayer to God for your marriage, your family, or your roommate.

My Prayer:

November 4

Pride—it goes before a fall. If this month is to be a month of harvest, a month of reaping a better family life, a month of reaping more security for your loved ones, you must put away *all* pride. Not others', yours! Only you can humble yourself.

432

One of the most harmful or threatening enemies of good, healthy relationships is poor communication. A solid relationship with another person cannot be built apart from communication. In the days to come, we will talk about communication. But, for now, we must talk about pride before you go into your family powwow! If pride is not taken care of in your life, then the powwow is doomed to failure.

Pride, for whatever reason it comes, can keep us from hearing —really hearing—what others are trying to say to us. It can cause us to erect walls of defense because we feel we must protect ourselves or keep our self-image intact.

It is hard to be vulnerable, to lay ourselves bare before another, isn't it? What if you are hurt? What if you find out that you have failed? What if they see that you are not perfect? You are afraid they will turn away in disappointment, in disgust, in despair of your ever being what you should be. Quite possibly. And, thus, bound by these fears, hiding behind your wall of pride, you never expose yourself to another and you're safe, in a sense! But there does remain a wall between you and others. And you are separated!

Today, you are going to sit down with your family and *listen* to them as they share what could be done to make them happier as individuals and as a family. Oh, dear one, I understand your vulnerability, I have been there. But do not defend yourself in any way, do not excuse yourself in any way, just listen and ask appropriate, *but not loaded,* questions. Make appropriate comments, like, "That's an interesting thought" . . . "Good idea" . . . "Sounds like fun." At this point, *do not* react saying, "But that is unreasonable, impossible, dumb, crazy" or "We do not have the time." *Just listen.* You do not have to resolve anything today. Have every member of the family share and let each one know that what they have said has worth, simply because of its source. They have worth. Set a time limit to the family powwow so that it won't drag on and so that they will be eager to have another one tomorrow, or if tomorrow is absolutely impossible, make it the next day.

When each one finishes, have someone collect the suggestions and write them out. Put them on the refrigerator or someplace for all to see. Then, tell them that at the next family powwow you will all talk about the suggestions and about what you can do to get started making home and family even happier.

Before you go, meditate on this Scripture, "A plan in the heart of a man [*or child or wife*] is *like* deep water, But a man of understanding draws it out. Many a man proclaims his own loyalty, But who can find a trustworthy man? A righteous man who walks in his integrity—How blessed are his sons after him" (Proverbs 20:5–7 NAS).

God, Show Me What Keeps Me From Being Vulnerable:

Things My Family Wants . . . Needs:

November 5

Communication—without it there can be no relationship. It is vital to life! Poor communication is the root cause of many of our problems.

How well do you know your mate, your son, your daughter? How often do you talk? How often do you share? Do you know more about them than just that which is seen, that which is evident? Do you understand the "whys" of their actions or responses? Are you aware of their fears and their frustrations because they have felt free to share these with you? Have you ever shared yourself with them—your fears, your frustrations, your longings?

Communication is not just verbal! We communicate much with our body; it is called body language. Our expressions, our position, our eyes, our hands, our tenseness or lack of it, all of these say something to those whom we are with. A touch, a pat on the back, a hand on the shoulder, a hug, a ruffled head, a squeezed hand, a love tap on the seat communicate so much.

How well do you communicate? Don't, please don't, excuse yourself saying, "I'm just not a communicator. I am not a toucher.

I am not a talker. I never will be, so let's forget it. I will never change, that is just the way I am. And furthermore, that is the way I am going to stay." Oh, beloved, don't say it! If that is your attitude, there is no hope for you, and there is little for your family. "He that refuseth instruction despiseth his own soul. . . . He is in the way of life that keepeth instruction: but he that refuseth reproof erreth" (Proverbs 15:32; 10:17).

Why don't you stop; take a minute; tell God that you want to learn all that He has for you to learn. Then, ask God to show you where you need to learn to communicate better: in verbal communication, in nonverbal, or in both. List below each member of your family, then ask God to show you how well you know and understand each one according to the questions you have read in today's devotional.

My Communication With My Family:

November 6

Today, you need to set up another family powwow for Sunday. It is important to set up the powwows ahead of time because it shows consideration of the family's time and plans. Share with them how much the powwow means to you because you love them and want to be a better parent.

Before you have that powwow, we need to share more on communication so that you will be ready for your family sharing time. Ask God to show you how to make these times special; maybe you can serve popcorn, a favorite meal, or dessert. Right after dinner, around the table, is one of the best times to share because you are already together. Let the dishes go; just push them aside. What is important? Do the important not the urgent! If the phone rings, don't answer it. This really impresses the kids with their importance. Also, when you have a powwow, act on what has been suggested. Carry through, or it will be just another disappointment.

There is so much I want to share with you. I'm so excited about writing this month's devotional for *us,* not only you, because Jack and I will go through it with you, day by day, powwow by powwow. I know God is going to use it greatly in our lives. Tomorrow, I want to begin sharing with you four major hindrances to openness in communication; but, before I do, I feel God would have me share with you that the very bedrock necessity for any communication is *accessibility.* You cannot communicate with someone who will not spend time with you. And, thus, we touch on the greatest weakness in the American family, and that is spending time together, *with* one another. There will never be any real communication without time. And without time for communication, there will never be a good, solid, healthy, whole family. Destroy the family and you will destroy a nation. Destroy the family, and living will cease—mere existence will continue!

A study in a small American community shows that the average time per day fathers spend with their very young sons is about thirty-seven seconds. Cross-cultural studies show that American parents spend less time with their children than parents in almost any other country in the world. Although both Russian parents work and Russian children spend a great deal of time in family collectives, emotional ties between children and parents are stronger and the time spent together considerably greater than in the United States.

May our prayer be, Lord, "So teach us to number our days, that we may apply our hearts unto wisdom" (Psalms 90:12).

God, Is My Time With My Children Adequate?

November 7

What keeps a person from opening up, from sharing? What hinders communication? I want to share four major hindrances to openness. I learned them years ago, probably from Henry Brandt or from reading James Mallory's book, *The Kink and I.* As I read these hindrances, God brought Scripture to my mind as He usually does.

Let me share one of the four hindrances today, then I'll share the others with you in the days to come. After you read each day's writing, take these things before the Lord and ask Him to speak to you on these issues. Then, listen for His still, small voice in your heart and write down **His Thoughts Toward Me.** Recording this is excellent therapy, and it is wonderful to look back upon! It is a good test of growth and obedience.

One of the reasons a person will not open up to another is because of the fear of being judged or criticized. We are very hesitant to open up to those whom we feel would reject or not accept what we have to say. Who needs critics! We have enough of those! This is one of the main reasons teens won't open up to their parents. "If I do tell them how I really feel, all I'll do is throw them into shock or get a lecture back! Who needs it!"

If you are going to lay a foundation for communication, next to the stone of "accessibility," lay the stone of "acceptance." If someone is really going to feel free to communicate their very heart with you, they first need to be assured of your acceptance of them as a person not your acceptance of their behavior. You can say, "That is wrong," as long as you do not reject them. Is this not the way it is with God? Our behavior may be wrong; He may have to chasten us; but we are ". . . accepted in the beloved" (Ephesians 1:6).

Things we say as parents show our children that there are certain things they can't communicate because to do so makes them unacceptable. Actually, we should teach them that the reason certain things should not be said is because the thing itself is not proper, appropriate, or right; but never should we say things like: "Don't say that, what will people say or think about you?" or "Hush, nice people don't feel that way." Also be careful about saying, "I don't understand you" because the implication there is that there is something wrong with them. If you don't understand, say, "I don't understand what you are saying." Then, you are not rejecting them as people.

Are you your child's (or your mate's) critic, or are you their coach? Are you on their team? Are they convinced of it? If so, they will share anything with you. Give them the opportunity!

"A friend loves at all times, And a brother is born for adversity" (Proverbs 17:17 NAS). If the heavenly Father accepts us just the way we are, should not the earthly father?

His Thoughts Toward Me:

November 8

Another thing or habit, on your part, that will keep your mate or your children from opening up and freely talking with you is giving advice too quickly, too patly, spilling out your counsel immediately. Sometimes, we do not even want to hear the other person out. We have already sized up the problem, analyzed it, and belched out the answer. If affects us like bad breath; we want to back away and go talk to someone else, someone who will give understanding before they give advice. Listen to God's words of wisdom. He is the Master Communicator! "The heart of the righteous ponders how to answer" (Proverbs 15:28 NAS). "He who gives an answer before he hears, It is folly and shame to him" (Proverbs 18:13 NAS).

Sometimes, when we hear certain things, we react to what we have heard in a shocked or a negative way. Reactions like that can end communication very quickly. Suppose your child told you, "I just don't believe in the Bible or God anymore." What would you say? Would you react in horror? Would you tell him that it is a dumb or stupid statement? Would you warn him that he would end up in hell for beliefs like that? OR would you remain calm, unmoved (externally at least), and say, "That is interesting. What brought you to that conclusion? I would like to hear it" . . . then, listen keeping the door of communication open, praying that God would let him see the folly of his arguments. Oh, beloved, how we need to learn to listen, to let our loved ones talk out their beliefs without getting all hot under the collar. "He who restrains his words has knowledge, And he who has a cool spirit is a man of understanding" (Proverbs 17:27 NAS).

One last word. When your mate or your child is in the midst of a strong emotion,—disappointment, hurt, anger, or bitterness— remember that they cannot usually accept advice at that time. What they need is someone who *understands* the emotion; note that I did not say *condones* but rather understands. If you'll say, "I understand *how* you feel," and then be quiet, when the emotion comes under control, they will want to share with you because you will understand.

For openness in communicating with your family, you'll never find two better words than, "I understand." Try it.

Why don't you set up another family powwow for Sunday lunch or dinner? Keep it without fail. Thanksgiving is coming!

His Thoughts Toward Me:

My Thoughts Toward Him:

November 9

Before we continue on hindrances to communication, I must share with you what to do at your family powwow. It is a practical exercise in communication for the family that will really get the talk going as long as you don't put your foot in your mouth and squelch the whole thing.

The whole purpose of this time is that you might become more sensitive to one another and to each other's needs. Knowing their needs will show you ways that you might express your love to them. If you don't have children or if they are grown and gone, then the two of you spend this time together. Or if you are single and live with others, share this time with them. You'll find it a great experience!

As the family gathers, have a piece of paper and a pen for each one, unless, of course, the children are too young to write. If they are, then just have them verbalize their answers when it is their turn to share.

First, have each one write down what they think about each

member of the family or what they wish that member of the family would do or wouldn't do and why.

The second thing they should write down is what they think each member of the family thinks about them and why.

When you finish writing out the answers, have the family share, one by one. As the sharing goes on, listen very carefully. This could be the most enlightening time of your life. Don't get angry . . . don't get hurt and go away mad. Be vulnerable; Christ was. You can explain yourself, but do not defend yourself.

Remember, the words, *I understand* are very valuable! If your children cry when they share or if they get vehement in what they are saying, watch and listen carefully. God is uncovering a need that has been bottled up. If you will respond to the need rather than react, healing is on its way.

Remember, dear one, "Let your speech always be with grace, seasoned, as it were, with salt, so that you may know how you should respond to each person" (Colossians 4:6 NAS).

Today, instead of writing **His Thoughts Toward Me** and **My Thoughts Toward Him**, write out a prayer for this family time.

My Prayer:

November 10

How did the family powwow go? How are you doing with your communication skills? Remember the old but true saying, "Practice makes perfect." I know that God is going to honor your desires, your prayers, your diligent efforts, and the time you are devoting to being all you should be as a marriage partner and as a parent.

Today, let me share with you the third major hindrance to openness in communication. This hindrance is the fact that others won't open up to us because we've closed up, we've closed our minds! We have them figured out; we have diagnosed their case, their problem. And so, we say things like, "You always have to have your own way," "You never listen; you will never change,"

"You are the same as the rest of them; you are no different," "That's typical of you," "I remember when you last . . ."

Oh, beloved, if you are one who always drags up the past, who never lets another forget what happened, you can know for certain there will be very little communication between you and another!

If you are going to effectively communicate with your mate, with your children, with anyone, never deal with their personality but rather with the problem. Remember, people will not open up to people they feel do not accept them! Be careful with words such as *never, always, typical.* Proverbs 18:19 (NAS), says, "A brother offended *is harder to be won* than a strong city. . . ." Words like these indicate an unforgiving spirit. We will deal more with this later; but, for now, just remember, beloved, that love forgives not condemns. Look at Calvary.

If you will give your family your assurance of unconditional love, of the fact that you are on their team; if you will be willing to forget the past, you can be greatly used of God in others' lives. We all need someone to be on our team.

Never break your child's or your mate's spirit, or you could destroy them. Believe in them. God does! "The spirit of a man can endure his sickness, But a broken spirit who can bear?" (Proverbs 18:14 NAS).

With God, there is always a new beginning. There is always hope.

God, My Prayer Is:

November 11

The last major hindrance to communication, at first glance, may strike you as being trite and rather obvious; yet, it is just what I said it is, a major hindrance. This hindrance is lack of openness. You cannot communicate with someone who will neither talk nor listen. You can talk to a person all day, share your heart with them, weep tears of longing, desperation, or bitterness. And they can sit there, apparently listening with no sign of impatience, wait for you to finish talking, and get up and walk away. Has anyone ever done that to you? Do you feel like you have communicated with them? Of course not! Why? Because they have not talked back; they have not discussed the problem with you; they have not let you know how they feel about what you have said. Oh, they have listened. And if you challenged them regarding hearing what you had said, they could, in essence, repeat what you had said. But there has been no communication because there has been no openness on their part. Possibly, the closed party won't open up because of some failure in the first three hindrances to communication that we have discussed, or maybe there are other reasons. Maybe they have said, "I'm just not a talker."

That could be; but, beloved, we can be certain of this: Relationships will never go below the surface apart from communication. If you refuse to open up, if you refuse to learn to talk no matter how painful it may be, then consider your self-centeredness. When you open up, you become vulnerable. To refuse to become vulnerable is pride. And "Pride goeth before destruction . . ." (Proverbs 16:18).

Instead of opening up, we expect people to read our minds. We say things like, "Well, you should know without me having to tell you." Maybe we should, but the safest way to make sure that they know is by opening up and telling them! If we expect others to understand, we must share! Therefore, if I am going to communicate, I must be willing to talk. But I must also be willing to listen, to truly hear what is being said. We will talk about listening tomorrow. But let me ask you about what we have learned today. Will you open up? Will you talk, share, bare your soul for your mate's sake, for your family's sake, for your Lord's sake? Tell God what you need, then tell your family. Remember, He said, ". . . You do not have because you do not ask" (James 4:2 NAS).

God, This Is What I Need:

November 12

"Never mind." "Just leave me alone." "Go away." "What's the use?" "It doesn't matter anyway." "Why talk, it won't do any good?"

Do any of those phrases sound familiar? Has anyone ever said any of these to you? They have been said to me, as a mother and as a Christian. To me, they were statements of debt sent special delivery showing me that I owed a listening heart. I had failed, failed to listen and, thus, failed in communicating! If I am going to communicate with my mate, my children, with people in general, I must hear and understand what they are saying not only with their lips but also with their body language. One of the reasons our children or our mates do not talk to us is simply because we do not take the time or make the effort to listen. We'll listen with one ear and keep on doing something else, like reading the newspaper, watching television, or fooling with notes on our desks. They can tell we are not listening because we will interrupt with thoughts of our own or with inappropriate statements. Why talk to someone who will not listen? Listening takes time. Listening takes effort—effort to pay attention, effort to watch their faces, effort to discern exactly what they are saying and why they are saying it, effort to ask appropriate and discerning questions that will let us know how they are feeling deep down inside.

Are you accessible? Do you have time to sit and talk? Are you available when your wife, your husband, or your children need you? Have you ever realized that your availability to your children is far more valuable than their college education, a car, other material possessions that you might give them? They want you to care, to be interested, personally, in what they are thinking, to listen to them not for the purpose of straightening them out but for the purpose of knowing how they feel.

If you neglect to give your loved ones a listening heart, if you

443

fail to be available, then know they will feel neglected and lonely.

"The hearing ear and the seeing eye, The Lord has made both of them" (Proverbs 20:12 NAS). O Lord, help us to hear . . . and let us see the need of others.

His Thoughts Toward Me:

My Thoughts Toward Him:

November 13

How do we block communication? Cut it off? Make others feel like it's not worth the effort?

Many just withdraw. They walk away excusing themselves with, "Well, I have to do my homework" or "I'd better get busy, or I'll never get finished." And they are off! Others withdraw behind a newspaper or a book. Some have to go back to the office. Others must go back to bed. Then, in other families, everyone is too busy doing their own thing, going their own separate way. And nothing is talked out. Depending on your personality type, you will handle difficult situations in a number of various ways; but usually none handle them in the ideal way. The ideal way is to talk, to listen, to make every effort that you can to understand, accept, appreciate, and respect one another. But then, for most, it is easier to turn on the television, "shush" one another, and escape from reality.

We have started this month with a desire to build a stronger, more secure, family unit. Our goal is to achieve a new depth of joy, happiness, and security as a family so that Thanksgiving Day really becomes a day of true gratitude.

Why not get a family discussion going at the dinner table tonight? Tell them how much you have enjoyed the family pow-wows and getting to share with one another. Then, ask them what they think keeps them from having the time to talk with one another. You might have each one share when they have wanted to talk to another member of the family but felt like they couldn't, and why they felt that way. Tell them that as each one shares they have to listen without interrupting. When everyone has finished sharing, questions can be asked. Parents, do not defend yourself; just listen; then, tell them that you want to do better.

"Listen to counsel and accept discipline, That you may be wise the rest of your days" (Proverbs 19:20 NAS). Don't withdraw. Draw near!

His Thoughts Toward Me:

My Thoughts Toward Him:

November 14

What expectations do you have for your mate . . . for your children?

Do you realize that, many times, the reason your child, or even your mate, will not communicate with you is because they feel like they cannot live up to your expectations of them? They just cannot fill the bill; they just cannot reach your goals for them; they just cannot be what you want them to be. They have tried, but they just cannot seem to please you no matter how hard they try. All these expectations bring pressure—pressure to perform, pressure to be, pressure to attain.

Spend your time today listing the name of each member of your family below. Then, after some honest meditation, write down your expectations or goals for each of them. Do this rapidly without evaluating what you expect. Then, next to each expectation, write out the reason why you expect that from that particular person.

445

My Family And My Expectations For Them:

November 15

Yesterday, we talked a little bit about expectations and how unrealistic expectations can hinder our communication with others. Today, review what you have listed as your expectations for each member of your family.

Begin by evaluating why you expect what you do. Is it a valid reason? A biblical reason? A reason born of tradition? Does the reason, in any way, elevate your flesh, your ego? Does the reason find God's stamp of approval? When you finish, look at the expectation itself.

It may have a valid, biblical, or common-sense reason, but is it appropriate to

their age,
their sex,
their temperament,
their abilities,
their desires,
their personality?

Why not take your expectations before the Throne of Grace today and talk with God about each of them. Tell your Father—their Father—that you want to know His heart, then write down below what comes to your heart about each loved one.

November 16

We've been sharing about expectations for our loved ones. And this is what you will share in your family powwow today if you are following our family-building plan. But, before you go into that family powwow, let me share with you something I have learned the hard way—by mistakes and by defeat. Maybe I can spare you some pain. I think that, many times, we, as Christians, put the so-called Christian expectations of others on our children. I would call them Christian "traditions" rather than biblical principles. I am referring to the "taste nots, touch nots, handle nots" that are deemed holy or unholy by the Christian community in which you live. I remember riding Tommy and Mark, trying to squeeze them into a molded behavior pattern to suit those inspecting them rather than respecting them as children—children who were created by God with definite personalities and abilities to be used for Him in accomplishing the work God ordained for them before the foundation of the world. Tom and Mark are extremely outgoing and, at times, their laughter and antics need curbing, but this must be done without squelching their God-given gregariousness. Our dear, active David has been criticized for holes in his pant-knees when Mom dresses so well (thanks to so many), but to keep him holeless was to tie him to a chair! Do you see what I mean? "Be quiet . . . be good . . . be polite because so-and-so is looking this way. What will they think?" Wrong expectations lead to "riding your kids" with constant criticisms, with do's or don'ts until, eventually, they feel defeated, unsuccessful, bitter, or rebellious. We will talk about it more tomorrow.

In your powwow today, have the children list what they think you, as parents, expect of them. Then, list what you think your children expect of you. Next, swap notes; have each one read what they wrote and discuss it.

Husband and wife, when you are alone tonight, share your expectations with each other. You will find it quite an eye-opener.

Remember, with regard to your family and to the community's expectations, "For am I now seeking the favor of men, or of God? Or am I striving to please men? If I were still trying to please men, I would not be a bond-servant of Christ" (Galatians 1:10 NAS).

His Thoughts Toward Me:

My Thoughts Toward Him:

November 17

One of the things God has shown me that is absolutely vital to my relationship with my children, my husband, and our staff is to let them know that I am on their team, that I am for them not against them, that I am committed to them as people, and that I love them with God's love, which never fails.

I must be honest with you and tell you that I have not always conveyed this to my husband, to my children, to our staff—and I have been wrong.

Just recently, God did a mighty work of healing in one of my son's lives when I looked at him through tear-filled eyes and told him that he was more important to me than my ministry. He almost came across the table! I love my sons so much, just the way they are. And they love me, just the way I am, "warts and all" as the saying goes. And I love my God—first and foremost. Without that love for God, knowing me, I know I couldn't love anyone but myself. It is God's love that enables me to love my husband, my sons, my staff, you! Sometimes, my zeal for God's work (not always according to knowledge) has overridden love's zeal for my family and my staff; this ought not to be!

Does your family have the security of knowing that you are committed to them no matter what? Does your Lord and your God know that you are committed to Him no matter what? I know that God has committed Himself totally to me—I am His forever. That blessed assurance draws me, calls me to loyalty not license! Ask God to show you how to assure your family of your total commitment to them—no matter what. Love "bears all things, believes all things, hopes all things, endures all things. Love never fails. . . ." (1 Corinthians 13: 7, 8 NAS).

His Thoughts Toward Me:

My Thoughts Toward Him:

November 18

How I wish I could sit down and talk with you face to face! As I write these devotions, I pray that God will give me the ability to convey, through words and punctuation, the message that I want to convey to you. It is a message that can be given only through words not through my countenance, my body, my language, my tone of voice. It's the facial expression, the tone of voice, the attitude of the body that colors the words and gives them proper expression rather than leaving them black or white! Do you understand what I'm trying to say?

The whole purpose of these devotions is to communicate with you as an individual because you are special to God, because He wants to minister to you in a personal way. Whether you realize it or not, you, and all that concerns you, are of primary importance to the Father. To show you this truth, God says, ". . . the very hairs of your head are all numbered" (Matthew 10:30 NAS). One little sparrow cannot fall to the ground apart from the Father. And you, created in His image and worth the death of His only Son, are of far more value than many sparrows (Matthew 10:29–31).

In these past seventeen days of November, as we have talked of the family and communication, I have made numerous references to body language. Why? Because body language is a vital part of communication. Your words are colored by the ease or tenseness of your body. If you relax, lean back, uncross your arms, your whole body is saying, "I'm listening, feel free to share with me; I have time for you." Or you can lean forward, smile softly, and give

449

your full attention, and they know you *want* to hear what they have to say. Your eyes, your expressions, your tone of voice—all of these confirm, deny, or contradict your words; all of these are as important as your words.

Now, can you understand my concern in writing to you? I must convey it all in words alone. That is why I break into "Oh, beloved . . ." because I long to convey His love, thus, my love, to you as I write.

What are you saying to your mate, to your children, through your body language? How do you color your words? Why not discuss it tonight during dinner?

His Thoughts Toward Me:

My Thoughts Toward Him:

November 19

Dinner, supper, whatever you call your evening meal, how important is it? What is its purpose? Is it simply to fill empty tummies, to satisfy crys of, "I'm hungry, when are we going to eat?" Could your evening meal serve another purpose besides that of pacifying growling stomachs? Obviously, it could, or I wouldn't bring the subject up; but before we discuss it, let me ask you a question. What are your evening meals like? Are they hurried trips to quick-service food stops? Are they split-shift meals with different members of the family eating at different times because everyone is going in different directions? Are they, "Shush, I can't hear what they're saying on television"? Are they let's give-an-ulcer meals when we are not only going to chew our food but also chew out certain worthy members of the family? Are they meals when you dine with "the General" who constantly speaks in commands,

"Quit that! . . . Don't do that! . . . Son, stop that . . . I've told you once, now I'm telling you again, don't . . . You had better . . . Put your hand in your lap . . . Get your elbow off the table"?

Or are your meals special times—so special that no one is in a hurry to go anywhere else? Are they times of good discussion when each person has the freedom to share what he believes? Are they times of reminiscing about the past? Are they times of story telling when the children learn to verbalize what is important to them? Are they times of laughter . . . that good old belly-shaking, doubled-up kind of laughter that releases the tensions of the day and is so good for body and soul? Are they times when the whole family pauses in the midst of a busy day just to be together?

What are you doing for dinner tonight?

His Thoughts Toward Me:

My Thoughts Toward Him:

November 20

How can I make the evening meal a special family time? And why should I? We will talk about it the next few days. How I pray that you will have eyes to see, ears to hear, the will to act so that your family life might know a new, rich depth of relationship.

There is much talk today about "the fractured family"—families that are divided rather than united. I think the term was primarily aimed at families that were broken by divorce. However, the term has taken on a broader meaning to include the family that lives together but very seldom spends time together because each one is going his separate way. Each is so busy doing his own thing, fulfilling his own desires, recognizing and achieving his own personal worth, that the family has ceased to be united. Or the family members have found it impossible to coordinate their personal schedules so that they really have time for one another. When can a family get together to talk, to share, to touch base with one another, to be whole instead of fractured into parts that never interlock to form a picture of solidarity that gives life its proper perspective?

One of our greatest problems today—and the root cause of a host of other problems—is the fact that we live totally individualistic, self-centered lives with little or no concern for others; we are only concerned for ourselves. Many find others important only if those others, in some way, can benefit their own personal, selfish needs or desires! We have countless activities and demands, even in church-related spheres, that pull us away from each other. When can we touch base with one another? When do we have time to communicate as a family on more than a superficial level? When can we learn of and take time to "Bear one another's burdens, and so fulfill the law of Christ" (Galatians 6:2)? When can we learn of one another's needs and learn not ". . . to be served but to serve" (Mark 10:45 NAS) . . . to lay down our lives for one another (John 15:13) . . . to rejoice with those who rejoice and to weep with those who weep (Romans 12:15)?

How fractured is your family? For whom does each family member really live? Write out below how much time your family spends together, as a unit, each day. How much time each week? When? Doing what?

November 21

When do you have time to talk as a family, to share with one another, to be involved as a whole in a relaxed and informal way? Are family powwows for an hour a week enough? When can you learn how your children think? When can you help them sort out their values, their concepts, their understanding of the precepts of life? When do you take the time to relate the practical aspects of God's Word to their situations of life?

Nowhere in the Word of God does God talk about family devotions. And, yet, some of you wives almost resent your husbands, at times, because they do not have family devotions. Now, please don't get upset with me and turn me off! I think family devotions are great; but even these are not to be a substitute for something much better and much greater that God has for us. His command to His people regarding their responsibility to their children is clearly stated in Deuteronomy 6:5–7 NAS:

"And you shall love the Lord your God with all your heart and with all your soul and with all your might. And these words, which I am commanding you today, shall be on your heart; and you shall teach them diligently to your sons and shall talk of them when you sit in your house and when you walk by the way and when you lie down and when you rise up."

Note the two instructions which God gives to His people regarding His Word. First, the parents are *to teach* His words diligently to their children; in other words, they are to teach with persistence and with thoroughness. Second, we, as parents, are *to talk of them* when we sit, walk, lie down, and rise up. The principles and precepts of the Word of God are to be an everyday part of our life and our conversation rather than just a Sunday-morning occurrence. The parents are to be the instructors rather than the Sunday school teachers! God ordained the parents as the instructors of His precepts. Sunday school teachers were man's invention because of failure on the part of the parents!

Who talks more to your children of God, you or the Sunday school teacher? When do you talk? How about a little "table talk" at dinner?

His Thoughts Toward Me:

My Thoughts Toward Him:

November 22

Because our lives are so busy, because so many women have to work outside the home, because so many of you find yourselves in single-parent situations, I know it is hard for you to maintain consistent family times with your loved ones.

I know, beloved, and I understand that, at times, you feel almost overwhelmed by the responsibilities and the pressures that come at you from so many different directions. At times, you wonder if you will ever make it! If you are like me, there have been times when you have just been tempted to walk away from it all—to escape. But if you did that, you know that you would have a hard time living with yourself. So what do you do? You have responsibilities to others!

Let's begin with dinner time. It is the one time during the day that, with a little effort and careful planning, you can be united as a family. It is a time when you can sit and talk to your family of the things of God as God instructs us to do in Deuteronomy 6. Note that God *never* said "preach" but rather "teach" (instruct) and "talk of." There's such a difference, and how some parents need to see this! My relationship with my sons just blossomed when I stopped preaching to them and started listening, when I let them share without going into shock at what they said or getting on my verbal bandwagon beating my own theological drum, when I started discussing God's Word and trusting the Holy Spirit as their Teacher who would lead them into truth as He has led me, when I realized it takes time to come to maturity, and that I was to lead, to teach, to guide but not to cram!

Sometimes, as parents, I think we have a tendency to overreact, to panic. I think a lot of this has to do also with a feeling of inadequacy or guilt on our part because of past failures. I understand. I've been there! We are so afraid that we are going to fail with our children! Oh, beloved, go to the Father, tell Him your fears. Then, rest, trust, pray, love, enjoy your family. It will do more than preaching, yelling, badgering, or threatening.

Woo them and win them by your life-style and by your love.

His Thoughts Toward Me:

My Thoughts Toward Him:

November 23

Has anyone ever made a promise to you that they never kept? Has anyone ever done something to you that caused you a great deal of hurt or disappointment? Has it been hard to forget that hurt, that disappointment? Or do you feel, in some way, that someone has failed you?

When you try to answer these questions, does it cause you pain of some sort? Is it unpleasant to think about? If so, beloved, it is a situation that has never been fully dealt with in your heart or resolved in your mind. And it needs to be; it should be talked out. Who knows, you could find the whole thing is a misunderstanding! Talking it out could heal a wounded relationship of a festering sore that might eventually poison the whole body.

In your family powwow today, why don't you share with your family *how important it is that we don't hold back anything we have against one another.* When we do hold back and things get difficult, the enemy, Satan, will bring that grievance, that hurt, that disappointment, before you and use it as a wedge to drive you apart. Therefore, it is important that these hurts, disappointments, and grievances (gripes) be talked out so that there can be understanding and complete peace by asking forgiveness and by forgiving or doing whatever is necessary.

So go around the table, one by one. It might go like this, "Son, when you think back over the years, is there anything that you can think of that I have done that hurt you . . . that disappointed you . . . that wasn't fair?"

As they share, listen, ask for forgiveness, don't defend yourself; you can explain any misunderstanding, but shoulder the responsibility and ask for forgiveness. Watch what God will do if you'll only take the time for sessions like this.

Remember, "A man's pride will bring him low, But a humble spirit will obtain honor" (Proverbs 29:23 NAS).

His Thoughts Toward Me:

My Thoughts Toward Him:

November 24

If dinner time is going to become a time when your family touches base with one another and when relationships with one another and with God are solidified, it is going to take some careful consideration and planning on your part. It is also going to take cooperation, but listen carefully. It cannot become a rigid family project that you have to do no matter what and that you do by bulldozing your way through leveling the family and scraping them the wrong way. So as we share, do not look at this in a legalistic way. Remember, the law kills (Romans 7:9–13) and can never conquer the flesh; only the Spirit can conquer the flesh (Romans 8:2–4). It will be God's Spirit working through you that will make these special and profitable times.

Mom, in a way, you will become the key person in making these times a success for you are the keeper of the home. Titus 2:4, 5 says that the young women are to be taught ". . . to be sober, to love their husbands, to love their children, To be discreet, chaste, keepers at home, good, obedient to their own husbands, that the word of God be not blasphemed." The word *keepers* means workers. Whatever our other responsibilities as women, this is our God-given one. First Timothy 5:14 says that women are to "guide [rule] the house." The word *guide,* in the Greek, shows us that we are responsible for the management or direction of the household affairs. Although I am a very busy woman doing "the work of the Lord," God has shown me that I must always make sure that my family's needs are met first. One thing that the Lord has shown me is the importance of family dinners. We have the best time around our table, sometimes sober sharing, sometimes reminiscing, sometimes doubled over in laughter as our three sons mimic one another or tell tales. Tommy, Mary Beth, and Meg live across the creek, and Mark and Leslie live a block away so we share meals quite often! These are such precious times, but they take some planning. We let the dishes sit while we talk around the table. If we have dessert, I have them keep talking while I fix coffee. When everyone starts to clear the table, it kills the table talk so the table is not cleared until we are finished talking. We've learned to keep the conversation going or to get it going by asking questions that have to deal with feelings or thoughts, like, "What do you think? How did you feel?" "Tell us about . . ." is a good opener. Saying, "Remember when . . ." always starts a conversation! I have sat at our table and prayed, in my heart, *Father, make this a special time.* Sometimes, we spend over an hour at the table. It may mean that I'll have to stay up later and work a little, but believe me, it is worth it! I just heard my oldest telling a guest today what fun we had at dinner! Another thing I do is plan good meals—colorful, balanced, healthy meals served on an attractively set table. No bottles or jugs are allowed on the table, pretty placemats are used. We enjoy the nice things we have rather than letting them sit and collect dust for rare holidays. These little touches, like daisies from the field, Queen Anne's lace weeds, candles, or something set in the center of the table as a centerpiece lets them know they are special. Also, the children, as they watch and help you set the table, see that you care. When we were kids, we colored the design on the paper napkins and made it special for Daddy! I learned where the fork went and how to put those special garnishes on food to make it attractive, like red flecks of paprika on pear salad!

One more thing, if you are going to have good table talk, you will have to turn off the television. "But I'll miss my program!" Right, you will miss your program; but if you don't turn that television off, you may miss your family.

Are they worth the time, the effort, the planning? Mom, it's up to you; you are the keeper of the home!

My Thoughts Toward Him:

Mom, What Do You Need To Do?

November 25

Armand M. Nicholi II, a faculty member of Harvard Medical School and a psychiatrist, has written quite a profound article entitled "The Fractured Family: Following It Into the Future" (from *An Evangelical Agenda: 1984 and Beyond*: William Carey Library). It is an article that needs to be read by every parent.

I feel the Lord would have me share, with you, some of the things Dr. Nicholi has to say so that you might meditate upon them and evaluate them in the light of your responsibility before God as a parent. The article states some rather alarming statistics. Only *one* American household *in three* consists of parents and their children. One-parent families are growing twenty times faster than two-parent families. There is now one divorce for every 1.8 marriages.

Dr. Nicholi goes on, "Early family experience determines our adult character structure, the inner picture we harbor of ourselves, how we see others and feel about them, our concept of right and wrong, our capacity to establish the close, warm sustained relationships necessary to have a family of our own, our attitude toward authority and toward the Ultimate Authority in our lives, and the way we attempt to make sense out of our existence. *No human interaction has greater impact on our lives than our family experience.*

"If any one factor influences the character development and emotional stability of an individual, it is the *quality* of the relationship he or she experiences as a child with 'both' parents. Conversely, if people suffering from severe non-organic emotional illness have one experience in common, it is the absence of a parent through death, divorce, *a time-demanding* job, or for other reasons. *A parent's inaccessibility, either physically, emotionally or both can profoundly influence a child's emotional health"* (italics added).

What has been shown to contribute most to the emotional development of a child is a close, warm, sustained, and continuous relationship with both parents.

Beloved, since the family was ordained by God, it is no wonder He says, "I hate divorce" (Malachi 2:16 NAS). For divorce destroys the incubator of the home, which provides the proper atmosphere that is desperately needed by children for survival in today's world. Yet God never intended it to be just a marriage for marriage's sake but rather a loving, sustaining, healthy union that would welcome and receive children and provide them with that relationship they so desperately need with both the father and the mother.

What is your relationship with your child like? What was, or is, your relationship with your parents like?

November 26

Yesterday, we heard that what influences the development and emotional stability of a child more than anything else is the quality of that child's relationship with his father and with his mother.

The other day, my heart just ached as I read my mail. Letter after letter told me of broken relationships, of husbands who had affairs with the wife's best friend, of how they had worshipped together and all the time they were carrying on an affair, of the confusion of the children as they wondered how Daddy could do such a thing, of a little girl who played that her daddy was dead because he never spent any time at home. And then I read another letter that seemed to show how this vicious cycle of wrong relationships gains momentum as it is passed down "to the third and fourth generation." The letter said, "Let me explain. All my life I have desired a mother's love. I have really yearned for the soft, sweet touch a mother can give. My mother was never one who showed her love to us kids. Her voice spoke mostly imperative sentences to us, 'Do this, Do that,' continually! She has never hugged me, and I have given up completely on her ever telling me that she loves me. . . . I have slipped into my mother's example of motherhood toward my daughter. *I don't know how* to love a daughter as I haven't experienced this first hand! . . . Please pray that God would help me to correct my errors, and that He would cover over in her life the mistakes I have made with her. I feel so super-defeated. Yet I know that with Jesus there is *Hope!* Please Kay, pray for me and show me *how to live. I beg of you!*"

And so we, as God's children, come along—strangers, in a sense—to show others how to live, to show them and to tell them of the One who has loved them with an everlasting love and who with lovingkindness has—is—drawing them to Himself (Jeremiah 31:3); of the One who will never leave them nor forsake them so that they can always say, the Lord is their helper (Hebrews 13:5).

And, yet, they should have been taught all this by example through their relationship with their father and with their mother. The earthly father should show the character of the heavenly Father. And, yet, many have abandoned their children when God would never abandon us! They have failed to reach out, to touch, to love, when God so loved that He gave His all at the greatest of personal costs!

What are you giving your children? Toys, education, clothes, cars, a roof over their heads—everything but the one thing they need, a quality relationship with you?

God, What Am I Giving My Children?

November 27

Thanksgiving, praise—do you know what these two expressions cause you to do? They cause you to focus on that which is good or worthwhile, that which is worthy of admiration or approval. They cause you to express appreciation to another for something which brings gratitude to your heart. They take your focus from the negative to the positive.

And what is accomplished in the heart of one who is the object of the praise or the thanksgiving? You know, don't you! You understand that when someone is grateful, you want to do even more for them. The giving has truly become a pleasure because it has been received with a grateful spirit. And when you are praised, well, it only spurs you on to greater heights . . . more challenging goals! You have succeeded! You have achieved! You have done it! You wondered if you could . . . you were afraid. What if you failed? What if others saw you had failed or heard of it? But you didn't— oh, you probably could do it better if you had another chance, but you made it this time. It was recognized; it was appreciated; there's hope! What relief! What joy! Someone has recognized worth in you. Praise helps you see your potential.

God showed me about a year ago a marvelous thing that has deepened my relationship with my sons in a precious way. It has drawn us even closer, and it has been used greatly of the Lord to encourage all three, even though two are grown and married. With the Lord's direction, I looked at the gifts, the abilities, and the potential that the Lord had given each of them. Jesus did the same thing with His disciples. Then, I shared what I had seen with them. For instance, our youngest son has the potential of leadership, so I shared this with him—what doors it has opened. David can see his worth, his potential! And now when I point out things in his behavior that would hinder this gift of leadership, these are received by him in a positive way. Why? Because of the power of

461

praise. I also tell him, and my other sons, how thankful I am to God for the gift of them. Are they perfect? No, they are not, but then neither am I! But I do know I am a person of worth, of value; my parents let me know that! Then, when at twenty-nine, I came to know God as my Father, it was confirmed to me in an everlasting way. God is for me (Romans 8:31); I am accepted in the Beloved (Ephesians 1:6); I am worth the death of His Son (Isaiah 53:10, 11).

Why don't you spend time with the Lord today asking Him to show you your mate's own special worth and also each child's worth? If you are unmarried, ask God to show you your roommate's or your friend's worth—and your parents' worth. Write their names in the space below, then after each name, write out what God reveals to you that is worthy of praise or thanksgiving in that life. When you finish, why don't you ask God for time to be alone with each one so that you might put your arm around them or hug them (touching is *so* important) and tell them of their worth and how thankful you are to God for them. If you cannot talk to each one in person, use the telephone—"reach out and touch," or write a letter.

Oh, beloved, if only you will do this, even if you have been disappointed, hurt or estranged, God will use it in a great way! You know what effect praise and thanksgiving has and you know, also, how hard it is to live without it! Let God do it *through you.*

November 28

"Reproach hath broken my heart; and I am full of heaviness . . ." (Psalms 69:20). It could be, beloved, that this month's devotions have depressed you more than they have helped you because of the state of your home! Maybe your home is so torn apart by anger, strife, rebellion, animosity that you feel the whole situation is hopeless. Or, possibly, your situation may be so critical, so beyond any glimmer of hope, that you feel like a complete failure.

Maybe you are so overwhelmed by guilt, frustration, anger, or a sense of inadequacy that the pain of it all seems like too much to bear. Maybe you could not honestly find or drum up one ounce of thanksgiving to God for anything. Maybe all you could do was ache with the pain of despair and belch the gall of bitterness! What about you? Is there any help for you?

There is so much teaching today on marriage, the home, and the family. Much of it gives pat formulas for successful marriages, homes, and families. Yet, by the time you have heard or have read of these success formulas, you feel as though it is too late! "I've blown it!" "There is no help for me!" . . . and the fog of guilt settles in, blotting out any possible glimmer of hope. You've discovered your child is involved in immorality, homosexuality, alcoholism, drugs, or thievery! Or your child has run away! You are a parent in pain. If you had been perfect, your children wouldn't be in this situation: they would be perfect; your home would be a happy one! Your relationship with your mate is strained; you are at one another's throats; accusations of failure echo down the corridors of your mind.

But is it true that if you were the perfect parent then your children would be perfect? No, it is not! God has shown me that He is a perfect parent, yet all His children are not perfect. He has not failed. His children have. I sat weeping. John White sat opposite me. My tears were tears of joy and gratitude. God had shown him the same truth he had shown me. It is all in his book, *Parents in Pain;* it is a book of comfort and of counsel.

Are you hurting? Will you not turn to God, "He healeth the broken in heart, and bindeth up their wounds" (Psalms 147:3).

His Thoughts Toward Me:

My Thoughts Toward Him:

November 29

John White begins the second chapter of his timely and much-needed book, *Parents in Pain* (InterVarsity Press) by sharing how parents live in fear when it comes to raising their children.

"Where did I go wrong? Am I still doing things wrong? Am I to blame? Such questions haunt many a parent. These are crippling questions. They can make you tremble inwardly with anxiety and self-doubt. Instead of setting you free, they impede your footsteps on an icy sludge of uncertainty, rendering you ineffective and indecisive. You become a pathetic victim of fears—fears of doing the wrong thing, fears of the future, fears of more problems, more pain."

Our lives are so confused today that many live in fear of parenthood rather than in joyous expectation! We are no longer confident parents, and, yet, we need to be! The lack of confidence on our part, as parents, has taken its toll on our children and on the homes of America for indecisiveness produces insecurity.

How am I to live as a husband and as a father? How am I to live as a wife and as a mother? These are good and legitimate questions, questions that need to be answered. But I believe, although seminars and books can help, the questions will only truly be answered in the school of life tutored by the Spirit of the Father. A good parent is not so much something that you do, as much as it is something that you become. It is not a process that, if followed, insures success; but rather it is a lifestyle to be lived no matter what the result. You see this truth when you look at the heavenly Father. There is a way in which He lives, and He never alters or deviates from His character which determines His way. Some of God's children are a success, some are a disgrace; but God is the same yesterday, today, and forever. He changes not! "If we are faithless, He remains faithful. . . ." (2 Timothy 2:13 NAS).

Are you afraid of going wrong? Do you live in fear of parenting? Do you want to know how to be the parent God would have you be? Then, go to the Father and ask Him to teach you the secrets of being a parent. How marvelous will be your instruction!

His Thoughts Toward Me:

My Thoughts Toward Him:

November 30

If you could pick the ideal parent, what would he or she be like? And if you could pick the ideal child, what would he or she be like? Stop and meditate upon these two questions, and then record your thoughts below.

The Ideal Parent:	The Ideal Child:

Now, looking at your list above, which of these characteristics would be possible for anyone to attain? Check these. How do these characteristics agree with what God's Word teaches? If they agree, put an "X" beside them. Now, if you are a parent, take each characteristic that is biblical and possible for all to attain and note what it would take in your life to meet this standard. What would it cost you? What dividends would it pay? Would it be worth it? Oh, beloved, do it! Don't just read this page and close the book. I could have written something better for you to read if that is all there is to it, but that is not what God laid upon my heart. This through, to do this exercise.

When you finish, if you are a parent, look at what you have written regarding the ideal child. Which, of the things you have written, are attainable and biblical? Mark these as you did the others. Now, note what you can do to help your child become "ideal." Then, help the child to the best of God's ability in your availability.

Today, if you have a family powwow, the children could do the list for the parent and then share what they have written and why. Then, you can do the same for the child. When you finish, talk about how you can help one another. If you do not have children, change "parent" to "mate" and make your list whether you are married or not! It will help you be prepared if you are still single!

DECEMBER

December 1

Four hundred years of silence. The heavens had been as brass. The prophets had gone. God had ceased to speak audibly to His people. All they had to cling to was the covenant and the promises. Year after year, they went to the temple to worship God, to bring their sacrifices, to say their prayers. Year in, year out, it was the same.

To some, the ritual of worship became routine, boring, a motion to go through because it was a part of life. But there were others who clung to the forms of worship, to the traditions of the elders, to the promises given by Jeremiah and Ezekiel of a new covenant. To some, it was a habit of life without meaning. To others, it was a way of life with purpose; they were to live for God, to keep His commandments and His regulations blamelessly. This is how Zacharias and Elizabeth lived, even though it seemed that God had not honored their fidelity and their wholeheartedness. God had not opened Elizabeth's womb. She was growing old, and she was barren. Yet they would serve their God. That time the lot had fallen on Zacharias. He was chosen to go into the temple to burn incense. The worshippers gathered, as usual, to pray as the priest entered the Holy Place.

Zacharias moved through that holy chamber guided by the burning oil of the candlestick past the table of shewbread. In deep reverence, he stood before the veil that kept him from viewing the ark of the covenant. There, he stood before the altar of incense.

Suddenly, unexpectedly, four hundred years of silence were broken! Gabriel had been sent from the presence of God to speak to Zacharias. Zacharias' prayers had been heard. Elizabeth would bear a son! A son who would go forth in the spirit and in the power of Elijah to make ready a people who would be prepared for the Lord (Luke 1:5–20).

Have you been praying for a long time? Has God been silent? Have you been tempted to quit, to give up? Has your worship become routine, boring? Oh, beloved, persevere, wait. God will speak . . . in His time.

His Thoughts Toward Me:

My Thoughts Toward Him:

December 2

The people never really knew, nor did they fully understand what had taken place that day in the Holy Place. Zacharias had been silenced, unable to speak until the day of John's birth; so almost another year went by without hearing from God. Little did the people realize that a prophet was on his way, that a prophet was being sent from God to prepare them for the coming of the Messiah. The promise of the Messiah was about 4,000 years old.

What rejoicing there was! Neighbors and relatives shared Elizabeth's joy. God had opened her womb and had given her a son. He was eight days old, and it was time for his circumcision. His mother had said his name was to be John, but great protest went up because Elizabeth and Zacharias had no relative named John. Those present said, "Name him after his father." But Zacharias ". . . asked for a writing tablet, and to everyone's astonishment he wrote, 'His name is John.' " Then, "Immediately his mouth was opened and his tongue was loosed, and he began to speak, praising God" (Luke 1:63, 64 NIV).

The silence of 9 months was broken—Zacharias could speak. The silence of 400 years had been broken—Zacharias was filled with the Holy Spirit, and he prophesied. And what God spoke through Zacharias was good news:

> Praise be to the Lord, the God of Israel, because he has come and has redeemed his people. He has raised up a horn of salvation for us in the house of his servant David (as he said through his holy prophets of long ago), salvation from our enemies and from the hand of all who hate us—to show mercy to our fathers and to remember his holy covenant, the oath he swore to our father Abraham: to rescue us from the hand of our enemies, and to enable us to serve him without fear in holiness and righteousness before him all our days (Luke 1:68–75 NIV).

Has the good news reached your ears yet? Has God spoken to you? Have you been enabled to serve God without fear in holiness and in righteousness in these days? If not, are you sure you have heard the good news?

His Thoughts Toward Me:

My Thoughts Toward Him:

December 3

When his son was born, Zacharias, filled with the Holy Spirit, prophesied of John's ministry. "And you, my child, will be called a prophet of the Most High; for you will go on before the Lord to prepare the way for him, to give his people the knowledge of salvation through the forgiveness of their sins, because of the tender mercy of our God, . . . to shine on those living in darkness and in the shadow of death, to guide our feet into the path of peace" (Luke 1:76–79 NIV).

John the Baptist was to tell them of the salvation that Christ would bring. This salvation is what Christmas is all about. This is the salvation that God has for men. Salvation is more than just dying and going to heaven. Salvation is more than living forever. Salvation is more than eternal benefits.

Salvation is forgiveness today for all of your sins—past, present, and future—that you might not live under guilt and condemnation.

Salvation is freedom from the kingdom of darkness and all of its fears. It is living life in the light of Jesus, who dispels the shadow of death which would keep you in bondage and in fear all the days of your life.

Salvation is peace, peace with God, peace of mind, peace of heart. It is being kept in peace as the storms of life rage round about you!

This salvation is for you not because you merit it, deserve it, or could possibly earn it, but because of the tender mercy of our God. Is this salvation, forgiveness, light, life—this peace yours?

If something seems to be missing in your salvation, why not tell God about it now? Ask Him to show you what the answer is to your need. He is waiting. He will answer.

His Thoughts Toward Me:

My Thoughts Toward Him:

December 4

The fullness of time had come! The Roman government was now permitted, by the sovereign Ruler of all the universe, to send forth its decree. It was time for the birth of the Son of God! God was to be born of woman, to be born under the law, to be born in Bethlehem Ephrathah. Out of this city, so small among the clans of Judah, would come Shiloh, the One who would be Ruler over Israel. Conceived by the Spirit of God in a virgin's womb, was the One ". . . whose origins are from of old, from ancient times" (Micah 5:2 NIV). The fullness of time had come, and most of the world would miss it.

The Roman census had been scheduled at an earlier date. As a matter of fact, it had been rescheduled more than once because of conflicts within Roman jurisdiction and problems with the Israelites. These seemed, at least to man, to be the reasons. But what man did not know was that this postponement was of God. It was not yet time to move Mary and Joseph. Then, finally, the word came: Caesar Augustus had issued his decree that a census should be taken of the entire Roman World. Everyone had to register in his own town. Joseph and Mary would have to leave Nazareth and travel south, past that famed city of Jerusalem, to Bethlehem.

What is going on today? Governments are making all sorts of plans—they are issuing many decrees involving the lives of multitudes, they are operating as if there were no sovereign God sitting upon His throne overlooking all of the universe. And yet God reigns in all of His majesty. Although the governments of this world do not know it, He permits them to go only so far, for He knows the time when He will restore the Kingdom to Israel. It will be when He, again, will say to His Son, "Come, for all things are ready." It will be in the fullness of *His* time. When God comes the second time, it will be to those who eagerly await Him for salvation. Will you be waiting and watching?

". . . I trust in you, O Lord; I say, 'You are my God.' My times are in your hands . . ." (Psalms 31:14, 15 NIV).

His Thoughts Toward Me:

My Thoughts Toward Him:

December 5

There was so much to treasure in her heart. The times of nursing passed by quickly, as Mary would sit and ponder all that had happened in this last year.

Her fingers caressed the unbelievably soft cheeks and then dropped down to play with the corners of her Son's precious mouth. She would rock Him back and forth in her arms until the surge of love would so overwhelm her that she would almost suffocate Jesus as she tried to absorb Him into her bosom. Her firstborn—her firstborn Son—given to her by God! Mary couldn't get over what had happened today in the temple when they went to circumcise Jesus and to consecrate Him to the Lord. Once again, she rehearsed in her mind the events of the day. First, the old man, Simeon, and then the prophetess, Anna. Both of them seemed to have an aura of holiness and joy about them.

She pondered Simeon's words once again. ". . . Behold, this *Child* is appointed for the fall and rise of many in Israel, and for a sign to be opposed—and a sword will pierce even your own soul —to the end that thoughts from many hearts may be revealed" (Luke 2:34, 35 NAS).

Her thoughts turned over and over in her mind, *What was it Simeon had said? A sword shall pierce my soul too! What did he mean? Jesus was destined to cause the falling and the rising of many in Israel. He was to be a sign to be spoken against so that the thoughts of many hearts will be revealed. Why would they fall, Lord? How could this precious baby, this dear Son of mine, cause people to speak against Him or to stumble? Oh, I know, He shall cause men to rise for He will tell them of You; He will save Your people from their sins. That is what You told Joseph. That was why we were to name Him Jesus. But how, Lord God, will He cause people to fall or to speak against Him?"*

When the question was answered in Mary's mind, we do not

know. Maybe it was when she remembered what Isaiah had said, ". . . He shall become a sanctuary; But to both the houses of Israel, a stone to strike and a rock to stumble over, *And* a snare and a trap for the inhabitants of Jerusalem" (Isaiah 8:14 NAS).

Or maybe it was when she stood at the foot of Calvary and heard their jeering taunts that pierced like a sword the breast that had once nursed Him. The pain was like a sword!

Has Jesus Christ caused you to rise or to fall? Do you speak against Him or do you speak for Him? Is His life foolishness to you?

His Thoughts Toward Me:

My Thoughts Toward Him:

December 6

He was born in Bethlehem. Like all true sons of Israel, He was circumcised the eighth day. Joseph and Mary took him to Jerusalem to present Him to the Lord; "as it is written in the Law of the Lord, 'Every firstborn male is to be consecrated to the Lord'" (Luke 2:23 NIV). ". . . they returned to Galilee, to their own town of Nazareth. And the child grew and became strong; he was filled with wisdom and the grace of God was upon him" (Luke 2:39, 40 NIV).

The next event we read of is Jesus' trip to Jerusalem with his parents. He was twelve years old. It was the Feast of the Passover. They lost Him. " 'Why were you searching for me?' he asked. 'Didn't you know I had to be in my Father's house?' " (Luke 2:49 NIV.) Jesus had been sitting among the teachers in the temple courts listening to them and asking questions! This was God, God incarnate sitting among those to whom He had given life and breath, and He was listening to them! Oh, they were amazed at

His understanding and His answers, but they did not know it was God sitting in the seat of a learner.

Jesus returned to Nazareth with His parents, and He was obedient to them. Nothing is told us of the next eighteen years of His life. Nothing, that is, except one vital sentence, "And Jesus grew in wisdom and stature, and in favor with God and men" (Luke 2:52 NIV). Here were the blind still blind, the lame still lame, the sick still sick, the possessed still possessed, Israel still waiting for the Messiah, the lost still perishing—and what was Jesus the Christ doing? He was growing in wisdom and stature and in favor with God and with men. He was developing, growing, maturing in four vital areas of life: intellectually, physically, spiritually, and socially. Why?

Why was He not out healing, delivering, preaching, teaching? He was God; He could have been doing these things! Because there was something more needful at that time than healing, than delivering, than teaching, than preaching, more important even than dying—it was growth, wholeness, balance in life. Man is not just spirit; he is spirit, soul, and body; each of these parts of man is to be preserved blameless before the Lord (1 Thessalonians 5:23). Our Lord's ministry was to be a balanced ministry, a ministry to the whole man. And to accomplish this ministry, He needed, as a man, to know this balance in His life. He was prepared intellectually, physically, spiritually, and socially.

Are you balanced? Have you given God the time to make you balanced? Or have you rushed off to do the work of the Lord unprepared, not realizing that you cannot minister to the whole man if you have not given yourself the time to mature in each of these areas?

My Thoughts Toward Him:

December 7

It was an opportune time for Satan to tempt Jesus. Jesus had just been baptized by John. God had opened the heavens and said, for all to hear, ". . . You are my Son, whom I love; with you I am well pleased" (Luke 3:22 NIV). Jesus was on the verge of beginning His public ministry. At last, the time had come, the time for which Jesus had been born. There was a confidence—a confidence that comes when you know you are in the will of God; but it was a confidence that could not go unchallenged by the enemy.

From the presence of people, from the words of God's blessing, Jesus was led to the wilderness. Now, all of a sudden, He was shut off in the desert, without food, alone. And for forty days, the enemy worked on Him—day in and day out without letting up. How Jesus was tempted, what Satan said to Him during that time, we know nothing of; we only know that ". . . for forty days he was tempted by the devil. . . ." (Luke 4:2 NIV). The Scriptures simply record for us what happened on that final day in the wilderness. But before we look at that in tomorrow's devotion, let's see what we can learn for our lives today.

God tells us, through Paul, that we are not to be ignorant of Satan's schemes lest Satan outwit us and take advantage of us (2 Corinthians 2:11). Many a child of God has walked into Satan's snare because of an ignorance of the enemy's tactics. It is my prayer that God will speak to you today, beloved, as you meditate on what God has laid upon my heart for you.

One of Satan's schemes is to shake your confidence as a child of God. How it disturbs the enemy when you know that you have been blessed and chosen of God to do a work for Him. It galls Satan to have you secure in the knowledge that God is pleased with you. And so one of the enemy's schemes is to try to make you unsure of your relationship with God.

Satan wants you to think that God is against you and not for you. Or he wants you to feel that you have disappointed God in such a way that God cannot use you. He might even whisper in your ear that you are not saved or that you have blasphemed the Holy Spirit and therefore you cannot be saved.

What do you do in times like these? You must take the shield of faith and stand in its protection. What does God say about you in

475

His Word? What has He spoken in the light? Do not doubt it in the dark hour of temptation. Submit to God; resist the devil; he will flee from you. Draw near to God, and He will draw near to you (James 4:7, 8).

His Thoughts Toward Me:

My Thoughts Toward Him:

December 8

For forty days, Jesus had gone without food. For forty days, the devil had tempted Him. Now, Jesus was hungry, so the enemy tempted Jesus as he tempted Eve. "Eat . . . satisfy yourself your way. You shall be as gods. God is holding out on you. Act independently." Satan wanted Eve to sin, and he succeeded. Now, Satan wanted Jesus to sin—acting independently of God, doing things in your own strength, according to your own ability—this is the root of all sin.

So now the enemy challenges Jesus to prove Himself as the Son of God, to take things into His own hands, to act independently, to supply His own needs by His own strength. But Jesus meets the enemy's fiery dart with the shield of faith, the precepts of God's Word. "It is written: 'Man does not live on bread alone, but on every word that comes from the mouth of God' " (Matthew 4:4 NIV). Life is not a matter of fulfilling our desires or our needs but rather of living according to God's words. The choice had been made by Jesus; He would trust in the Father and wait upon Him to supply all of His needs according to the Father's way.

When this temptation failed, Satan tried another tactic. He offered Jesus a crown apart from the cross. He showed Jesus the kingdoms of the world and said, "I will give you all their authority and splendor, for it has been given to me, and I can give it to anyone I want to. So if you worship me, it will all be yours" (*see* Luke 4:6, 7 NIV). But in this temptation, Satan also failed. Jesus knew there was no crown without a cross. He would not prefer the temporal to the eternal. The sufferings of the present time were not worthy to be compared with the glory which was to be revealed when He would stand with us before the Father's throne. He was born to die. He came to give His life a ransom for many. He would not sell His birthright for Satan's mess of pottage.

It was quite a day; Satan would not give up! The devil also tried to get Jesus to put God to the test by challenging God to do a miracle on His behalf in order to prove God's protection. And so once again, Jesus put up His shield of defense, the truth of God's Word. How vital it is that we know the Word of God, that we can say with authority, "It is written."

Have you esteemed His words more precious than your necessary food, or have you neglected them? Maybe that is why you have weakened under Satan's temptations. Can you blame it on God, or are you responsible?

His Thoughts Toward Me:

My Thoughts Toward Him:

December 9

When does Satan usually tempt us? It is usually in times of weakness—physical or mental weakness—when you are alone, when all is quiet and you have time to think, and think, and think.

Sometimes, Satan will just seek to wear you down or distract you by some train of thought that you cannot seem to shake. Jesus' temptation went on for forty days! Can you imagine?

Let me share with you what Satan has been doing to me for the past ten to fourteen days. I keep thinking of how I should have designed our home differently. We built it in 1976. And when we built it, I did it with an underlying fear that people would criticize. We built it in a hurry and did not make it as large as our board of directors instructed us to do because of fear, which was not of God but of Satan. Now the thought of failing in something as vital as designing and building a house has almost done me in; the thoughts have come at the most inconvenient and inopportune times. They come when I'm praying, when I'm teaching, when I'm counseling, when I'm alone at night or in the morning—whew! They have almost distracted me from things that are vital to our ministry.

I know it all sounds so carnal, so fleshly, so worldly, but I share it with you so that you might see how Satan attacks. I have been wrestling for days with this. But victory is here! Satan must depart. It is over for now. I think what finally broke his attack was when, embarrassed though I was, I shared with some other dear sisters in Christ and asked them to pray for me. They listened to me with love and understanding and without condemning me for being tempted with such fleshly things. Also, I determined to start praising God for our home just the way it is laid out. Oh, Satan will probably come back, "When the devil had finished all this tempting, he left him until an opportune time" (Luke 4:13 NIV).

But praise God, when Satan does return, I will know that it is because he is panicked at the work God will do through me if I will only persevere.

When the temptation comes, even though it may last awhile, still I can say, "Thanks be to God who always causes us to triumph through Christ Jesus our Lord."

His Thoughts Toward Me:

My Thoughts Toward Him:

December 10

Nazareth—tourists go there to see the place of Jesus' childhood, to drink from Mary's well. This is where the Son of God came with His mother to help her fetch water. A Son who did not complain; a Son upon whom Mary must have looked with awe, with joy, and yet with sorrow. And so the people of Nazareth watched this Son of Israel grow in wisdom and in stature and in favor with God and man. Jesus, Joseph's Son, was a good lad. How blessed of Jehovah were Mary and Joseph to have One such as this open Mary's womb. The heads of those in Nazareth surely nodded in agreement as they passed Him daily going to the well to draw the water that sustained them. Little did they realize that He was the fountain of living waters, the One of whom they could drink and live forever.

As the tourists leave Nazareth, I wonder if they look for the brow of the hill where it happened? I wonder if they stop long enough to hear the echoes of the angry cries of the multitude. The Son of Mary and Joseph came to Nazareth, where He had been brought up. And as was His custom, He entered the synagogue on the Sabbath and stood to read (Luke 4:18). But this time, they didn't like what they heard. Oh, the reading of Isaiah was fine; He read with such clarity, such authority; the men of Nazareth shook their heads in wonder at the gracious words of this Nazarene as they whispered among themselves, "Is this not Joseph's Son?"

As Joseph's Son, they would listen because He was One of them. But when He spoke as the Son of God and took away their cloak of self-righteousness that covered their hard hearts of sin, it was too much! They were filled with rage; they rose up and cast Him out of the city; they led Him to the brow of the hill in order to throw Him down the cliff (Luke 4:28, 29).

What about you? Do you look with sweet sentiment on the baby Jesus and sing the traditional carols to put you into that good feeling of Christmas? And how do you feel about Jesus as He assumes His place as God uncovering your sin and calling you to righteousness, to submission? Do you bow before Him as Lord, or do you seek to push Him from the brow of the hill in anger because He calls you to conform to Him and does not, will not, conform to your conception of Him?

His Thoughts Toward Me:

My Thoughts Toward Him:

December 11

"For if you forgive men when they sin against you, your heavenly Father will also forgive you. But if you do not forgive men their sins, your Father will not forgive your sins" (Matthew 6:14, 15 NIV).

Just preceding this statement, our Lord had given His disciples instruction in prayer, "When you pray, say . . . 'forgive us our debts *AS* we forgive our debtors.' " It is part of what we call the Lord's Prayer . . . a prayer prayed by countless lips in countless churches on the Lord's day week after week. They are words said with lips, lips that speak words from hearts. What lies in those hearts? What is in your heart toward others?

Next Sunday, as you stand or sit in church, as you sing your Christmas carols praising the One who was born to die that you might have forgiveness of your sins, look around you. Are there *any, any at all,* in your church whom you have not forgiven *as* your heavenly Father has forgiven you? And as you sit and think, are there any in your family, any among your friends, any among your acquaintances, any at work that you have *anything at all* against? Can you look at each one and treat them with complete love and with total forgiveness so that it is just as if they had never hurt, never offended, never disappointed, never wounded you? Stop and walk back down the galleries of your mind. Do you see hanging on those walls the memory of anything that would cause you to murmur or to turn away in revulsion as you remember that particular person? If so, then go with Christ to Calvary, and listen to your Savior as He hangs upon that cross beholding, through eyes filled with the agony of torture and rejection, those who have gladly put Him there. Listen to the words spoken from that cross, "Father, forgive them, for they do not know what they are doing" (Luke 23:34 NIV).

Have you claimed God's, Christ's, forgiveness for your sins and your trespasses? Has He forgiven you? Now, look at the one who has sinned or trespassed against you. Which debt is greater, yours to God or theirs to you? If you have been forgiven the greater, you must forgive the lesser. If you do not, you shall be as the debtor in the parable in Matthew 18:21–35, and that is how your ". . . heavenly Father will treat each of you unless you forgive your brother from your heart" (Matthew 18:35 NIV). Jesus said it with His own lips!

His Thoughts Toward Me:

My Thoughts Toward Him:

December 12

Are there some people you just cannot please no matter what you do? There is just no satisfying them no matter how hard you try? You try and you try, but everything you do is wrong. You long with all that is within you to show them the reality of the Christian life, but all they can do is find fault with your life.

Has this caused you to become disappointed, discouraged, defeated? Have you despaired of ever being Christ-like enough to win them to your Lord? Do not despair, beloved, not if you have sought with God's leadership to live before them in His strength and according to His precepts of life. Do not give up on being "holy" and think, *What is the use? I'll never be what I should be! I'll never do anything right! I'll never convince them!"*

Jesus understands your frustration. He lived among the same type of people. Listen to what He said; it is a word written for you:

> To what, then, can I compare the people of this generation? What are they like? They are like children sitting in the marketplace and calling out to each other: "We played the flute for you, and you did not dance; we sang a dirge, and you did not cry." For John the Baptist came neither eating bread nor drinking wine, and you say, "He has a demon." The Son of Man came eating and drinking, and you say, "Here is a glutton and a drunkard, a friend of tax collectors and 'sinners.'" But wisdom is proved right by all her children (Luke 7:31–35 NIV).

No matter what Jesus or His disciples did, they could not please some men. So God understands your frustration. Therefore, may your one goal be to please God. ". . . If God is for us, who can be against us?" (Romans 8:31 NIV.)

His Thoughts Toward Me:

My Thoughts Toward Him:

December 13

Have you ever heard some news that has so torn at you, that made you so sick at heart you had to walk away; you had to be alone, you needed to be by yourself, you had to be away from people?

The news came to Jesus—John the Baptist had been beheaded. John's disciples had just buried his body; then they came to tell Jesus. Of course, they had to tell the full story. It helped to explain, to go into the details of how it all came about. And so they carefully related how John had stood before Herod, the Tetrarch, and told him face to face that it was wrong to take Herodias, his brother's wife. John was right, "He stood, he feared the face of no man." John was imprisoned. But at this point, John was not killed for Herod feared the people, and they looked upon John as a prophet.

Then, the disciples continued telling Jesus of Herod's birthday celebration. Herodias' daughter had danced for Herod, and, in his extreme delight, he promised her anything her heart desired. At that point, Herodias, her mother, saw that her hour of vengeance had come. As Herodias whispered in her daughter's ear, the request was passed on for all to hear, " 'Give me here on a platter the head of John the Baptist' " (Matthew 14:8 NIV). The disciples told of some who were there that said Herod was distressed at the request. They had said his distress was visible, but what could he do for he had sworn an oath?

The disciples told the Lord of how John's head had been brought into that banquet hall on a platter and given to Herodias' daughter, of how she took it triumphantly and gave it to her mother! There was no more to say; the story was finished; John the Baptist was dead. The prophet that would have fulfilled Elijah's role if only they would have listened, if only they would have believed, was beheaded at Herod's command (Matthew 17:11–13). It seemed that evil had triumphed over good. Evil seemed the victor, the conqueror rode on the lips of the people through the streets of Jerusalem.

"When Jesus heard what had happened, he withdrew by boat privately to a solitary place" (Matthew 14:13 NIV).

Here was God walking in the midst of men, knowing their beginning and their end. Here was the sovereign ruler of the

483

universe, and He had to be alone. Because He had become flesh, because He could be tempted as we, because He could be touched with the feeling of our infirmities, grief drove Him to a solitary place.

I believe that grief tore at His soul—grief over John, who was the greatest among men and yet not recognized as such; grief over Herodias' triumphant gloating and her blindness that would remain until she faced God's judgment in the final day, only to see John the Baptist with his head intact standing with the triumphant children of God; grief over man's inhumanity to man because of sin's destructive lusts.

He had to get away from man, but they followed Him. And when He ". . . saw a large crowd, he had compassion on them and healed their sick" (Matthew 14:14 NIV).

May we, no matter how grieved we may be because of man, always have compassion on them, even as Christ did!

His Thoughts Toward Me:

My Thoughts Toward Him:

December 14

". . . their teachings are but rules taught by men," and it was because of this that Jesus said, " 'They worship me in vain . . .' " (Matthew 15:9 NIV).

So many Christians are living their Christian lives according to man-made rules—traditions of men but not of God. Somehow, somewhere along the line, we have picked up a code of do's and don'ts for the Christian, and these have become our standard for living rather than the Word of God. We live by man's traditions instead of by the Word of God. How well we know our traditions, and how quick we are to look down our noses and judge as non-spiritual those who do not walk by our code! Yet as we walk within the confines of these do's and don'ts, what are our hearts like? What comes out of our mouths? That which comes out of your mouth, not your traditions or your code of do's and don'ts, shows what you are really like. What comes out of your mouth makes you clean or unclean. "Out of the same mouth come praise and cursing. My brothers, this should not be. Can both fresh water and salt water flow from the same spring?" (James 3:10, 11 NIV).

Some Pharisees and teachers of the Law had come down from Jerusalem to Galilee where Jesus was ministering. The express purpose of their visit was to criticize Jesus and His disciples because they had broken the Pharisees' tradition; Jesus' disciples ate with unwashed hands and, therefore, they were unclean! So Jesus proceeded to teach them where uncleanness really came. "But the things that come out of the mouth come from the heart, and these make a man 'unclean.' For out of the heart come evil thoughts, murder, adultery, sexual immorality, theft, false testimony, slander. These are what make a man 'unclean'; but eating with unwashed hands does not make him 'unclean' " (Matthew 15:18–20 NIV).

How does your heart compare with your traditions, with your Christian do's and don'ts? Are you like the Pharisees, critical of those who don't follow your particular "Christian" traditions so that from your mouth comes slander regarding them?

Have you put your traditions *above* or even beside God's Word? Do your children know the do's and don'ts, or do they know the Word of God? Which do you live by?

"Thus you nullify the word of God for the sake of your tradition. You hypocrites!" (Matthew 15:6, 7 NIV.)

His Thoughts Toward Me:

My Thoughts Toward Him:

December 15

What would make Jesus address Peter as "Satan"? What would make Him say, "Out of my sight, Satan! You are a stumbling block to me; you do not have in mind the things of God, but the things of men" (Matthew 16:23 NIV)?

Jesus was born for one purpose, and that purpose was to die— to give His life as a ransom for many so that those who were dead in trespasses and sins might live (Matthew 20:28; Ephesians 2:1). It was through Jesus' death that He would ". . . destroy him who holds the power of death—that is, the devil—and free those who all their lives were held in slavery by their fear of death" (Hebrews 2:14, 15 NIV).

The time had come in Jesus' life to explain to His disciples that He must go to Jerusalem and, there, suffer at the hands of the elders, the chief priests, and the teachers of the law. This suffering would end in death—He must be killed; but on the third day, He would be raised to life.

Apparently, when our Lord said this to His disciples, all that they heard was suffering and death! They completely missed His words, ". . . and on the third day be raised to life" (Matthew 16:21 NIV). And so Peter began to rebuke Jesus, " 'Never, Lord!' he said. 'This shall never happen to you' " (Matthew 16:22 NIV).

And, thus, in return, Jesus addressed Peter as "Satan," and He gave His rebuke. Then, our Lord taught them the principle that is true for every man. "If anyone would come after me, he must deny himself and take up his cross and follow me. For whoever wants to save his life will lose it, but whoever loses his life for me will find it" (Matthew 16:24, 25 NIV).

The work of the cross was God's doing not Satan's! It pleased the Father to give His Son as a ransom for you and for me (Isaiah 53:10).

And it pleases the Father when you and I are willing to follow in Christ's stead, to lay down our lives, to give our lives, in a sense, as a ransom for others. What will you give to God in gratitude, in love for His unspeakable gift? *Don't listen to Satan as he uses the lips of others to keep you from the cross.* Think of the pain that would have been spared Peter and the others if they hadn't gotten caught up with Christ's death and missed His words, ". . . and on the third day be raised to life." Life comes only through death!

His Thoughts Toward Me:

My Thoughts Toward Him:

December 16

Little children—they thought Jesus was too busy, too important, too occupied in the work of God to be bothered by them. But, oh, how the children wanted to be around Him! For when Jesus was around, there was excitement! And so, they would make their way through the forest of tall people searching and pushing through the flowing garments that blocked their paths like the undergrowth of the woods.

You could hear their whispers, their giggles, their calls to their playmates until all of a sudden, the forest was gone; they stood in the clearing dazzled by the unexpected light. There He was. Timidly, they walked to Him, uncertainty clapped its hands over their mouths quieting their giggles and their childish chatter. Would He smile or would He scold them? Would He be kind or would He be mean? Would He even pay any attention to them? Would He put out His arms or would He be angry and impatient? As their little sandaled feet crept closer, they were suddenly brought to a halt! The iron gate of a man's arm swung back stopping them. "Don't bother the Master!" And in their little minds, they must have talked to themselves as little kids do, *Why do grown-ups always have to be so busy? Why do kids always seem a bother? Why do we always have to go away or wait until later?*

All of a sudden, Jesus reached out and gently drew one of them to His side, tucking him under His arm. Then, Jesus gave him that special squeeze of love, and a tiny smile crept out of the cloud as the upturned face caught the reflection of the Son's smile. And Jesus began to speak, "And whoever welcomes a little child like this in my name welcomes me. But if anyone causes one of these little ones who believe in me to sin, it would be better for him to have a large millstone hung around his neck and to be drowned in the depths of the sea" (Matthew 18:5, 6 NIV).

With that, I'm sure their eyes opened wide in amazement while their little arms poked one another, and again they talked to themselves, *Hey! We do matter! We're not a bother! Jesus of Nazareth does care about little children! See, He's not too busy for us because we are important!*

Children are important. They matter to Jesus so much that God has given you this warning. Are you careful with children? Do you welcome them? Do you demonstrate to them the love of God, the character of God? Or do you, by your life, your behavior, your example, cause them to sin? How great will be your punishment!

Fathers, will your children have a hard time accepting and understanding God the Father's love because they have never really known, never really seen, never really felt your love? Or will it be easy for your children to go to Jesus because they have lived tucked under your loving arms?

His Thoughts Toward Me:

My Thoughts Toward Him:

December 17

Jesus looked at him, and He loved him. But His love did not alter what He said to him. Here was a rich young man with a zeal for the things of God. He had kept the commandments since he had been a boy, or at least he thought he had kept them! Now, seeing Jesus, he had fallen on bended knee to ask what he must do to inherit eternal life.

"What must *I do?*" Today, so many of us would be so quick to reply, "Why, nothing! It is a gift. All you have to do is *believe* that Jesus is God, that He has died for your sins and paid for them in full. You must believe that Jesus Christ was then buried and that He rose from the dead conquering death by His perfect sacrifice. And you must believe that He lives. If you will accept the Lord Jesus Christ as your Savior, you will be saved." And, doctrinally, our answer would be right. But would our answer be appropriate? Would it be an answer that would bring this rich young man to salvation?

The Apostle Paul would later say to a Philippian jailer who asked what he could do to be saved, "Believe on the Lord Jesus Christ and thou and thy house shall be saved."

But Jesus did not say this to the rich young man, and the rich young man went away lost. Why? Because the rich young man did not do what was necessary to be saved. "Do? Do, you say! But there is nothing to do to be saved! It is by faith! All you have to do is believe!"

Are you sure there is nothing to do? Carefully read Mark 10:-17–30. Ask God to reveal truth to you. Then, write below why the rich young ruler was not saved; afterwards, meditate upon this passage.

His Thoughts Toward Me:

My Thoughts Toward Him:

December 18

When the rich young man came to Jesus, he called Him, "good teacher." With that, Jesus replied, "Why do you call me good? . . . No one is good—except God alone" (Mark 10:18 NIV).

Why did Jesus pick up on the word *good?* Why did He need to say that there is none good except God? I believe that Jesus was attempting to bring this young man face to face with the fact that He is God. When Jesus quoted the commandments to the young man, He skipped over the first and foremost commandment—the commandment which required men to love God with all and above all! The commandments that Jesus did reiterate, the young man had kept since he was a boy. But what about the first and the foremost commandment?

The Scriptures tell us that Jesus looked at and loved this young man. Then, our Lord put His finger on this young man's idol—his possessions, his earthly treasures. He could not forsake his possessions; he could not give them up. He had broken the first commandment, but he was totally unaware of it!

What did the rich young man have to do to be saved? He had to put Jesus first. He had to be willing to leave everything for Christ. Why? Because Jesus is God, and He must have the preeminence in our lives. If you and I are not willing to acknowledge Him as God, and if we are not willing, if necessary, to forsake all for Him, we cannot be saved. That is the "doing" of salvation—not the working but the doing! It is giving God His rightful place as God. Have you ever done this? When did you do it? If you have never

490

done this, will you do it?

". . . The kingdom of heaven is like a merchant looking for fine pearls. When he found one of great value, he went away and sold everything he had and bought it" (Matthew 13:45, 46 NIV).

His Thoughts Toward Me:

My Thoughts Toward Him:

December 19

During our Summer Family Camp at Reach Out, I decided that I would take the eight- through thirteen-year-olds for an outing so that we could be together—just the kids, a couple of helpers, and I. I wanted to spend some time with them because their little lives are so precious to God. So we piled into our van and our station wagons taking thirty-three kids along! But, at that point, I didn't know how many I had, and I was taking them to a neighbor's pool! We had a lot of rambunctious boys along—just my cup of tea since we have three sons of our own who are of the same sort! Therefore, I called for a lineup so that I could quiet them, give orders, and count noses! What a push there was among many of them to be the first in line! Of course, they were thinking, *First in line, first in the pool.* I watched several of them push and shove for first place, and I could understand their aggressiveness for my personality is anything but introverted! Then, I watched some finagle their way in front of others. The smaller or quieter ones lost the prime places. As I watched, it seemed unjust, not right, not fair, but I did nothing for I knew what I would do *later!*

When the line was finally formed and the count-off was finished, I looked at the hurting faces of those who were to be last in the pool because their number was closer to thirty than it was to one!

491

I looked at other little faces; they didn't care where they were in line; they were there! They would get in the pool sooner or later! There was no anxiety, only the joy of getting to go.

Then, I quoted the Scripture and made my brief application, "So the last will be first, and the first will be last" (Matthew 20:16 NIV).

I wish that I had taken a little more time to make it more effective, but someday God will bring it back to their remembrance.

How these verses hit me this morning in my quiet time:

> Peter answered him, "We have left everything to follow you! What then will there be for us?" Jesus said to them, "I tell you the truth, at the renewal of all things, when the Son of Man sits on His glorious throne, you who have followed Me will also sit on twelve thrones, judging the twelve tribes of Israel. And everyone who has left houses or brothers or sisters or father or mother or children or fields for my sake will receive a hundred times as much and will inherit eternal life. But many who are first will be last, and many who are last will be first" (Matthew 19:27–30 NIV).

What a shock it will be when we see so many who, seemingly, have had it made as God's children in this life with their "fame," with their notoriety, with their position within Christian circles, with their acclaim and acceptance, with their prominence, with their lack of want in any area. Many of these who were seemingly first will be last. O Father, stamp eternity upon my eyes . . . upon our eyes! May we be able to say, "There is not anything that will keep me from following you freely."

His Thoughts Toward Me:

My Thoughts Toward Him:

December 20

My heart was in conflict. He sat me down in the chair, and ever so gently, he began to remove my sandals. As he placed my feet in the basin and began to wash them, I thought, *No, this isn't right. I should wash his feet first. I'm the woman; he is the man. God's Word says that I was made for him.* But Jack had taken the initiative. He had come to me and led me across that Upper Room. There was no question, no hesitation, Jack was going to wash my feet first. Then, I would be given the opportunity of washing his in return. It was so easy to wash his! I didn't want him to do a thing, not even to untie his shoe. I wanted to do it all. Now, I could fulfill my role; now, I could serve him in this act of love as he had served me. As I held his foot in the towel, I bent to kiss that which stood as my earthly shield and protector, that which stood for righteousness, that which stood, in picture form, as my heavenly Lord.

The service proceeded. The walls of that "Upper Room" in Jerusalem echoed back our hymns of praise and adoration. Not only were feet washed, but eyes, cheeks, even hearts were washed by tears sent from the Spirit of God. As my eyes moved from one precious face to another, they were suddenly arrested by a new face aglow in worship as he sang with us. Now, I was to go, to ask if I could wash his feet. I did not know his name; I did not even know if we spoke the same language; I only knew that I was to wash his feet, and that he would understand. Although we did not know one another, I knew we were not strangers.

Now, the conflict was gone. I could see that it was only right that Jack should wash my feet first. He is the man, he is the husband, he was to first wash the feet of his bride. "What I do you do not realize now; but you shall understand hereafter" (John 13:7 NAS). Christ sought me longing to make me His. It was He who gave Himself up for me that He might sanctify me, set me apart, make me holy by cleansing me by His blood and then through the washing of the water of the Word (Ephesians 5:25, 26). And so it was right; although it seemed hard at first for me to let him, it was right that Jack, my lord, should first wash my feet. "You call me Teacher, and Lord; and you are right; for so I am. If I then, the Lord and the Teacher, washed your feet, you also ought to wash one another's feet" (John 13:13, 14 NAS). And so I went to wash another's feet; his name was John.

His Thoughts Toward Me:

My Thoughts Toward Him:

December 21

Although they had all gone to the garden at Gethsemane together, only three of them were taken apart to pray with Jesus. But even that prayer meeting did not last long; His sorrow was too great. He had to be alone. Alone, where, in the throes of the conflict, He could fall on His face and allow the cry of His heart to become confession. There are times when the conflict is so great that you must be alone; your lips cannot keep silent anymore! The conflict must be verbalized aloud to the God of all flesh. And so He prayed, "My Father, if it is possible, may this cup be taken from me. Yet not as I will, but as you will" (Matthew 26:39 NIV). As Jesus returned to His disciples, He found them sleeping! Now was not the time for sleep but for prayer and vigilance. Soon, they, too, would be faced with temptation; and so Jesus, in concern, said, "Watch and pray so that you will not fall into temptation. The spirit is willing, but the body [flesh] is weak" (Matthew 26:41 NIV).

How well Jesus knew the truth that He was imparting to them. He must do the will of the Father; ". . . I have come to do your will . . ." (Hebrews 10:7 NIV), but the flesh, His body, was weak.

And so He went back to wrestle alone in prayer, to watch and pray. Three times, Jesus, the Son of God, had to pray ". . . if it is possible, may this cup be taken from me. Yet not as I will, but as You will."

I stood, not too long ago, in Gethsemane's garden reading these words and sharing their truths with those we were teaching on our Bible tour of the Holy Land. All of a sudden, my heart understood what our Lord was really saying. No longer could I read; tears flooded my eyes, sweeping away the words from my sight. Then, my soul reached out, grabbing this truth and clinging to it for its very life. I was rescued from the awful current of temptation which would seek to carry me away and to toss me lifeless and gasping among the wreckage of the storm. I had been tempted in a way in which I had not been tempted in a long time. My flesh had longed to flirt with sin; but, in my spirit, I knew I couldn't. I didn't want to sin, to walk in disobedience. Why, a few hours earlier, it was the farthest thing from my mind for I was walking in joyous fellowship with my God. But then it came, that desire, that longing, that temptation to yield. Only through diligence in watching myself carefully and through persistent praying, was I able to say, "Not my will but thine be done!" Now, I saw how well Jesus understood the truth that He tried to share with His disciples for in Gethsemane He, Himself, experienced that truth, "Watch and pray. . . . the spirit is willing, but the body is weak." Jesus knew. He knew because He was wrestling with the weakness of His flesh!

This is my Savior who was tempted in all points such as I. One who can be touched with the feeling of my infirmities . . . my weaknesses.

He knew. He understood that although my spirit was willing to do God's will . . . to walk in obedience, still my flesh was weak.

Have you almost been caught in sin's snare? Are you ashamed for even being tempted? He understands, and He says, "Watch and pray."

His Thoughts Toward Me:

My Thoughts Toward Him:

December 22

"Watch and pray . . . the spirit indeed is willing but the flesh is weak" (Matthew 26:41). But they did not watch, nor did they pray; instead, they slept.

Jesus knew the temptation that Peter would very soon encounter. He had told him that Satan had demanded permission that he might sift him as wheat. But Peter was confident; he knew his own spirit. "Even if I must die with You, I will not deny You" (Matthew 26:35 NAS). Peter was willing to die for Christ. He was not lying. He meant those words; they came from the depths of his heart.

Now, Peter was awakened to participate in a nightmare. Before him stood a large crowd armed with swords and clubs. Suddenly, they seized Jesus. Peter would not have it. His sword was drawn, and in a flash, he had honed it on the enemy's head. An ear was gone. Then, the rebuke came. They could not fight! They could not defend themselves! Jesus was to be arrested. Suddenly, Peter, the warrior, the defender of Jesus, was called to a cease-fire. Yet the enemy marched on. It was too much for his flesh; his flesh was weak. "Then all the disciples deserted him and fled" (Matthew 26:56 NIV).

Peter was not prepared. Oh, he had been warned, "Watch and pray . . ."; but instead, he had slept. Peter knew his spirit, but he had not soberly reckoned with his flesh. And so in a little while, he would find himself weeping bitter tears of defeat and condemnation.

Are you, beloved, aware of the weakness of your flesh? Oh, the zeal is there and so is the dedication and the commitment; but, also, there is the flesh! May you, may I, thus remember to watch ourselves carefully, and may we pray much. For only that constant vigilance and that close communion will keep us from the bitter weeping.

So many who were once standing in zeal are today falling into temptation. Zeal alone cannot keep you from falling; it takes vigilance and prayer.

His Thoughts Toward Me:

My Thoughts Toward Him:

December 23

It is so much easier when what you are doing has the support of those around you! It is easy to go along with the crowd. As a matter of fact, they kind of spur you on; they give you impetus or courage to do what maybe you wouldn't do if you had to do it by yourself.

Jesus had been arrested and taken to the house of Caiaphas, the high priest. The chief priests and the Sanhedrin were waiting. All they wanted was evidence that would enable them to fulfill the desire of their hearts—to kill Jesus. The witnesses gathered, all of them false. One by one, they stepped forward to testify lies without compunction. They were in the company of liars. Finally, the high priest put Jesus under oath. Now, He had to speak. His words came, confirming that He was the Son of God, " '. . . In the future you will see the Son of Man sitting at the right hand of the Mighty One and coming on the clouds of heaven' " (Matthew 26:64 NIV). With this, the high priest tore his clothes and accused Jesus of blasphemy. There! The crowd had it! The high priest had said it.

Jesus was guilty! The high priest said to the crowd, "What do you think?" They answered, "He is worthy of death." Yet every one of them was wrong. And, I believe, if they had gone away to be alone, to think it through, they would have recognized how wrong they were. There was no evidence. They were simply walking by the present desires of their flesh; they were encouraged by others of the same weaknesses.

But, as if it were not enough, one emboldened by the verdict of the high priest spit in Jesus' face, and so others followed his example. Then, one hit Jesus with his fist, and others followed. Still others slapped Him and said, "Prophesy to us, Christ. Who hit you?" (Matthew 26:68 NIV.) The crowd was enjoying its sport.

He sat alone . . . the only One who was right; yet He looked like He was the guilty party. At the present, He was unvindicated! But He knew He was right; it was the multitude who was wrong.

Days are coming, beloved, when, if you are going to do what is right, you may have to sit alone. You may have to take the unjust abuse of men, men who are wrong. There may be no justice; you may have to suffer—unjustly. When it happens, remember, there is One who understands, who sat where you are sitting. He is, now, at the right hand of the Mighty One, where someday you shall be also. So sit alone if need be. It won't be long. He is coming soon.

His Thoughts Toward Me:

My Thoughts Toward Him:

December 24

Tomorrow is Christmas. How do you feel?

Numb ... busy ... exhausted ... pushed ... carnal ... guilty ... frustrated?

Lonely ... forsaken ... forgotten ... empty ... hurt ... rejected ... unwanted ... unloved ... uncared for?

Disappointed ... disillusioned ... filled with despair?

or

Excited ... loved ... warm ... happy ... secure ... content ... full of joy, anticipation, love, gratitude?

Ask God to show you the reason you feel the way you do. Then, write out below **His Thoughts Toward Me.**

Now, beloved (for that is what you are to God), ask God to show you what to do about your feelings. If all is well, write **His Word To Me** in joy! If all is not well, ask Him to heal you and write below what you have asked to be healed from under **His Healing For Me.**

Sleep well tonight knowing that you are wrapped in the same tender care that you knew, or that you wish you had known, as a child—protected in your Father's arms of love. Your heavenly Father is holding you closely. Remember that He said He would never leave you nor forsake you.

His Thoughts Toward Me:

His Word To Me or His Healing For Me:

December 25

Christmas! Christmas is God saying, "I love you. Look in My manger and see what was born for you . . . what is given by Me. Come. See. It is My Son, My only begotten Son. He means all the world to Me. He is there, My gift to you on My Christmas tree. It's Calvary. Hush! Listen! Can you not hear the carols that are being sung? They were composed for you to tell you over and over again that I love you."

What is man, that thou shouldest magnify him? and that thou shouldest set thine heart upon him? (Job 7:17).
. . . Yea, I have loved thee with an everlasting love: therefore with lovingkindness have I drawn thee (Jeremiah 31:3).
. . . God commendeth his love toward us, in that, while we were yet sinners, Christ died for us (Romans 5:8).
. . . God, Who is rich in mercy, for his great love wherewith he loved us, Even when we were dead in sins, hath quickened us together with Christ . . . (Ephesians 2:4–5).
In this was manifested the love of God toward us, because that God sent his only begotten Son into the world, that we might live through him (1 John 4:9).
. . . God so loved the world, that he gave his only begotten Son, that whosoever believeth in him should not perish, but have everlasting life (John 3:16).
Behold, what manner of love the Father hath bestowed upon us, that we should be called the sons of God . . . (1 John 3:1).
Behold, for peace I had great bitterness: but Thou hast in love to my soul delivered it from the pit of corruption: for thou hast cast all my sins behind thy back (Isaiah 38:17).
. . . The beloved of the Lord shall dwell in safety by him; and the Lord shall cover him all the day long, and he shall dwell between his shoulders (Deuteronomy 33:12).
Behold, I have graven thee upon the palms of my hands . . . (Isaiah 49:16).
. . . If God be for us, who can be against us? He that spared not his own Son, but delivered him up for us all, how shall he not with him also freely give us all things? . . . Nor height, nor depth, nor any other creature, shall be able to separate us from the love of God, which is in Christ Jesus our Lord (Romans 8:31, 32, 39).
. . . he hath made us accepted in the beloved (Ephesians 1:6).

God says to you, "What more can I say? What more can I do? What more can I give to show My love to you? If there is anything, will you tell Me?"

What Would You Say To Him This Christmas Day?

December 26

The pastor stood before the coffin in his church and pointed his finger threateningly to the congregation. His staccato-pointing finger seemed to direct the beat of his words. "This will never happen again in this church. This woman never should have died. It is your fault."

A mist of guilt rolled over the congregation blocking out the warmth and the light of the Son that was meant to comfort those who sorrowed but not as those without hope. The responsibility of this young mother's death drenched their garments of mourning. Someone in the church had lacked faith. Someone had made a negative confession. And so this young mother had died leaving her husband and her young children without a keeper of the home.

The true story above could be repeated in numerous ways as similar pronouncements come from pulpit after pulpit: "Your daughter wouldn't have died in that accident if someone had prayed properly." "What you confess with your mouth is what you get . . . you can be healed by the faith of a positive confession. . . ." "Job brought his problems upon himself for he said, 'What I feared came upon me'" (Job 3:25). "No Christian ever need die of sickness if he has enough faith because healing is in the atonement. Jesus bore all our sicknesses in His death. He carried them to Calvary. Just believe; just confess your health. Do not doubt, and you will be healed; according to your faith be it unto you."

And so guilt, condemnation, and anxiety rest like a heavy cloud over many a church, over many a Christian. They are told that their lack of faith or their negative confession permitted disease or brought premature death. If this is true, and it is not, apparently their lack of faith had caused Jesus, who had the keys of hell and death, to open the door before God, who had numbered their days, intended for them to die. Apparently, this loved one's times were not in God's hands (Psalms 31:15), but their times were in the hands of their own faith and confession or in the faith and confession of other believers!

Just recently, a precious man said to me, "I lost my children and my wife some time ago. When I heard this teaching, I began to wonder if I was responsible for their death. I thought, maybe if I had only prayed differently or spoken differently they would still be alive. It was really beginning to trouble me." The furrows of anxiety showed in his elderly face. Trouble and confusion had hung as shades over his eyes until truth pulled the cords; then, the shades went up, and the light dispelled his darkness. Finally, he understood the prophecy from Isaiah 53:4 NAS: "Surely our griefs He Himself bore and our sorrows He carried" for he saw in Jesus' life when this Scripture was fulfilled. We will look at this verse in depth tomorrow, but let me first ask you a question: Beloved, are you a student of God's Word who has learned for yourself to compare Scripture with Scripture, or do you simply live by what you hear others preach? Do you believe something because you have studied it in God's Word or rather because of someone's testimony?

His Thoughts Toward Me:

My Thoughts Toward Him:

December 27

Do you know someone who has what men call an incurable disease such as cancer or leukemia? Or do you possibly know someone who is lame, blind, or deaf?

Have you heard that they could be healed if only they would believe? Have you heard that if, in faith, they would confess that healing with their mouth and believe it in their heart, then healing would come to pass?

Have you watched Christian television programs as they have televised healing services where the lame abandon their crutches, wheelchairs, and walkers, where the deaf utter words spoken into their ears? Have you listened to interviews of people who have been miraculously healed of cancer and other incurable diseases or who have been raised from the dead?

And when you see all these things, what do you think? How do you feel? Does Jesus heal today? Are miracles still possible? Are these healings real healings? Are these healers really men of God? Does my faith or my positive or negative confession determine the length of my own, or of another's life or health? Is healing of physical illness and infirmity ours through the Lord Jesus Christ's atonement?

Beloved, these are legitimate and valid questions. Questions to which we need answers. Did Christ, who was born to die, carry all of our physical sicknesses to the cross and there atone for them so that through faith we can be healed of all that would afflict us? This is something we will discuss for the next two days as we look at Christ's ministry to mankind in His life and in His death. May God, by His Spirit, lead us into truth through a study of His Word as we compare Scripture with Scripture. Let's begin by reading Matthew 8:14–17, in the New American Standard. "And when Jesus had come to Peter's home, He saw his mother-in-law lying sick in bed with a fever. And He touched her hand, and the fever left her; and she arose, and began to wait on Him. And when evening had come, they brought to Him many who were demon-possessed; and He cast out the spirits with a word, and healed all who were ill; in order that what was spoken through Isaiah the prophet might be fulfilled, saying, 'He Himself took our infirmities, and carried away our diseases.'"

Now, compare these verses with Isaiah 53:4 NAS. "Surely our griefs (sicknesses) He Himself bore, and our sorrows He carried; Yet we ourselves esteemed Him stricken, Smitten of God, and afflicted."

According to the verses in Matthew, beloved, when did Jesus bear or take our infirmities and carry away our diseases? Write your answer:

Does Jesus heal today? Yes. Are miracles still for today? I believe so. As a matter of fact, I am acquainted with a number of legitimate miracles that have occurred in our time. These were miracles of God, but is all healing, are all miracles from God? No. Satan can heal and perform miracles also, as we are warned of in 2 Thessalonians 2:9, 10.

So, then, what do I feel the Scriptures teach? I believe they teach us that Jesus did and can heal. But I do not believe that the Scriptures teach that physical healing of these temporal bodies is ours because of His atonement. You may possibly retort, "But what about the verse that says that by His stripes we are healed." Tomorrow, we will look at that verse. Today, it is my prayer that God will use these lessons to free those of you who are under bondage—the awful bondage that this false teaching brings when you or your loved ones are not healed. Remember, beloved, our heritage through death is to be absent from the body, present with Christ (2 Corinthians 5:8).

His Thoughts Toward Me:

My Thoughts Toward Him:

December 28

It was the prophet, Isaiah, who told us that by Christ's stripes we would be healed. Listen to the magnificent words of promise given to him by God. Isaiah 53:4–6 NAS:

4 Surely our griefs He Himself bore, and our sorrows He carried; Yet we ourselves esteemed Him stricken, Smitten of God, and afflicted.
5 But He was pierced through for our transgressions, He was crushed for our iniquities; The chastening for our well-being fell upon Him, And by His scourging we are healed.
6 All of us like sheep have gone astray, Each of us has turned to his own way; But the Lord has caused the iniquity of us all To fall on Him.

There is, in these few verses, a progression of events. Let's follow them closely and hear what the Spirit of Truth would speak to our hearts.

We saw yesterday that Christ bore our sicknesses or griefs and carried our sorrows or pains during His earthly ministry as He healed the sick and set free those possessed of demons. "Yet we ourselves," God's Israelites, "esteemed Him stricken, smitten of God and afflicted." What a paradox it was! Christ came and manifested to Israel—to the world—His miraculous powers of healing, His complete authority over Satan and his kingdom; yet at the cross of Calvary, they taunted Jesus with statements, like, "He believes in God, let God rescue Him" (See Matthew 27:43). They were statements that implied that Jesus was being smitten by God. What audacity! What sin lay in their darkened hearts! What blindness!

Then, Isaiah, in verse 5, goes on to explain the why, the reason, the purpose of the cross. He was pierced through for our transgressions. He was crushed—killed—for our iniquities. Our deserved chastening fell on Him that we might have peace, reconciliation with God. Jesus was born to die for your sins and my sins that we, dead in sins and trespasses, might be made the righteousness of God in Him (Ephesians 2:1, 2 Corinthians 5:21). By His scourging, or stripes, we are healed. Healed? Healed of what?

Peter tells us in his first epistle, "and He Himself bore our sins in His body on the cross, that we might die to sin and live to righteousness; for by His wounds [welt] you were healed. For you were continually straying like sheep, but now you have returned to the Shepherd and Guardian of your souls" (1 Peter 2:24, 25 NAS).

By His stripes we were healed of our sins . . . of their power and their dominion over us (Romans 6). What a healing! What a Savior!

His Thoughts Toward Me:

My Thoughts Toward Him:

December 29

There He stood—God in the flesh—being scourged by men whose very breath He controlled. The leather straps coiled around His body like a serpent striking the flesh with its fangs of bone and metal.

The momentum of the blow to His back caused the flailing straps to wrap themselves around his abdomen. Just as each hook caught His flesh, the arm of the soldier would wrench back his whip, flipping the flesh from Jesus' back and abdomen. There Christ stood, the New Covenant being written in His blood.

I gave My back to those who strike Me, and My cheeks to those who pluck out the beard; I did not cover My face from humiliation and spitting. For the Lord God helps Me, Therefore, I am not disgraced; Therefore, I have set My face like flint, And I know that I shall not be ashamed (Isaiah 50:6, 7 NAS).

Why did God permit all this? Why the scourging? Why not just the crucifixion? Why did God permit His Son's appearance to be "... marred more than any man, and His form more than the sons of men" (Isaiah 52:14 NAS)? The literal Hebrew rendering of this verse says that Christ was so marred that His appearance was not human. Was not death on a cross enough without these stripes?

No, crucifixion was not enough. A certificate of debt, a list of decrees against mankind and hostile to us, had to be written out. We had broken God's holy law, and we were indebted to Him by virtue of our unrighteousness. And so God wrote out that certificate of debt in the flesh of His Son. He wrote it with a scourge as Jesus bore our sins in His own body. Then, God took that certificate of debt and nailed it to the cross (Colossians 2:14). Finally, from the cross, the cry came, "Tetelestai (It is finished!)" (*see* John 19:30).

When a man incurred a debt against another, a certificate of debt was written out and held until that debt was paid in full. When the debtor finally paid off the debt, the word "tetelestai" was written across that certificate of debt. The certificate was then nailed to the door of the debtor's home. Thus all could see and know that his debt had been "paid in full."

God has written out your certificate of debt. He has engraved your sins in the body of His only begotten Son that by His stripes you might be healed . . . healed so that you might die to sin and live to righteousness. Have you been healed? Do you live a righteous life?

"No one who is born of God practices sin, because His seed abides in him; and he cannot sin, because he is born of God. By this the children of God and the children of the devil are obvious: any one who does not practice righteousness is not of God, nor the one who does not love his brother" (1 John 3:9, 10 NAS).

His Thoughts Toward Me:

December 30

"Let God rescue Him. . . ." But God did not rescue Jesus. He let Him die. And if God had rescued Him, where would we be? We would be lost, for there would have been no sacrifice for our sins. Jesus was our substitute. He was the One who died for us, in our place, and, thus, He paid the penalty for our sins. He was born to die.

We live in a time when men flee from suffering and from anything that would bring great personal cost. We live in a time when it is rare to see men and women willingly lay down their lives for the sake of others, for the cause of righteousness. We live in a day and age that has made man the goal, the purpose, the end of all things rather than God and others. We live in a world that lacks true leadership because few are willing to pay the high cost of leadership. Men are doing what is right in their own eyes, for their own benefit!

And all of this has crept into the theology of the church in America.

Whatever our problem, whatever our trial, whatever our suffering, the cry is, "Let God rescue them." It seems that we want to escape, to flee, to be taken from the hardships of life, from the testings, from the trials, from the temptations. "O God, I believe; give me my exemption from this trial"; this seems to be the motto of the church today, "Give me a miracle."

Now, please, beloved, do not write me off as one who has such little faith that I could not receive a miracle. I believe God can do anything today that He has done in the past. But that is not the issue! The issue is this, "Is it always to God's glory and to man's good for God to rescue us?" And if it is not, are you willing not to be rescued, to suffer?

> Those who passed by hurled insults at him, shaking their heads and saying, "You who are going to destroy the temple and build it in three days, save yourself! Come down from the cross, if you are the Son of God!" In the same way the chief priests, the teachers of the law and the elders mocked him. "He saved others," they said, "but he can't save himself! He's the king of Israel! Let him come down now from the cross, and we will believe in him. He trusts in God. Let God rescue him . . ." (Matthew 27:39–43 NIV).

And so, also, the word comes to the followers of Jesus, "Come down from the cross . . . save Yourself . . . let God rescue You." But God does not always remove the instrument that would bring us to death of self. If we would save ourselves from all unpleasant and difficult situations, how would others in the same situations see the sufficiency of our God for those situations and, thus, be saved? If we save ourselves, we cannot save others. Let God rescue me? " 'Now my heart is troubled, and what shall I say? 'Father, save me from this hour'? No, it was for this very reason I came to this hour. Father, glorify your name!' " (John 12:27, 28 NIV).

Oh, beloved, whatever your trial, your difficulty, your circumstance, will you not ask God to glorify His name in whatever way it pleases Him? Will you not say, "Rescue me, Father, only if it is Your will? Otherwise, I shall be faithful unto death for I know that if I am to remain at this cross, through my obedience, You will rescue and save others!"

His Thoughts Toward Me:

My Thoughts Toward Him:

December 31

There was no escape for Jesus. He tasted it all. He drank the dregs of the cup of suffering. He partook of temptations, of trials, of testings. He learned obedience through the things that He suffered even though He was the Son of God. There was no escape for Jesus.

Why was there no escape? Because you and I need a great High Priest who can be touched with the feeling of our infirmities (Hebrews 4:15). We need a Priest who can understand our temptations because He has been there.

There was no escape for Jesus. Shall there be escape for you
... for me ... for His children? It seems that this is what many
are seeking in Christianity—a way to escape. It seems that this
teaching makes popular preaching. But is this what God has for
His children? Escape?

If we are to be priests in Christ's stead, in His place, as His
representatives, which God says we are to be (Revelation 1:6; 5:9,
10; 1 Peter 2:9), doesn't the world need people to minister to them
who can be touched with the feeling of their infirmities? Then,
why are we trying to escape trials, testings, afflictions, sufferings,
discomfort?

> ... For Thy sake we are killed all the day long; we are accounted
> as sheep for the slaughter. Nay, in all these things we are more than
> conquerors through him that loved us. (Romans 8:36, 37).

Why, then, are we trying to escape? What kind of priests do you,
do I, want to be? He was born to die that we might live, and we
were born to die that others might live.

> ... The hour has come for the Son of Man to be glorified. I tell you
> the truth, unless a kernel of wheat falls to the ground and dies, it
> remains only a single seed. But if it dies, it produces many seeds.
> The man who loves his life will lose it, while the man who hates
> his life in this world will keep it for eternal life. Whoever serves me
> must follow me; and where I am, my servant also will be. My
> Father will honor the one who serves me (John 12:23–26 NIV).

His Thoughts Toward Me:

My Thoughts Toward Him: